LANGUAGE IN SOCIETY 5

The Sociolinguistics of Society
Introduction to Sociolinguistics Volume I

LANGUAGE IN SOCIETY

GENERAL EDITOR:
Peter Trudgill, Professor of Linguistic Science,
University of Reading

ADVISORY EDITORS:
Ralph Fasold, Professor of Linguistics,
Georgetown University
William Labov, Professor of Linguistics,
University of Pennsylvania

1 Language and Social Psychology
Edited by Howard Giles and Robert N. St Clair

2 Language and Social Networks
Lesley Milroy

3 The Ethnography of Communication
Muriel Saville-Troike

4 Discourse Analysis
Michael Stubbs

5 Introduction to Sociolinguistics
Volume I: The Sociolinguistics of Society
Ralph Fasold

6 Introduction to Sociolinguistics
Volume II: The Sociolinguistics of Language
Ralph Fasold

The Sociolinguistics of Society

RALPH FASOLD

Basil Blackwell

© Ralph W. Fasold 1984

First published 1984

Basil Blackwell Publisher Limited
108 Cowley Road, Oxford OX4 1JF, England

Basil Blackwell Inc.
432 Park Avenue South, Suite 1505
New York, NY 10016, USA

British Library Cataloguing in Publication Data

Fasold, Ralph
  Introduction to sociolinguistics.—(Language in
  society; 5)
  The sociolinguistics of society
  1. Sociolinguistics
  I. Title   II. Series
  401'.9   P40

  ISBN 0-631-13385-2
  ISBN 0-631-13462-X Pbk

. Also included in the Library of Congress Cataloging in Publication Lists

Typset by Communitype, Wigston, Leicester
Printed in Great Britain by
T. J. Press Ltd, Padstow, Cornwall

7ω216978-4

Contents

	Editor's Preface	vii
	Introduction	ix
1	Societal Multilingualism	1
2	Diglossia	34
3	Qualitative Formulas	61
4	Statistics	85
5	Quantitative Analysis	113
6	Language Attitudes	147
7	Language Choice	180
8	Language Maintenance and Shift	213
9	Language Planning and Standardization	246
10	Language-Planning Cases	266
11	Vernacular Language Education	292
	Bibliography	316
	Index	333

To Gae
who shares everything

Editor's Preface

Sociolinguistics, as the term itself suggests, is a discipline that is capable of combining linguistic and societal concerns in varying degrees. In this book Ralph Fasold deals with interests that lie towards the societal end of the language and society spectrum. Many of the chapters, consequently, will be relevant reading for sociologists, anthropologists, and social psychologists. In a subsequent volume in Blackwell's Language in Society series, Fasold will deal with the other end of the spectrum and will examine the implications of sociolinguistic research for the study of language and linguistic theory. Taken together, these two books will provide thorough and clearly written coverage of the entire field of sociolinguistics. They will therefore make an excellent introduction to the field for readers with relatively little background in the subject. These, however, are more than just introductory textbooks in sociolinguistics. Unlike a number of other authors of sociolinguistics texts, Fasold is himself a *practitioner* of sociolinguistics. He has carried out empirical research in a number of areas of sociolinguistics, and has also been very keen to apply the results of his research to the solution of educational and other problems. He therefore writes from considerable experience and with considerable insight. Throughout *The Sociolinguistics of Society,* original interpretations, evaluation and theoretical contributions abound, with the result that these books will also be important reading for academic sociolinguists and others with research interests in the field. The book is, too, highly contemporary in its concerns, and very wide-ranging in the languages and sociolinguistic situations it covers.

Peter Trudgill

Introduction

This book is the first volume of a pair of introductory textbooks in sociolinguistics. Although the size of the subject area dictates a second volume, the division into two books is also useful since it reflects the idea that there are two large subdivisions in the field. One of these subdivisions takes *society* as the basic starting point and language as a social problem and resource. The topics in this volume belong to this subdivision. The other major subdivision starts with *language*, and social forces are seen as influencing language and as contributing to an understanding of the nature of language. The second volume will be about this kind of sociolinguistics. Another way of looking at the subdivisions is to consider this volume to be about a special kind of sociology and the second one to be about linguistics from a particular point of view.

The essence of sociolinguistics, in my view, depends on two facts about language that are often ignored in the field of linguistics. First, language *varies* – speakers have more than one way to say more or less the same thing. In this context, I include the entire range of linguistic variation from the subtle differences in the pronunciation of individual vowels such as those described by Labov (1966) and Trudgill (1974) to choices among whole languages by bilingual or multilingual speakers. Second, there is a critical purpose that language serves for its users that is just as important as the obvious one. It is obvious that language is supposed to be used for transmitting information and thoughts from one person to another. At the same time, however, the speaker is using language to make statements about who she is, what her group loyalties are, how she perceives her relationship to her hearer, and what sort of speech event she considers herself to be engaged in. The two tasks (communicating information and defining the social situation) can be carried out simultaneously precisely because language varies – speakers can choose among alternative linguistic means, any of which would satisfactorily communicate the propositional information. It is the selection among these alternatives that defines the social situation. The study of the interplay between these two facts about language is exactly sociolinguistics.

As a linguist, I take linguistic theory seriously – a linguist who is interested in sociolinguistics should never be content with descriptions of interesting phenomena, but should constantly be considering how the social function of language relates to whatever the correct theory of language turns out to be. (So far, I know of no convincing reasons to take a position on the issue of whether the theory of language should directly account for the social function of language or whether the theory of language itself makes no reference to social function but interacts with a more general theory of communication. On an emotional level, I favor the latter approach.)

It will become clear in this volume that I consider anthropological linguistics and another subfield of anthropology, the ethnography of communication, to be part of sociolinguistics. In the second volume, it will be apparent that I consider the theoretical syntactic and philosophical approaches to speech acts and pragmatics also to be part of sociolinguistics. Since the study of pidgin and creole languages is scarcely possible without a consideration of the social environments where these linguistic systems develop, there will be a chapter on pidgins and creoles in the second volume.

Some readers will probably question the emphasis in chapters 3 and 5 of this volume on qualitative and quantitative methods of analyzing societal multilingualism; in particular, the qualitative typologies and formulas that received considerable attention in the past seem to have gone out of vogue in recent years. It will become clear in chapter 3, however, that I find the qualitative formula method an insightful starting point for the naturalistic approach to the sociology of language. It provides one framework for thinking about what the social functions of languages are at the level of sociopolitical organization and what characteristics a language needs to have to fulfil one of them. Chapter 5, on quantitative analysis, presents tools for analyzing societal multilingualism in terms of numbers. Although neither quantitative nor qualitative formulaic approaches are extensively utilized in the study of the sociolinguistics of society, it seems to me that students in sociolinguistics should be introduced to these aids to orderly thinking. There is also a chapter on statistics (chapter 4), which is so placed because I need to refer to fundamental statistical concepts in chapter 5, and a rudimentary understanding of statistical procedures at least is needed in the later chapters of the book.

Apart from these, the topics that will be taken up in these two volumes are unexceptionably sociolinguistic. Societal multilingualism, diglossia, language attitudes, language choice, language maintenance and shift, language planning and standardization and the use of language in education are well within the mainstream of anyone's idea of the sociolinguistics of society. All of them are concerned with the social meaning of choices among linguistics variants and so are also consistent with the concept of sociolinguistics I have just given.

I think it would be helpful for the prospective reader to know the principles

I have tried to follow. To begin with, I have attempted to be more comprehensive than some introductory discussions of sociolinguistics have been. I have also tried to pay scrupulous attention to the distinction between what might be called 'received knowledge' and my own original thinking on the topics I have written about. It is important for an introductory student in any discipline to be exposed to the foundation knowledge that practicing scholars presuppose. The idea of an introductory course or textbook is to provide an efficient way for a student new to the field to catch up with current issues. The beginner should be made familiar with the fundamental concepts and leading scholars that he will find cited in the books and articles he will subsequently read. It is the responsibility of the author of an introductory text and the teacher of an introductory course to provide this foundation, even if he disagrees with some of it or thinks some parts are overemphasized.

On the other hand, it is not reasonable to expect either the author or the teacher not to think creatively about the issues they are dealing with, or to refrain from presenting their own original thinking about the issues. Neither author nor teacher, if they have any talent at all, is a simple compiler or conduit of other people's ideas. The danger in all this is that the two kinds of material might be indistinguishable to the student. Unless teacher and author are aware of their responsibilities, students might take a quite idiosyncratic notion of the textbook writer or teacher to be generally accepted knowledge in the field. I have tried to be aware of this responsibility in developing this book. I have made an effort to include the information that practicing sociolinguists can be presumed to have, regardless of my personal opinion of the value of it. Where I have added my own original thinking, I have tried to identify it as such. I very much hope no user of this book will mistake an idea of my own, which may never be generally accepted as valid or important, for an item of received knowledge. I appeal to teachers who may use the book as a course text to reinforce this distinction.

I have made an effort to write in an informal, quasi-conversational style. A lot of the concepts in the sociology of language are rather complex and it seems to me that a more traditional, perhaps aloof, textbook style would make them more difficult to grasp than the less formal style does. As a consequence of this effort, I have quite deliberately ignored some of the usually prescribed rules of English usage. Readers will find, for example, quite a number of sentences that end with a preposition. I realize that there are many potential readers who will find this practice distasteful, but I think that the majority of students will find the less formal style more helpful than distracting. This means, of course, that my editors should not be blamed for my deliberate 'lapses' in style!

Another feature of this volume is the relatively large number of case studies. Wherever I have been able to get detailed information from some part of the world where a sociolinguistic principle is exemplified, I have presented the information as a case study. The major criterion for selecting a society to be featured as a case study was the availability of information. In some cases, the result has been an emphasis on a society in a small corner of the world. For example, because of Susan Gal's (1979) very fine study of language choice, maintenance and shift in the Hungarian community of Oberwart, Austria, this small village is used as a major case study in chapters 7 and 8. Similarly, I have used my own work on data from the Tiwa Indians, a small native American group in the southwestern part of the United States, as another example of maintenance and shift. I am reasonably satisfied that each of the case studies I have chosen are typical of the principles I am using them to illustrate, in spite of their lack of general prominence. A possible exception is the use of the South American nation of Paraguay as an example of societal multilingualism. Typical of multilingual nations in most ways, Paraguay is unique on the South American continent because of the prominence of one of its indigenous languages, Guaraní, relative to its colonial language, Spanish. I find Paraguay fascinating for this reason and have indulged myself by using it as a multilingual case study alongside India in chapter 1. A hazard in using case studies in this way is that I have had to rely more than I would like on secondary sources. Undoubtedly, this has led me to make mistakes in emphasis in some of the cases I write about, if not outright errors. Some of the people who have read earlier drafts of the manuscript have pointed out some examples of this type, but I would be surprised if similar mistakes (minor ones, I hope) do not remain. I am willing to assume the risk because I am convinced that going over an example is far superior to simply trying to explain a principle abstractly.

Where I thought it helpful, I have included maps, figures, and tables as aids to explication. At the end of each chapter, I have included a briefly annotated set of bibliographical notes referring to further readings on the subject, many of which I could not cite directly in the chapter. I anticipate that the bibliographical notes will, among other uses, be helpful for students writing research papers related to the subject matter in the various chapters. Of course, the notes will become dated fairly quickly and student researchers will have to search for more recent material. Following the notes to each chapter, there is a list of 'objectives'. These 'objectives' are really study questions that point readers to information that I consider particularly important. I intend the objectives to be a tool that may be used or ignored. Some teachers might want their students to learn the information highlighted by the objectives; others may choose to ignore them. I don't think the usefulness of the book depends crucially on the objectives.

The objectives are, in fact, part of an instructional technique developed by Frederick Keller (1968) and others. This method, called the 'personalized system of instruction' (PSI), allows students to move through a course of instruction at their own speed, within limits. Classroom activity is considerably different from what is found in a lecture and readings format.

In a PSI format, courses are divided into 'units', each with its own set of readings. Students are assigned the unit readings and a set of objectives of the sort found at the end of the chapters of this book. The objectives are supposed to be explicit and to cover precisely what students are to learn from the readings; they are not held responsible for anything else. If a student is uncertain whether or not she has mastered one or more of the objectives, or if there is something in the readings she does not understand clearly, she comes to the next class period to ask questions. Students are dealt with individually. When a student thinks he has mastered the unit readings, he takes a 'mastery test'. The mastery test contains exactly one question designed to test mastery of each of the objectives. These are, for the most part, short-answer questions, like multiple-choice, but brief essay questions can also be used.

I have briefly described the personalized system of instruction in case an instructor is inclined to use the book in this fashion. This volume contains (as will its companion) the readings and objectives, but the purpose of the mastery tests would be defeated if they were included in the book. A teacher could construct her own mastery tests based on the objectives. I would be happy to advise anyone on mastery test construction. Of course, the book can be used with the PSI format, but it in no way *depends* on it. It can be used as a general course text or a supplementary text in a standard course format. Mastering the objectives can be part of a course requirement, the objectives can be used as a basis for review discussion in class, or ignored entirely. I have attempted to survey the sociolinguistics of society. I have also tried to make it possible to use the book in an alternative teaching method. The survey is usable with or without the methodology.

I extremely grateful to a number of people who have read portions of the manuscript. Each one without exception has helped me materially improve the part they read. If I had been bold enough to impose on them even more than I did, the book would, I am sure, be better than it is; as it is, I must accept full responsibility for its shortcomings. I wish to acknowledge expressly the help I received from Peter Trudgill, himself the author of a fine introductory sociolinguistics textbook, Deborah Tannen, Shaligram Shukla, Roger Shuy, Malcah Yeager-Dror, Walt Wolfram and Ulla Connor. I am also grateful to the anonymous scholars who reviewed the manuscript for the publisher. I used a pre-publication draft of this volume with two different classes of students at Georgetown University, and I am grateful to several students who alerted me to various errors in this draft. In particular, I wash to thank Elisabeth Aasheim, Maria Clara DaSilva, Gina Doggett, Donna Kim, Elizabeth Lanza, Maria Carmelia Machado, Catherine Neill, Marianne Phinney-Liapis, and Theodora Predaris.

Finally, I am grateful to John Davey of Basil Blackwell for his kindness, support, and seemingly infinite patience while I was completing this project.

1

Societal Multilingualism

NATIONS AND LANGUAGES

The sociolinguistics of society is about the social importance of language to groups of people, from small sociocultural groups of a few hundred people to entire nations. If everyone in the group spoke exactly the same as everyone else in the group, there would be no such thing as the sociolinguistics of society. Not only do people use language to share their thoughts and feelings with other people, they exploit the subtle and not so subtle aspects of language to reveal and define their social relationships with the people they are talking to, with people who can overhear them, and even with people who are nowhere around.

In many countries of the world, a lot of this kind of social identity work can be accomplished simply by choosing one or another of the two or more languages a speaker knows. A large number of countries are so linguistically diverse that it is not uncommon for even children to be bilingual or multilingual. Many countries in Africa and Asia (for example, Nigeria, Tanzania, India, Indonesia and the Philippines) have literally hundreds of languages within their borders. It's not the case that these countries have one language that almost everyone speaks, with the rest belonging to small isolated tribes. Of course, there *are* small-group languages, but there are others spoken by substantial populations. India, for example, recognizes 14 languages in its constitution, all but one of which is spoken by at least two million people (the exception is Sanskrit, a classical language). The Philippines has six major regional languages and Nigeria has three. Nigeria, at least, also has a second echelon of important languages within each region. Lewis (1972a) lists 85 nationalities within the Soviet Union, most of which have their own languages. Canada, in addition to English and French, has numerous Indian and Eskimo languages within its borders as well as substantial populations of immigrants who maintain their own languages to one degree or another. The United States is not so monolingual as is sometimes thought;

there are three major Spanish-speaking populations: Puerto Ricans, Cuban immigrants, and Chicanos. There are also speakers of native American languages and European and Asian languages, due to earlier and recent immigration.

Concepts

In order to understand what multilingualism means to a society, it will be helpful to have certain concepts in mind. The ones we will use are those developed by Joshua Fishman (1968b, 1972c). Fundamental to Fishman's thinking is the difference between *nationality* and *nation.* Nationalities are 'sociocultural units that have developed beyond primarily local self-concepts, concerns, and integrative bonds' (Fishman 1972c:3). In other words, a nationality is a group of people who think of themselves as a social unit different from other groups, but not just on a purely local scale. Two important points should be kept in mind about the concept 'nationality'. First, it is to be distinguished from a closely related notion, *ethnic group,* which is just like a nationality except that it is a level of sociocultural organization that is 'simpler, smaller, more particularistic, more localistic' (Fishman 1972c:3). As usual in sociolinguistics, 'nationality' and 'ethnic group' are points on a continuum rather than discrete distinctions. In other words, we will find it difficult, in some cases, to decide whether a sociocultural unit is a nationality or an ethnic group. Nevertheless, a given group's relative position on this continuum is sometimes important.

The second important point about the nationality concept is that nationalities do not necessarily have their own autonomous territory. In Fishman's words, 'the term "nationality" is neutral with respect to the existence or nonexistence of a corresponding political unit or polity' (Fishman 1972c:4). Civil wars, then, can often be understood as an armed struggle by a nationality to get control of its own territory.

By Fishman's definition, a nation is 'any political-territorial unit which is largely or increasingly under the control of a particular nationality' (Fishman 1972c:5). There is a certain indeterminacy in Fishman's definition; one might ask how much control a particular nationality has to have over its territory before the unit qualifies as a nation. A nation is distinct from a state, polity or country in that the latter may not be independent of external control, whereas a nation is. More to the immediate point, a state, unlike a nation, does not always have a single predominant nationality (Fishman 1972c:5). As a result, Fishman's terminology can be used to speak of multinational states, but not multinational nations, which would be a contradiction in terms. A nation, though, can consist of a variety of ethnic groups. Combining Fishman's distinction between 'nationality' and 'ethnic group' with his distinction between 'nation' and 'state', we get a new continuum. On one end, we have *multinational states* and, on the other, *multiethnic nations.* Politically, multinational states are less stable than multiethnic nations. To the extent that sociocultural groups in a country feel that they themselves are a nationality who merely happen to live under someone else's governing control, to that extent the country is a (possibly unstable) multinational state. If the members of the sociocultural groups in a country feel that they are simultaneously citizens of the nation they live in and members of their particular group, then the country is close to the multiethnic nation end of the continuum. A third possibility – one that is not at all uncommon for small, geographically remote sociocultural groups – is that ethnic groups have no interest whatsoever in the country they live in, either as its loyal citizens or as an oppressor to be resisted. If all the groups in a country except the controlling nationality were of this type, the country would be a multiethnic nation.

The role of language in nationism and nationalism

We are led to a distinction, then, between *nationalism,* feelings that develop from and support nationalities, and *nationism,* or the more pragmatic problems of governing. As we will see, the requirements of nationalism and nationism can be in conflict where language is concerned.

The role of language in nationism is fairly straightforward (Fishman 1968d:7, 9). There are two large arenas in which language becomes a problem for nationism: general government administration and education. The process of governing requires communication both within the governing institutions and between government and the people. This means that a language or languages must be selected for use in governing. As far as nationism is concerned, whatever language does the job best is the best choice. Education requires a medium of instruction (or several) that efficiently transmits knowledge to school children. Again, as far as nationism is concerned, the languages that do the job best and at the least cost are the ones to choose.[1]

The role of language in nationalism is more subtle. Language, together with culture, religion, and history, is a major component of nationalism. Language, as Fishman (1972c:44–55) points out, serves as a link with 'the glorious past' and with authenticity. These are abstract and very emotional concepts, but ones with immense power. A language is not only a vehicle for the history of a nationality, but a part of history itself. As far as 'authenticity' is concerned, it is a great advantage to a nationality if it can claim a language of its own. In Fishman's words 'the mother tongue is an aspect of the soul', or essence of a nationality (Fishman 1972c:46).

Another role that language plays in nationalism is what Fishman (1972c:52) calls 'contrastive self-identification' and Garvin and Mathiot (1956) call the 'unifying and separatist functions'.[2] Simply stated, these terms refer to the feeling of the members of a nationality that they are united and identified with others who speak the same language, and contrast with and are separated from those who do not. The notions of unification and separation go deeper than the simple fact that it is difficult to communicate with people who speak a different language. A person can be bilingual and have good control of a second language and still feel 'unified' with speakers of his first language and 'separated' from speakers of his second language.

Given the powerful symbolic importance of language for nationalism, it is possible that we may have an indicator that we can use to decide whether a given sociocultural group is more a nationality or more an ethnic group. Fishman (1972c:62) writes: 'Nationalisms consciously undertake to produce self-consciously modern, authentic, and unifying standard languages, which are to be consciously employed and conscientiously espoused, where previously there existed only regional and social varieties, unconsciously employed and unemotionally abandoned.' In an earlier article, Fishman (1968d:6) speaks of language as a 'symbol of contranational ethnic-cultural identification on the part of smaller groups who, resisting fusion into the larger nationality, develop a localized nationality consciousness of their own.' So a useful indicator of nationality versus simple ethnicity might be the degree to which a group maintains and advocates the use of its language versus the degree to which it is prepared to abandon it. In our case studies of Paraguay and India, we will test this indicator.

Multilingualism as a problem and a resource

Problems for nationalism. It is obvious that multilingual states have problems that more nearly monolingual ones do not. On the strictly practical level, difficulties in communication within a country can act as an impediment to commerce and industry and be socially disruptive. But more seriously, multilingualism works against nationalism. Given that nation-states are more likely to be stable than multinational states, and given the importance of language for nationalism, the development of a sense of nation is more difficult for a multilingual state than for a monolingual one. Multilingual states can approach the problem in one of two ways: they can either attempt to develop a national language, or they can try to develop nationalism on grounds other than language.[3] Historically, most countries have taken the former route. This leads immediately to the problem of selecting the national language, promoting its acceptance by those who are not its native speakers, and, often, developing the language itself so that it can serve the needs of a modern state. None of these problems is trivial.

Problems for nationism.   Since the problems language presents for nationism are pragmatic rather than symbolic, a solution to a nationist problem often creates a nationalist problem. For example, on pragmatic grounds, the best immediate choice for the language of government in a newly independent colony might be the old colonial language. The colonial governing institutions and records are already in place in that language and those nationals with the most government experience already know it. But the old colonial language is usually a terrible choice on nationalist grounds. For a nationality which has just acquired its own geographical territory, the last language it would want as a national symbol would be the language of the state that had denied it territorial control. So pressing are the immediate problems of nationism, however, that nationalist needs usually have to be postponed in new states with respect to the language of government. One solution, that adopted by Ireland, is to declare both the nationalist language and the language of the deposed power as official (Irish and English, respectively, in the case of Ireland), and use the colonial language for immediate nationist purposes while working on the promotion and development of the nationalist language.[4] India's solution was similar; it declared the chosen nationalist language (Hindi) as official, while allowing *de facto* retention of English as a second language of government, without granting it constitutional recognition. A deadline (which, as it turns out, could not be met) was set for the total replacement of English by Hindi. Other countries, for example, Mali, don't make any official selection and use the colonial language for government, while they search for a solution to the national language problem.

In education, the conflict between nationalism and nationism is likely to be of a different sort. In some respects, the best strategy for language in education is to use the various ethnic–group languages. After all, these are the languages the children already speak and subject-matter instruction can begin immediately without waiting until children learn the nationalist language. According to one point of view, however, this strategy could be hazardous for the development of nationalism. If children receive their education in their ethnic languages, these may increase in importance and become symbols of contranational nationalism. We will address these nationist–nationalist conflicts in education in more detail in chapter 11.

Measurable effects of societal multilingualism. If it is true that multilingual nations have problems that monolingual ones do not, it may be possible to show that multilingual countries are disadvantaged, compared to monolingual ones, in some way that can be measured. Is it demonstrably the case, for instance, that monolingual countries are better off economically than multilingual ones? To show this, it would be necessary to have a measure of economic well-being. We would also need to measure the degree of language diversity in some way, since there are very few totally monolingual nations and many degrees of multilingualism. Then, if those nations whose level of multilingualism is very high are also very low on a scale of economic well-being, that would be evidence of a measurable deleterious effect of multilingualism.

Fishman (1968a) and Pool (1972) are two scholars who have attempted to carry out such an investigation. Both point out that actually carrying out research of this type is not nearly as straightforward as I have described it. Three of the difficulties Pool (1972:215–18) mentions are: first, what to measure and how to measure it; second, unreliability in sources of statistical information, and third, causal inferences. One can think of any number of ways to measure either economic well-being or linguistic diversity.[5] Any measure that is chosen will be approximate at best. The statistics available for whatever measures are selected must be taken from censuses and other survey reports. These sources are often misleading or unreliable, as we shall see later in this chapter and in chapter 5. Most dangerous, perhaps, is the risk of making erroneous causal inferences. For example, suppose it were discovered that most people who prefer bowling to tennis as a leisure-time activity also prefer beer to wine as a beverage. One might try to argue from such data that bowling creates a thirst for beer and tennis creates a similar craving for wine. Or it could be argued that beer makes people feel like bowling and that one effect of drinking wine is an urge to play tennis! If this beverage–sport affinity could be demonstrated (which it never has been, as far as I know), it would be far more likely that some common cause, say a set of values associated with a particular kind of life-style, is responsible for both kinds of preference. One has to be careful in drawing causal inferences from correlational data. If A and B are correlated, it could be that A causes B, that B causes A, or that some third factor C causes both. Even if A ultimately causes B, it could be indirect; A causes X, which causes Y, which causes B.

With these cautions in mind, it is nevertheless instructive to examine Pool's results. As a measure of economic well-being, Pool chose gross domestic product per capita. Gross domestic product per capita measures the value of the economic output of a country in a given year, divided by the number of people in the country. The year used was 1962, or the closest year for which Pool could get data. As his measure of societal multilingualism, he used the size of the largest native-language community in the country relative to the size of the total population. With a moment's thought, it is easy to see why the multilingualism measure works. Suppose the largest language group makes up only 25 per cent of the population of some country. That means the remaining 75 per cent of the population is divided among language groups, the largest of which is *less* than 25 per cent of the total. On the other hand, if the largest group comprises 90 per cent of the population, that leaves only 10 per cent for all the other language groups.

After painstaking research using numerous sources, Pool was able to calculate these two values for 133 countries. The values were placed in a scatterplot, with the gross domestic product (GDP) value on the vertical axis and the proportion of the largest language group to the total population on the horizontal axis. The result is presented in Figure 1.1[6] The upper left quadrant of figure 1.1 has been marked to emphasize the fact that it is nearly empty, compared with the rest of the figure. It appears that the following generalization, in Pool's words, is very nearly true (Pool 1972:222):

a country can have any degree of language uniformity or fragmentation and still be underdeveloped; and a country whose entire population, more or less, speaks the same language can be anywhere from very rich to very poor. But a country that is linguistically highly heterogeneous is always underdeveloped or semideveloped, and a country that is highly developed always has considerable language uniformity.

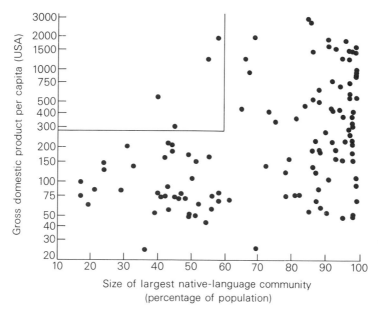

Figure 1.1   Gross domestic product per capita and size of largest native-language community, c. 1962. Each dot represents one nation.
Source: Adapted from Pool (1972:221)

Fishman (1968a:60) has 'the decided impression' that 'linguistically homogeneous polities are usually economically more developed.' In view of our earlier discussion, it is important not to jump to the conclusion that a high degree of multilingualism prevents economic development. It could equally well be the case that economic well-being promotes the reduction of linguistic diversity. Or uniformity and economic well-being might reinforce each other. We should also be open to the possibility that there might be a single cause for the fact that the same countries are so often both highly multilingual and economically underdeveloped. For example, it is arguable that both linguistic diversity and economic disadvantage are the legacy of colonialism. Furthermore, it is entirely possible that the available data are of such poor quality that no confidence can be placed in any patterns that emerge from them. We will look at the issue of multilingualism as related to economic development again in chapter 5 as an example of the use of statistical methods. Still, there is a definite relationship between linguistic uniformity and economic development, though it may not be a causal one.

Societal multilingualism as a resource.   It would be altogether too one-sided to view societal multilingualism only as a problem. In many ways multilingualism can be seen as a resource. First, multilingualism can be at least a temporary solution to nationist–nationalist conflicts in language policy. The use of both a colonial language (for nationist reasons) and a national language (for nationalist reasons) as official government languages can be one solution to nationist-nationalist conflicts at that level. In education, the conflict between using ethnic group languages as media of instruction for nationist reasons of efficiency versus using the national language for nationalist reasons of unity can sometimes be resolved by using the ethnic languages for *initial* education, and later switching to the national language for more advanced education. This, as we will see later in the chapter, is the official policy in India. The policy may contribute to the maintenance of the ethnic-group language alongside the national language, thus maintaining diversity, but this result is part of the solution.[7]

At the individual level, multilingualism serves as an interactional resource for the multilingual speaker. Typically, multilingual societies tend to assign different tasks to different languages or language varieties. One language, for example, might normally be used as the home language and with close friends, whereas another is used for doing business with government agencies. To take a simple scenario, imagine two friends who are both bilingual in the same 'home' and 'government' languages. Suppose one is also a local government official and that his friend has official business with him. Suppose, further, that the government employee has two pieces of advice to give his friend: one based on his official status as a government representative, and one based on their mutual friendship. If the government man gives the official advice in the 'government' language and the friendly advice in the 'home' language, there is little chance that there would be a misunderstanding about which advice was which. The friend would not take the advice given in the 'home' language as official. In a similar monolingual situation, the friendly advice might easily be mistaken for official advice.

A more subtle example is given by Abdulaziz Mkilifi (1978). The example is about language use during arguments of a Swahili–English bilingual married couple in Tanzania. The husband uses Swahili, whereas his wife argues in English. Abdulaziz Mkilifi suggests that the explanation might be that Swahili is symbolic of the traditional, more clear-cut role relationships between husbands and wives, whereas English is associated with less traditional, more converging roles. By using Swahili, the husband is appealing to his traditional role without saying a single word on the subject. At the same time, his wife is appealing to a less submissive view of her role, simply by her choice of English.

These, I take it, are examples of what Southworth (1977:224, cited in Apte 1976:927) means when he says: 'bilinguals develop functions of linguistic heterogeneity which (potentially at least) go beyond the expressive possibilities available in a single code.'

In addition to multilingualism as a solution to nationist– nationalist policy conflicts and as an individual interactional resource, societal multilingualism can contribute to a more dynamic society. A multiethnic society, possibly with concomitant multilingualism, is arguably a richer society than a nation with only one dominant ethnic group. The multiplicity of life-styles and world views can make such a nation a more exciting and stimulating place to live. The ideal situation, from this point of view, is a multiethnic nation where sociocultural groups are aware of their cultural and linguistic identity at the local level, but still consider themselves part of the nation as a whole. In short, the nation is closer to the multiethnic nation end of the continuum than to the multinational state end.

How multilingual nations develop

It is impossible to understand societal multilingualism fully without understanding something of the historical patterns that lead to its existence. Four of these patterns are discernible, although they are not mutually exclusive. Cases that I will give as examples of some of these might justifiably be taken as examples of one of the others instead. Furthermore, a given multilingual society is usually an example of more than one of the historical patterns at the same time. These patterns are: (1) migration, (2) 'imperialism', (3) federation and (4) border area multilingualism.

Migration. Migration can be divided into two broad types, in the first of which a large group expands its territory by moving into contiguous areas, simultaneously taking control over smaller sociocultural groups who are already there. Some of the indigenous populations eventually become nationalized to the larger group and become linguistically and culturally assimilated to one degree or another. Others maintain their own nationality and remain a problem for the unity of the nation controlled by the dominant nationality. The Catalonians in Spain and the Bretons in France are two such incompletely assimilated nationalities. In the United States, the western migration of the descendants of the British colonists after independence can be seen as an example of this type of migration, with various native American cultures being swallowed up along the way. Some native American groups have been assimilated linguistically, if not culturally, but others have not. It is only because the groups involved are so small that their nationalist aspirations are not more noticeable.

The other kind of migration occurs when a small number of members of an ethnic group move into the territory already under the control of another nationality. Immigrants, of course, arrive speaking their native languages, thus adding to the host nation's multilingualism. The United States is a prime example of this kind of immigration, with the nineteenth- and early twentieth-century European and Chinese immigration and the more recent immigration

from the Indo-Chinese countries, Korea, Cuba, and Haiti.[8] Other examples
include immigration to Great Britain from Commonwealth nations and the
'guest worker' immigrations to Germany and Switzerland. Lieberson et al.
(1975) have noticed that the US experience, by and large, has been that
immigrant groups have been fairly quick to assimilate linguistically, whereas
sociocultural groups that were overwhelmed by dominant-group migration –
such as Chicanos, Acadian French, and some native American groups – have
maintained their languages for much longer. Nevertheless, there are exceptions in both directions and it would be dangerous to generalize.

Imperialism. 'Imperialism' is a loaded word and I would have preferred a
neutral term for what I want to talk about, but have not been able to find one.
The subtypes of imperialism are colonization, annexation, and 'economic
imperialism'. 'Imperialism' differs from large group migration only in relative
terms. In large group migration, relatively large numbers of people from a
given nationality move into contiguous geographical areas and take control of
them. In imperialist processes, control is taken with relatively few people from
the controlling nationality actually taking up residence in the new area.
Colonialism and annexation are both types of imperialism, differing only, as
far as I can see, by whether or not people have to cross an ocean to do it.[9] Both
types of imperialism have become less common over time. The absorption of
the Baltic republics (Lithuania, Latvia, and Estonia) into the Soviet Union
after the Second World War may be a modern example of annexation. In the
case of Latvia and Estonia, where Lewis (1972a) reports that 26 per cent and
20 per cent of the populations, respectively, were Russians in 1959, we may
wish to say that we have a case of large group migration.[10] In Lithuania, only 8
per cent of the population was Russian in 1959 (Lewis 1972a:330). Colonialism, of course, can be exemplified by any number of former British, French,
Spanish, Portuguese, and Dutch colonies in Africa, Asia, and South America,
most of which have achieved independence in this century.

In 'economic imperialism', a foreign language makes inroads into a country
without the associated nationality ever taking political control, partly because
of the economic advantage associated with it (Fishman et al. 1977). The use of
English in Thailand, a country which has never been the colony of any
English-speaking country, but which has attempted to teach English to a large
segment of its population none the less, is a good example (Aksornkool 1980).

All three varieties of what I am calling 'imperialism' have the effect of
introducing the language of the imperialist countries into other societies. In
spite of the fact that relatively few people from the imperialist nation take up
residence in the subjugated territories, their language eventually takes on
considerable importance. In annexation and colonization, the imperialist
language is likely to be used in government and education; in economic
imperialism, the imperialist language becomes necessary for international
commerce and diplomacy. Annexation and especially colonialization have a

further effect on multilingualism – forced federation.

Federation. The third historical pattern contributing to multilingualism is federation. By federation, I mean the union of diverse ethnic groups or nationalities under the political control of one state. Federation may be voluntary or forced. Cases of voluntary federation are rare, and the best example is Switzerland, where there has been a union of states (called cantons); these for the most part joined the federation voluntarily. Switzerland has four languages with official status: German, French, Italian, and Romansch, although there are not many speakers of Romansch. Another example might be Belgium. Belgium is a country consisting of two major linguistic groups: the French-speaking Walloons in the southern part of the country and the Flemish in the north. The Flemish speak a language of the same name, which is similar to Dutch. When Belgium became independent in 1830, the Flemish elite spoke French, and Flemish nationalism, with language as its symbol, was not well developed. In this century, Flemish nationalism has increased greatly, causing considerable unrest in Belgium (Lorwin 1972). Thus, Belgium is undergoing some of the same stresses that forced federations undergo, although historically its federation was not forced.

Cameroon is another example of voluntary federation, but only in the sense that it is a federation of a former French and a former British colony. The fact that French and English are both used in Cameroon is a consequence of this federation. With respect to the indigenous languages of Cameroon, its multilingualism is, as in other former colonies, a product of forced federation.

By forced federation, I mean primarily the effect of European colonization in Africa and Asia and, to a lesser extent, in the western hemisphere. Various multilingual states put together by force also rose and fell in Europe throughout history, and the sociolinguistic effects of some of them exist today, but we will concentrate our attention on the more recent cases of colonization. The boundaries of European colonies were established largely on grounds other than the ethnic affinities of the subjugated peoples. As a result, many colonies brought together sociocultural and linguistic groups under a single administration that had never had a common government before and may never have become part of the same nation if left to themselves. The result is a *de facto* federation of numerous sociocultural groups who never had much say in the matter. When former colonies become independent, the new state remains a federation. Occasionally, a force-federated nationality will attempt to secede, as did Biafra from Nigeria, Katanga from Zaire, and Bangladesh from Pakistan. Only Bangladesh was successful. It then becomes a task for the new nation to develop a society that is more a multiethnic nation than a multinational state. This necessity is reflected in language policy. Most former European colonies, then, are examples of both imperialism and forced federation.

Border areas.   The fourth historical origin of multilingualism is concerned with border areas. Every state must have reasonably definite geographical boundaries so that, for example, it is clear from whom it can collect taxes, what areas it is committed to defend militarily, and where it is obliged to provide government services. However, sociocultural groups do not always select their area of residence for the convenience of political boundary drawing. As a result, in many areas near the borders between countries, there are people who are citizens of one country, but members of a sociocultural group based in the other. One example among many of this phenomenon is the presence of French-speaking people in the northeastern United States who live in the United States, but are ethnically closer to the citizens of the Canadian province of Quebec.

A complication in the case of border areas is connected with the spoils of war. A nation that loses a war is often forced to give up territory to neighboring victorious countries. Sometimes these are multiethnic or multi-national areas that have been contended for by neighboring countries for long periods of time and end up as part of whichever country was on the winning side in the most recent war. Alsace-Lorraine is one example. Inhabited by speakers of varieties of both German and French, the two provinces have been part of both countries during their histories. Alsace and Lorraine are now part of France, where the German-speaking population contributes to multi-lingualism in that country.

There is an American case which might be viewed from the perspective of any of the four patterns. This is the acquisition of a huge area of the southwest United States by cession from Mexico at the conclusion of the Mexican–American War in 1848. This can be taken as an example of the shifting of a multiethnic border area as a result of war. Or, it can easily be argued that it is actually a case of annexation-type imperialism on the part of the United States. To the extent that American interest in the territory was due to the fact that Americans had moved into it, it can be taken as a case of large group migration. As far as the various groups of native Americans in the southwest are concerned, it is a case of forced federation. I point out this ambiguity to emphasize the fact that the four historical patterns are not to be taken as hard and fast categories, such that every multilingual society is an example of one and not the others. Rather, they are historical strands, some of which, like annexation and large group migration, are not clearly distinguished from each other. Furthermore, two or more of these strands often converge in the history of some particular society or country.

With this discussion as background, we will examine Paraguay and India as examples of multilingual polities.

PARAGUAY

Background

Paraguay is a land-locked country in central South America (map 1.1). It has had a checkered history involving European colonization, varying degrees of independence from Spain and from neighboring South American countries, and devastating wars with its neighbors. Like all countries in the western hemisphere, part of its multilingualism has its origins in the colonization and

Map 1.1   Paraguay, showing the Chaco region

forced federation of indigenous peoples. But in Paraguay there is a difference which is unique in the western hemisphere and perhaps in the world. Beginning in the sixteenth century, the Spanish colonists and their descendants began adopting one of the indigenous American languages, Guaraní. The result is that in 1950, nearly 95 per cent of the population spoke Guaraní; far more than claimed to know Spanish (Rona 1966, Rubin 1978). In no other country in the New World has an indigenous language been so thoroughly adopted.

The most important language issues in Paraguay, then, involve the relationship between Guaraní and Spanish, but there are two other, minor sources of linguistic diversity in Paraguay. One is small-group immigration, largely Mennonites who have established semi-autonomous colonies in the western half of the country; as well as other German immigrants, Slavs, and Japanese. The other is the result of the forced federation of unassimilated native sociocultural groups, who, like the Mennonites, are located largely in the western Chaco region (Klein and Stark 1977). We will have more to say about the languages of the Indians in the Chaco later.

Bilingualism patterns

Spanish is used in Paraguay as the language of government and, at least until very recently, as the exclusive language of education in state schools. In urban areas, majorities of the populations claim to know Spanish, mostly as a second language. According to the census data from 1950, presented by Rona (1966:284), 89.1 per cent of the population of Asunción, the capital, knew Spanish. By far the greatest proportion of them (76.1 per cent of the city's population) were bilingual in Spanish and Guaraní.[11] The picture in the rural areas is far different. Outside the capital, the census data indicate that 45.8 per cent report monolingualism in Guaraní and 49.5 per cent report themselves as bilingual.[12] Rona, however, believes that the bilingualism percentage is exaggerated even at that. He points out that transportation and communication in Paraguay in 1950 were very poor, with the inevitable result that some remote areas were not reached. These are the very areas where Guaraní is spoken almost exclusively. Furthermore, it seems likely that many rural people who told census takers that they 'knew' Spanish actually knew no more than a few words.

When these two factors are taken into account, Rona estimates that less than half the total population of Paraguay actually knows Spanish and less than 40 per cent is really bilingual. In the rural areas, knowledge of Spanish and bilingualism would be far less. Except for Asunción, census data for Paraguay are reported only by *department* (roughly equivalent to US states). The departments include both rural areas and towns, and it is known that knowledge of Spanish is much more common in towns than in the country. Using the data from the department of Caaguazú, which has two major towns,

Rona (1966:285) estimates that if 60 per cent of the population of the towns spoke Spanish (compared to over 89 per cent in Asunción), then there would be *nobody* in the rural areas of the department who knew Spanish. Rona's estimation seems to be on the right track; according to Rubin (1978:189), Guaraní monolingualism reported outside Asunción rose from 45.8 per cent in the 1959 census to over 52 per cent in the 1962 census. Presumably, more of the remote areas of the country were reached by the census in 1962.[13] The picture we get is of a nation with few Spanish monolinguals, almost universal knowledge of Guaraní, substantial bilingualism between the two languages in urban areas, especially the capital, and mostly Guaraní monolingualism in the rural areas.

Language attitudes

An important factor in Paraguay is the feelings of the people toward the two major languages. It turns out to be very ambivalent. On the one hand, Guaraní fills the unifying and separatist function of Garvin and Mathiot (the same as Fishman's 'contrastive self-identification'); in fact Guaraní was the language they used to illustrate these functions (Garvin and Mathiot 1956, Rona 1966:286). It seems to be a common attitude that anyone who does *not* know Guaraní is not really Paraguayan (Rona 1966:282), thus excluding out the small-group immigrant, the unassimilated Indians, and even monolingual Spanish speakers. Paraguayans argue that Guaraní is especially fit to express abstract notions, and that it is a great language (Rona 1966:287-8). On the other hand, there are urban Paraguayans who believe that Paraguay cannot make progress until the knowledge of Spanish becomes more widespread. Monolingual speakers of Guaraní are held in disdain by bilinguals and often consider themselves stupid because they cannot speak Spanish (Rubin 1978:479). For most Paraguayans, there is a nagging feeling that Guaraní is not quite respectable, because it is a 'mere' Indian language. Paraguayans have a profound sense of devotion to their language; they want to be proud of it and are. Nevertheless, there is a covert sense of uneasiness about it and a feeling that somehow Spanish is really more elegant and better.

In terms of social status for the two languages, these feelings about Guaraní and Spanish interact in a rather intricate way. Guaraní is simply a prerequisite for status as a genuine Paraguayan. It conveys no special status within the nation. Spanish is used for the elevated functions of the society and so conveys prestige on those who speak it *in addition* to Guaraní. 'Those who speak only Spanish have no social rating at all' (Rona 1966:286).

Nationalist–nationist conflicts in government and education

Until 1967, only Spanish was officially recognized. In 1967, the constitution was revised to recognize both Spanish and Guaraní as 'national' languages, but only Spanish as 'official' (Rubin 1978:191). It appears that nationist concerns have prevailed in the choice of the language of government. The colonial language remains in place in this function. Apparently Guaraní, clearly the symbolic language of nationalism, is not ready to be used as an official governing language, due to the lack of development of its technical vocabulary (Rona 1966 presents evidence of this). In any case, Paraguay has been independent of Spain for more than 150 years and the use of Spanish is not perceived as a threat to nationalism. There seems to be no agitation for the adoption of Guaraní as the official language of government. Paraguay seems to be a classic case of the value of a multilingual solution to the nationist–nationalist conflict. Guaraní can serve as the national language (in Fishman's sense), whereas Spanish is allowed to serve nationist purposes.

It is not immediately clear why there should be a nationalist–nationist conflict in the area of education. At first glance, Guaraní would seem to be the choice as the language of education on both counts. To use Guaraní as the language of education would strengthen the symbolic value of the national language and so serve the goals of nationalism. Since nearly 95 per cent of the population speaks Guaraní and only about half speaks Spanish, it would appear that the business of educating children would go most smoothly through a Guaraní medium. In fact, Spanish has *always* been the exclusive language of education in Paraguay, and Guaraní was not even permitted in the classroom at all until 1973 (Rubin 1978:191). Children were forced to give up using Guaraní not only in class but on the playground, sometimes with flogging as the penalty (Rubin 1968a:480, 1978:190–1). Rubin paints a grim picture of the effects of this policy, especially in rural areas; slow, inadequate acquisition of Spanish, a high drop-out rate, and an astonishing amount of grade repetition are some of them.[14]

If nationalist considerations would dictate the use of Guaraní and the practical concerns of nationism seem not to be met by the use of Spanish as the medium of instruction, why has the Spanish-only policy persisted? Indeed, why was it instituted in the first place? To answer these questions, let us take the nationalist and nationist considerations separately. As far as nationalism is concerned, Guaraní simply does not and never did need support from the educational system as a national language. Guaraní was firmly established as a unique national language for Paraguay well before independence. The issue of whether or not to use the education system to teach people their national language simply never arose. On nationism, although it may seem reasonable that children would learn better if their teachers used a language they could understand, and although the Paraguayan experience shows that Spanish-medium instruction is not working, the situation is not *perceived* in these terms. Guaraní simply has not been and, to a great extent, still is not considered adequate for the lofty task of educating the nation's children. At the practical level, there is also a shortage of educational materials in Guaraní and teachers who can teach in it.

In sum, Guaraní has not been used as the language of education in Paraguay because the education system was not needed to shore up Guaraní in its nationalist function and Guaraní was not perceived as the appropriate language for the nationist goal of efficient education. From this perspective – directly the opposite of our initial discussion – Spanish is the obvious choice as the language of education.

This is not the end of the story. Perhaps it can be argued that Guaraní is not sufficiently developed for higher or even secondary education (whether it is or not, it is very unlikely that Paraguayans will soon *believe* that it is). But maybe Paraguayans can be convinced that it is best to use Guaraní for *initial* education, simultaneously with the teaching of Spanish as a second language, and then later to switch to Spanish as the medium. The government has taken a few steps in that direction. In 1973, a 'New Curriculum' was initiated by the Ministry of Education which authorized and even encouraged the use of Guaraní in primary education as a way of facilitating the transition to Spanish (Rubin 1978:191 – 2). Few concrete steps have been taken toward implementation of the bilingual education approach, and Rubin outlines a number of issues that have to be addressed if the program is to be successful. None the less, the initial use of Guaraní does no violence to nationalist goals, and if it proves to be efficient from a nationist point of view, Paraguay may well be the better for it.

The Indians of the Chaco[15]

It will be interesting and instructive to examine more closely the minor Paraguayan multilingualism that is the result of forced federation. Paraguay is thought of as having two major parts – the eastern section, known as the Oriental, and the west, called the Chaco (see map 1.1). The Chaco is extremely sparsely populated, having 60 per cent of the nation's geographical area and only 3 per cent of its population (Klein and Stark 1977). The Chaco is the home of most of Paraguay's unassimilated Indian ethnic groups. Klein and Stark (1977) recognize 13 languages in five linguistic groups spoken by only some 24,000 people. This seems a large number of languages for so few people, and it is true that there is a high degree of linguistic diversity among the Indians of the Chaco. On the other hand, some of these languages are closely related and can be understood to some degree by speakers of the others. The five 'languages' in the Mascoi family are all somewhat inter-intelligible and all are called Enlhit or Enenlhit by their speakers.

In general, these Indians have been forced to give up their traditional economies, based on fishing, hunting, and gathering, and to try to find places in the Paraguayan national economy. Some have been able to participate in both systems by hunting wild game and selling the skins, but, with increasing agricultural development in the Chaco and new laws against selling the skins of wild animals, this practice is also diminishing. Others have worked for generations in factories that manufacture chemicals for treating skins, but this industry is dying for the same reason. The opportunities that are left consist mostly of employment on ranches as agricultural workers, in agricultural jobs in the large, semi-autonomous Mennonite colonies in the central Chaco (a surprisingly large proportion of these Indians are employed by the Mennonites), and on military bases. Some live in areas administered by various Christian missionary groups, some of whom are teaching Indians agricultural techniques with a view to their achieving self-sufficiency.

The linguistic practices of these sociocultural groups vary substantially from 100 per cent maintenance of the tribal language to a total shift away from it. The fate of any one of these languages depends very much on the recent history of its speakers and on their cultural values. A brief discussion of two groups, the Angaité and the Chulupí, illustrates this point.

The Angaité speak one of the varieties of Mascoi. Some have been working for several generations in the chemical factories, which have also employed Indians speaking other Mascoi language varieties. There has been considerable intermarriage as a result. Even though there is a moderate amount of inter-intelligibility among these languages, husbands and wives from different languages will use Guaraní with each other and with their children. Other Angaité work on ranches or on Mennonite farms. Like the factory workers, they consider Guaraní to be prestigious and either speak Guaraní to their children or encourage them to learn it from other Paraguayans. Only one band of 250, who live on a mission facility where they are learning agriculture, retain Angaité as a home language. Except for this one band, it seems likely that the Angaité will have shifted from their tribal language to Guaraní within two generations.

The Chulupí speak a language of the Mataguayo group and are considered the ethnic group with the greatest linguistic and cultural pride in the Chaco. Although some have had to learn Spanish or Guaraní for reasons of employment, they generally do not learn these languages well and do not mix them with their tribal language. Unlike the Angaité, their home language is invariably Chulupí. Also in contrast with the Angaité, a Chulupí Indian will make a great effort to understand a speaker of another Mataguayo language without resorting to Guaraní as a contact language. This is true in spite of the fact that the Mataguayo languages are much less similar than the Mascoi languages are. In many places where Chulupí Indians live, there are bilingual education programs in Chulupí and Spanish, some of which use materials developed by the Indians themselves. In the Mennonite town of Filadelfia the Mennonites operate a radio station which broadcasts some programs in Indian languages. The Chulupís have requested that Spanish loanwords be removed from the Chulupí broadcasts so that only pure Chulupí will be heard. It is easy to predict that the Chulupís will maintain their language for the foreseeable future.

Earlier, I mentioned the possibility of using Fishman's statements about language maintenance, shift and espousal as an indicator of whether a given sociocultural group was more an ethnicity or a nationality. Recall that Fishman spoke of nationalisms being consciously concerned with the use, promotion, and authenticity of their languages. This pattern is contrasted with the unconscious use and unemotional abandonment of languages by ethnic groups who are not small-group nationalities. The former pattern is clearly true of the Chulupí. They consciously use their own language whenever possible and teach it to their children at home, they promote it through their active involvement in bilingual education programs, and they protect its authenticity by refusing to use or allow the use of loanwords from Spanish and Guaraní. They qualify, on these criteria, as a subnational nationality.

The Angaité, on the other hand, seem to regard their language as nothing but a communication tool. As soon as the tool is found to be inefficient, even when the addressee speaks a similar language, it is unemotionally abandoned in favor of a better tool, Guaraní. The Angaité, on the language-as-symbol criterion, are an ethnic group rather than a nationality.

Finally, we should mention briefly the languages of the Tupi-Guaraní group. Klein and Stark (1977) distinguish two of these, both of which are called Guaraní-eté by their speakers. They are both related to the national language, Guaraní. One of them is sometimes called 'tribal Guaraní' and is distinguished from 'Paraguayan Guaraní', the national language. The tribal languages are linguistically very close to the 'national' language and may be more conservative varieties of the same ancestor language. Partly due to the linguistic similarity, though mostly due to cultural values, both Tupi-Guaraní groups are rapidly shifting to the national language.

Paraguay – multiethnic nation or multinational state?

Paraguay is clearly very close to the multiethnic nation end of the continuum. It has a national language spoken by the overwhelming majority of its citizens. The Guaraní language fulfills the symbolic functions of a national language, especially the unifying and separatist functions. Nationist functions are fulfilled by Spanish with no threat to nationalism. It is possible that one nationist function – language of education – may soon be partly carried out by Guaraní, further strengthening the national language, and probably improving primary education in the bargain. The immigrant groups are not considered real Paraguayans, but are not considered a threat or disruptive force either. The indigenous populations seem to include both ethnic groups, such as the Angaité, and subnational nationalities, such as the Chulupí. But even the groups with their own incipient national consciousness are so small as to pose no real threat to unity (there are only about 5,000 Chulupís, for example). There can be no real doubt that Paraguay is among the genuine nation-states of the world.

INDIA

Background

India – the sociolinguistic giant – is one of the most multilingual countries in the world.[16] No one knows definitely how many languages are spoken within its borders, but they number several hundred. Khubchandani (1978:553) refers to 'about 200 classified languages'. Grimes (1978:266) lists 312 languages for India. The languages referred to by Le Page (1964:54) total 844, including 63 'non-Indian' languages. The 1961 census lists 1,652 'languages and dialects' (Apte 1976:141), but this number is unrealistically high, mainly because it includes hundreds of mother tongues with very few speakers (210 of them have only one or two speakers) and because some languages get counted more than once under slightly different names (Apte 1976:142). The real number of languages, whatever it is, is certainly a large one.

As a British possession until independence was achieved in 1947, the present-day pattern of India's multilingualism is largely due to the usual effects of colonialism and forced federation. Of course, there had been a long history of multilingualism in India before it became a British possession.[17] Whatever political arrangements might have evolved if there had been no European intervention, they would no doubt have involved some nationalities and ethnic groups being governed by others. It is probably also true that many of the social and political conflicts that India has faced involving language would have been avoided, if it had not been a colony.

Not all the hundreds of languages in India, of course, have the same status. Hindi, as we will see, was selected as the national language and is so designated in the constitution. English is not mentioned in the constitution, but is in fact used as a government language at the federal level and in some states. The VIIIth Schedule, a section of India's constitution, lists 14 languages as 'the languages of India' (Le Page 1964:53). India is divided linguistically into two major language families, the Indo-Aryan languages in the north and the Dravidian languages of the south, although there are a number of languages that belong to neither linguistic family. Of the VIIIth Schedule languages, ten are Indo-Aryan (Assamese, Bengali, Gujerati, Hindi, Kashmiri, Marathi, Oriya, Panjabi, Sanskrit, and Urdu). The other four (Kannada, Malayalam, Tamil, and Telegu) are Dravidian languages. The VIIIth Schedule languages account for 90 per cent of India's population. In the 1971 census, each of them was claimed by 10 million speakers or more except Assamese (8.95 million), Kashmiri (2.42 million), and Sanskrit (Apte 1976:159). Sanskrit is a classical language; its relationship to the Indo-Aryan languages is similar to the relationship between Latin and the Romance languages. Although it is often considered a dead language, 2,544 people claimed it as a mother tongue in the 1971 census.[18] In any case, it is included in the VIIIth Schedule because of its religious and cultural importance for the majority Hindu population, rather than because of the number of its speakers.

In addition to the VIIIth Schedule languages, there are another 19 that have one million or more speakers, and 49 others with at least 100,000 speakers (Apte 1976:142). The remaining languages are small-group languages, somewhat comparable to the indigenous languages of the Chaco in Paraguay.

Bilingualism patterns

With the degree of diversity that exists in India, a great deal of individual bilingualism and multilingualism is to be expected. The 1961 census figures indicate that 9.7 per cent of the population of India is bilingual (Khubchandani 1978:559) – a surprisingly low figure. However, there are reasons to

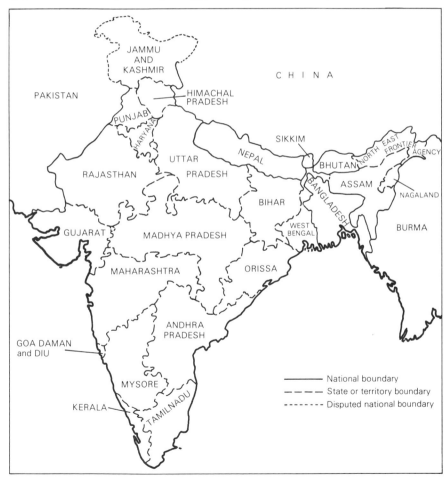

Map 1.2   Political subdivisions of India, 1966

believe that the census figures on bilingualism are misleading, especially in the north-central part of the country (Khubchandani 1978). Examining these will give us new insights into Indian language diversity.

To begin with, classifying and labeling languages in India has proved to be a source of controversy. Part of the reason for this is that, especially among the Indo-Aryan languages, one language tends to fade into a related one with no clear break between them. An important example of this, although not altogether typical, is the relationship between Hindi and Urdu. Hindi and Urdu share substantially the same phonological and grammatical systems. However, they are written with different writing systems, their historical and cultural statuses are different and, in written prose style, their vocabularies are partially distinct. The Hindi side of the language complex has historically been used by the Hindu segment of the population. It is written in a script called Devanagari, the same script used to write Sanskrit. Hindi speakers, as opposed to Urdu speakers, use vocabulary derived or borrowed from Sanskrit. Urdu is the language of the Muslims and is written in Perso-Arabic script. Its vocabulary is borrowed from Persian and Arabic, rather than from Sanskrit. It is clear that one could immediately identify any written text as being either Hindi or Urdu, because of the sharp script differences. In written style, there would be some lexical items that belong to either Hindi or to Urdu, but in the spoken language, where Hindi-Urdu is used as a link language to accomplish everyday communicative tasks, the two merge into one. Many writers dealing with the sociolinguistics of India tend to emphasize the similarities between Hindi and Urdu and refer to Hindi-Urdu (for example, Kachru and Bhatia 1978; Khubchandani 1977, 1978).[19] Although much less closely related to either Hindi or Urdu than they are to each other, Panjabi has at times been considered part of the same language complex, even by its own speakers (Kachru and Bhatia 1978:532). The 1951 Indian census counted all three languages as one, but each has been counted separately in subsequent censuses.

Another aspect of the problem is that some speech varieties are hard to classify. A case in point is Maithili. Maithili was claimed as a mother tongue by over six million people in the 1971 census (Apte 1976:160); it has its own script and literary tradition. It is structurally similar to Bengali and would no doubt be considered a variety of that language from a technical linguistic point of view. Yet it contains considerable vocabulary borrowed from Hindi. If the status of Maithili were to be decided on linguistic criteria alone, there would be little problem, since borrowing of vocabulary is not a criterion for determining language relationships. But Maithili is officially considered a dialect of Hindi – a state of affairs which Kachru and Bhatia (1978:51) find regrettable. They would prefer a third option, that Maithili be considered a language separate from both Hindi and Bengali. Clearly, the decision on what status to accord a speech variety like Maithili is made more on political than linguistic grounds.

All this means that when the census-taker comes around to ask an Indian citizen what his mother tongue is and what other languages he speaks, it is not so easy to answer. For some people, it may be the first time they have even had to think about what language they speak. The answer is likely to be based more on the desire to be associated with a prestige language, to appear patriotic, or to claim allegiance to a local ethnic group. For example, imagine a speaker who uses an Indo-Aryan speech variety at home that she does not have any name for. She is likely to think it is not really a language at all. She may be able to understand Hindi to some degree and to use colloquial Hindi for interethnic dealings. Hindi is the national language; it has status and prestige. She tells the census-taker she speaks Hindi. Another speaker speaks a segment of Indo-Aryan called Rajasthani. Should he claim Rajasthani? Rajasthani is not an VIIIth Schedule language, it is noticeably similar to Hindi, and Hindi is the national language. He wishes to appear patriotic; he claims Hindi. According to Kachru and Bhatia (1978:53–4), this was a motivation many people responded to in the 1951 census, immediately after independence. In each of the 1961 and 1971 censuses, the number of people who claimed Hindi rather than one of its 'dialects' declined.

On the other hand, some people have a very local self-concept. Not knowing a name for their language, and unwilling for one reason or other to name one of the major languages, they give the name of their caste, locality, or even their occupations as the name of their language (Apte 1976:142). It is now up to the census officials to decide how to count such a response.

The lack of clear lines of demarcation among some of the Indo-Aryan languages leads to a situation that Khubchandani calls fluidity (for example, 1977:40, cf. Gumperz and Naim 1960). A speaker may control a verbal repertoire which makes him a native speaker of a range of speech that is labeled with more than one dialect name. Much of what is called 'bilingualism' in India is more a matter of inherent variability than of code-switching. What is confusing is that different parts of this variation get called by different names. If we can imagine that what an American lawyer spoke in his office were called 'English' and what he spoke at home were called 'American' and they were regarded as separate languages, we have something of what is meant by fluidity. Of course, the language varieties in India differ from each other more than these imaginary English varieties would.

Knowing all this, it is still not completely clear whether we ought to say there is more bilingualism in north-central India than the census figures indicate or not. It is probably the case that people understand each other a lot better than the census figures would lead us to believe. The statistical tools discussed in chapter 5 will allow us to throw more light on the issue of the extent of Indian bilingualism.

Language of government

Federal government.   Like most newly independent states, India was left with a colonial language, English, as the language of government. At that moment, the nationist imperative that the new nation immediately carry out government functions dictated that English continue to be used. Nationalist motivations, on the other hand, dictated that an indigenous Indian language be adopted as the national language. Hindi seemed to be the most qualified candidate. It had more native speakers by far than any other Indian language and was widely used as a means of interethnic communication.

However, there were three problems with selecting Hindi. First, although it is a widely-known and used language, it is far from evenly distributed throughout the country. At one extreme is the northern (Indo-Aryan area) state of Uttar Pradesh, where a calculation from some of the 1961 census figures given by Khubchandani (1978) indicates that 96.7 per cent of the population claimed Hindi or Urdu as either a first or second language. At the other extreme is Tamilnadu, a state in the Dravidian language-speaking south; less than 0.0002 per cent of the population said they knew Hindi or Urdu. Second, its selection offended the subnational nationality sentiments of the speakers of other languages. Other Indian languages (for example, Tamil and Bengali) had literary traditions as rich as Hindi's and, in the minds of their speakers, had as much right to be 'national' languages as Hindi did. Third, in comparison with English, it seemed that Hindi might need vocabulary development before it could be used efficiently as a language of government. Nevertheless, these problems were considered tractable and Hindi was named as the national language in the constitution. The task of language development was begun and a fifteen-year deadline was set for the complete replacement of English by Hindi. That deadline passed in 1965. Due to continued opposition to Hindi in the south, it was not politically possible to make the changeover. A law was passed in 1967 allowing the use of both Hindi and English for all official purposes and that situation still exists.

The nationist–nationalist conflict with respect to the language of government was much more complicated in India than in Paraguay. In Hindi's favor, there was much less a feeling that the language was not good enough for official use than there seems to have been in Paraguay concerning Guaraní. On the other hand, at the time of Paraguayan independence, Guaraní actually *was* the national language, and did not have to be made so. This, of course, was not true of Hindi. Most important of all, Guaraní has no competition from other indigenous languages and there are no other languages serving as symbols of large-group nationalisms. India is not so fortunate in that respect. The bilingual solution at the official federal-government level in India is not so much a resolution of nationist-nationalist conflicts as it is a solution to the requirements of nationalism in a country as a whole versus the nationalist sensibilities of its component groups.

The question of whether or not Hindi is a viable candidate as a national language, in the sense that it might be used by a substantial portion of the population throughout the country, is a matter of considerable debate. Using the 1961 census figures, Khubchandani (1978) analyzes the status of Hindi-Urdu and other Indian languages as contact languages. One of his conclusions is the following:

[The] H[indi]-U[rdu] amalgam, by virtue of being the most dominant language of the largest region, exercises a good deal of influence in intergroup communication throughout the country (of course with varying degrees of intensity in different regions). It had virtually acquired the position of a *lingua franca* for trade, entertainment, and informal communication in heterogeneous situations (mainly urban, industrial, and military settlements) throughout the country, *well before the hectic involvement of official and semiofficial agencies in the promotion of H.* (Khubchandani 1978:563; italics in the original)

Kelley (1966:304), using the 1951 census figures, comes to the opposite conclusion:

the census figures show little evidence for the assertion that Hindi is already known (or at least is already in daily use) throughout the country. Bombay alone of all the major cities which lie outside the Hindi heartland provides evidence to support the claim that Hindi functions as a lingua franca.

Anyone reading the two articles would see that the different conclusions reflect the authors' different points of view, not a difference between the two censuses. In fact, a careful reading of the two quotations will show that they both could be factually true.

The most reasonable conclusion I have seen on this issue is the remark made by Ferguson in response to Kelley's paper (Bright 1966:307): 'If you look all over the country as a whole and measure the use of second languages everywhere, which one is more widely used as a second language than any other? I am sure the statistics would support Hindi as meeting that criterion.'

State governments. India is subdivided into two kinds of political units, states and centrally administered 'union territories'. The states were established on linguistic grounds. As a result, the majorities of the populations of all India's states, except two, speak the same language. The two states without a linguistic majority are Himachal Pradesh and Nagaland. The majorities range from just under 55 per cent in Bihar (Hindi-Urdu is the majority language) and the state of Jammu and Kashmir (Kashmiri) to over 95 per cent in Uttar Pradesh (Hindi-Urdu) and Kerala (Malayalam) (Apte 1976:161–3). None of the states are totally monolingual. The states and union territories were left free to determine their own official government languages at that level. Most states chose the language of their linguistic majorities, but some selected English. Nagaland, one of the two states without a linguistic majority, uses English. The other, Himachal Pradesh, chose Hindi. Jammu and Kashmir bypassed its majority language, Kashmiri, and made Urdu official. The states have expended considerable effort in developing special vocabularies, shorthand systems, typewriters, and educational materials for their official state languages. Translations of federal and state laws, rules, and regulations are available in regional languages as are official forms of various types.

This freedom to use and develop state languages is something of a calculated risk. On the one hand, since language can be a symbol of subnational nationalism, to allow such freedom could encourage divisive nationalistic feelings on the state level. On the other, attempting to suppress the regional languages might have caused sharp resentment. The political impossibility of making Hindi the sole official language at the federal level may be an indication that India has taken the less hazardous route. In fact, there is reason to believe that linguistic diversity is less a political threat in India than it would be in Europe. We will return to this issue later.

Linguistic minorities.   The federal government's pluralistic approach to the major regional languages is extended to the minority languages in official policy. Speakers of minority languages have certain legally guaranteed rights, and there is an official, the Commissioner for Linguistic Minorities, whose function it is to deal with their complaints. However, it is well known that the minority languages are woefully neglected by the state governments, compared to the official state languages. The Commissioner for Linguistic Minorities has only advisory powers and cannot force state governments to follow his recommendations. States typically follow policies that, in practice, discourage the retention of minority languages and encourage the acquisition and use of state languages. Having achieved linguistic autonomy at the state level, state governments are most reluctant to grant it within their states. In relation to the state governments, linguistic minorities are considerably less numerous and less powerful than are the linguistic states in relation to the federal government. As a result, the states are more successful at using language to promote subnational nationalism than is the federal government at using Hindi in support of nationalism in the country as a whole. It should be pointed out that one linguistic group, led by Panjabi-speaking Sikhs, was able to get control of its own state by bringing about the partition of the old state of Panjab. One of the new states, which retained the name 'Punjab', has Panjabi as its official language. The other, called Haryana, kept Hindi. This incident, however, is very much the exception.

We are now in a better position to see why the issue of whether or not a language variety like Maithili is a language or a dialect is a political issue. If it is simply a dialect of Hindi, then it will be presumed that its needs are taken care of by efforts to develop Hindi. If it is declared a separate language, then it has some legal rights to official support of its own.

Language in education

The educational policies and practices in India will be clearer if we first have in mind the hierarchical structure of the languages of India (Apte 1976:155–6). At the top of the structure are the two official government languages at the federal level, Hindi and English. Next come come the official state languages. At the third level, we might place languages which have no official government function at the federal or state level, but are spoken by more than one million people (Bhojpuri and Magahi are two examples).[20] Finally, there are small-group and tribal languages, which not only are not recognized at either level of government, but have scant hope of receiving anything but indifference or hostility from official sources.

The British policy was to use English as the medium of instruction. The philosophy of the colonial administration was succinctly outlined in a short speech by a member of the Supreme Council of India named Thomas Babington Macaulay in 1835. In his famous speech, known as 'Macaulay's Minute', he expressed despair that the administration would ever be able to educate all of the people of India. Rather, he said, the goal should be to develop 'a class who may be interpreters between us and the millions whom we govern – a class of persons Indian in blood and colour, but English in tastes, in opinions, in morals and in intellect' (quoted in Khubchandani 1977:35). English, of course, was the appropriate medium. Although the policy later changed to one of making education available to all the people, and official policy recommended the use of indigenous languages for lower-level education in some instances, in practice English was almost always the medium of instruction. This in itself tended to make formal education a training ground for the elite, in accordance with Macaulay's perspective, whatever the official policy. Even today, English is a language of the highly educated in India.

After independence, the federal government of India took a very pluralistic stance with regard to the languages to be used in instruction, as it did concerning the linguistic rights of the state and linguistic minorities. The official policy is in accordance with what is called the 'Three Language Formula' (Apte 1976:149). According to it, three languages must be taught at the secondary level: the regional language, Hindi, and English. In areas where Hindi is the regional language, another Indian language is to be substituted. Some of the states with Hindi as the regional language have thwarted the spirit of the Three Language Formula, in the view of the other states, by substituting Sanskrit for Hindi. Their position is similar to what would be the position of Spanish speakers in the United States if there were a law that said that schools had to teach both Spanish, if that is the mother tongue of most children in a local school, and English. Imagine, further, that the law states that if the mother tongue of the children is English, any other language could be used as the second language. No doubt Spanish speakers would expect that Spanish might be selected in a large number of schools where English is the mother-tongue of the children, and would resent it if Chaucerian English were a common choice instead.

The government also endorses the idea that children should receive initial education through their mother tongue, whatever it is. To the extent that this is carried out, the Three Language Formula translates into a *four* language formula for speakers of languages in the lower two tiers in the Indian language hierarchy. These youngsters would receive primary instruction in their first language, begin studying the regional language of the region they live in by the time they reach secondary school, and then study Hindi and English as well. In the incredibly multilingual state of Nagaland, many people end up learning, or at least studying, *five* languages. In addition to the four languages that children of other linguistic minorities learn, many Nagas also learn an Assamese-based creole, Nagassamese. Nagassamese has no official status, but is an important medium for ordinary inter-group communication in Naga-land (Sreedhar 1979).

The idea of providing education through 'mother tongues' is far more complicated than it seems. Even if the problems of materials development and teacher training are left aside, deciding just what a 'mother tongue' is is far from easy. Historically, there have been two definitions of mother tongue used in India: the broad definition and the narrow definition. According to the broad definition, any language without a written tradition is automatically considered a dialect of the regional language. Thus, a child who speaks an unwritten small-group language could end up being assigned a 'mother tongue' that she scarcely understands. The narrow definition regards the home language of a child to be the mother tongue, regardless of the level of development. According to Khubchandani (1977:44), the official policy has largely been settled in favor of the narrow definition, but actual implementation is slow. In come cases, state governments seem to be hoping that the minority languages will die out before they have to be used in education.

Even under the narrow definition, another aspect of the mother-tongue problem can arise: the *form* of the mother tongue to be used in school. As we have seen, the linguistic fluidity that is typical in India means that the designation 'speaker of Hindi' may refer to a large range of linguistic variation. The form of Hindi which is selected as a school language is likely to be a high-prestige urban standard. This standard form might be at least understandable to an adult from a small village, and he may use it occasionally in formal or official circumstances, but his children may know only a very different colloquial kind of Hindi. As a result, the 'Hindi' a child encounters at school might not match her home language very well at all. On the other hand, the same fluidity phenomenon could, in some instances, mean that a speaker who gives a minority language as his mother tongue may have considerable ability in the regional language.

The pluralistic policy is often publicly justified on the pragmatic nationist grounds that it is educationally more efficient. However, it seems clear that the advocacy of mother-tongue education in India, unlike Paraguay, is really more a *nationalist* decision than a nationist one. In education, more than in the selection of the language of government, the real threat to nationalism is not from the large numbers of indigenous Indian languages, but from *English*. The use of English in education smacks of the colonial exploitation of the education system along the lines of Macaulay's Minute. Nationalistically, then, it is more important to reduce the reliance on English than it is to promote Hindi. Since it is not possible to introduce Hindi as the universal medium of instruction, it is better to turn to the various indigenous Indian languages than to continue to use English. It may be the case that the use of mother tongues is also the better decision on *nationist* grounds as well, at least at the earlier levels of education. Whether or not India would be better off retaining English in higher education than to attempt to convert university education to the Indian languages, from a pragmatic point of view, is open to debate (cf. Apte 1976:152).

India – multiethnic nation or multinational state?

Using Fishman's comments about espousal and retention of languages as a barometer of national consciousness, you would have to conclude that most of the VIIIth Schedule languages function as symbols of subnational nationality, and that the majority of the remaining Indian languages represent ethnic groups. This would place India very close to the multinational-state end of the continuum. As a multinational state, it would consist of a group of multiethnic nationalisms, roughly the linguistic states. Viewed in this way, there would be grounds for serious concern for India's political stability, as there typically is for multinational states. This view may, in fact, be correct. It seems to be the point of view taken by Kelley (1966:299), who considers India an 'experiment' that 'bears comparison with a United States of Europe'. In his view, the experiment is threatened by the 'large number of regional languages which serve as a focus of cultural and political loyalty below the national level'.

On the other hand, there is a widespread feeling among Indian intellectuals that such comparisons with Europe are seriously misleading. In their view, a national language, in the sense of a single language actually known and used by almost all citizens, is not essential to Indian nationalism. One statement of this point of view is given by Pandit (1975:81):

In order to settle down among other language speakers, an Indian does not have to give up his language. He is welcome despite his different language; speaking a different language does not make him an alien. The underlying acceptability of any Indian in any Indian cultural setting is symptomatic of a cultural identity and homogeneity at a deeper level.

Le Page (1964:60) provides the following quotation from the Report of the

1962 Committee on Emotional Integration: 'All down the ages, there has been an awareness of an India that transcends all differences of province, caste, languages and creed.' These are not just two isolated voices. Apte (1979) reports that this point of view was a strand running through a symposium on Indian bilingualism held in India in 1976. The pluralistic policies of the Indian government seem to be based on the view that Indian nationalism does not crucially depend on a single universally-known language.

If this alternate view is accurate, India seems to be much more of a multiethnic nation than it did before. If so, the test of nationalism based on the retention and espousal of language does not work very well in India. At the very least, we should be warned not to base sociolinguistic generalities on European or North American experiences, or even on a Western interpretation of non-Western social orders. The way the members of a society view their own situation should be considered, before we decide that they are an example of one principle or another.

SUMMARY

Many, perhaps most, of the countries of the world are decidedly multilingual. Understanding what multilingualism means to a society is at the core of the sociolinguistics of society. Fishman's concepts of *nationality* (as opposed to ethnic group) and *nation* (as opposed to country or state) provide a useful framework for the study of multilingualism. Nationalism and nationism motivate language policies in different and often conflicting ways. Societal multilingualism is in some ways a problem for a country. It may impede nationalist and nationist goals and there is some evidence that it is associated with economic underdevelopment. On the other hand, there are ways in which it is a resource. Although it sometimes causes problems for nationalism and nationism, official multilingual policies may ironically be the best solution to nationalist–nationist conflicts as well. In addition, multilingualism provides individuals with interactional resources and societies with social and cultural enrichment.

Historically, there are four distinguishable strands which have produced multilingual states: migration, 'imperialism', federation, and border-area phenomena. A given state may have become multilingual due to the effects of more than one of these strands, and it is not always easy to decide which one applies in a particular case.

Paraguay and India were examined in some detail as cases of multilingual states. Many of the initial concepts were useful in these cases. However, although it seemed to work in Paraguay, the use of language espousal and maintenance as an indicator of nationality versus ethnicity, is of debatable value in India. Paraguay emerges as very much a nation; one which is only marginally multiethnic. India is either close to being a multinational state or is rather a multiethnic nation, depending on what viewpoint on the importance of language as a component of nationalism is taken.

BIBLIOGRAPHICAL NOTES

Several important studies of societal multilingualism in India and Paraguay were not directly referred to in the text. The marked tendency of the languages of India to influence each other in linguistic form has led to the study of India as a 'linguistic area'. Emmeneau (1956) is a classic study of this tradition. Important early studies of sociolinguistic significance of multilingualism in India are to be found in Bright (1976), Gumperz (1971) and Ferguson and Gumperz (1960). Rubin (1968c) is the authoritative study of Paraguayan bilingualism.

NOTES

1   Even without bringing in conflicts with nationalist requirements, it is by no means easy to decide which languages 'do the job best at the least cost' in education.

2   Garvin and Mathiot speak of these as functions of a standard language, but it seems clear that a language need not be standardized to serve these functions. They also discuss two additional functions, the prestige and frame-of-reference functions, at least the second of which apparently *does* require a standard language.

3   There are three nationalistic movements in American history in which there was little or no appeal to language as a symbol of nationalism. The first was the American Revolution, where American nationalism replaced nationalism toward England. The second was the nationalism that led to the establishment of the Confederate States of America and the Civil War. The third is the American black nationalist movement that reached its peak in the late 1960s and early 1970s, and which Fishman (1972: viii) cites as one of three nationalist movements he has witnessed that have partially motivated his study of language and nationalism.

4   The latter task has not so far been accomplished in Ireland.

5   A sophisticated measure of linguistic diversity will be examined in detail in chapter 5.

6   Pool explains the uneven intervals on the vertical axis with the statement: 'Variances are approximately standardized in the Figure by subjecting the economic variable to a logarithmic transformation, such that each unit of vertical distance represents an equal proportionate, rather than absolute, change' (Pool 1972:222, footnote 51).

7   As Bull (1955) points out, using ethnic languages, or 'vernaculars', as media of instruction in some cases actually hastens their extinction.

8   The movement of Puerto Ricans from Puerto Rico to the continental United States is technically not a case of immigration, since Puerto Rico is part of the United States. But since Puerto Rico is surely another nationality, in Fishman's sense, the Puerto Rican case is an example of immigration from the sociolinguistic point of view.

9   Another difference might be that in annexation, but not in colonization, the subjugated populations are supposed to become part of the 'mother country'. This was sometimes also attempted by colonizing countries as well. Prior to their independence, Portugal claimed that the citizens of its African colonies, Angola and Mozambique, were 'overseas Portuguese'. Incorporation of subjugated populations is much easier when they are geographically contiguous.

10   Russia has a long history of territorial expansion by annexation.
11   These figures are rather dated by now, but Rubin (1978) reports that the bilingualism figure for Asunción was almost identical in the 1962 census.
12   It was necessary to make a slight correction in Rona's percentages concerning the population outside the capital because of arithmetic errors in the original.
13   The 52 per cent figure might be slightly inflated due to a difference in the form of the language question on the 1962 census (Rubin 1968a:486, footnote 1). This problem with census data will be discussed in more detail in chapter 5.
14   In one rural school, 40–60 per cent of the class in the first three grades were repeating the grade (Rubin 1968a:485). It takes 7.3 years, on average, for a Paraguayan student to get through the fourth grade (Rubin 1978:190).
15   The discussion in this section is based on the information in Klein and Stark (1977).
16   I am indebted to my colleague, Shaligram Shukla, for several suggestions on an earlier draft of the section on India. He is not, of course, responsible for any remaining mistakes.
17   For a study of dialectal variation and phonological change in Middle-Indo-Aryan, see Shukla (1974).
18   There is a Sanskrit University in Benares where Sanskrit scholars from all over the country, having no other language in common, use Sanskrit as a medium (Shaligram Shukla, personal communication).
19   The relationship between Hindi and Urdu is the exact opposite of what you usually find. Normally, it is in the written and most formal spoken styles that language is most uniform; it diverges in informal colloquial styles (cf. Trudgill 1974:40–3 for a discussion of the relationship between received pronunciation and English regional dialects in this regard). The Hindi-Urdu situation is most divergent 'at the top'; most uniform 'at the bottom'. Space does not allow us to explore the reasons why Hindi-Urdu seems to go against this sociolinguistic generality.
20   Some of these languages are considered dialects of VIIIth Schedule languages, for some purposes.

OBJECTIVES

1   Be able to recognize the differences among nationality, nation, and ethnic group.
2   Be able to recognize the difference Fishman makes between nations and countries (states, polities).
3   Be able to distinguish nationalism and nationism.
4   Be able to give the definition (not necessarily in exact words) of 'contrastive self-identification' or 'the unifying and separatist functions'. (Both sets of terms mean the same things.)
5   Be able to state one way in which a group treatment of its own language can indicate whether it is more a nationality or more an ethnic group.
6   Given a problem that multilingual states might have, be able to state whether it is a problem for nationism or a problem for nationalism.
7   Be able to state the relationship that Pool seems to have found between linguistic diversity and economic well-being.
8   Be able to recognize the ways in which multilingualism can be a resource at the national and individual levels.
9   Be able to recognize definitions of the four ways multilingual countries become multilingual.

10 Be able to recognize the general geographical distributional patterns of Paraguay's two main languages.

11 Be able to recognize the contribution to social status that comes from a knowledge of Guaraní and a knowledge of Spanish.

12 Be able to recognize the reasons in favor of Guaraní as a language of education and the reasons in favor of Spanish.

13 Be able to give the reason why linguistic diversity in the Chaco is actually somewhat less than it seems to be at first.

14 Given several rough estimates of the number of languages spoken in India, be able to identify the most accurate.

15 Be able to state the number of languages listed in the VIIIth Schedule of the Indian constitution and the proportion of the total population that they account for.

16 Be able to recognize a definition of Khubchandani's term 'fluidity' (pp. 23).

17 Be able to identify the characteristics of Hindi or Guaraní that relate to their choice as national languages (pp. 14-15, 24-5).

18 Be able to state how many Indian states are monolingual and how many do not have a single language spoken by a majority of their populations.

19 Be able to state the attitude of the federal government of India toward the major regional languages and the attitude of the state governments toward minority languages within the states.

20 Be able to identify the position of the four types of language in India according to a heirarchy of political importance.

21 Be able to identify the attitude toward Indian education represented by 'Macaulay's Minute'.

22 Be able to state the policy called the 'Three Language Formula' and the number of languages that children will actually learn or study if it is practiced.

23 Be able to state the 'broad' and 'narrow' definitions of 'mother tongue' that have been debated and to name the one that has been officially adopted.

24 Be able to recognize the difference in motivation for advocating mother-tongue education in India from the motivation in Paraguay.

25 Be able to state which of the two nations selected for case study in this chapter is a better example of a multiethnic nation rather than a multinational state.

26 Be able to recognize the view of some Indian intellectuals on the extent to which India's societal multilingualism is a threat to unity.

2

Diglossia

In the discussion of multilingualism as an interactional resource in chapter 1, I mentioned that different languages were commonly assigned different tasks in multilingual societies. This relationship of language form and social function has been much studied from the perspective of a phenomenon known as *diglossia*. The term was first used in English by Charles Ferguson in 1959 (the French word *diglossie*, which inspired Ferguson's coinage, had earlier been used by the French linguist Marçais). Ferguson's article is now considered the classic reference for diglossia. An important modification of the concept was introduced by Fishman (1967). To get an idea of what diglossia is, we will review in detail what these two scholars have said on the subject.

FERGUSON'S DESCRIPTION OF DIGLOSSIA

Ferguson's attention had been drawn to the general fact that speakers often use more than one language variety in one kind of circumstance and another variety under other conditions. He also noticed that there was a special case of this 'where two varieties of a language exist side by side throughout the community, with each having a definite role to play' (Ferguson 1972:232).[1] This special case, which he called 'diglossia', was to be distinguished from the alternate use of a standard language and regional dialect, and also the case where 'two distinct . . . languages are used . . . throughout a speech community each with a clearly defined role' (Ferguson 1972:233). In time, I will explain the importance of these distinctions; for now it will suffice to say that we will eventually try to decide whether the two situations Ferguson is excluding are really distinct from diglossia. Using as examples four speech communities and their languages – Arabic, Modern Greek, Swiss German, and Haitian Creole – Ferguson proceeded to explain diglossia under nine rubrics: function, prestige, literary heritage, acquisition, standardization, stability, grammar, lexicon, and phonology.

Function

Function is the most crucial criterion for diglossia. In Ferguson's concept, there are two moderately distinct varieties of the same language, of which one is called the *High dialect* (or simply H) and the other the *Low dialect* (or L). In Arabic, H is Classical Arabic, the language of the Koran, and L refers to the various colloquial forms of the language which differ from one Arab country to another. In Greek, H is called *katharévusa* ('puristic') and L is called *dhimotiki* or demotic. Demotic Greek is the spoken language and katharevusa is a kind of purified Greek with some linguistic features of classical Greek restored. In German-speaking Switzerland, H is standard German and the various Swiss German dialects are the L (French is H in Haiti, whereas L is French-based Haitian Creole. The functional distribution for H and L means that there are situations in which only H is appropriate and others in which only L can be used, with very little overlap. The functions calling for H are decidedly formal and guarded; those calling for L are informal, homey and relaxed. Table 2.1 is Ferguson's list of typical situations in which the two varieties are distinguished.)

Table 2.1. Typical situations and choices of H or L in diglossia

Situation	H	L
Sermon in church or mosque	x	
Instructions to servants, waiters, workmen, clerks		x
Personal letter	x	
Speech in parliament, political speech	x	
University lecture	x	
Conversation with family, friends, colleagues		x
News broadcasts	x	
Radio 'soap opera'		x
Newspaper editorial, news story, caption on picture	x	
Caption on political cartoon		x
Poetry	x	
Folk literature		x

Source: Ferguson (1972:236)

It is a serious social gaffe to use the wrong variety in an inappropriate situation. If a university professor were to give a lecture in L, he would be considered very foolish, or perhaps a political radical. A speaker who used H in an informal conversation would either be made fun of or avoided as someone who is unbearably pompous.

As for poetry and folk literature, some poetry in L is common, but in most communities, only H poetry is thought of as 'real'.[2] H is officially the language of formal education , but a good deal of L is necessarily used in schools.[3] The reason for this is that facility in H is often restricted to a small elite, whereas everyone in the community speaks L. Teachers, then, have to spend time explaining in L material that has been presented in lectures and textbooks in H.

Prestige

The attitude of speakers in diglossic communities is typically that H is the superior, more elegant, and more logical language. L is believed to be inferior, even to the point that its existence is denied. Ferguson (1972:237) reports that many educated Arabs and Haitians insist that they never use L, when it is quite apparent that they always use it in ordinary conversation. This insistence is not a deliberate lie, but rather a sort of self-deception. Even people who do not understand H well insist that it be used in formal settings such as political speeches or poetry recitations. High regard for H and its appropriateness for elevated functions outranks intelligibility as a criterion for the choice of dialect in these situations.

Literary heritage

In three of Ferguson's four example languages, there is considerable literature in H which is much admired by the speech community (the Greek case is exceptional in this respect, as we will see). Contemporary literary work in H is felt to be a continuation of this great tradition. The High dialect literary tradition is, at least in the four example cases, remote from the contemporary society in one of two ways. The body of literature has its roots either in the distant past (as in the Arab countries and, in a sense, in Greece) or in another speech community (France and Germany, respectively, for Haiti and German-speaking Switzerland).

Acquisition

A very significant aspect of diglossia is the different patterns of language acquisition associated with the High and Low dialects. L will be used to speak to children and by children among themselves, so that L is learned in the normal, unselfconscious way. H is always an 'add-on' language, learned after L has been substantially acquired, usually by formal teaching in school. This acquisition pattern has two typical effects. First, those who leave school in the early grades, not an unusual phenomenon in many parts of the world, may never learn H at all. Secondly, those who do learn H almost never become as fluent in it as they do in L. The reason for this is that L is used regularly for everyday communication, whereas H is learned by memorizing rules of grammar, similar to the way foreign languages are studied in school. Most reasonably well-educated people in diglossic communities can recite the rules of H grammar, but not the rules for L. On the other hand, they unconsciously *apply* the grammatical rules of L in their normal speech with near perfection, whereas the corresponding ability in H is limited. In many diglossic communities, if speakers are asked, they will tell you that L has no grammar, and that L speech is the result of the failure to follow the rules of H grammar.

Standardization

Not surprisingly, it is the H form of the language that is standardized by the usual means of formal codification. Dictionaries, grammars, pronunciation guides, and books of rules for correct usage are written for H. The alphabet and spelling rules for H are established and do not vary much. It is rare for any studies of L to exist at all (this is to be expected as long as L is thought not to exist, or to be just corrupt H). Those that do exist are likely to be conducted by scholars from other speech communities and written in other languages. Writing in L is difficult because of the lack of established spelling rules, but in most cases no one wants to write in L anyway.

Stability

Diglossia is commonly an extremely stable phenomenon and there are many cases that have lasted for centuries. In fact, depending on how broadly we want to define diglossia, it can be argued that diglossia is *required* in order for more than one language variety to be maintained in one community. Tension between H and L in diglossia is relieved to some extent by the development of mixed, intermediate forms of the language which share some of the features of both H and L. Borrowing of H words into L is usual; use of L vocabulary in H is less usual, but does occur.

Grammar

Although Ferguson's view of diglossia requires that H and L be forms of the same language, there are considerable differences in the grammars of H and L. For example, standard German has four noun cases and two simple indicative tenses. Swiss German has only three cases in the noun and one simple tense. French nouns show agreement of number and gender, whereas Haitian Creole nouns have neither. In syntax, complex sentences with numerous subordinate constructions are appropriate in H, but seem stilted and artificial on the rare occasions when they are attempted in L. In short, based on an intuitive notion of 'simplicity' in grammar, the grammar of L is simpler than the grammar of H.[4]

Lexicon

For the most part, the vocabularies of H and L are shared. As you might expect, learned words and technical terms like 'nuclear fission' exist only in H. At the same time, there are words in L for homey objects such as farm implements and some cooking utensils that have no equivalents in H. But the most striking feature of diglossia, as far as lexicon is concerned, is the existence of *paired* items, one in H and one in L, for very commonly referred-to concepts. An example Ferguson gives in Greek is the pair of words for 'wine' – H: *ínos*, L: *krasí*. The menu in a restaurant will say *ínos*, but the patron orders *krasí* from the waiter (Ferguson 1972:242–3). The closest parallel in American English, Ferguson suggests, are pairs like the relatively formal 'children' versus the more colloquial 'kids'. But the parallel is not perfect; it is perfectly acceptable to use either 'children' or 'kids' in ordinary conversation and both can be written. In diglossic communities, only the H form is normally written and only the L form is expected in everyday conversation (Ferguson 1972:243).

Phonology

There is a substantial range of differences between H and L phonologies, from quite close in the case of Greek to quite divergent, as in the Swiss German case. None the less, Ferguson, thinking in terms of the phonemic theory of phonology that was prevalent in 1959, says it is a valid generality that 'the sound systems of H and L constitute a single phonological structure of which the L phonology is the basic system and the divergent features of H phonology are either a subsystem or a parasystem' (Ferguson 1972:244). A study of Greek by Kazazis (1968) suggests that, in terms of generative phonology, H phonology is, as a rule, closer to the common underlying forms in the whole language (fewer rules have been applied in the phonological derivation of H forms) and that L phonology is farther from underlying forms (relatively more rules have been applied in L derivations). This interpretation would be consistent with Ferguson's original insight, since phonological derivations in both dialects start with the same underlying phonological structure. One form may also have a few underlying contrasts and ways of combining sounds that the other does not, but not enough so that you would want to say that there are two different structures.

Ferguson's complete definition

Having discussed the nine features of diglossia, Ferguson gives a complete and often-quoted definition of diglossia (Ferguson 1972:245):

DIGLOSSIA is a relatively stable language situation in which, in addition to the primary dialects of the language (which may include a standard or regional standards), there is a very divergent, highly codified (often grammatically more complex) superposed variety, the vehicle of a large and respected body of written literature, either of an earlier period or in another speech community, which is learned largely by formal education and is used for most written and formal spoken purposes but is not used by any sector of the community for ordinary conversation.

In addition to the points made in the definition that we have discussed already, notice that H and L are to be taken as varieties of the same language (that is, as not too distantly related; they cannot be separate languages). At the same time, compared with L, H is 'very divergent' (that is, H and L cannot be linguistically too similar; they cannot just be different styles or registers). Notice that the diglossic pair is 'in addition to the primary dialects of the language' and that H is not used in conversation by 'any sector of the community'. This last point, as it turns out, is crucial for distinguishing diglossia from standard dialect with regional dialects. We will have occasion to return to these points later.

Outcomes for diglossia

One of the three outcomes cited by Ferguson (1972:248) for diglossia is, of course, that it may simply remain stable for a very long time. Under certain conditions, though, pressures may arise that lead to its demise. Ferguson cites increased literacy and broader communication throughout a country as two such pressures. A wider familiarity with H and increased use of written language is likely to cause a blurring of the linguistic distinctions between H and L. A third factor is the development of nationalism with the desire for a national language as its symbol; a phenomenon we became familiar with in chapter 1. In this case, there will often be a great deal of heated argument between proponents of H and proponents of L about which is the appropriate national language, but usually the form of the language that wins out will win out for reasons that have nothing to do with the arguments or even legislation on the language issue. The best bet by far is that the L spoken in the communication center of the speech community will be the basis for the standard, national language, but some considerable mixture with H is a possibility. The third possible outcome is for H to become the eventual standard, but Ferguson believes, probably correctly, that this can happen only under two conditions. H may become the standard: (1) if H is already the standard language in some other community; and (2) if the diglossic community merges with that other community. If Ferguson is right, then there is no chance that Classical Arabic will become the actual national language in any Arab country (although it may be named the 'national' or 'official' language) or that katharévusa will ever be the functioning national language of Greece. Standard German or French could become the national languages of German-speaking Switzerland and Haiti, respectively, only if they were to merge with Germany and France. Needless to say, the prospect of that happening in either case is extremely remote.

FISHMAN'S DESCRIPTION OF DIGLOSSIA

In 1967, Joshua Fishman published an article in which he revised and
expanded the concept of diglossia.[5] Fishman believes that diglossia ought to
be carefully distinguished from bilingualism. In this connection, bilingualism
is a subject for psychologists and psycholinguists; it refers to an individual's
ability to use more than one language variety. Diglossia is a matter for
sociologists and sociolinguists to study; it refers to the distribution of more
than one language variety to serve different communicational tasks in a
society. Fishman modified Ferguson's original proposal in two crucial ways.
First, Fishman places less emphasis on the importance of situations with only
two language varieties. He allows for the presence of 'several separate codes',
although the separation is said to be '*most often* along the lines of a H(igh)
language, on the one hand . . . and an [sic] L(ow) language on the other'
(Fishman 1972d:92; my italics).[6] Second, whereas Ferguson restricts the term
'diglossia' to cases in the middle range of linguistic relatedness (more
difference than there is between styles, less than there is between separate
languages), Fishman would ease that restriction. He endorses the view, which
he attributes to John Gumperz, that: 'diglossia exists not only in multilingual
societies which officially recognize several "languages", and not only in
societies that utilize vernacular and classical varieties, but also in societies
which employ separate dialects, registers, or *functionally differentiated
language varieties of whatever kind*'(Fishman 1972d:92; italics in the original).
Fishman's use of the term 'diglossia' can refer to any degree of linguistic
difference from the most subtle stylistic differences within a single language to
the use of two totally unrelated languages, including, of course, the range
allowed by Ferguson. The crucial test is that the linguistic differences must be
functionally distinguished within the society. Fishman, in addition, finds the
degree of individual bilingualism found in the society to be an important
typological criterion. His display, reproduced here as table 2.2, illustrates the
interaction between bilingualism and diglossia. The term *bilingualism* in table
2.2 should be understood in a somewhat special sense to mean something like
'control of both H and L is found throughout the society'. *Diglossia* refers to
the functional distribution of H and L.

For a society to be characterized as a speech community with both
bilingualism and diglossia, almost everyone would have to know both H and
L, and the two varieties would have to be distributed in a manner typical of
diglossia. Fishman cites a country we are already familiar with as an example
of a nation which approximates this situation – Paraguay. Quite obviously,
Guaraní serves as the Low language and Spanish as the High. Fishman's
reference to Paraguay illustrates how far apart linguistically two languages
may be and still be in a diglossic relationship, as Fishman sees it. Spanish is an
Indo-European language and Guaraní is an indigenous American language;

there are great structural differences between them.[7] Taking each German-speaking Swiss canton as an individual subnational speech community, we have other examples of bilingual–diglossic speech communities. Due to a highly efficient education system, almost all school-age or older German Swiss citizens alternate between Swiss German and standard German, and distribute their usage in a typically diglossic manner.

In order to have diglossia without bilingualism, two disjunct groups within a single political, religious, and/or economic entity are required. One is the ruling group and speaks only the High language. The other, normally a much larger group, has no power in the society and speaks exclusively the Low language. Such situations were not particularly rare before the First World War in Europe, for example, but they are a bit harder to find in more recent times. An example might be one period in the history of czarist Russia

Table 2.2 *The relationship between bilingualism and diglossia*

		Diglossia	
		+	–
Bilingualism	+	1 Both diglossia and bilingualism	2 Bilingualism without diglossia
	–	3 Diglossia without bilingualism	4 Neither diglossia nor bilingualism

Source: Fishman (1972d:75).

during which it was fashionable for nobles to speak only French, whereas the masses of Russians spoke only Russian. Asian and African colonies of European countries might also be examples, although, of course, there might have been several Low languages, not just one. Diglossic communities without bilingualism are not *speech communities,* since the two groups do not interact, except minimally through interpreters or by using a pidgin language.

Bilingualism without diglossia is the designation Fishman gives to communities in which there are large numbers of bilingual individuals, but they do not restrict one language to one set of circumstances and the other to another set. Either language may be used for almost any purpose. Such communities exist during major changes in diglossic relationships and are extremely unstable, or transitional (Fishman 1972d:105). Bilingualism without diglossia is the result when diglossia 'leaks'. Leaky diglossia refers to cases in which one variety 'leaks' into the functions formerly reserved for the other. The outcomes of bilingualism without diglossia, as far as the language varieties themselves are concerned, will be either a new variety that is a mixture of the old H and L varieties (especially if H and L are structurally similar), or the replacement of one by the other (especially likely if H and L are structurally dissimilar). An example of bilingualism without diglossia in which L is receding before H is the German-speaking area of Belgium, as reported by Verdoodt (1972:382–5). There, the shift to French from German is being preceded by widespread bilingualism in which either language may be used for nearly any purpose.

The final logically possible pattern is neither bilingualism nor diglossia. Because Fishman is willing to admit even style-level linguistic differences into his concept of diglossia, it is extremely difficult to come up with examples for this quadrant of the figure. For such a situation to exist, a very small, isolated, and egalitarian speech community is required. There must be only one linguistic variety in existence and no differentiation of roles requiring even stylistic differences in speech, at least stylistic differences that would result in High and Low styles. The double negative quadrant of table 2.2 is, according to Fishman, 'self liquidating' (Fishman 1972d:106).

Of the four types of communities, only two are examples of diglossia (diglossia with and without bilingualism), and these are the only stable ones. It will be instructive to examine more closely the exact difference between these two types. Both are characterized by diglossia, so the difference is to be found in 'bilingualism'. One is said to be a society 'with bilingualism' and the other to be 'without bilingualism'. That is, either bilingualism in H and L is nearly universal or does not exist at all. But the typical case in diglossia, as Ferguson points out, is for there to be partial bilingualism. Since L is known by everyone and H is learned by those with substantial education, bilingualism in H and L is limited to those who have had the required amount and type of education. Bilinguals make up a more-or-less elite group which comprises anywhere from a very small segment of society – not more than 12 per cent in Haiti (Stewart 1963:151), or 15 per cent with respect to English–Swahili diglossia in Tanzania (Abdulaziz Mkilifi 1978:137) to about 40 per cent of the population in Paraguay (Rona 1966:285) to nearly everyone in Swiss cantons (Weinreich 1968:89, Fishman 1972d:95). (Of course, 'elite' does not mean too much in the Swiss case!) In the past, the elite group may not have even been bilingual, but monolingual in H; that pattern, however, has virtually disappeared and is not characteristic of a speech community in any case. Of the four quadrants in table 2.2, what we have left as truly characteristic of diglossia is diglossia with (a wide and varying range of) bilingualism (cf. Johnson 1975).

COMPARISON OF FISHMAN'S AND FERGUSON'S CONCEPTS OF DIGLOSSIA

The two studies of diglossia have raised several important issues in the definition and concept of the phenomenon. Recall that Ferguson wished to distinguish diglossia from the relationship between standard languages and regional dialects, and also from the diglossia-like distribution between distantly related or totally unrelated languages. Fishman has nothing to say about regional dialects, but it is clear that his concept of diglossia does include whole language diglossia. Fishman mentions the possibility that more than two language varieties can be reserved for specific functions in a society, although he does not discuss such cases as diglossia. Ferguson's view of diglossia is limited to two language varieties. The greatest agreement between the two scholars is in the area of functional distribution in society; both have the same basic concept of H varieties being used for formal purposes and L varieties being reserved for less formal, more personal uses. This leaves us with four questions that need to be further pursued. The first is the standard-with-dialects question: is diglossia to be distinguished from standard languages with their dialects? The second is the binarity question: must the phenomenon that has been called diglossia be restricted to the distribution of only two language varieties? Third, we have the relatedness question: is diglossia to be understood as applying only to the intermediate degree of linguistic related-ness specified by Ferguson, or may it apply to any degree of relatedness whatsoever? Fourth, and last, is the function question: what is the exact nature of the social functions which H and L varieties are associated with?

The standard-with-dialects question

As Ferguson (1972:232) himself points out, speakers of regional dialects of some languages frequently use their local dialect and the standard language in ways that parallel the diglossic distribution. The local dialect is used at home and among local friends and the standard is selected for communicating with speakers of other dialects or for public functions. He goes so far as to suggest that 'some instances of the relationship may be close to diglossia or perhaps even better considered as diglossia' (Ferguson 1972:245). What is crucial for Ferguson, however, is that no segment of the community uses H in ordinary conversation. This certainly seems true of the diglossia cases we have seen. In the standard-with-dialects situation, 'the standard is often similar to the variety of a certain region or social group (e.g., Tehran Persian, Calcutta Bengali) which is used in ordinary conversation more or less naturally by members of the group and as a superposed variety by others' (Ferguson 1972:245). In other words, as long as you can find some group in the speech community that uses the putative H in normal conversation, even though there are other groups which do not, we do not have a case of diglossia, but rather a standard-with-dialects. This criterion, however, depends heavily on the meaning of the term 'speech community'. There are surely people who use the Haitian H (French) in ordinary conversation, but they live in France, not Haiti. Similarly, the German Swiss H is used for normal interaction, but in Germany, not in Switzerland. Ferguson does not define 'speech community', but his discussion indicates that his tacit notion of speech community is roughly 'all those within the borders of some country who speak the same language'. The term 'speech community' has been much discussed in sociolinguistics (for example, Labov 1966:125; Hymes 1974:51; Bailey 1973:65; Gumperz 1962:31; Milroy 1980; Saville-Troike 1982); and it is hard to find exact agreement on what it should mean. However, there is no reason to think that it has anything crucial to do with political boundaries.

I will not attempt to define 'speech community' in general, but I propose that *diglossic community* be defined as a social unit which shares the same High and Low varieties.[8] Each speech community must share not only the same H, but the same L as well. This means that German-speaking Switzerland is not a single speech community with respect to diglossia, but there is one speech community for each distinguishable Swiss German dialect. By 'distinguishable', I mean distinguished by the people who use them, not distinguishable by technical linguistic criteria. Typically, several diglossic communities so defined will share the same H, but be distinguished by their L varieties.[9] Figure 2.1 illustrates this situation. Figure 2.1 applies to the German-speaking Swiss communities, but also applies to various regional dialects sharing the standard language of only one country. Therefore, each regional dialect distinguishes a different diglossic community, and within each of them, no one uses the standard for normal conversation. If there is a group within the same country that uses the standard, or something close to it, for all functions, then it is not a sector of any of these diglossic communities. Rather, it is a separate community (not necessarily a diglossic one, at least not in the same sense) because it does not share a Low variety with any of them. If this definition of diglossic speech community is accepted, then the distinction between diglossia and most instances of standard-with-dialects cannot be maintained.

Figure 2.1   Speech communities sharing the same H but distinguished by different Ls. Squares represent separate diglossic communities.

The binarity question

Is it profitable to distinguish the functional differentiation of two languages from the similar differentiation of more than two? To answer this, we will have to look at some instances of multiple-language differentiation. There are three fascinating types of multiple language 'polyglossia' that have appeared in the literature: (1) double overlapping diglossia (in Tanzania) (Abdulaziz Mkilifi 1978); (2) double-nested diglossia (Khalapur, India) (Gumperz 1964); and (3) linear polyglossia (Singapore and Malaysia) (Platt 1977).

Double overlapping diglossia.   Abdulaziz Mkilifi (1978) describes the situation in Tanzania as triglossia, but more profoundly as a 'situation of intersection between two developing diglossia situations, one involving Swahili and some vernacular and the other involving Swahili and English' (Abdulaziz Mkilifi 1978:134). This intersection between diglossia situations is what I am calling double overlapping diglossia. Tanzania is the former British colony of Tanganyika, later federated with Zanzibar. As one would expect in a former colony, it is, in the terms of chapter 1, a forced federation of numerous sociocultural groups with a colonial language added.)In addition, there is a widespread lingua franca, Swahili, which is currently being developed as the national language. At the moment, Swahili is involved in two diglossic systems: as the High language with the various Tanzanian vernaculars as Lows, and as the Low language with English as the High. The situation can be illustrated as in figure 2.2.

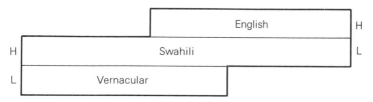

Figure 2.2   Double overlapping diglossia in Tanzania

Abdulaziz Mkilifi explains in fascinating detail how it all works. The discussion is based on data collected from 15 Swahili–English bilinguals, all but two of whom also spoke one of the vernaculars. In spite of the small number of subjects, the picture we get from their reports seems not to be atypical in any way. All but two subjects, whose first language was Swahili, learned vernacular languages first at home before beginning school, although most of them learned some Swahili as well. This, of course, is the typical pattern of acquisition for L varieties. Those who were exposed to Swahili in addition to their vernaculars said that they did not even realize that they were speaking (or mixing) different languages until they got to school. This state of affairs is partly due to the fact that all the vernaculars involved and Swahili itself are Bantu languages and have similar linguistic structures and a basic vocabulary core. It is reminiscent of the fluidity found in north India and of the closely related languages in the Paraguayan Chaco. In primary school, Swahili was the medium of instruction, either from the beginning or after the vernacular had been used in the first two grades. This introduction of a new language variety in school is typical of the acquisition of a High variety. Since the primary schools were located in the area in which the vernaculars were spoken, the vernaculars could be used in all conversations with family members and local people. Swahili was a school language only. In this manner, the vernacular–Swahili diglossia pattern was established.

Things changed when secondary school was reached. At the time Abdulaziz Mkilifi's informants attended secondary school, there were only a handful in the entire country so students were obliged to leave their home areas to attend school. No longer able to use their vernacular languages for conversations with friends, since most of them spoke different vernaculars, Swahili began to be used for these typical 'Low' functions.[10] At the same time, English was taught as a subject, used as a medium of instruction, and enthusiastically learned by the young people. English was stressed as a requirement for success and was insisted upon as the only language to be used on the school compound under threat of punishment, something like the insistence on Spanish in schools in Paraguay. In this way, English took on the functions typical of a High variety, while Swahili was taking on the Low functions. In the nation as a whole, then, the vernaculars are used only in very local situations. Educated speakers use pure vernacular only with those few Tanzanians who do not speak Swahili, although it is common to mix Swahili and the vernacular to express local solidarity when someone is talking to a fellow speaker of the same vernacular. Swahili is 'the language of culture and communication at the national level' (Abdulaziz Mkilifi 1978:136). As such, it is the High language with respect to the vernaculars and the Low with respect to English. English is used for official government business, in commercial and legal interaction, and in higher education. It is also the vehicle for access to world literature and technological information. As for writing, most subjects said they read and wrote English for the most part, although some read and wrote in both languages. The vernacular languages are rarely used for writing and letters to vernacular language speakers are written in Swahili, if the recipient does not speak English. All of this supports the impression of a dual status for Swahili with respect to diglossia.[11]

Double-nested dilgossia.   The situation in Khalapur, India – a rural village north of Delhi described by Gumperz (1964) – can be called double-nested diglossia. Although Gumperz does not use the term, the account he gives shows all the earmarks of diglossia.[12] The High variety is Hindi and the Low is the local dialect, which Gumperz refers to simply as 'Khalapur'. Khalapur is one of the unnamed varieties of Hindi that exemplify north Indian fluidity, and the villagers report themselves as speakers of Hindi for census purposes (Gumperz 1964:143). In linguistic structure, the phonological, grammatical and lexical differences between the two are of the sort that Ferguson found to be characteristic of diglossia. In phonology, Khalapur has two or three special consonantal distinctions that Hindi does not have and lacks one that Hindi has. There are three diphthongs in Khalapur that do not occur in Hindi, and medial geminate consonants are allowed which do not appear in Hindi. Otherwise, the two are phonologically the same. In grammar, Khalapur lacks the Hindi feminine plural suffix, and there are several minor differences in verb morphology and syntax. In the lexicon, there is a list of paired items, one for Hindi, one for Khalapur, which Gumperz (1964:144) gives. This kind of pairing of commonly used words is, as we know, one of the striking characteristics of diglossia.

Khalapur is spoken by everyone in the village and is always used in local relationships. Hindi is superposed in the manner typical of diglossia, either by being learned in school, or through residence in cities, or through outside contacts. Hindi is spoken by the better educated and socially prominent villagers for dealing with matters like commerce and politics, that go beyond village concerns. Hindi is also the language used in classroom teaching and formal lectures. Villagers who do not speak Hindi none the less modify their speech in its direction when the occasion makes it appropriate. In short, the Khalapur community is a garden variety example of a diglossic community.

The striking fact about Khalapur is a second level of diglossic relationships that appear *within* both the main High and Low varieties. Within the Khalapur dialect, there are two sub-varieties, which have local names: *moti boli* and *saf boli*. Moti boli (literally 'gross speech') is used in informal relationships such as with family members and close relatives, children, animals and untouchable servants. Linguistically, it has a few minor features not characteristic of the Khalapur dialect as a whole, and the most distinctive features of the local vernacular are very frequent. Saf boli (literally 'clean speech') is used with relatively more distant acquaintances and to show respect for elders. Linguistically, saf boli avoids the features characteristic of moti boli and leans in the direction of Hindi with respect to the other Khalapur–Hindi contrasts.

There are two subvarieties in the Hindi spoken in the village, as well. Gumperz calls these *conversational* and *oratorical* style. The conversational style is typical of the general spoken Hindi of the region, but the oratorical style is distinctive in its heavy use of Sanskrit loanwords, as well as the use of special consonant clusters. The oratorical style, as might be expected, is used in more formal lectures. Since it is maximally different from the local Low dialect, a lecture delivered in oratorical Hindi may be difficult for an audience to understand. The lecturer is obliged to explain parts of the lecture in conversational Hindi or in Khalapur.

The picture we get of the Khalapur diglossic community is of a continuum from the superHigh oratorical style of village Hindi to the superLow moti boli variety of the Khalapur vernacular. Within the High and the Low varieties can be distinguished a higher and lower Low and a higher and lower High, which appear, in form and function, to be microcosms of the larger diglossic contrast. This situation, with two 'little diglossias' within the 'big diglossia', can be illustrated as in figure 2.3.

Neither double overlapping diglossia nor double-nested diglossia require anything more than a refinement of the concept of binarity. In the one case there are two sets of two, the Low member of the one being the same as the High member of the other. In the other case, there is a large diglossic pair,

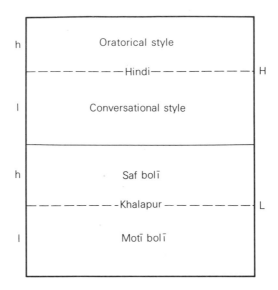

Figure 2.3   Double-nested diglossia in Khalapur, India

within each member of which there is a more refined diglossic distribution. All the relationships involved, however, are arrangements of binary sets.

Linear polyglossia.   Such is not the case for the English-educated Chinese communities in Singapore and Malaysia described by Platt (1977). The verbal repertoires of both communities consist of various Chinese languages, of which one is likely to be regionally dominant, formal and colloquial kinds of English, and standard and 'bazaar' versions of Malay. So far, it appears that perhaps the dominant vs. nondominant Chinese languages, formal vs. colloquial versions of English, and standard vs. bazaar Malay might conveniently arrange themselves in a series of diglossic pairs, giving a 'triple-nested diglossia' similar to the double-nested diglossia in Khalapur. This arrangement would require that the Low form of any of the languages be 'higher' than the High form of the next language in the series, just as the lower form of Hindi, conversational Hindi, is higher than the High form of Khalapur, saf bolī. This turns out not to be the case for English-educated Malaysians. The High form of Malay, Bahasa Malaysia, is the second-highest linguistic variety used in the community and gaining in status. But the Low form, Bazaar Malay, far from being the next-highest, is the lowest variety of all; both forms of English and all the Chinese varieties exceed it. Besides this, there is a special status for Mandarin Chinese that has to be included with the other languages. The actual arrangement can be called linear polyglossia.[13]

For a typical English-educated Chinese individual in Malaysia, a common speech repertoire would include: (1) her mother tongue, one of the Chinese languages spoken in Malaysia; (2) one or more other southern Chinese languages, probably including the dominant one of the region, if that language is not her mother tongue; (3) some formal Malaysian English; (4) some colloquial Malaysian English; (5) a certain amount of Bahasa Malaysia (the recently standardized national language); and (6) Bazaar Malay, a low-prestige lingua franca. In Platt's view (1977:366–7), these language forms fit into a complex glossic model which includes one or more High varieties, one or more Medium varieties, and one or more Low varieties. In addition, Platt's model allows for a subLow (symbolized L–), to accommodate lingua francas, such as Bazaar Malay, which are used exclusively for transactions on a local level, as well as a 'Dummy High' (DH). The two criteria Platt used to assign the languages to these categories are domains, a concept introduced by Fishman (1971, 1972d) that is basically an expansion of what we have been calling 'function', and *speaker attitudes*. Platt finds it reasonable to arrange domains, or functions, along a linear scale defined by public versus private interaction and degrees of formality. In this, he is well within the spirit of the studies of diglossia we have seen. In addition, Platt takes into account how highly the members of the community evaluate the varieties in their repertoires, that is, speaker attitudes. Recall that Ferguson says that High dialects have much more prestige than Low dialects do, and Platt uses attitude data to help set up his polyglossic scale.

It is his attention to attitude that leads Platt to the notion of a Dummy High. By his definition, DH 'refers to speech varieties of which some of the members have a certain knowledge, and which are given prestige ratings by the speakers ... but which *are not in fact utilized extensively in any domain*' (Platt 1977:373-4, my italics). A DH owes its significance in the community almost exclusively to the high regard in which the people hold it; it is not used for any real communicative purpose. Mandarin, a major language of northern China, is a DH for the English-educated Chinese in Malaysia. Mandarin is not used in that community for any purpose, and few members have more than a smattering of knowledge of it, but it carries a great deal of prestige for them. A near example, which Platt does not give, is Sanskrit in India. As we saw in chapter 1, it is listed among the 14 constitutional languages solely for its value to the majority Hindu population. Sanskrit is not quite a DH, since it is used as a language of religion and in the study of literature, but these are comparatively limited functions. We will meet another setting in which we have to consider the symbolic value of a language for a community apart from its communicative function when we study Irish language planning in chapter 10.

I will not give the details of Platt's methods, but his final analysis for the Malaysian English-educated Chinese is presented in figure 2.4. There is no reasonable way to subdivide this figure into groups of two. If the polyglossic Malaysian case is to be included under the same general heading as the other situations we have seen, then the binarity requirement must be given up.

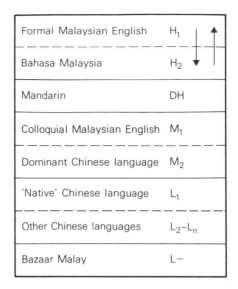

Formal Malaysian English	H_1
Bahasa Malaysia	H_2
Mandarin	DH
Colloquial Malaysian English	M_1
Dominant Chinese language	M_2
'Native' Chinese language	L_1
Other Chinese languages	L_2-L_n
Bazaar Malay	$L-$

*Figure 2.4   Linear polyglossia for English-educated Malaysian
Chinese. The vertical arrows between the two Highs are
intended to indicate that Bahasa Malaysia is gaining
ground at the expense of English as the 'higher' High (Platt 1977:374).
Source: Platt (1977:375, table 5.)*

The relatedness question

Ferguson's original definition of diglossia required an intermediate level of
linguistic relatedness between clearly separate languages and mere style
shifting. The Malaysian case, together with the situation in Tanzania and what
we know of Paraguay from the previous chapter, shows that some sociolinguists have found it reasonable to apply the term to situations in which the H
and the L are separate languages, and I am in sympathy with this approach.
But we have had little to say about whether or not diglossia should be allowed
to cover situations in which there is more than the level of relatedness that
Ferguson allows.

A number of linguists have noted facts that lead them to the conclusion that
subdialectal variation works in the same way as diglossia. In an early and
insightful discussion of Haitian diglossia, Stewart (1963) was struck by the
fact that Haitians seemed to switch to French from Creole exactly where an
American would switch from an informal to a formal style of speech. In the
following overheard example, a Haitian businessman switches from French to
Creole in mid-sentence (with the Creole portion of the utterance between
phonemic brackets) (Stewart 1963:158):

Je comprende très bien pourquoi vous demandez l'argent d'avance,
/wap proteže tet u/.

It seemed to Stewart that the impact of the switch from French to Creole could be captured to some extent in a translation into American English of the following sort:

I certainly understand why you're asking for the money in advance – ya gotta look out fur yaself, I guess.[14]

The formal 'High dialect' part of the sentence is marked by a somewhat more deliberate pronunciation, and the use of certain lexical items, like 'certainly', 'you're asking for' (instead of 'you want'), and 'in advance' (instead of 'up front'). The informal 'Low dialect' part is marked by more casual pronunciation, and the use of lexical choices like 'I guess', 'gotta' (rather than 'have to') and 'look out fur yaself' (instead of 'look out for your own interests'). Thus it seemed that speakers of American English could accomplish the same sort of interactional task by exploiting stylistic variation in their language as could members of a diglossic community using their High and Low varieties.

Another interesting fact that Stewart noticed is that foreigners who know French often find Haitian French rather stiff and bookish in comparison with the French used in France. Haitians themselves say that their French is more 'pure' than the language is in France. A plausible explanation is that Haitians never have to develop an informal sort of French; in any situation in which informal speech is needed, they switch to Creole. By contrast, French speakers from France, like speakers of American English, have no distinctive L to switch to, so 'Low' styles of French must be developed.

More recently, Krysin (1979), studying diglossia-like phenomena in Russian, found that the concept seems to apply to what he calls *codified* and *colloquial* forms of standard Russian, in addition to the diglossic relationship between standard and dialectal forms of the language. It appears that there is a large diglossic relationship between standard Russian and non-standard Russian dialects and a smaller-scale one between the two forms of the standard. This, of course, reminds us of the double-nested diglossia in Khalapur. To take a different perspective of the Khalapur situation, it seems that it can be viewed as a continuous blend of styles from the formal, Sanskritized oratorical Hindi to the informal, relaxed motī bolī, with four points on the continuum happening to have names. In Greek diglossia, there is a difference of opinion as to whether katharévusa and demotic Greek are distinguishable forms that may be mixed (Householder 1963:121; Sotiropoulos 1977:9 *et passim*), or whether they are points on a linguistic continuum (Kazazis 1976:370). Another example of a probable continuum from H to L is found on Norfolk Island, an Australian possession in the South Pacific (Flint 1979).

It appears that people have a universal tendency to reflect their perception of the intimacy or formality of a situation in their speech. This may be done by means of subtle stylistic shifts within the same language, by switching between two moderately distinct 'dialects', or by selecting entirely different languages.[15] The social phenomenon is the same, regardless of the nature of the linguistic means used to accomplish it.[16]

If the notion of diglossia is to be expanded to include not only separate languages, but style-shifting as well, then there is a further reason to relax the binarity requirement. Since style-shifting is a continuous blend of varying linguistic alternatives from very colloquial to very formal, it is impossible to divide styles into two sections on any principled grounds.

The function question

If there is agreement on any aspect of diglossia, it is in the area of function. Everyone agrees that H speech is used in formal, public settings and L in informal, private ones. As we saw in table 2.1, Ferguson has given us some specific examples of situations in which H or L would be selected in the four defining languages. A cursory examination of the general discussions of diglossia by Ferguson (1959a/1972) and Fishman (1967/1972d), and the studies of diglossia in Tanzania (Abdulaziz Mkilifi 1978), Khalapur (Gumperz 1964), Malaysia (Platt 1977) and Greece (Householder 1963), shows that certain specific functions tend to recur in connection with both H and L.

H varieties are said to be used for sermons (Ferguson, Fishman, Householder), for official government business (Abdulaziz Mkilifi, Platt, Householder), in education (the probability of this use increases with the education level) (Ferguson, Fishman, Abdulaziz Mkilifi, Gumperz, Platt, Householder), modern commerce (Abdulaziz Mkilifi, Gumperz, Platt), and they are associated with urban, rather than rural, life (Abdulaziz Mkilifi, Gumperz). The H varieties are typically used for written purposes, especially 'serious' ones (Greece is an exception to this).

L forms are used in speech with family and friends (Ferguson, Fishman, Abdulaziz Mkilifi, Gumperz, Platt, Householder) and to servants and lower status workers (Ferguson, Fishman, Gumperz). L is also said to be related to local or rural cultural identities (Abdulaziz Mkilifi, Gumperz).

Ferguson (1972:235–6) says that the two sets of situations overlap 'only very slightly' and that appears to be true for the most part. But there are a few areas where some overlap is common, for example, although everyone agrees that H is the language of education, L may be used in some communities for initial education, and informal explanations in L of material presented in H is not uncommon at any level. None the less, if there is substantial leakage of H or L varieties into the functions of the opposite variety, this is usually a sign of the incipient breakdown of the diglossic relationship.

REDEFINITION – BROAD DIGLOSSIA

Ferguson (1959a/1972) rather carefully defined diglossia so that it explicitly excluded the functional distribution of separate languages and standard versus regional dialects. Implicitly, it is clear he intended that diglossia refer only to situations with just *two* language varieties and that the two be moderately divergent. Fishman (1967/1972d) explicitly expanded the notion to include cases of both closer and more distant degrees of language relatedness, and indicated that the sort of functional distribution of languages found in diglossia need not involve only two languages. I have discussed these limitations on the definition as questions about standard-with-dialects, binarity and relatedness, and proposed relaxing Ferguson's original limitations in each case. Ferguson depends on the fact that H is not used as a medium of ordinary conversation by anyone in the speech community to exclude the standard-with-dialects cases, but that criterion no longer applies if the term 'diglossic community' is redefined to make it less correlated with political boundaries. Binarity is shown to be more complex than Ferguson's early article seems to reveal; there are intricate binary cases that I have called double overlapping diglossia and double-nested diglossia. Platt (1977) showed that diglossia-style language distribution need not be limited to binary sets at all. As for relatedness, it can be argued that the relationship between language form and the situation defined on a formality–informality continuum can exist whether the language forms are separate languages, major subsystems of the same language, or subtle shiftings of a stylistic sort. Only function remains unchallenged; it is the very heart and soul of the diglossia concept.

Although reasonable people may well disagree with my conclusions on these scores, I suggest the following definition of 'broad diglossia':

> BROAD DIGLOSSIA is the reservation of highly valued segments of a community's linguistic repertoire (which are not the first to be learned, but are learned later and more consciously, usually through formal education), for situations perceived as more formal and guarded; and the reservation of less highly valued segments (which are learned first with little or no conscious effort), of any degree of linguistic relatedness to the higher valued segments, from stylistic differences to separate languages, for situations perceived as more informal and intimate.[17]

Since the above definition does not require that only two repertoire segments be involved, it might seem that the term 'diglossia' is no longer appropriate. But 'diglossia' is a term with a considerable and respectable history, and it would be a shame to give it up. We can keep the term if we understand the prefix to refer loosely to the two ends of the formality–intimacy continuum of language use, rather than to two linguistic varieties. If this justification seems far-fetched, we can simply keep the term without trying to match meanings to its morphological parts, as is done for the term 'co-ed'. 'Co-ed', as an abbreviation for 'co-educational', is a slang term used in the US to refer only to women students. Going by its component parts, if it refers to students at all, it ought to mean a student of either sex at a co-educational institution. But we don't go by its component parts, and I propose the retention of 'diglossia' on the same grounds, if on no other.

At the same time, we should not give up Ferguson's original concept entirely. Once we have decided that we have a case of broad diglossia, it will be worth while to inspect the degree of relatedness between the H and L forms. At this point, we need the notion *classic diglossia,* and I do not think Ferguson's 1959 definition can be improved upon, except to remove the phrase 'in addition to the primary dialects of the language (which may include a standard or regional standards)' (Ferguson 1972:245), so that functionally distributed standards and regional dialects are not excluded. Classic diglossia gives us a convenient midpoint in the possible range of relatedness to be found in broad diglossia. Where High and Low language varieties are *less* closely related, we have *superposed* bilingualism. Where H and L are more closely related, we can speak of *style-shifting.* The relationships among these terms are illustrated in table 2.3. The distinctions among the three subtypes are relative.

Ferguson emphasized that diglossia can remain stable for centuries and often does. None the less, diglossic relationships do change, and show characteristic signs of change when they do. Two characteristics of changing diglossia are: (1) *leakage* in function; and (2) *mixing* in form. These two characteristics seem to be present in one case of classic diglossia (Greece) and in one case of superposed bilingualism (Tanzania).

Table 2.3   Subtypes of broad diglossia

Linguistic relatedness	Subtype of broad diglossia
Separate languages	Superposed bilingualism
Divergent dialects	Classic diglossia
Stylistic differences	Style shifting

SIGNS OF CHANGE

Greece

It appears that the classical diglossia relationship between katharévusa and demotic Greek is coming to an end. Ferguson (1972:249) predicted that Greece would develop a single national language based on the demotic Greek of Athens, with considerable admixture of katharévusa vocabulary. Kazazis (1976:369) agrees that modern Greek is on its way toward 'monoglossia' and that some katharévusa elements will persist. Browning (1982:66) says that the basic language conflict between katharévusa and demotic has been resolved 'resoundingly' in favor of demotic, although exactly which features of the old

Low variety will be part of the common national language is still being decided.

Greek diglossia began leaking in a serious way in the late nineteenth century, when a group of Greek literary figures, such as the poet Kostis Palamas, began writing in demotic Greek in a conscious rejection of katharévusa.[18] In 1888, Yannis Psycharis published an account of a journey in Greece called *To taxidi mou,* which became a sort of demoticist manifesto (Browning 1982). Psycharis's work created a normative, regularized demotic that was criticized as too artificial by some advocates of demotic. Nevertheless, the publication of *To taxidi mou* marked the beginning of a movement that was so successful that nearly all literary work and criticism of the arts is now written in demotic. This change in the linguistic situation did not happen smoothly. The publication of a New Testament translation in demotic in 1901 not only elicited a condemnatory encyclical from the Ecumenical Patriarch Ioakeim, but sparked riots in the streets of Athens (Browning 1982:55). Furthermore, the ascendancy of demotic over katharévusa in the cultured arts outstripped its advance in the society at large. Although demotic was perfectly well accepted in literature, to speak in demotic would make someone sound like 'a stevedore' (uneducated) or 'a Communist' (radical) (Kazazis MS).[19] A person's use of Greek was so socially and politically charged that, until very recently, it was possible to 'draw sweeping conclusions regarding a speaker's social status or political affiliations from the manner in which he decline[d] third-declension nouns' (Browning 1982:67).

Greek diglossia has changed in the wider society, but more slowly. Although demotic had been used as the medium of instruction earlier in this century, katharévusa was reintroduced by the regime that came to power in 1967. In 1976 demotic was made the only language of instruction through secondary education (Sotiropoulos 1977, Browning 1982).[20] At present, katharévusa is still commonly used in the courts (it is the language in which most laws are written), in the armed forces, and in official forms and public notices. The only other domains where it is even partially dominant are parliamentary and political speeches and university lectures. The official communications of the Orthodox church are written in a form of Greek which is 'not so much Katharévusa as Byzantine' (Browning 1982:58).

This large-scale leakage seems to have made people unsure of how to distribute their use of H and L, so that today there is considerable mixture of the two, especially in speech. In an article published in 1963, Householder (1963:121) insisted that H and L in Greek could always be distinguished, but he was referring only to written texts (he admitted that there was some mixture, even in writing). Kazazis (1976:370) states that the boundaries between katharévusa and demotic are 'indeterminate' and that 'we are dealing with a continuum rather than two well-defined linguistic modes.' Browning (1982:67) refers to the 'numerous doublets and the multiplicity of choice open to speakers and writers' of modern Greek. The Greek case is showing both signs of the demise of classical diglossia – leakage in function and mixture in form – and Ferguson's prediction seems accurate.

Tanzania

Abdulaziz Mkilifi's description of the double overlapping diglossia in Tanzania gives the impression that Swahili is expanding in use both higher and lower from its middle position. The vernacular languages of Tanzania, the Low languages to Swahili as a High, are used primarily as languages of 'ethnocultural identification and solidarity' (Abdulaziz Mkilifi 1978:135). Swahili, on the other hand, marks the resocialization of individuals on the national level. As Abdulaziz Mkilifi (1978:135) puts it: 'Among the younger and more detribalized speakers there is a merging of role and value distinctions based on Swahili and the vernacular, with Swahili systems often dominating.' Eleven of Abdulaziz Mkilifi's subjects reported that they speak pure vernacular only with those who do not understand Swahili, a minority of Tanzania's population.

There is some evidence of leakage of Swahili into the English functions, as well. Although English is largely the language of government administration at the national level, considerable correspondence with regional authorities is conducted in Swahili. Political meetings involving large general audience participation are in Swahili, as are the meetings of the dominant political party. There are both English and Swahili versions of official government forms. In Dar-es-Salaam, the capital city, Muslim sermons are delivered in Swahili; other religious services are conducted, at different times, in Swahili and English. In general, the policy and practice is to 'use as much Swahili as possible, except where not yet possible for some technical or linguistic reasons' (Abdulaziz Mkilifi 1978:139).

Along with leakage, Abdulaziz Mkilifi reports widespread mixing of Swahili with both the vernaculars and with English. The mixing of the vernacular languages with Swahili seems to be the result of a conflict between loyalty to a speaker's ethnic group and its values and loyalty to national life and its values. As for English, part of the motivation for switching seems to be due to the conflict between the desire to express nationalist values, on the one hand, and the need for technical vocabulary and the desire to demonstrate one's educational attainments, on the other. An illustration of the switch between Swahili and English for reasons of vocabulary is the following passage given by Abdulaziz Mkilifi (1978:140, Swahili portions in italics):

> *Zile* hormones *za uvyazi za* tilapia *zategemea zile* environmental factors *zinazowaathiri hawa* tilapia. (The reproductive hormones of tilapia depend upon how the environmental factors have been impinging on tilapia.)

English appears to be resorted to only when technical terms are needed. This passage is not totally representative, however. Abdulaziz Mkilifi (1978:140) reports that rapid switching between Swahili and English takes place 'even if equivalent Swahili–English lexical items exist'. An example is later given of apparently 'equivalent' items in the two languages which were not equivalent in the mind of the bilingual speaker at all. One bilingual speaker included the English word 'fruit' in an otherwise Swahili sentence. When asked why he didn't use the Swahili word *matunda,* he replied that *matunda* is picked from trees and *fruit* is bought at a market (Abdulaziz Mkilifi 1978:143).

In any case, it seems that Swahili is expanding its usage at the expense of both the vernaculars and English, and experiencing the code-mixing that typically accompanies such expansion. To the extent that Tanzanians develop nationalism, coming to think of themselves as Tanzanians as well as, or even more than, members of a subnational ethnic group, to that extent we may expect the vernaculars to be given up in favor of Swahili. Paraguay appears to be a nation which has reached an advanced stage of that sort of development, with the national language, Guaraní, having all but totally replaced the ethnic languages. Abdulaziz Mkilifi (1978:145) foresees that Tanzania might get 'perhaps increasingly a simple diglossia for many who will be bilingual in Swahili and English', quite similar to Spanish–Guaraní bilingualism in Paraguay. It appears, though, that this is a change that may take several generations. Swahili in Tanzania seems to be more acceptable than is Guaraní in Paraguay for High functions; it is being used as the medium of instruction in primary education, whereas the same use of Guaraní is being gingerly approached in Paraguay. The total replacement of English by Swahili seems not to be imminent. It appears that English will continue to be needed as a language of international commerce and diplomacy and of science and technology for the foreseeable future.

Greece appears to be destined to undergo diglossic change in the direction of a more unified linguistic system containing elements of both the old H and the old L, with the old L predominating. The 'lower' portion of Tanzania's double overlapping diglossia may eventually change; the old H may some day replace at least some of the old Ls. Both the H and the L of the 'upper' portion will probably be maintained, although the L language will probably squeeze the H into an increasingly narrower range of functions. In neither case do we speak of the end of diglossia. Diglossia never ends; it is a human universal. The changes we have discussed will simply mean that diglossia will begin to be expressed through a more unified set of linguistic options, that is, more what we have called style-shifting and less what we call superposed bilingualism or classic diglossia.

BIBLIOGRAPHICAL NOTES

A few studies of Ferguson's four defining cases of diglossia are as follows: Ferguson (1959b,) Kaye (1970), and Zughoul (1980) on Arabic; Householder (1963), Kazazis

(1976), Sotiropoulos (1977) and Browning (1982) on Greek (Browning 1982 is particularly valuable as a historical sketch of Greek diglossia); Stewart (1963) and Valdman (1968), (1971) on Haiti; and Moulton (1963) and Weinreich (1968) on Swiss German. Some recent studies of other cases of diglossia include: Flint (1979) (varieties of English on Norfolk Island), Hughes (1972) (French and English in Montreal), Jaakkola (1976) (Swedish and Finnish in Sweden), Krysin (1979) (Russian), Magner (1978) (Standard Croatian and local dialect in Split, Yugoslavia), Meeus (1979) (standard Dutch and Flemish in Belgium) and Parasher (1980) (English and mother tongues in India).

NOTES

1   Ferguson's article 'Diglossia' was originally published in the journal *Word* in 1959. Citations in this chapter will be to its reprinting in Giglioli (1972).

2   Diglossia in Greece, as we will see later and as Ferguson predicted, seems to be coming to an end in the classical sense of the term 'diglossia'. The language of literature in the Greek case has undergone an interesting reversal.

3   The Greek and Swiss cases are, to some extent, exceptions to this.

4   This is also true when Ferguson's more technical definition of simplicity is used (1972:241–2).

5   Citations from Fishman's article will be taken not from the original source, but from the slightly revised version in Fishman 1972d.

6   Although it is clear that Fishman realizes that more than two language varieties can be used for separate purposes in a society, it is not clear that he thinks such cases should be called 'diglossia'; indeed, presumably he does not think so. What is less clear is to what extent Fishman considers the two-variety case to be special.

7   As we saw in chapter 1, it would be an exaggeration to assume that almost everyone in Paraguay speaks both Spanish and Guaraní.

8   A similar notion of the relationship between linguistic community and the linguistic varieties they use is found in Gumperz (1962:32). It is my intention that the term 'social unit' be interpreted broadly enough to include Fishman's cases of 'diglossia without bilingualism'.

9   The opposite case, where speakers have the same L but different Hs, would also distinguish speech communities under my definition. It is not clear that any such cases exist. Allan Bell has suggested to me that one place to look for such an example would be along a national border where a single sociocultural group lived on both sides. In such a case, the L might be the same small group language for both, whereas the H would be a different national language for group members on either side of the border.

10 This is as good a time as any to point out that, in spite of the term 'Low', the functions served by Low varieties are far more important to an individual as a person than the functions served by the High varieties.

11 We will encounter Tanzania again in chapter 10 as an example of language planning.

12 In at least two articles, Gumperz (1962, 1964) discusses the functional distribution of languages within a community and lists Ferguson (1959a) in the bibliography, but avoids using the term 'diglossia'.

13 Platt is aware of the possiblity of grouping subcodes within codes, which he explicitly distinguishes from what he found in Singapore and Malaysia (Platt 1977:363).

14 I have modified the informal part of the translation and so it differs slightly from the one Stewart gives (Stewart 1963:158).

15 Looked at in this way, native English-speaking readers of this book are now using their knowledge of 'High' style English. In the next conversation with a family member or close friend, 'Low' English will be used.

16 For a repartee between proponents of opposite sides of the relatedness question, see Fellman (1975) and Johnson (1975).

17 There is no doubt that there will be cases one would wish to call diglossia that won't quite fit this definition in one respect or another. One case I am already aware of is the great pride German-speaking Swiss take in their Lows, the Swiss dialects. As Moulton (1963) points out, there have been grammars written for some of them, a school set up to teach Swiss German to returning Swiss expatriates, and a preference for pronunciation rules for standard German, the High dialect, that make it sound more Swiss. It is therefore not clear that the Swiss German Ls are 'less highly valued' than standard German. As we saw in the previous chapter, Guaraní is 'less highly valued' than Spanish in Paraguayan broad diglossia only in a limited sense.

18 One novelist and short-story writer of this period, Alexandros Papadiamantis, wrote the dialogue in his works in the spoken Greek of his day, the narrative in katharévusa with many demotic features, and descriptions and lyric digressions in classicizing katharévusa (Browning 1982:54).

19 This led to a state of affairs, anomolous for diglossia, in which writers of serious literature write 'lower' than they speak (Kazazis 1976).

20 Browning (1982:57) finds it 'most unlikely' that any Greek government will again restore katharévusa as the medium of education.

OBJECTIVES

1 Be able to state which of the nine characteristics of diglossia is the most crucial.

2 Be able to identify the reaction to the use of either High or Low in a given situation (appropriate or not), such as the ones given in table 2.1.

3 Be able to identify the acquisition pattern for the H and L dialects and which one is learned more fluently.

4 Be able to state the striking fact about H and L lexicons that is pointed out by Ferguson.

5 Be able to recognize the relationship between the grammars of H and L and the phonologies of H and L.

6 Be able to recognize 'the best bet by far' for an outcome to diglossia if it does not remain stable.

7 Be able to identify the two important modifications Fishman made to Ferguson's concept of diglossia.

8 Be able to state the central factor in diglossia on which Fishman and Ferguson agree.

9 Given the description of a situation like those on pages 41–2, be able to identify which of Fishman's four categories it would fit into.

10 Be able to state the factor that in Fasold's opinion makes the distinction between diglossia with bilingualism and diglossia without bilingualism less useful (see p. 42–3).

11 Be able to distinguish Ferguson's implicit notion of diglossic (speech) community and Fasold's definition.

12 Be able to state the major feature of double overlapping diglossia.

13 Be able to recognize a description of double-nested diglossia as exemplified in Khalapur, India.

14 Be able to state the importance of linear polyglossia for the binarity question.

15   Be able to recognize the conclusion on the relatedness question that studies of Haitian French, Russian and 'a different perspective' on the Khalapur situation lead to.

16   Be able to recognize the 'question' on which Fasold's definition of 'broad diglossia' agrees with Ferguson's original definition.

17   Be able to recognize the degree of linguistic relatedness associated with 'classic diglossia' and the two other kinds of broad diglossia it is opposed to. (Table 2.3)

18   Be able to name the two characteristics of changing diglossic relationships.

19   Be able to state whether or not Fasold believes diglossic change can involve the end of diglossia, in the broad sense.

3

Qualitative Formulas

FORMULAIC APPROACHES

We have explored the social and political aspects of societal multilingualism enough to see that certain patterns tend to recur, involving different languages in different parts of the world. For example, we find European colonial languages as the official government language of Paraguay (Spanish), Tanzania (English), and, in part, India (English). At the same time, we find indigenous languages designated as national languages in the same three countries (Guaraní in Paraguay, Swahili in Tanzania and Hindi in India). It should be noticed that these nations are located on three different continents and the indigenous languages involved are totally unrelated. Two countries we have looked at have extremely multilingual, relatively undeveloped sub-areas (the Indian state of Nagaland and the Paraguayan Chaco). Both of these areas have numerous related languages spoken by small numbers of people who are just beginning to join the national life. We also saw strikingly similar diglossic patterns between Spanish and Guaraní, Classical and Colloquial Arabic, and the *saf bolī* and *motī bolī* styles of the Khalapur vernacular. These are just a few examples of sociolinguistic generalities that seem to recur regardless of location or language.[1]

Typologies and formulas

If there are such generalities that apply all over the world, is it possible to make general sociolinguistic statements that apply to all the countries of the world, or at least to groups of them? During the 1960s there was an effort to discover general patterns in the sociolinguistics of language that would facilitate comparisons among countries. This effort developed into two kinds of approach: typologies and formulas. The typologies were attempts to set up categories based on a few variables into which any nation could be placed. They emphasized the historical development of nations (somewhat in the same spirit as the four historical strands of chapter 1), the legal status of various languages in countries, the relative position of the ruling nationality to the country as a whole, questions of language development and relatedness, and the size of the populations speaking various languages. Two such typologies were developed by Kloss (1966, 1968) and Rustow (1968). The second approach was begun by Stewart (1962), modified by Ferguson (1966) with some development of his own earlier work (Ferguson 1962), and modified again by Stewart (1968).[2] To see how the formula approach works, we will examine in detail the systems proposed by Ferguson (1966) and Stewart (1968).

Ferguson's formula.   Ferguson's goal was to continue Stewart's earlier search for a succinct notational system that could be applied to nations and quickly reveal the important sociolinguistic facts. Ferguson began by setting up three general categories into which the languages of a nation might fit. A language is a *major language* (Lmaj) if it meets at least one of the following three qualifications:

1   it is spoken as a native language by more than 25 per cent of the population or by more than one million people;
2   it is an official language of the country;
3   it is the language of education of over 50 per cent of those completing secondary school in the nation.

A language is a *minor language* (Lmin) if it meets none of the requirements for a major language, but does have one of the following characteristics:

1   it is spoken as a native language by more than 5 per cent of the population or by more than 100,000 people;
2   it is used as a medium of instruction above the first years of primary school and has textbooks other than primers published in it.

The third category is designed to catch languages that seem to be significant, but do not meet any of the above qualifications.[3] A *language of special status* (Lspec) may be used as a language of religion, for literary purposes, widely taught as a subject in secondary schools, or used as a lingua franca.[4]

    Beyond these general categories, both Ferguson's and Stewart's formulas involve *types* and *functions.* The idea of types and functions was adopted by Ferguson from Stewart's earlier work (Stewart 1962). The five language types that Ferguson recognizes are these:

1   A *vernacular* (symbolized by a V), the unstandardized native language of a speech community.
2   A *standard* (S), a standardized vernacular.
3   A *classical* language (C), a standard which has died out as a native language.
4   A *pidgin* (P), defined as a hybrid language with lexical stock from one

language and the grammatical structure of another language or languages.

5   A *creole* (K), a pidgin that has become the native language of a speech community.

Ferguson gives the following functions as being fulfilled by various types of languages (functions are symbolized by lower case letters):

1   *Group* function (g), used primarily for communication within a particular speech community, identifying it as a specific sociocultural group in the country.

2   *Official* use (o), designated legally as official or used for government purposes at the national level.

3   *Language of wider communication* (w), or lingua franca, used within a given country for interethnic communication.

4   *Educational* use (e), used in education beyond the first years of primary school, with textbooks published in it.

5   *Religious* purposes (r).

6   *International* use (i), for communication with other nations.

7   *School-subject* function (s), widely studied as a subject in schools, rather than being used as a medium of instruction.

These three classes of information are then combined in a formula. The format can be illustrated with Ferguson's formula for Paraguay, a nation we are familiar with (1966:314):

$$3L = 2Lmaj(So,Vg) + 0Lmin + 1Lspec(Cr)$$

The formula is to be read:

Paraguay has three languages, of which two are major languages, one a standard language fulfilling the official function and the other a vernacular fulfilling the group function, none are minor languages, and one is a language of special status, a classical language fulfilling the religious function.

It is not possible to read off directly which language is which from a Ferguson formula, but it is not difficult to work out that the standard language is Spanish, the vernacular is Guaraní, and the classical language is Latin.[5]

This basic notational system can be elaborated with three supplementary devices. Diglossia can be indicated by the use of a colon between the High and Low varieties. For example, the formula for Morocco contains the entry C:Vorw for Arabic.[6] This is to be read as:

There are classical and vernacular forms of a language in diglossic relationship, with the classical as the High dialect and the vernacular as the Low dialect; and the official, religious and wider communication functions are distributed between them as is expected in diglossia (that is, the classical form fulfills the official and religious functions, and the vernacular the wider communication function).

To indicate that one of the major languages is a 'nationally dominant language', defined as being used as a first or second language by over three-quarters of the population, the language type and function designation is printed in bold type (Ferguson 1966:313). Finally, there are countries in which there are numerous small group languages, none of which qualifies as either a major language, a minor language, or a language of special status on its own. Nevertheless, taken together as a bloc, these languages represent a total that should be represented in the formula. Ferguson uses braces and the plus sign to indicate such blocs, which, as it turns out, are always vernacular languages that together are of minor language size. To illustrate how this works, consider the formula for Taiwan (Ferguson 1966:314):

$$5^+ \text{ L} = 3\text{Lmaj(Sow,2Vg)} + 0^+\text{Lmin([V])} + 2\text{Lspec(Cr,Ssi)}$$

This is to be read as:

There are five languages, plus a bloc, of which three are major languages, one a standard language fulfilling the official and wider communication functions, and two vernaculars fulfilling the group function; there are no minor languages, but there is a bloc of vernacular languages that, taken together, would qualify as a minor language; and there are two languages of special status, the other a classical language fulfilling the religious function and one a standard language fulfilling the school-subject and international communication functions.

Stewart's Formula.   Stewart's (1968) formula is a modification of the notational system he proposed in 1962. Like Ferguson's formula, Stewart's contains language types and functions, allows diglossia to be expressed, and provides for indications of the size of the populations speaking different languages (the latter two tasks, though, are handled differently by Stewart). One important aspect of Stewart's approach is his definition of language types by means of *attributes*. He proposes a set of four attributes, different combinations of which give the seven language types he recognizes. These include the five that Ferguson uses plus *dialects* (symbolized by D) and *artificial* languages (A), which are deliberately constructed languages (Esperanto is perhaps the best-known example). The four attributes are:

1   *standardization,* the codification and acceptance of a designated set of norms for correct usage;
2   *autonomy,* the status of a linguistic system as independent – one that does not have to be referred to in connection with another language;

3 *historicity*, the acceptance of the language variety as one that developed normally over time;

4 *vitality,* the existence of an unisolated community of native speakers of the language variety.

The seven types are defined by these attributes as in table 3.1.

Table 3.1 Language types defined by attributes

Attributes				Language type	Symbol
St	*Au*	*Hi*	*Vi*		
+	+	+	+	Standard	S
+	+	+	−	Classical	C
+	+	−	−	Artificial	A
−	+	+	+	Vernacular	V
−	−	+	+	Dialect	D
−	−	−	+	Creole	K
−	−	−	−	Pidgin	P

Source: Adapted from Stewart 1968:53

Stewart's attributes can perhaps be better understood if it is explained why they have minus values for the types in table 3.1. Vernaculars, dialects, creoles, and pidgins are −standardization because they typically do not have grammar books, dictionaries and similar codifying materials developed for them.[7] Dialects, creoles, and pidgins are −autonomy because they are popularly considered varieties of some other languages; in the case of pidgins and creoles, they are considered varieties of the languages from which they draw most of their lexicon. Artificial languages, creoles, and pidgins are −historicity because their histories are not considered 'normal' in one way or another: for artificial languages, because they come into existence 'suddenly' when they are invented; for pidgins, because they are born out of contact with another language; and for creoles, because they develop from pidgins. An important aspect of historicity is the association of a language with the tradition of some sociocultural group; something all these three lack. Classical, artificial and pidgin languages are all −vitality, because none of them, by definition, have communities of native speakers.

The language functions that Stewart recognizes are the seven that Ferguson uses, plus the following three:

1 *provincial* function (p), indicating official use at the level of some political subdivision smaller than the country as a whole;

2 *capital* function (c), indicating that the language variety is the dominant means of communication in the area of the national capital;

3 *literary* function (l), meaning the use of the language mainly for literary and scholarly work.

In addition to language types and functions, Stewart places each language in one of six classes, based on the percentage of the population that speaks it.[8] This system replaces Ferguson's major and minor language categories, as well as his use of the boldface type convention. Another important difference between the two systems is that Ferguson counts only native speakers when classifying languages as major, minor, or neither (but not for the use of boldface type), whereas Stewart counts all speakers – native and second language speakers – in assigning languages to classes. Table 3.2 gives Stewart's classes.

Table 3.2 Stewart's classification of languages by proportion of populations speaking them

Class	Percentage
Class I	75 +
Class II	50 +
Class III	25 +
Class IV	10 +
Class V	5 +
Class VI	below 5

Source: Stewart (1968:542)

Like Ferguson, Stewart has added a few special conventions to express additional information. If a standard language has two norms by which it is standardized (an example he gives is 'Hindustani', with both Hindi and Urdu norms), then it is given the subscript 2 along with the type symbol (for example, S_2). If a language in a given country is standardized according to the norms originating in another country, this is called *exonormative standardization* and indicated with an x subscript. The exonormative standard must then be specified. For example, the English used in Nigeria is standardized on a British norm, and therefore Stewart's formula for Nigeria would include:

English S_xo   (British norm)

Diglossia is indicated by the notation '(d: H=Language A)' next to the Low variety and the notation '(d: L=Language B)' next to the High variety. The High and Low varieties must be listed separately. Stewart (1968:544) gives the following example of his formula for the Curaçao Island group of the Netherlands Antilles:

Class I	Papiamentu	K	(d: H=Spanish)
Class IV	Dutch	So	
	English	Sigs	
Class V	Spanish	Sisl	(d: L=Papiamentu)

Class VI	Hebrew	Cr
	Latin	Crs

The way this formula should be read is reasonably transparent.

THE FAILURE OF FORMULAIC APPROACHES

Although a great deal of thought was put into these two and other typological schemes by scholars of considerable ability, none of them has been widely accepted as *the* conventional method of representing societal multilingualism. In fact, no attempt has been made to develop a formulaic model by a noted sociolinguist for more than a decade. If indeed there are sociolinguistic generalities of the sort exemplified at the beginning of this chapter, why has no one been able to develop a notational system that captures them?

One fact to consider, as Ferguson pointed out in the discussion of his 1966 paper (Bright 1966:316), is that 'this is a very small universe of discourse – there are somewhere between 100 and 200 countries in the world'. Since there are relatively so few countries to talk about, perhaps it would be pointless to develop general statements. Perhaps a prose description of the multilingualism of each country would do as well. I believe, however, that we can profit from the study of another 'small universe of discourse' in another field for which important general principles have been discovered.[9]

The chemical elements number about 100, give or take a handful of laboratory elements. Nevertheless, steady progress has been made in the discovery of the nature of elements over the past 150 years. The German chemist Johann Döbereiner discovered that there was a relationship between atomic weight and certain physical and chemical properties of elements. Döbereiner's way of presenting this fact was in the form of triads of elements arranged by atomic weight. Within each triad, some of the physical and chemical properties of the element in the middle could be predicted from those of the other two. Some 35 years later, in 1864, an English chemist named John Newland noticed that if the elements were arranged in eight columns of seven elements each, the eight elements in the horizontal rows showed striking similarities in properties. This 'law of octaves' was the forerunner of the modern periodic table of the elements. There were a few gaps in the table expressing the law of octaves, and the great Russian chemist, Dmitri Mendeleyev, predicted that elements would be discovered to fill those gaps and he also predicted what properties these elements would have. Sure enough, three rare earth elements – gallium, scandium, and germanium – were later discovered; they fit in three of the blank spaces and had the properties Mendeleyev predicted.

Until this point, elements were assigned positions in the table by atomic weight. Mendeleyev also noticed that two elements seemed to be out of place when positioned strictly by atomic weight, since their other properties would be better predicted if they switched places with their neighbors. At that time (around 1870) there was no explanation for why atomic weight was such a good organizing principle in general, but seemed to be slightly faulty in these two cases. In 1914, another English chemist, Henry Gwyn-Jeffreys Moseley, using a procedure based on the measurement of the wavelengths of X-rays emitted by various elements, was able to show that the correct ordering principle would be based on atomic number (the number of protons in the atomic nucleus). When elements are arranged by atomic number, the disorders noticed by Mendeleyev disappear. The explanation for the fact that atomic weight is a good, but not perfect, predictor of periodicity is to be found in the theory of the structure of the atom. Virtually all the weight of an atom is accounted for by the nucleus. The nucleus contains both protons and neutrons, each of which has about the same mass. Since atomic number reflects the number of protons, the higher the atomic number, the greater the atomic weight value. However, small discrepancies are to be expected between neighboring elements when they are ordered by atomic weight due to variation in the number of neutrons. The chemical properties of elements are accounted for largely by the number of extra-nuclear electrons in their atoms; a number equal to the number of the protons. This, of course, is the same as the atomic number. Properties of elements are thus predicted by the atomic number, and atomic weight is a good but not perfect predictor, because atomic weight is closely, but not perfectly, correlated with atomic number.

This brief lesson in the history of chemistry is designed to show how the study of a 'small universe of discourse' can lead to greater and greater accuracy in ordering its members, constant refinement of principles, and ultimately a superior understanding of just how a phenomenon works. This is in stark contrast with the work on qualitative formulas. Here, various schemes were proposed and modified without a convincing increase in their accuracy. The effort led to little gain in the understanding of societal multilingualism. Ultimately the entire enterprise was abandoned. The study of the elements, it seems to me, proceeded on the basis of two principles that did not underlie the development of the sociolinguistic formulas. These might be called the principle of naturalism and the principle of prediction.[10]

The principle of naturalism simply means that the object of study is to be taken as an observable phenomenon and the job of the scientist is to find out how it works. This was the obvious approach to take in the study of elements, some of which are found simply lying around on the earth. In the study of social organization, naturalism is not quite so obvious an approach. The various typologies and formulas had to apply to some unit and the unit invariably chosen was the *nation*.[11] Nations may be a natural social unit, but they may well not be, since nations, as we now understand the term, are a relatively recent invention. In any case, there are facts that make us doubt that nation is always the unit we would be drawn to if we followed the principle of naturalism. For example, in India we find subnational political units – the states – to which Ferguson's or Stewart's formulas would apply as well as to the nation as a whole. In some countries, geographical differences would lead to totally different formulas. This seems to be particularly true in island countries. Stewart (1968) gives strikingly different formulas for the Curaçao Island group and the Leeward Island group of the Netherlands Antilles, for example. Another problem is the case of ethnic groups that have not settled primarily within the boundaries of one country. As was pointed out by Einar Haugen in the discussion of Ferguson (1966) (Bright 1966:318–19), Lappish is a language spoken by Lapps in Sweden, Norway, Finland, and the Soviet Union, but by small numbers in each country. By Ferguson's criteria, Lappish would not appear in the formulas for any country. The language is, to some extent, relevant for all four countries, but the Lapps should probably be viewed as a transnational group as well. The Jews of the Diaspora represent another sociolinguistically important social group that transcends any one country.[12] Naturalism, it seems, would lead to the application of a formulaic system simultaneously to whole countries, subdivisions of countries, transnational geographical regions (like the Indian subcontinent, Scandinavia or the Iberian Peninsula) and transnational sociocultural groups like the Lapps.

Another area in which naturalism would lead to a new perspective is connected with some of the functions (the category of items that Ferguson and Stewart represent by lower-case letters). The official function, for example, has almost invariably been assigned to whatever languages have been declared official in the constitutions and laws of countries, regardless of whether or not they actually perform that function. English was actually an official language of India before the 1967 law declared it so; Irish still is not much of a functioning official language in Ireland, in spite of being so designated in the Irish constitution. The language of education is another such function. The existing formulas will list languages as having the education function if the school policy is to use that language, regardless of whether or not teachers actually end up speaking some other language most of the time in the classroom, and regardless of whether or not much educating is really accomplished if the designated language is strictly adhered to.

The principle of prediction was not a basis for the formulas and typologies of the 1960s; instead, the purpose was categorization and comparison. If an ordering principle is not required to predict anything, then a great many different systems will do. For example, if one simply wanted a classification of apples that would allow all apples to be placed in one category or another, one could use size groupings, color, part of the world in which they are grown, or any of a number of other criteria. But if the classification must fit in with a predictive theory of botany, then the number of acceptable classifications is immediately sharply reduced. Similarly, the existing formulas and typologies were required only to organize languages with respect to nations (or the reverse), and allow comparisons among nations. Any of a great number of possible systems would provide reasonable organization and, as long as the same system is used for all countries, comparison is possible as well. It is only when prediction is expected of the organizing principle that we can begin to speak meaningfully of right and wrong systems, and hope to find the right ones.

One further principle we will introduce, even though it seems not to be one that guided the research on elements, is the *continuum* principle. Part of the difficulty in the formula concept is that overly rigid categories were often set up. Take for example the notion of 'standardization' or 'standard language'. This was the defining criterion distinguishing standard languages from vernaculars for both Ferguson and Stewart. If a language was standardized, or codified, or had accepted norms, or the like, it was said to be a standard language, otherwise it was a vernacular. But there are all sorts of levels of codification and some languages are more standard than others. Kloss (1968:78) distinguishes six levels of standardization. The five that form something of a continuum are listed below.[13]

1   Mature standard language. All modern knowledge can be taught through a mature standard language at college level.
2   Small-group standard language. Norms have been in place for some time, but the speech community is so small that broad domains of modern civilization will never be pursued through it.
3   Young standard language. The language has been codified, with dictionaries, grammars, and similar devices, very recently in time. The language may be adequate for primary education, but not yet for more advanced study.
4   Unstandardized alphabetized language. There are no dictionaries and grammar books for the language, but it has been reduced to writing.
5   Preliterate language. The language is rarely or never used in writing.

Levels of standardization may be set up on other criteria and a different number of levels may be more useful, but Kloss's list illustrates the fact that standardization is not a binary category.

We find that language functions are fulfilled by different languages from one country to another to varying degrees, rather than being either fulfilled or not. The official function is one of these. As we saw, Stewart (1968) recognized this to some extent in his distinction between the o function, at the level of the national government, and the p function for official languages at the province level. Kloss (1968:79) distinguishes between languages that are the only official language at the national level, coequal official languages at the national level, regional official languages, languages not designated as official but promoted by the government in some way, languages that are ignored by the government, and languages that are actually legislated against. We will consider the 'officialness continuum' again shortly.

A NEW BEGINNING

Perhaps the principles I have been talking about will not work in socio-linguistics as they do in the physical sciences. It is possible that the physical phenomena are much more regular than the behavior of human society, and that a naturalist outlook and the expectation of successful predictions are not appropriate in sociolinguistic research.

There are two reasons not to give in to this kind of pessimism too soon. First, there do seem to be generalities in sociolinguistic phenomena that are applicable, regardless of language or location. It is reasonable to believe that there may be basic reasons for these and that these reasons can be discovered. Second, not all areas of the sociolinguistics of society have had such a disappointing history as profile formulas and typologies. In chapter 2, we saw the development of the concept of diglossia from Ferguson's original proposal to an important and general principle that seems to apply to a wide variety of cases around the world. The definition of broad diglossia which we gave in chapter 2 can even be interpreted as a set of predictions:

1 Most or all societies have a verbal repertoire that includes a substantial range of variation.
2 Some parts of this repertoire are more highly valued than others by the community.
3 The lower-valued parts are learned earlier and informally; the higher-valued ones are learned later and more formally.
4 An important subset of the language functions in a society can be ordered along a continuum from formal and guarded to informal and relaxed.
5 The more highly-valued segments of the community repertoire will be used for the formal and guarded functions, and conversely.

If the study of diglossia can have a lively history, lasting for more than 20 years, with at least the illusion of progress, then perhaps a new formulaic approach can be as profitable.

William Stewart is to be credited with two of the largest blocks in the foundation of our fresh approach. It was Stewart who first noticed that every function was not equally likely to be fulfilled by every language type:

although the possibilities of co-occurrence of a given language function with a given language type are varied enough so that both need to be specified for each case, there is nevertheless a certain correlation between the two in that the o, p, l, and r functions will almost always be associated with S or C types, the i function with S, C or A types, and the g function with S, V, or K types. (Stewart 1968:541)

In other words one could almost predict that, given a certain language function, only a few of the language types could possibly fulfill it in any country. To Stewart, it seemed that these predictions were not reliable enough to be built directly into the formulas, but his discovery that the relationship between types and functions is not random is extremely important.

Stewart's second seminal insight was that language type was not a prime category; the types could be further broken down into combinations of *attributes*. Although not all the particular attributes Stewart proposed prove useful, the notion that languages can be defined by constellations of sociolinguistic properties, or attributes, is also very important. In fact, we will dispense with the notion 'language type' entirely, and utilize only functions and attributes.

These two ideas can be carried one step further. Given that social groups, nations or other units, have language functions drawn from a universal set (Ferguson's or Stewart's language functions might be a first approximation to this set), then languages that fulfill these functions have to be *qualified* to fulfill them. To be qualified, a language must possess the required set of sociolinguistic attributes. At first, it will be necessary to guess what these attributes might be. In examining a wide range of actual nations or other polities around the world, we will be able to refine and revise the functions, the attributes, and the match between them, somewhat in the manner in which the periodic table of the elements was refined.

Let us begin with the *official* function. To be consistent with the principle of naturalism, we won't regard a language as official simply because there is a national law or section of a constitution that says it is. Rather, a language will be judged official only if it actually operates as an official language in the country. That is, it must be used for some or all of at least the following tasks. First, it must serve as the spoken language of government officials in their official duties at the national level (they may speak other languages in friendly conversation). Second, it must serve as the language of written communication between and within government agencies at the national level. Third, it must be the language in which government records are kept at the national level. Fourth, it should be the language in which laws and regulations governing the nation as a whole are originally written (they may be translated into other languages). Finally, it should be the language in which forms, such as tax forms and various applications related to the national government, are published. The expression 'at the national level' is stressed to exclude two other functions. The official language at the subdivision level (states, provinces, departments) may fulfill these same tasks at the subdivision level without detracting from the status of the national official language. Above the level of the whole country, another language might be used as the language of international diplomacy or international commerce. This is the international function and will be considered distinct from the official function.

What if a language is used for some, but not all of the above tasks? This is where the continuum principle comes in. It is possible for a language to be official to one degree or another. It is also possible that more than one language can be used for the same task, as when government forms are printed in two or more ιanguages. Perhaps it will one day be possible to agree on a precise list of official function tasks, and to weight them by importance so that we can say that a language is 'o_5' on an officialness scale of ten, where the higher numbers mean the language fulfills more, and more important, official tasks, and the lower numbers, fewer and less·important ones.

A *nationalist* function needs to be distinguished from the official function. Official languages are in place primarily for *nationist* reasons, those concerned with the day to day practical tasks of governing. The nationalist function is concerned with *nationalist* motivations, the unifying and separatist functions, the link with the glorious past, and authenticity. As a result, the official and nationalist language functions require of a language different sociolinguistic attributes. In fact, although many nations have the same language serving both the official and the nationalist functions (and this situation is generally considered the ideal one), it is common for nations to have different languages serving these two functions. One of the clearest examples is Paraguay, where Spanish is the functioning official language and Guaraní is the nationalist language.[14]

The continuum principle must also be applied to the nationalist function. The two ends of the continuum are fairly clear. At one end would be languages such as Manx (cited by Myles Dillon in Bright 1966:317), which are extinct but are used on some public occasions. At the other end are languages that are so obviously nationalist languages that they are not even expressly advocated within their nations, and may not even be designated as national languages by law or constitution. Some examples are Icelandic in Iceland, French in France, Thai in Thailand, and Japanese in Japan. Between these two extremes are languages whose statuses as nationalist languages are being consciously promoted, with varying degrees of success. The nationalist function resembles the group function used by both Ferguson and Stewart, except that it applies to the national level of social organization, not just to subnational socio-cultural groups. It turns out, however, that the nationalist function is not simply the group function applied at the national level. The nationalist and group functions require of a language similar, but distinct, attributes.

There are other functions and these will be brought in during the discussion of the attributes required for the fulfillment of functions. Before we consider that, let us try a first approximation of the attributes required by the official and nationalist functions. The official function seems to require, first, a sufficient level of standardization, probably something equivalent to Kloss's (1968:78) 'young standard' or higher, which implies status at or very near the High end of the community's diglossia repertoire, and second, a sufficiently large cadre of well educated citizens who can use the language well (this cadre must be reasonably well distributed geographically within the country, but can be a very small proportion of the population). If a language is proposed or designated as official in some polity and does not have these two attributes (or whatever attributes experience shows to be the correct ones), then we would predict that it will not successfully fulfill the official function. This is where the principle of prediction comes in. Of course, a language may lack some crucial attribute, such as sufficient standardization, when it is chosen, but it may acquire that attribute reasonably quickly. In that case, we would predict success, provided the missing attribute is acquired.

Before I discuss the attributes required for the nationalist function, it will be helpful to look at those required for the group function. As an initial guess of what is required I propose, first, that language is used for ordinary conversation by all members of the group (implying that it is acquired early, which implies that it is at the Low end of the diglossic repertoire); and second, that language must be seen by its speakers as fulfilling the unifying and separatist functions. With respect to the second requirement, notice that the language need not be seen as a symbol of authenticity or a link with the glorious past. These are strictly nationalist function requirements, that is, a sociocultural group that has these feelings about its language is a nationality, in Fishman's sense. Furthermore, the contrastive self-identification provided by the language may even be seen as *regrettable*; the speakers may be embarrassed to be identified as members of their group, or at least feel ambivalent about it. With respect to the nationalist function, contrastive self-identification is always a matter of pride.

The nationalist function requires, I propose, the following sociolinguistic attributes. First, the language serves as a symbol of national identity for a sizable and powerful proportion of the population. Second, the language is used for some everyday, unofficial purposes by a sizable proportion of the population, although not necessarily as the home language. Third, the language is spoken fluently and with ease by a sizable proportion of the population. Fourth, the major sociocultural groups in the country, although they may have other languages fulfilling the group function, have no alternative nationalist language. Any nationalist aspirations they develop will be associated with this one language. An example of this last point is Quechua in Ecuador. There is a substantial number of Quechua speakers in Ecuador, but they typically acquire Spanish as they enter the mainstream of national life. Hindi in India does *not* have the fourth attribute; it is not accepted in the nationalist function by speakers of other major languages, especially speakers of Dravidian languages. Requiring this attribute of a nationalist language means that a language may fulfill the nationalist function for some subdivision of the country without being a nationalist language for the country as a whole. Fifth, the language must also be acceptable as a symbol of authenticity; it must be 'good enough'. This usually, but not always, implies a fairly high degree of standardization and a position at the High end of the diglossia repertoire. Finally, and sixth, the language must be seen as a link with the glorious past.[15]

The second and fifth attributes can conflict in distressing ways. If a language is widely used for everyday, unofficial purposes, it implies that it is rather 'Low' in the terminology of diglossia. To be 'good enough' means that it cannot be so Low as to lose credibility as an authentic language. For some nationalities, authenticity requires that the language be used to fulfill the highest of the diglossic functions, including higher education and official use at the national level. Others are willing to accept their national language as authentic, while tolerating a higher language for some purposes. The smoothest situation occurs when there is single-code diglossia within the nation; High and Low functions are distributed among the styles of the national language. This allows the community to see the 'same' language being used for all purposes from the most erudite university lectures to cuddling 2-year-olds. Another way of resolving the potential conflict is when diglossia is distributed among varieties of a linguistic system at the level of relatedness described by Ferguson (1959a), but the population nevertheless sees the whole linguistic complex as a single language. The Arab countries are a good example of this. Classical Arabic is seen as the 'real' national language, with the colloquial dialect as a more-or-less deviant variety of the same language. According to Ferguson (1959b), it is typical for citizens of each Arab country to believe that its own colloquial is closer to Classical Arabic than the colloquials of its sister nations. This no doubt helps to reinforce the idea that the Classical and colloquial varieties are really part of the same language in that country. There seems to be a similar tendency in Haiti to consider French and Creole as varieties of the same language.

A few nationalities are willing to allow another language to be used for High purposes, while a lower language serves the nationalist function. We have already seen three examples of this. In Switzerland, the Swiss German dialects fulfill the nationalist function for the subnational nationalities in the German-speaking cantons, while standard German remains in place as a High dialect. In Paraguay, Guaraní and Spanish coexist with Spanish given the High functions of official use and higher education. The same pattern can be found in Tanzania, where Swahili has achieved considerable status as a nationalist language, while English continues as High language in some respects. Notice that, in all three cases, the Low variety is 'raised' somewhat. The Swiss German dialects are remarkable for the fact that there have been grammar books written for them within their own communities, schools have existed in which they were taught, and their speakers take considerable pride in them. Guaraní has also been standardized to some extent and Paraguayans fervently insist on the logic and adequacy of the language (Rona 1966). Swahili is steadily encroaching on the High functions formerly reserved for English in Tanzania, and at the same time it is receiving formal standardization.

The *educational* function appears to require at least three attributes. First, the language must be understood by the learners; second, there must be teaching resources available in the language (teachers able to teach in it and textbooks must exist); and third, it must be sufficiently standardized, entailing a relatively High position in the diglossic repertoire. The level of education must be taken into account in applying these attributes. The first attribute decreases in importance and the other two increase as the level of education is raised. Of course, even university students have to understand the language used as the medium of instruction, but it is more reasonable to place the burden of *learning* a qualified language on university students than it is to place it on small children going to school for the first time. Furthermore, the second and third attributes become harder to meet with an increase in educational level. A higher degree of knowledge on the part of teachers, more highly technical books, and greater standardization and prestige are required for higher levels of education.

The problem that arises when there is no single language possessing all three attributes is the source of one of the most widespread kinds of language conflict in the world. We have already seen a little of India's attempts to deal with speakers of languages that lack the second and third attributes by means of the Three Languages Formula. Very often, a country will select a language of education that has the second and third attributes even when it lacks the first. This can have only two results: either the students come to understand the language of education (that is, they learn it), or almost no education takes place. Some of the educational problems in rural Paraguay, as only one example, can be traced to the fact that the learners do not know the designated language of education, Spanish. From the naturalist point of view, we would say that Spanish does not fulfill the educational function for these youngsters.

For a *language of wider communication,* there seems to be one required attribute: it must be learnable as a second language by at least one linguistic minority in the country. Of course, *any* language can be learned or it would not exist, but by 'learnable' I mean it must be *considered* learnable by the relevant populations. If the learning population is overwhelmed numerically and politically by the native speakers of the language of wider communication, the tendency is to learn it more or less the way the native speakers speak it, although with an accent. If there is less of a numerical and power discrepancy, or if no group within the country claims the language of wider communication as their own, then the second-language learners, in effect, *make* it more learnable by the process that Hymes (1971) calls 'pidginization'. The result is a pidgin or creole; or a simplified lingua franca, or 'bazaar' language.

As for the attributes of languages of *international* commerce and diplomacy, it seems that the best we can do is to say that the language must come from a short list of languages, mostly European: English, French, Spanish, Russian, German, perhaps Mandarin Chinese, and maybe one or two others. The reason these languages are used for this function reflects the historical fact that their speakers have control of these international activities.

The fundamental requirement for a *school-subject language* seems to be that its level of standardization must be equal to or greater than the standardization level of the languages of the students. A young standard language might be taught to speakers of an unstandardized, alphabetized language, but not the reverse. Similarly, it would be expected that speakers of a young standard language might study a mature standard language or a classical language (assumed to have equivalent levels of standardization); the reverse, however, is far less likely.[16] The exception, in the case of the schools that taught Swiss German dialects to returning Swiss expatriates (Moulton 1963), is easily understandable. The schools were designed to replace the natural language-learning process that would have taken place if these students had spent their childhood in Switzerland. Of course, it is common to teach languages to people who are native speakers of a language at the same level of standardization, like Spanish or Latin to speakers of English.

The *religious* function must be carefully defined. From their practice, it is clear that Ferguson and Stewart do not intend this function to apply in the case of religions in which the ordinary language of the adherents is used. They

Table 3.3 Language functions and attributes required

Function	Sociolinguistic attributes required
Official	1 Sufficient standardization 2 Known by a cadre of educated citizens
Nationalist	1 Symbol of national identity for a significant proportion of the population 2 Widely used for some everyday purposes 3 Widely and fluently spoken within the country 4 No major alternative nationalist languages in the country 5 Acceptable as a symbol of authenticity 6 Link with the glorious past
Group	1 Used by all members in ordinary conversation 2 Unifying and separatist device
Educational (level specified)	1 Understood by learners 2 Sufficient teaching resources 3 Sufficient standardization
Wider communication	1 'Learnable' as a second language
International	(1 On the list of potential international languages)
School subject	1 Standardization equals or exceeds that of the language of the learners
Religious	(1 Classical)

Particularly tentative attributes in parentheses

mean a language especially reserved for religious activities and used for very little else, except perhaps as school subjects or literary and scholarly languages. These languages have special status, often as the original language of the scriptures of the religion, the language historically used in its rites, or both. It is tempting to say that the key attribute for a language of religion is that it must be a classical language, in the sense that it is fully standardized, but no longer has native speakers. This has been true for an impressive number of major religions: Latin in Roman Catholicism, Classical Hebrew in Judaism, Classical Arabic in Islam, and Sanskrit in Hinduism. Although the use of ordinary language is a historical tenet of Protestantism, some conservative Protestant sects have developed a religious use of 'Classical English', in the use of *thee* and *thou* forms and the accompanying verbal concord in public prayers. These forms are taken from the sixteenth-century English of the Authorized Version of the Bible. But there are minor religious movements that have special languages of religion that may not be classical. Whiteley (1973:171), for example, applying Stewart's formula to Kenya, lists a vernacular language, Konkani, as a language of religion. The exact specifications of the attributes of a language fulfilling the religious function must await further research. The proposed language functions and the sociolinguistic attributes required for fulfilling them are given in table 3.3. All the proposed attributes are tentative, but the ones in parentheses are particularly so.

APPLICATION

The way one would use these concepts to make predictions is to compare the attributes of the language with the attributes required by the function. If a language proposed for a particular function lacks a required attribute, we predict that it will fail in that function. The format we will use is illustrated in the examples below. A plus sign indicates that the language has the attribute; a zero indicates the language does not have the attribute, but it is reasonable to expect that it will be acquired, and a minus sign indicates that the language lacks the attribute and will not acquire it in the foreseeable future. As an example, let us look at Guaraní as the potential national language of Paraguay.

Sociopolitical group: Paraguay
Function: Nationalist
Language: Guaraní

Attributes required	*Attributes possessed*
1 Symbol of national identity	+
2 Widely used for everyday purposes	+
3 Widely and fluently spoken	+

4 No major alternative language   +
5 Symbol of authenticity   +
6 Link with glorious past   (+)

Guaraní has all the attributes required, so we would predict that it can satisfactorily serve as a nationalist language, which it does. It is not clear that Guaraní serves as a link with the glorious past, but interestingly, there seems to be a tendency to construct a glorious past for the language. Rona (1966:287) reports that there have been scholarly efforts to demonstrate that Guaraní was of great importance in South America before the Spanish Conquest. These efforts are based on rather fanciful Guaraní etymologies for place names all over the continent. As another example, take Spanish as the language of primary education in rural Paraguay.

Sociopolitical unit: Rural department in Paraguay
Function: Educational (primary level)
Language: Spanish

Attributes required	*Attributes possessed*
1 Understood by learners	–
2 Sufficient teaching resources	+
3 Sufficient standardization	+

Spanish lacks a crucial attribute for primary education; it is not well understood by the learners. Unless it is effectively taught before it is used as a medium of instruction, Spanish will not be effective in the educational function for this group.

A third example will be Hindi as the designated nationalist language in India.

Sociopolitical unit: India (whole country)
Function: Nationalist
Language: Hindi

Attributes required	*Attributes possessed*
1 Symbol of national identity	+/–
2 Widely used for everyday purposes	+/–
3 Widely and fluently spoken	+/–
4 No major alternative language	–
5 Symbol of authenticity	+
6 Link with glorious past	+/–

It is certainly *not* true that there are not major alternative nationalist languages in India, and it certainly *is* true that Hindi is qualified as a symbol of authenticity in the sense that it is 'good enough' (it is a standardized language with a literary tradition). Whether or not it has the other four attributes depends on how much of the country's population is involved in the definition of them. Hindi is a symbol of national identity, is widely known and used for everyday purposes and is a link with the glorious past for its native speakers and perhaps for some second-language speakers in the northern part of the country. It does not have these attributes elsewhere. In any case, the many major competing languages cost Hindi a crucial attribute, which means a prediction that Hindi will not serve very well as a national language for the foreseeable future.

Next, we will examine Swahili as a proposed official language in Tanzania.

Sociopolitical unit: Tanzania
Function: Official
Language: Swahili

Attributes required	*Attributes possessed*
1 Sufficient standardization	0 or +
2 Cadre of educated citizens	+

Swahili is the language of late primary and some secondary education and is known by the vast majority of Tanzanians. Therefore, there is no particular problem finding government workers who can use it. Swahili is being standardized and developed for use as an official language and can reasonably be expected to qualify on the standardization criterion in the near future if it does not already. The prediction is that Swahili will succeed as an official language.

As our last example, we will look at a proposal that is investigated in Volume II, concerning the use of Vernacular Black English in language arts education in the USA.

Sociopolitical group: VBE-speaking American children
Function: Education (primary level)
Language: Vernacular Black English

Attributes required	*Attributes possessed*
1 Understood by learners	+
2 Sufficient teaching resources	0
3 Sufficient standardization	−

Vernacular Black English is certainly understood and used fluently by most working class black youngsters in the United States. Although trained teachers and printed materials for VBE do not now exist to any great extent, they could be developed without too much difficulty. VBE will not be sufficiently standardized in the foreseeable future, however. There would be no problem writing grammar books, spelling rules, dictionaries and so on for Vernacular Black English – in fact there already exists a small amount of material of this kind. But standardization as used in these formulas implies that the codification is overtly *accepted* by the community. That is, whatever formal standardization devices are proposed, they would have to be accepted as legitimate authorities on the correct use of VBE by its speakers. It is this aspect of standardization that has such a poor prognosis. The use of Vernacular Black English in primary education would not succeed.[17]

The notational system developed can be modified for use as a profile for comparative purposes as well. Instead of listing languages and associating functions with them, as Ferguson and Stewart do, the present system would list functions and then the languages that fulfill them. Where possible, the *degree* to which a function is fulfilled will be indicated. As an example, we will give a partial profile formula for Paraguay in Table 3.4. Parentheses indicate attributes that are doubtful or are being developed. The remaining functions would be listed in the same format. In addition, it would probably be useful to append a list of all the languages that appear in the formula, together with the numbers of speakers each has and the percentage of the population that speaks each.

Table 3.4   Partial profile for Paraguay

Function	Language	Attributes	Notes
Official–9	Spanish	1,2	Estimated that Spanish would be 9 on a 10-point officialness scale
Nationalist–9	Guaraní	1,2,3,4,5,(6)	Estimated 9 on a 10-point nationalist scale
Group	Guaraní	1,2	Group: 'Real' Paraguayans
	Spanish	1,2	Group: Monolingual Spanish speakers
	Chulupí	1,2	Group: Chulupí Indians
	(Other indigenous languages)		
	Plattdeutsch	1,2	Group: Mennonites
	(Other immigrant languages)		
Educational (primary)	Spanish	(1),2,3	Attribute 1 absent in rural areas
	Guaraní	1,(2),3	

table continues

Table 3.4 contd.

Function	Language	Attributes	Notes
	Chulupí	1,(2), 3	Mennonite and mission schools
	(Other indigenous languages)		
	German	(1),2,3	Mennonite colony schools
Educational (secondary)	Spanish	1,2,3	Students reaching the secondary level are assumed to have learned Spanish
Educational (higher)	Spanish	1,2,3	

SUMMARY

It seems clear that there are legitimate generalizations to be discovered in the interaction between multilingualism and society. During the 1960s, various typologies and formulas were designed to apply to any nation in the world. Two of these, those proposed by Ferguson (1966) and Stewart (1968), were examined in detail. None of the attempts at formula construction was very successful and the formulaic approach was soon abandoned. A brief review of the history of another 'small universe of discourse', the chemical elements, shows how generalities were progressively discovered and how understanding deepened over time. A new formulaic approach was proposed, conforming to the principles of *naturalism* and *prediction* (which seem to have applied in the study of the elements), and one additional principle, the *continuum* principle. Expanding on the insights of William Stewart, the formulaic system is based on (near-)universal language functions and the sociolinguistic attributes required of a language in order to fulfill them. By comparing the sociolinguistic attributes required by a function with those possessed by a language designated to fulfill it, it is possible to predict how successful that language will be in that function. A few examples of how the new formulaic system can be used were given.

NOTES

1   A minor, but still striking 'coincidence' was pointed out to me by Deborah

Tannen in connection with diglossia. The High language in Greek diglossia, katharévusa, translates as 'puristic'. Half a world away in a small Indian village, the High style of the Khalapur dialect is called saf bolí, 'clean speech'. It is probably a near-universal that High languages are seen as 'clean' or 'pure' compared with Low languages.

2   Ford (1974) is a later attempt to develop a formula, somewhat similar to the Stewart–Ferguson approach.

3   A language qualifies for any of these classifications as long as it meets at least *one* of the requirements. For example, Irish would be considered a *major* language in Ireland, although it is spoken by less than 3 per cent of the population and less than one million people, because it is legally an official language of the country.

4   Ferguson gives a fifth special use, a major language for an age-sector of the population, but this seems to be a rather rare and transient situation.

5   With more recent information than Ferguson had at his disposal, we might wish to designate Guaraní as a standard language (Rona 1966), although it is not clear that Guaraní is standardized *enough* to be a standard language in Ferguson's view. Guaraní[4] by now may also have the educational function (Rubin 1978). Notice that the indigenous languages of the Chaco and the immigrant languages do not appear in the formula, since they do not meet the requirements for any of the three general categories. This coincides with the Paraguayan point of view that treats these languages as irrelevant to Paraguayan nationality (cf. chapter 1).

6   There is a discrepancy between pages 312 and 314 of Ferguson (1966) for this notation. In one place, Moroccan Arabic is designated as I have designated it here; in the other, it is given as Corw:V. I believe that the format I have chosen is what Ferguson intended.

7   There are always exceptions. Stewart would most likely consider the varieties of Swiss German to be 'dialects'. Yet, grammars have been written for some of them (Moulton 1963).

8   Kloss (1968:81) proposes a similar classification system.

9   The discussion of the history of research on the elements is taken from 'Element' (*Encyclopedia Americana*, 10:203–9, 1976), and 'Periodic Law' (*Encyclopedia Americana*, 21:587–91, 1976).

10   Explanation was also a goal in the research on elements, but explanation is only possible when prediction has been achieved.

11   'Nation' in the popular sense, not according to Fishman's definition. In Fishman's terms, we would have to say that the formulas applied to states or countries.

12   Kloss's 'fragmented-unfragmented' distinction (1968:73) touches somewhat on this issue.

13   Kloss's sixth level, the 'archaic standard language', corresponds to Ferguson's and Stewart's 'classical language' and perhaps belongs in a different list.

14   The 1967 revision of the Paraguayan constitution recognizes Spanish as official and both Spanish and Guaraní as national languages, thus coming very close to the distinction I have in mind (Rubin 1978:191).

15   This attribute no doubt helps a language fulfill the nationalist function, but I am not sure it is a *requirement*.

16   The school subject function requires that the language fulfilling that function be *widely* taught at the secondary level or higher. The study of rather exotic languages by university students in language and linguistics departments doesn't count!

17   It is important to remember that Vernacular Black English is not *linguistically* unqualified to serve in education, but lacks a crucial *socio*linguistic attribute.

OBJECTIVES

1   Be able to identify the feature of the sociology of language that inspires the hope that typologies and formulas might be possible (p. 60).
2   Given the relevant descriptions, be able to classify languages as major, minor and special status, using Ferguson's methods. For example, given:

> *Lg. A.*   Spoken natively by 1.5 million people in a country with a population of 10 million people, but not used for education nor is it officially recognized, although it is an important lingua franca.
> *Lg. B.*   Spoken natively by 3 per cent of the population of the country, used as the medium of instruction in upper elementary grades with educational material printed in it, but is not officially recognized, although it is an important religious language.
> *Lg. C.*   Not officially recognized, nor used as a medium of instruction, it has a negligible number of native speakers but is the language used in the rites of a major religion.

you would conclude that Lg. A is a major language, Lg. B is a minor language and Lg. C is a language of special status. Note: If a language meets even *one* of Ferguson's criteria for a category, it belongs in that category. For example, Lg. A is not officially recognized, not used as a medium of education and is spoken by less than 25 per cent of the population. Nevertheless, it is a major language because it has over 1 million speakers.
3   Be able to recognize the definition of five language *types*.
4   Given the lower case letters indicating *function*, be able to name and explain these functions. Be especially sure you can distinguish e from s and i from w.
5   Be able to recognize the meanings of the following special notations in the Ferguson formula (where X stands for any *type* and x for any *function*): X:Xxxx, X, [X].
6   Be able to supply each of Stewart's 'attributes', given the definition.
7   Be able to define and give the symbols for the functions 'literary' and 'provincial', which are used by Stewart but not by Ferguson.
8   Given a formula written with either the Ferguson or the Stewart notation system, be able to interpret its meaning and state which scholar's system it conforms to.
9   Be able to name a smaller 'universe of discourse' than the countries of the world to which steady progress was made in developing a formulaic description (pp. 67-8).
10   Be able to explain how a *naturalistic* treatment of the 'official' or 'educational' functions would differ from the ones used in the early sociolinguistic formulas.
11   Be able to name a second principle that was used in the field mentioned in objective 9 that Fasold thinks should be applied to the development of sociolinguistic formulas, and a third principle that he endorses although it was not a factor in the other field.
12   Be able to recognize William Stewart's two insights that contribute to Fasold's proposed 'new beginning'.
13   Be able to recognize a description of Fasold's way of dealing with Stewart and Ferguson's *types* and *functions* (p. 72).
14   Given a language and its sociolinguistic attributes in a hypothetical country, be able to judge if is probable, possible, or improbable that it will succeed as an *official* language.
15   Similarly, be able to make the same kind of judgement as to whether a hypothetical language will succeed as a *nationalist* language, in the fullest sense.

4

Statistics

INTRODUCTION

Why is it necessary to include a chapter on statistics in this book? Statistics is in part a tool; one that can be used to make sense out of a mass of numbers. In chapter 1, we found out that numerical data were a useful way of studying the relationship between national economic strength and linguistic diversity. But it is not always obvious just what numerical data mean, once they are assembled. There are procedures in statistics that can be used to tell a researcher whether or not the data support the idea she is trying to test. This use of statistics is called *inferential statistics*; we will have more to say about this later. In linguistic research that focuses on language structure alone, inferential statistical tests are generally considered unnecessary, since language structure is regular enough so that qualitative analysis is usually sufficient. But when language use in context is the object of study, as it is in sociolinguistics (especially the sociolinguistics of society), we often need a method for distinguishing the real from the spurious. Statistics gives us that method.

If statistics is necessary, then we had better begin with an explanation of what it is about. In brief, statistics provides the researcher with a way of finding out what his observations mean, using numbers. The analysis of economic well-being and linguistic diversity in chapter 1 showed that many undeveloped countries are also highly diverse linguistically. But what does that observation mean? Is it totally spurious; an association that seems to exist, but is really only the result of random distributions? If the association is a real one, can it be interpreted causally; does either the lack of economic development or linguistic diversity cause the other? If one phenomenon is associated with the other, how confident can we be of the association? Statistical techniques can help deal with problems such as this one; in fact, this very issue is taken up in the next chapter with rather surprising results.

An understanding of the rudiments of statistics is important for the further study of the sociolinguistics of society, but it is beyond the aim of this chapter to make working statisticians of its readers. Understanding the content of the chapter will not make you able to *carry out* statistical analysis, but rather, to *understand* and *interpret* the statistical analyses of others. Anyone who contemplates doing original research in the sociolinguistics of society will have to have a working knowledge of statistics and that will have to come from some other source. Nevertheless, I hope that this brief introduction will give a head start to people who decide to study statistics in more detail.

FOUR BASIC NOTIONS

An understanding of how statistical analysis works depends on an understanding of four fundamental notions: (1) population; (2) characteristic; (3) quantification; and (4) distribution. There is much more to statistics than these four concepts, but all of the rest begins with these.

Population

The first and most basic component of any statistical analysis is the population. A population consists of a group of individuals the researcher is interested in, or, more accurately, a set of numerical values associated with these individuals. A population need not consist of *people*, it may be any well-defined class of objects of whatever kind. For example, the countries of the world, or the states or provinces of a given country can be populations. In the sociolinguistics of language, we might want to examine the population of all final-consonant clusters uttered by a given speaker during an interview. Sometimes populations, in the statistician's sense, do consist of people. For example, a population of interest to a sociolinguist may include all the citizens of some country who speak a particular language.

Very often, a whole population is too large to deal with in its entirety. It would be impossible to interview all the citizens of India, for example, or listen to all the final consonant clusters uttered by an individual in a year. It is necessary, in the usual case, to resort to a *sample*. A sample consists of a small number of members of a population which can be studied in detail. The results can then be projected to the population as a whole. In order for this projection to be accurate, the sample should be a microcosm of the whole population. If a researcher wanted to discover the attitudes of Americans toward the use of 'whom' rather than 'who' as a relative pronoun in the objective case, it would be important that the sample she selected did not differ from the population in any crucial way. If the sample included all college students, for example, or had a larger proportion of immigrants than the US population as a whole does, the results would not be typical of the population. If the sample had an especially large number of underweight people, though, it probably would not matter. Making sure that the sample represents the population in all crucial ways is not easy. Sampling is discussed in some detail in Hatch and Farhady (1982:8–10), in Shavelson (1981:10–12) and in Anshen (1978:37–40). A detailed, technical and innovative discussion with special reference to sociolinguistics is given in Wölck (1976).

Characteristic

There is always some characteristic of the population that the researcher is interested in. In a study of a population of nations, for example, you might be interested in characteristics such as geography, population density, economic development, linguistic diversity, urbanization, or any of a number of others.

Characteristics under analysis are often called variables, and there are two types – *independent variables* and *dependent variables*. The dependent variable is the one the researcher is interested in learning about, and independent variables are other characteristics that are assumed to be related to or to influence the dependent variable. For example, if someone wanted to find out if laboratory mice gained weight faster as the amount of protein they were fed was increased, he might take several mice and feed them different measured amounts of protein. Since weight gain is the characteristic of interest, the weight of the mice is the dependent variable. Weight is hypothesized to be related to the amount of protein eaten, so amount of protein is the independent variable. To take a sociolinguistic example, let us suppose we wish to explore the possibility that government operations become more efficient the more standard the official language is. We would need measurements of standardization and of efficiency (the second is particularly difficult to measure, but it doesn't matter, the hypothesis is a dubious one anyway!). Since we are guessing that efficiency is influenced by standardization, efficiency is the dependent variable and standardization the independent one.

Which variable is which depends entirely on the way the research question is framed. For example, in the problem concerning the relationship between economic well-being and linguistic diversity discussed in chapter 1, you could ask if linguistic uniformity makes it easier for a country to develop economically. If this is how the question is put, then the economic factor is the dependent variable and the linguistic factor is the independent one. On the other hand, you could put the problem the other way around and ask if an economic development leads the citizens of a country to switch from many languages to only a few. In this case, the linguistic factor would be the dependent variable and the economic factor would be the independent variable.

Quantification

Once a population, or a sample of it, and the relevant characteristics are selected, quantification is the next step. The way you go about quantifying data depends on which of two classes of characteristics your research problem is about. The two kinds are *namable* characteristics and *measurable* ones. If we were interested in some aspect of African nations as opposed to nations of other continents, for instance, we would have a namable characteristic – a country is either located on the African continent or it is not. It makes no sense to try to measure how much it is in Africa.[1] On the other hand, a characteristic like national wealth is of a different sort. Although it is possible to divide countries into rich and poor categories, obviously there is a range of degree of national wealth. Every country has or lacks wealth to one degree or another. In this case, the characteristic is measurable and it is up to the researcher to find some way of measuring it.

If the characteristic is only namable, then the only possible method of quantification is to count the members of the population or sample that have the namable characteristic. For example, we could count the number of nations that are located in Africa and those on other continents. The number of male and female members in a human population or sample can only be counted, gender being a namable characteristic. If the characteristics under study are measurable, then the questions we can ask and the answers we can find are far more interesting. In this case, we are not just counting members who do or do not have the characteristic, but we are measuring how much of the characteristic the sample member has.

Measurement requires an instrument and a scale. Physical properties, such as temperature and linear distance, are measured with physical instruments like thermometers and meter sticks. The kinds of characteristics we are interested in here are measured with question-and-answer paper instruments, such as census questions, written tests, and questionnaires. Scales are systems designed to tell us how much of a measurable characteristic a member of the population has. A scale consists of a reference point or points and units. For instance, the measurement of heat has the freezing and boiling points of water as reference points and the degree as the unit. In the next chapter, we will encounter the Greenberg–Lieberson diversity measure which has total diversity and total uniformity as reference points and an 'A' value as a unit. Although we tend to think of the standard physical scales as the only possible way of measuring what they measure, most scales are fundamentally arbitrary. The establishment of the freezing and boiling points of water as reference points on the Celsius temperature scale, and the degree as one one-hundredth of the difference between them, was at first an arbitrary decision. It later became accepted as a standard. It sometimes becomes necessary for a sociolinguist, or any other researcher, to invent a new measuring system – including instrument, scale, and unit – to measure something that has never been satisfactorily measured before. This is perfectly legitimate.

The two kinds of quantification – enumeration (counting) and measurement – give rise to the four types of measuring scales commonly discussed by statisticians (for example, Shavelson 1981:16–18). Of these, one applies to namable characteristics, two to measurable ones, and one scale falls between the two. Namable characteristics are assigned values on a *nominal scale*. These values merely identify which namable characteristic a member of a sample has. If we were using continental location as a namable characteristic for a sample of nations, we could assign a value of 1 to an Asian nation, 2 to an African nation, 3 to a European nation and so on. These numbers have no particular significance; we do not mean that an African nation has more or less of the characteristic than an Asian nation, for instance. We could equally well use 'X, Y, Z' or 'green, blue, and yellow' as symbols for designating continental location. Whenever each individual member of a sample or population could receive another symbol as well as a number for a characteristic, we are dealing with a nominal scale.

Measurable characteristics are assigned values on an *interval* or *ratio scale*. Shavelson's (1981:17) definition of an interval scale is:

Interval measurement is possible when the differing levels of an attribute can be identified, and *equal distances* between the levels of the attribute can also be identified.

The key terms are 'differing levels' and 'equal distances'. A sample member assigned a 2 on an interval scale is at a higher level with respect to the characteristic in question than a member who is assigned a 1. The difference in level between a sample member assigned a 3 and a member assigned a 2 is just the same as the difference between the member with the 2 and a member with a 1. Take a simple example concerning the measurement of heat. Suppose we have four bowls of water: the temperature of bowl A is 10°C, of bowl B is 12°, of bowl C is 20°C, and of bowl D is 22°C. Since the Celsius scale is an interval scale, the difference in temperature between bowl A and bowl B is the same as the difference between that of bowl C and bowl D, namely, 2°C.

The difference between interval and ratio scales is of minimal importance for our purposes (Hatch and Farhady 1980 do not even mention ratio scales). Interval and ratio scales have the same properties, except that ratio scales have an absolute value for zero and interval scales have an arbitrary zero. The Celsius temperature scale has an arbitrary zero value, the freezing point of water. The Kelvin scale is a ratio scale; its zero is the absolute absence of heat.

The fourth kind of scale is the *ordinal scale*. In an ordinal scale, the numbers are assigned to members of a sample in order, but the intervals are not equal. The quickest way to understand an ordinal scale is to imagine a list of the finishers in a marathon race. The first runner to cross the finish line is given a 1, the second a 2, and so on. But the intervals between the runners need not be the same. The winner might finish 30 seconds ahead of the second-place finisher, who finishes only 2 seconds ahead of the third-place finisher. The numbers assigned give rank order, but tell us nothing about the intervals between them. If, on the other hand, the runners are listed with their times, then the times constitute ratio-scale data. The units (hours, minutes, seconds and tenths of seconds) have equal intervals for all runners, and the zero is absolute (no time at all).

If research results are to make sense, experimenters must keep clearly in mind which kind of scale matches the numerical data they have, and to choose statistical procedures accordingly. If a researcher assumes the characteristic he is investigating has been measured on an interval scale when it has only been measured on an ordinal scale, his statistical procedures may be perfectly valid in a purely mathematical sense, but be pure nonsense when interpreted in the real world (cf. Shavelson 1981:18).

Accuracy of measurement is evaluated in terms of *reliability* and *validity*. A measure is reliable, if it gives the same results every time; if it is consistent. A measure is valid, if it measures exactly what it is designed to measure. Validity is the stricter of the two criteria. A measure cannot possibly be valid, if it is not reliable. If it gives different results on successive applications, it is obviously not measuring accurately what it is supposed to be measuring. On the other hand, a measure can be entirely reliable, but not valid. Imagine someone who believes that an accurate measurement of intelligence is to be gained by measuring people's foreheads. A high score (a large forehead) is taken to indicate a very smart person, and a low score (small forehead) a stupid one. If the measuring device is good and the procedures careful enough, the measure would be reliable. Every time a person's forehead is measured, she would get the same score. But the measure would not be a valid measure of *intelligence,* merely of forehead size.

Distribution

When the characteristics of a population, or its sample, have been appropriately measured, we are interested in aspects of the distribution of the scores. By distribution, we simply mean how many members of the population or sample got each of the scores up and down the scale. Ordinarily, we expect a population to have a symmetrical distribution of scores measuring most characteristics. Most members of the population would have scores near the middle of the range, with few members getting scores at the very high or very low ends of the scale. Oversimplifying somewhat, a distribution of this type is called a *normal curve*. A distribution is *skewed*, if more members of a population get scores toward the high end of the range than the low end, or the opposite.

Descriptive statistics give us an idea of the distributional nature of a particular set of data. The two most important descriptive statistics are the *mean* and the *standard deviation.*[2] The mean is simply the average score, calculated by adding the scores for each member of the sample and dividing by the total members in that sample. The standard deviation is an indication of how scores are distributed about the mean. A small standard deviation means that the scores are fairly well bunched up close to the mean. A large one means that the scores are widely scattered up and down the range or there are a few scores very far from the mean. If displayed in curve form, a set of scores with a small standard deviation would have a sharp peak in the middle. The curve associated with a large standard deviation would be fairly flat or very irregular.[3]

If we have a sample and not the whole population, we probably will want to know how the descriptive statistics of our sample compare with those of the whole population. If the sample really were an exact microcosm of the whole population, its mean and standard deviation will be exactly the same as those of the population. But if the members of a sample are drawn at random from the population, it is virtually certain that the sample is a little different in its score distribution than the whole population would be. Statisticians, however, have developed ways of estimating what the population and standard deviation are, once we know these statistics for the sample. This is usually expressed as a range and a probability. Statements such as this are made: 'There is a 95 per cent chance that the population mean is between 51 and 59.'[4]

STATISTICAL PROCEDURES

The descriptive statistics of a sample, or even the estimated descriptive statistics of a whole population, are important but are not the most interesting uses for statistics. The most interesting aspect is *hypothesis-testing.* Hypothesis-testing involves procedures for taking quantifications and using them to determine whether or not a certain hypothesis is right. Before I explain how it works, we need to understand what hypotheses in statistics are like.

Hypotheses

Hypotheses, as they are thought of in statistics, come in pairs. For every problem there is a *research hypothesis* and a *null hypothesis.* The null hypothesis, to put it simply, always states that 'there is nothing special going on here'. In other words, there is nothing to explain. The research hypothesis is some statement to the effect that there is an extraordinary relationship among quantified characteristics of a population and it *does* have to be explained. A particular null hypothesis is always the negation of the research hypothesis it is paired with. For example, if we were to entertain the hypothesis that the taller a child between the ages of 5 and 15 is, the heavier she is, the null hypothesis would be that there is no special tendency for children in this age-range to have a greater weight when their height is greater. In statistical procedures, we never set out to *prove* the research hypothesis directly, but to establish it indirectly by *rejecting the null hypothesis*. If we find that we can reject the null hypothesis that I have just stated, then the only logical alternative is to accept the research hypothesis. Specifically, if it is not reasonable to believe that there is *no* tendency for the weight of children in the designated age-range to be greater when height is greater, then the only alternative is to believe that there *is* such a relationship.[5]

A null hypothesis is usually not stated, but is implicitly present every time statistical hypothesis-testing takes place. When reading statistical results in research reports, it is useful to be prepared to work out precisely what the null hypothesis is. For instance, in our height and weight example, suppose we could not reject the null hypothesis. That does not necessarily mean that there is *no* relationship between height and weight, just that the relationship is not such that taller children are heavier. It is logically possible that shorter children are heavier; a possibility that has not been checked by testing the research hypothesis as I stated it.

Hypotheses need to be stated with precision, related to a particular set of quantified data. For example, 'Students who have good teachers learn more' is a miserably poor hypothesis, as far as statistics is concerned. We have no definition of what is meant by 'good teachers' nor have we been given a measurement of amount of learning. An adequate hypothesis would be something like: 'Students who have been taught by teachers rated "excellent" or "good" by their colleagues will score significantly higher on a standardized final examination than will students taught by teachers rated "fair" or "poor" by their colleagues.' Furthermore, a hypothesis needs to be consistent with the type of data available. Suppose we have, for a given high school, a list of all the male students and ratings by their guidance counselor as to whether they are 'aggressive' or not. Suppose we also have lists for all the sports teams at the school. Further, suppose we have the idea that aggressive boys are more likely to be good athletes than those who are not. With the data I have described, we *cannot* test the hypothesis: 'The more aggressive a boy at this high school is, the better athlete he is.' This hypothesis requires that we treat aggressiveness and athletic ability as *measurable* characteristics, and that we have measurements for them on an interval or ratio scale; but the data we have treat the two variables as *namable* only. That is, we have judgements of aggressive versus not aggressive, and being listed on a team list versus not being listed. These are nominal-scale data. A hypothesis we *can* test is: 'Boys at this high school who are judged to be aggressive by their counselors are significantly more likely to be included in sports teams than boys who are judged to be not aggressive.'

How it works

There is a standard format followed in statistics in attempting to reject null hypotheses. Each of the procedures used in hypothesis-testing that will be discussed (except one – correlation) results in a numerical value which can be compared with the known theoretical distribution of such values. For example, a statistical test called the '*t*-test' gives a *t*-value that can be compared to the theoretical distribution of values of *t*. If the value you get is sufficiently close to the mean t-values, it could have been obtained simply by chance. If the value you get is sufficiently far from the mean, it means that it probably didn't arise by chance, that something caused it. How far is 'sufficiently far'? This is a matter to be decided, within limits, by the researcher. If the value found is in a range where we might expect to find 80 per cent of the theoretical distribution of *t*-values, we would be quite comfortable with the null hypothesis that there is nothing to explain. But suppose the *t*-value we find is in a range where only 10 per cent of the theoretical distribution of *t*-values are located. Most statisticians would *still not* reject the null hypothesis; 1 chance in 10 is too great a likelihood. In practice, your value would have to be in the 5 per cent range at least before you would reject the null hypothesis. This is usually expressed as 'the results were significant at $p < 0.05$', meaning that the probability is less than 5 in 100 hundred that your value could have been obtained by random forces only. Often statisticians are not satisfied unless their results are significant at $p < 0.01$ (less than 1 chance in 100 that the null hypothesis is valid) or $p < 0.01$ (less than 1 chance in 1,000).

As an example, imagine that you and I are next-door neighbors and have vegetable gardens next to each other. Suppose we both follow the same gardening practices, except that you use a special fertilizer which you have developed yourself and I use only composted cow manure. At the end of the summer, we each pick 100 tomatoes at random and calculate the average weight of them.[6] The research hypothesis is that tomatoes treated with your fertilizer will be significantly heavier, on the average, than the ones that got only cow manure. The null hypothesis is that there is no difference in the average weights in favor of your tomatoes that is not due to random variation. Of course, the research hypothesis would be disproved if my tomatoes are actually heavier than yours, but even if yours are heavier, we cannot reject the null hypothesis if we can attribute the difference to random factors. You, of course, hope that there will be something to explain, because you have a ready explanation concerning the superiority of your fertilizer, so you would like to be able to reject the null hypothesis. Suppose that the average weight difference is 20 gm in favor of your tomatoes. Suppose that this difference, using the relevant statistical test, is significant at $p < 0.01$, the significance level we had chosen. That would mean that we had only 1 chance in 100 of getting a 20-gm weight difference with only normal variation in the growth of the tomatoes. It is almost a certainty that something was causing the weight difference. Since fertilizer treatment is the only difference in the way the two gardens were managed, it is reasonable to believe that this is the cause.

It is important to notice two things about this conclusion. First, we have not ruled out the null hypothesis *absolutely*. Suppose I got my 100 tomatoes for weighing by picking every third one I came to, and you used the same procedure. Now it is possible that every third tomato in my garden happened to be among the smallest ones I have and every third one in yours happened to be one of your biggest. If we had selected every second tomato in each garden, perhaps there would have been no weight difference. This is a possibility, of course, but extremely unlikely. Statistics is a way of estimating just *how* unlikely. In the second place, we have only proved that it is very likely that something is causing the tomatoes in your garden to grow larger than the ones in mine. The statistical test does not show that that something is your fertilizer. We had hoped to set up the experiment so that fertilizer treatment was the only difference, so that if your tomatoes are significantly heavier, fertilizer is the only possible cause. To the extent that we succeeded, we have proved the superiority of your fertilizer. To the extent that there are *uncontrolled variables*, to that extent the cause of the result is in doubt.

Suppose we hadn't thought of making sure that we each planted the same strain of tomatoes and had, in fact, planted different varieties. It still *might* be the case that the fertilizer is causing the difference, but we now have an uncontrolled variable that might also be the cause. Its presence casts doubt, not on the fact that there is a significant difference in tomato weights, but on the inference that the difference is due to fertilization. In sociolinguistic research, as in most social science research, it is very difficult to control all the variables.

TYPES OF STATISTICAL TESTS

Statistical tests can be divided into two general categories: parametric and non-parametric. This distinction has some relationship to the distinction we made in quantification scales (nominal and ordinal versus interval and ratio). The most common parametric statistical procedures are used only when our quantifications involve interval or ratio scales. The non-parametric procedures you are likely to come across are designed for use when quantifications are made on nominal or ordinal scales. It is of fundamental importance not to use the wrong type of procedure with the wrong type of data, because fundamentally different assumptions underlie the two kinds of procedures. The likely result of using the wrong kind of procedure is that null hypotheses that ought to be rejected will be accepted, or some that should be accepted will erroneously be rejected.

In the sections that follow, I will briefly describe four of the most commonly used statistical procedures, the chi square test, the *t*-test, analysis of variance, and correlation. There are, of course, a great many other statistical procedures used in research. Virtually all of them depend on the basic procedure of comparing some value or other with the known theoretical distribution for values of that type and estimating the probability that the value obtained is due only to random factors. Therefore, if you read that the results of some statistical procedure are 'significant at $p<0.01$', you will understand something about the credibility of the author's hypothesis, even if you don't really know how the procedure works.

Chi square

Description. The chi square test (pronounced 'kye square' and symbolized by χ^2) is a non-parametric statistical procedure most often used to test the independence or interdependence of the distribution of two namable characteristics within a population. It is always easier to explain how a statistical procedure works by working through an example than to explain it in the abstract.

In chapter 1, a study by Joshua Fishman (1968a) was referred to in which linguistic diversity was compared to various measures of national development. In one of those comparisons, Fishman compared an economic measure, gross national product (GNP), with linguistic diversity. These are two characteristics that can be treated as measurable, but they are treated as namable characteristics in Fishman's study. Each of 114 nations is judged as having 'very high or medium' per capita GNP or else 'low or very low' per capita GNP. The same 114 nations were also named either 'homogeneous' or 'heterogeneous' as designations of linguistic diversity.[7] When this had been done, it was possible to place all 114 nations in four categories, based on the two values of each of the two characteristics. Each one of the countries could be unambiguously assigned to one of the four categories. The results are displayed in table 4.1.

The research hypothesis to be tested is that the assignment of nations to the homogeneity–heterogeneity categories is not independent of their assignment to two levels of per-capita GNP. It is hard to tell just from looking at table 4.1 whether the hypothesis can be accepted or not. A large majority of the linguistically heterogeneous polities have low or very low per-capita GNP, but the homogeneous polities are about evenly distributed on the GNP scale. We need a way of telling if the 114 countries might have landed in the four categories just by chance, or if it is so unlikely to have occurred by chance that we can conclude that there is a genuine relationship between the two characteristics. The way to go about this is to compute what the distribution would be, if there were no relationship between the two characteristics, and then to discover if the distribution in table 4.1 is sufficiently different from that distribution. This 'hypothetical' or 'theoretical' distribution is given in table

Table 4.1   *Arrangement of polities by linguistic homogeneity–heterogeneity and per-capita gross national product*

Gross national product	Linguistic factor	
	Homogeneous	Heterogeneous
Very high/medium	27	15
Low/very low	25	47

Source: Fishman 1968a:62

4.2.[8] A chi square value measures the difference between the actual distribution of the data and the hypothetical distribution.[9] The chi square value in our example is 8.19. When we check this on a table showing the expected distribution of chi square values, we find that it is significant at $p < 0.005$.[10] If this is a level of significance that is acceptable (which it usually is in social science research), then we can reject the null hypothesis and accept the research hypothesis.

Table 4.2   *Hypothetical distribution of the data in table 4.1*

Gross national product	Linguistic factor	
	Homogeneous	Heterogeneous
Very high/medium	19.2	22.8
Low/very low	32.8	39.2

As is usual with statistical tests, we should be careful to note what the results do and do not tell us. We now know that the distribution of nations among the values of the two characteristics in table 4.1 is very probably *interdependent* rather than independent. We do *not* know, just from the fact that we obtained a significant chi square value, whether homogeneous countries are likely to a have very high or medium GNP, or whether heterogeneous countries are likely to have a low or very low GNP, or both. We are even farther from having proved that homogeneity promotes economic development, that economic development promotes homogeneity or even that there is a causal relationship at all.

The chi square test is not limited to hypotheses involving two characteristics with two distinctions each. In Fasold (1980), I reported on a series of experiments concerning two pronunciations of the word 'nine' by speakers of various social classes, ages, and racial ethnicities.[11] Each speaker was recorded as having used one of two pronunciations, either [na^{I}n] or [na:n]. When the two pronunciations are tallied by social class (middle or working) and race (white or black), the result is the distribution shown in table 4.3. The research hypothesis was that the pronunciations would be disproportionately disturbed

Table 4.3   *Numbers of speakers using two pronunciations of 'nine' in Washington, DC, in 1977, by class and race*

Pronunciation	Race and class			
	White middle	*Black middle*	*White working*	*Black working*
[naɪn]	150	23	37	12
	82.9%	62.2%	52.1%	15.0%
[naːn]	31	14	34	68
	17.1%	37.8%	47.9%	85.0%

among speakers of the two classes and two races. The chi square value calculated for table 4.3 was significant at $p < 0.001$. The null hypothesis was rejected. It is important to realize that all the chi square test lets us state with certainty is that it is very likely that the distribution of speakers using one pronunciation rather than the other is not random among classes and races. We have not proved anything about what is significant about the distribution. Of course, looking at the table makes it reasonably clear what the distribution is; the [naɪn] pronunciation tends to be associated with middle-class speakers and with speakers of white racial ethnicity, and that class is more important than race. This more interesting inference, though, is not *directly* demonstrated by the chi square test. I point this out because the distinction between the research hypothesis established by a statistical procedure and what the researcher makes of it can easily be missed. It is a very crucial distinction; typically only part of an author's conclusions is supported directly by the statistical procedure employed. The rest is inference, based more or less on common-sense reasoning, and is open to challenge on common-sense grounds.

When to use the chi square test.   Data requirements.   To use the chi square test to determine independence versus interdependence, you must first have data on a single population or sample. For each member of the population or sample, you must have information on at least two *namable* characteristics. These characteristics each have two values defined in such a way that if a member of the population or sample has one value, it cannot have the other. For the data in table 4.1, we had a sample of nations and for each nation we knew: (1) the value of the homogeneity/heterogeneity characteristic – either it was homogeneous or not (if not, it was heterogeneous); and (2) the value of the gross national product characteristic – either it was very high/medium or not (if not, it was low/very low). The chi square test is used when *all* the characteristics are namable; no measurable characteristics are involved at all.

Hypothesis.   Your hypothesis concerns whether or not the two (or more) characteristics work together. You want to know whether members of the population or sample that have (or do not have) are particular value of one of the characteristics tend also to have (or not have) a particular value of another. For the data in table 4.1, we wanted to know if there was a tendency for nations that were homogeneous also to have a very high or medium GNP.[12]

The t-*test*

Description. The *t*-test is a parametric statistical test that tests whether the means of sets of scores from two samples are significantly different from each other. If they are not sufficiently different, we cannot reject the null hypothesis that the two means could have come from two samples of the same population. If they are different enough, we are justified in concluding that the means are of samples from different populations. Before we work through a sociolinguistics example, let me illustrate what I mean with a slightly silly preliminary example.

Suppose we had the measurements of the neck lengths of 50 giraffes and of 50 camels. Presumably, the mean neck length of the sample of giraffes would be so much larger than the mean of the neck length of the camels that we could accept the research hypothesis that the giraffes and camels were drawn from two different populations with respect to neck length. On the other hand, if we had measured the necks of two samples of 50 giraffes, the mean length of the two groups would most likely be so close that we would have to conclude that they might have been drawn from the same population. In short, we set out to see whether or not two samples are drawn from two separate populations with respect to some measurable characteristic by testing the significance of the difference between the two means. The data required are scores for the same measurable characteristic (the dependent variable) for two different samples. The characteristic defining the two groups is a namable characteristic (the independent, or grouping, variable).

As an example with sociolinguistics data, we will use some of the data given by Milroy (1980:204–5) on the pronunciation of certain vowels in the speech of working class people in Belfast. Among the data given in Milroy's appendix are data on the pronunciation of the vowel in words like 'hut' and 'mud'. The vowels in this word class can be pronounced either [ʌ] or [ɔ̈], the latter the more local pronunciation.[13] According to her system of quantification, the numerical value for these vowels for a given speaker is the percentage of words that were pronounced with the second of the two variants. If 10 words with the vowel of 'hut' or 'mud' were transcribed for a certain speaker and 8 of them had [ɔ̈], then that speaker would receive a value of 80.0.

For many phonological variables in Belfast, men and women speakers have different patterns of frequency, with men using the local vernacular forms more frequently than women do. This is also true of the vowels of the 'hut' class; the mean frequency of use for the local vowel pronunciation by male speakers is 52.0. The mean for female speakers is 34.7. These means are substantially different, but the *t*-test allows us to test the specific research hypothesis: 'The mean use of the [ɔ̃] variant by men and by women in Belfast is sufficiently different so that it is likely that men and women represent different populations with respect to the pronunciation of this vowel.' The *t*-value is 3.06, which is significant at $p<0.01$.[14] The null hypothesis is rejected, and we can accept the conclusion that men and women differ significantly in their treatment of this vowel. As it turns out, there are several socially significant variables for which this is true (Milroy 1980:123–31).[15]

When to use the t-*test.* Data requirements. For the *t*-test, two samples are needed. Often the samples are subsets of a larger sample. The subset is defined by some *namable* characteristic. For each member of each subset, you have measurements for the same characteristic. This characteristic must be measureable and the scale type must be interval or ratio. In the example from Milroy's work, we had two subsets of the Belfast sample defined by the namable characteristic, gender. For each member of the male and female subset, we had a measurement of the same characteristic, vowel pronunciation. The measurement was in percentage form, a ratio scale. The namable characteristic that defines the subsets is the independent variable; the measurable characteristic is the dependent one.

Hypothesis. The *t*-test hypothesis is always concerned with whether or not the two samples are drawn from the same population, with respect to the characteristic for which there are measurements. In less technical terms, you want to find out if the two subsets are significantly different with respect to the measured characteristic. In the example case, we wanted to know if Belfast men and Belfast women are so different in their use of vernacular vowel pronunciations that they have to be considered statistically as two different populations. A bit less technically, we wanted to know if Belfast men and Belfast women were significantly different in their use of vernacular vowel pronunciations.[16]

Analysis of variance

Analysis of variance (often abbreviated ANOVA) is a parametric statistical procedure that can be applied in a number of ways in different research designs. We will describe it in terms of its two fundamental variations: the *one-way design* and *factorial designs* (often *two-way* designs). With the one-way design, the goal is similar to the goal of the *t*-test, that is, to test whether samples drawn from different groups represent different populations with respect to a measurable characteristic. There is at least one difference. Whereas the *t*-test is designed to to be used with only two samples at a time, one-way analysis of variance can be applied to any number of samples, provided they represent different *levels* of the same general characteristic. To return to our silly example about the neck length of hoofed mammals, suppose we wanted to add zebras' neck lengths to the data we already have on camels and giraffes. If we were restricted to the *t*-test, we could only test the three samples in pairs – giraffes vs. camels, giraffes vs. zebras, camels vs. zebras. In analysis of variance, we can regard the three kinds of animals as levels of the same general characteristic, hoofed-mammal species, and test the neck-length hypothesis with a single test.

As it turns out, it would not only be easier to use ANOVA with this kind of hypothesis than to use the *t*-test, but the *t*-test, for technical reasons, would be likely to give very misleading results if used repeatedly in the way I just described.

In analysis of variance, we test the difference between means by asking if there is more variation *between* the group scores than there is *within* the group scores. In other words, we want to know if there is a lot more variation around the grand mean than there is around the group means. For our example, that means we want to know if there is more variation comparing giraffes as a group with camels as a group with zebras as a group than there is comparing one giraffe (camel, zebra) to another. In the example, we would certainly expect that there would generally be a wider difference between giraffe necks as a group and zebra necks as a group than there would be between two individual giraffes or two individual zebras. On the other hand, suppose we had taken three samples of 50 giraffes each. There would be no reason to expect that the variation from one group of giraffes to the next would be any larger or smaller than the variation from one individual giraffe to the next. Briefly, if scores come from different populations, we expect the variation *between* groups to be many times greater than the variation *within* each group. In analysis of variance, this ratio is computed and called an *F*-ratio. An *F*-ratio of 5.50, then, would mean that the variance between the groups in the experiment is 5.5 times greater than the variance within the groups. To find out if 5.50 is a big enough value to allow the null hypothesis to be rejected, a table of *F*-ratios needs to be consulted, from which we would get the significance level associated with that particular *F*-score.[17]

An example of the application of one-way analysis of variance to a problem in sociolinguistics brings us back to Milroy's work on phonological variation in Belfast. In our discussion of the *t*-test, we tested the hypothesis that men and women in Belfast are different populations with respect to variation in the use of the vowel in 'hut'. In her own discussion of her work, Milroy used analysis of variance as her vehicle for testing the same hypothesis (Milroy 1980:122–3). Vowel usage, the percentage of the local variant used, was the dependent variable, measured on a ratio scale (percentages). The independent characteristic was sex, with the obvious two 'levels'. The *F*-ratio Milroy calculated was 6.38. Variance between men and women speakers was well over 6 times the variance within each gender group. This ratio is significant at $p < 0.05$. As a result, Milroy was able to reject the null hypothesis.

You may have noticed that the significance level for analysis of variance was lower than it was for the similar hypothesis tested by the t-test. By a t-test, the significance level was $p<0.01$; by analysis of variance, it is only $p<0.05$. If $p<0.01$ were selected as the minimum level of significance for rejecting the null hypothesis (the hypothesis that men and women do not constitute different populations with regard to this vowel variable), and you decided to use the t-test, you would be able to reject the null hypothesis. On the other hand, if you had used analysis of variance, the resulting F-ratio would *not* have been large enough to allow you to reject the same null hypothesis. Analysis of variance is more *powerful*, where the term *power* is a technical term referring to the probability of rejecting a null hypothesis that is actually false (Shavelson 1981:355). If men and women in Belfast are actually *not* separate populations with respect to variation in the vowel of words like 'hut', it is easier to come to that conclusion with analysis of variance than with a t-test.[18]

With factorial analysis of variance, more than one namable characteristic is used to define groups. Some of Milroy's analyses involve groupings not only by sex, but by age as well (Milroy 1980:121–30). In her work, age was treated as a namable characteristic, with two age-groups – 19–25 years and 40–55 years - being distinguished. This allowed her population to be divided into four groups for purposes of factorial analysis of variance. The four groups are: young women, older women, young men, and older men. Factorial analysis of variance allows the variance between each of these groups to be compared with the variance within them. The end result is an F-ratio as in the one-way design. The F-ratios make it possible to test the hypotheses that the age groups are different populations with regard to vowel pronunciation scores independently of sex, and that the sex groups are different populations independently of age. These hypotheses – that is, those involving the namable characteristics that define the groupings – are called *main effects*. But factorial analysis of variance allows the testing of *interaction effects*. If an interaction effect is significant, it means the dependent variable is affected by a combination of two or more independent variables *quite apart from the effect of each independent variable itself*. In fact, for one of Milroy's vowel variables, neither age nor sex main effects were significant, but the interaction between them was. What this tells us is that neither age nor sex, by themselves, has a significant effect on the pronunciation of this particular vowel. But the combination of the two factors, working together, *is* significant. As it turns out, what is happening in this case is that there is nothing extraordinary about the use of the vowel by the young men, the young women or the older men. The older group of women, however, show a different pattern from the men of the same age and also from the younger women. Hence the significant interaction (Milroy 1980:125–9).

When to use analysis of variance.   Data requirements.   For one-way analysis of variance, the data requirements are the same as the ones I have described

for the *t*-test. For factorial analysis of variance, a large sample is subdivided by
two or more namable characteristics at the same time. In our example from
Milroy's work, the Belfast sample was subdivided by the namable characteristics of age (old or young) and gender (male or female) in such a way that each
male speaker could be either young or old and so could each female speaker.
For each member of the entire sample, you have a measurement of the
particular characteristic you are interested in on a ratio or interval scale. In the
example, the characteristic was vowel pronunciation, measured as a percentage. As in the *t*-test, the namable characteristics that subdivide the sample are
independent (grouping) variables and the measurable characteristic is the
dependent one.

Hypothesis. For one-way analysis of variance, the hypothesis will be
similar to the *t*-test hypothesis, except that more than two groups can be tested
at once. For factorial analysis of variance, we want to find out if at least one of
the subgroups of the whole sample that possesses a namable, defining characteristic is so different from the other subgroup(s) with respect to the
measurable characteristic that it has to be considered statistically as a different
population. In our example, we wanted to know if females and non-females
(males, of course!) were different populations with respect to percentage of
vernacular vowel pronunciations in their speech. We also wanted to know if
old and non-old (young) speakers were different populations. Less technically, we were interested in finding out whether vowel pronunciation was
significantly different according to age and gender. This part of factorial
analysis of variance deals with the main effects. We can also find out if at least
one of the smaller subsets defined by *more than one* of the namable
characteristics is significantly different from the others. In our example, we
found that the subset that was both older and female was significantly
different, in their treatment of the vowel variable under investigation, from all
other subsets defined by age and gender. When more than one of the defining
characteristics is used at the same time, we are dealing with an interaction
effect.[19]

Correlation

The final statistical procedure to be introduced is correlation. Correlation is a
procedure for determining the extent to which two or more characteristics
vary together in a given population. Returning briefly to an example I used
earlier, imagine we had height and weight measurements for a group of 100
children between the ages of 5 and 15. We would expect that the taller children
would weigh more and the shorter youngsters would weigh less. If we were to
list all the children in order by height, they would automatically be very nearly
also in order by weight. This would be an example of *positive* correlation; a
youngster with greater height would also probably have greater weight, and
vice versa. If we were to take the same children and compare two different

characteristics, this time age and the amount of time it takes a child to run 50 meters, we would expect a *negative* correlation. By and large, older children should be able to run 50 meters in *less* time than younger children. In neither case would the correlation necessarily be perfect. There would probably be some shorter youngsters who happen to weigh more than a taller child, and also a few older children who took more time to run 50 meters than some younger children. Correlation gives a measure of how much one characteristic varies with another. If the two vary together perfectly in a *positive* direction, then we would obtain a *coefficient of correlation* of +1.00. If they varied in the exact opposite direction from each other, the correlation coefficient would be −1.00. If they were not related to each other at all, the coefficient of correlation would be 0.00. Thus, coefficients of correlation vary in value between −1.00 and +1.00. A coefficient of correlation of 0.83, for example, would represent a very strong positive correlation. A value of −0.53 would be a moderate negative correlation.

The correlation procedure I have been describing is called the *Pearson product-moment correlation* and the coefficient of correlation it gives is sometimes called a *Pearsonian r* or just *r*. The Pearson procedure is a parametric statistical method and therefore requires that both characteristics being correlated be measurable ones. There is also a non-parametric correlation procedure that we will describe shortly.

We can use the data in table 4.4 to illustrate the usefulness of the correlation. The data come from an intelligibility study of the 'contact vernacular' of Norfolk Island, an Australian possession in the South Pacific (Flint 1979). Flint tested the intelligibility of 17 dialogues in this variety, apparently an English-based creole, by having a native speaker of Australian English listen to the dialogues and report, sentence by sentence, what he thought the meaning was. This person was a linguist who was familiar with creole languages, but not this particular creole. These ratings were then compared to other characteristics of the dialogue, including the percentage of English cognate words with a meaning close to their standard English meaning. The dialogues are listed in table 4.4 by intelligibility ratings. An examination of the 'percentage of English words' column shows that the dialogues are not listed in order by this ranking. Nevertheless, on closer inspection, we find that there is some relationship. The mean intelligibility rating is 59.46 and the first eight dialogues are, naturally, above this mean. The mean percentage of English words is 91.05. The percentage of English words is above the mean in 7 of the first 8 dialogues. So there is some tendency for the more highly intelligible dialogues to have a relatively high percentage of English words. But how strong is this relationship? The coefficient of correlation is designed to give this answer. The value of *r* for the data in table 4.4 is +0.544.

Unlike the other statistical procedures that we have looked at, the magnitude of an *r* value must be interpreted by a rule of thumb. A typical interpretation system is the following (from Guilford 1956:145, quoted in Williams 1968:134):[20]

0.01–0.20   slight; almost negligible relationship;
0.20–0.40   low correlation; definite but small relationship;
0.40–0.70   moderate correlation; substantial relationship;
0.70–0.90   high correlation; marked relationship;
0.90–0.99   very high correlation; very dependable relationship.

*Table 4.4   Percentage intelligibility and percentage of
English words in 17 Norfolk Island dialogues*

Dialogue number	Percentage intelligibility	Percentage of English words
9	79.7	93.9
11	79.1	95.5
17	75.6	94.3
12	74.9	97.8
16	68.9	87.3
13	65.6	93.5
15	62.5	92.0
7	60.2	95.3
9	59.1	87.7
10	58.8	93.6
5	56.0	85.9
4	55.5	91.0
3	53.4	84.6
8	50.4	90.5
6	43.6	85.6
2	34.1	90.6
1	32.5	89.5

Source: data from Flint (1979:320-1)

Accordingly, the relationship between intelligibility and the percentage of English words in the Norfolk Island dialogues is a substantial one, showing moderate correlation. However, this interpretation is useless, if the coefficient of correlation is due to a sampling error only. If there is a high enough probability that we could have obtained a *sample* correlation coefficient of 0.544, even if the *population* value were zero, then we have to ignore the sample correlation. To test this, we use a special application of the *t*-test to test whether our *r* value is significantly different from zero. The research hypothesis, of course, is that our value *is* significantly different from (in this case, greater than) zero; the null hypothesis is that it is equal to zero, meaning that there is no real correlation. The *t*-test calculation gives a value which is significant at $p < 0.05$, an acceptable level.

When we have established the *significance* of the coefficient of correlation, the *interpretation* can be accepted as well. The coefficient of correlation has another handy use in addition to giving an indication of the strength of a relationship. Squaring r gives another statistic, r^2. The value of r^2 is a measure of the amount of variance that the measures of the two characteristics have in common. It is often multiplied by 100 and reported as the *percentage* of the variation of one measure that is 'explained' or 'accounted for' by the other (Shavelson 1981:203). In the case of the Norfolk Island dialogues, we can say on this basis that 29.6 per cent of the variance in intelligibility is explained by the variance in the percentage of English words.

As usual, care should be used in arriving at secondary conclusions. All that we have established by our statistical procedure is: (1) that there is a substantial positive relationship between intelligibility and the percentage of English words; (2) that the coefficient of correlation we calculated is probably not due to a sampling error; and (3) that 29.5 per cent of the variance in the two measures is in common. We haven't shown anything about the *reason* for the relationship. In this particular case, it makes sense to say that a dialogue is understandable to an English speaker partially owing to the degree to which it has English words. It does *not* make sense to say the proportion of English words it has is partially due to the degree to which it is understandable! A third possible cause for the relationship, that there is some third force that produces both understandability and the proportion of English words is conceivable as the explanation, but it seems justified to interpret our results in the first way suggested. In other words, it seems reasonable to say that 30 per cent of the intelligibility of a Norfolk Island dialogue to a standard English speaker is due to familiarity of vocabulary. But the same would not be true of our hypothetical example of the heights and weights of children. If a high correlation were found (it no doubt *would* be), we could not infer that growing taller makes children heavier or that getting heavier makes them taller. The two characteristics go together because of the influence of a third factor, physical maturation.

Another correlation procedure is used when at least one scale of measurement is only ordinal. Imagine that we have the order of finish in both the Boston Marathon and the New York City Marathon for 25 runners who ran in both races, but we do not have their times. Recall that this means that we know that the third-place finisher finished ahead of the fourth-place finisher and that the fifth-place runner finished ahead of the sixth-place runner. But the third place finisher may have crossed the finish line two or three minutes ahead of his nearest rival, whereas the fifth-place runner may have only barely beaten the sixth-place finisher. We have to treat the order-of-finish data as ordinal rather than interval or ratio. The correlation we would compute for order of finish in the two races would be the *Spearman rank order correlation*. This non-parametric correlation procedure gives a value called *Spearman's rho* (written ρ), which is interpreted just like a Pearsonian r. However, its computations are limited to the arithmetic operations that are possible with ordinal data.

For an example, we will return to Milroy's Belfast research. In addition to ratio and interval measures of phonological variables, and nominal data on sex and age, she used a *network-strength score,* which can best be interpreted as an ordinal measure. The network-strength score was designed to give a quantified measure of how tightly an individual's social relationships were bound within the community. It can be expected that a person who has a high network-strength score will be strongly governed by community norms, including linguistic ones. This led to the hypothesis that there would be a positive correlation between the phonological indexes and network-strength scores, where the phonological indexes were so constructed that high values meant more frequent use of local vernacular variants. The network score was based on five conditions, such as 'Having substantial ties of kinship in the neighborhood' and 'Working at the same place as at least *two* others from the same area'. The five conditions allow a six-point scale, allowing for 0 for anyone who did not meet any of the conditions (Milroy 1980:139–44). Since there is no particular reason to believe that each of the five conditions is of equal value as an indicator of network strength, the resulting scale is only ordinal. It is reasonable to believe that a person with a 4 on the scale is more closely bound to community values than one with a 3, but there is no reason to believe that the interval between a 4 and a 3, for example, is exactly the same as the interval between a 2 and a 1.

Table 4.5 is the correlation data between network strength and the index for one of the vowel variables, for 18 Belfast women. The vowel is the (a) variable

Table 4.5   Index for (a) and network-strength score for 18 Belfast women

Speaker	(a) Index	Network-strength score
1	2.78	2
2	2.74	5
3	2.70	5
4	2.63	2
5	2.50	3
6	2.48	3
7	2.42	1
8	2.38	1
9	2.35	4
10	2.33	5
11	2.33	3
12	2.25	2
13	2.16	1
14	2.13	1
15	1.75	1
16	1.73	1
17	1.45	0
18	1.05	0

Source: data from Milroy 1980:204-5

and refers to the vowel in 'hat'. The vowel variants are not important for our purposes, except that the index is related to a five-point phonetic scale (it is not a percentage) and high values mean more, and more frequent, use of local vernacular pronunciations. When speakers are listed in order by their vowel indexes, we see that high values on the network scale tend to collect near the top and low ones near the bottom. The Spearman's ρ-coefficient calculated by Milroy (1980:155) is 0.683 – another substantial, moderate relationship. Testing the coefficient by a t-test, Milroy obtained a value which is significant at $p<0.01$. The hypothesis that the population correlation might be zero (the null hypothesis) can be rejected and the research hypothesis accepted. A reasonable secondary hypothesis is that Belfast women tend to have a more marked local accent (with respect to this vowel at least) the more loyal they are to local group norms in general, and that this tendency is a substantial one.[21]

When to the use the Pearson product-moment correlation. Data requirements. For correlations, you have only one sample and it is *not* divided into subsets. Instead, you have measurements for two characteristics of the one sample. To use Pearson product-moment correlation, both characteristics must be measurable on a ratio or interval scale. In the Norfolk Island data, the sample was composed of dialogues. Each dialogue was measured on a ratio scale for two characteristics, percentage of English words and percentage intelligibility.
Hypothesis. Using the Pearsonian r, we test the hypothesis that the two measurements have a large proportion of their variation in common. More informally, we are trying to discover to what extent the two characteristics go together (or go in opposite directions) in the sample. The value obtained by Pearson product-moment correlation, the coefficient of correlation, must be tested for significance by a t-test and also interpreted by rule of thumb. The percentage of English words and intelligibility went together in the Norfolk Island dialogues to a moderate, but significant degree.

When to use the Spearman rank-order correlation. Data requirements. As in the Pearson procedure, we have measurements for two characteristics for a single sample. But with the Spearman procedure, the characteristics are measured on an ordinal scale only. In other words, we know how the members of the sample are ordered by the characteristics, but we have no information on the distance between one member and another. Quite often, we actually have interval or ratio data on one of the two characteristics, but only ordinal data on the other. The interval or ratio data is treated as if it were ordinal. In the Belfast data, we had the same speakers ranked by network strength (an ordinal scale) and by percentage of vernacular vowel pronunciation (a ratio scale treated as an ordinal scale).
Hypothesis. Using Spearman rank-order correlation, we attempt to find out to what extent our sample is ranked in the same (or opposite) order by the two characteristics. Like the Pearson procedure, the result must be tested for

significance by a *t*-test and interpreted. Milroy found that Belfast women tended to be ranked in the same order by network strength and by their pronunciation of the vernacular variant of (a) to a moderate but significant extent.

USING STATISTICAL PROCEDURES

I have tried to explain the workings of statistics as clearly as possible so that the reader will be able to understand references to statistical methods in books and articles on sociolinguistic research. There is not enough information in this chapter to enable a reader to apply statistical procedures to her own research. Yet, some readers might like to try their hand at statistics in their own work, even if it is just a small research project lasting only a few weeks. There are numerous textbooks available covering introductory statistics, many of which are excellent. The authors of three recent ones have gone out of their way to demystify the procedures for uninitiated readers. Anshen (1978) has written precisely for linguists and his book is lucid and entertaining. However, it is somewhat too brief and omits important detail and some commonly-used statistical procedures. For the chi square test, his discussion is clear enough so that you can use the test simply by following his instructions. The book by Hatch and Farhady (1982) is also extremely clear and unintimidating, and is much more thorough. It is written primarily for applied linguists, but many of the examples the authors use are similar to some of the topics in this book. For more depth, with little sacrifice in clarity and friendliness of style, Shavelson (1981) is unsurpassed. It is directed at the behavioral sciences in general but a few of his example cases are of direct sociolinguistic interest. Although all three are well written, each one I have mentioned asks more of its readers than the previous book, but provides more breadth and depth in return.

For people who need to work out statistical operations on paper with the help of a pocket calculator, Yuker (1958) is invaluable. For chi square, *t*-test, and the two types of correlation, Yuker provides step-by-step instructions for the computations, making them as simple as possible. For analysis of variance, you will have to rely on Hatch and Farhady (1982), Shavelson (1981), or another introductory statistics text.

For medium- to large-scale research, the use of a computer is almost a necessity. An easily learned statistical package that is available in many university computation centers is called Minitab. Minitab accepts statements in plain English and has a very helpful user's guide (Ryan, Joiner, and Joiner 1976). Minitab is somewhat limited in the amount of data it can accept and in the power of some of the statistical procedures built into it. Two other widely available packages are the Statistical Package for the Social Sciences (*SPSS*) and the Statistical Analysis System (*SAS*). Both have far greater capabilities than Minitab, but are slightly more complex to master. Both have user's guides (Nie et al. 1975 for SPSS; and *SAS User's Guide* 1979 for SAS). Hatch and Farhady show how to execute each of the procedures they discuss with SPSS, but they assume readers are already familiar with the package. SAS also has a very clear and usable introductory guide (Helwig 1978), designed to cover only those capabilities of the system that most users need, and the system is also noted for its graphics capabilities. Neophyte users of computer facilities may find using these systems less intimidating than they imagine. The Bio-Medical Data Package, available at some computer installations, has some capabilities that SPSS and SAS lack. The increasingly popular microcomputers, like the Radio Shack TRS–80 Model III, the Apple II Plus, The IBM Personal Computer and the BBC computer, have statistical package software available that makes it comparatively easy to do statistics with them.

Even if all this computer technology is not available, statistical calculations can be made less tedious with a calculator that computes mean and variance (the square root of which is standard deviation) automatically. Even better is a programable calculator that can be 'taught' to do repetitive calculations by itself. One or two pocket computer models are available that are much more limited than microcomputers, but still far more powerful than programable calculators.

SUMMARY

The quantified results of research activity in sociolinguistics often do not permit conclusions based simply on inspecting the numbers. A principled method is needed to distinguish valid numerical differences from those that are due to mere random factors. Statistics gives us the tools for accomplishing this.

Four basic concepts – population, characteristic, quantification, and distribution – underlie the two major uses of statistics. One of these is description. Descriptive statistics, such as mean and standard deviation, give an overall statistical picture of a body of quantified data. A more important use of statistics is hypothesis-testing, that is, a set of procedures that allows the researcher to establish the validity of certain kinds of hypotheses with a designated degree of confidence. Four hypothesis-testing procedures were discussed: the chi square test, the *t*-test, analysis of variance, and correlation. Of the first three, the chi square test is a non-parametric test. It requires namable characteristics quantified on a nominal scale. The *t*-test and analysis of variance are parametric procedures. They require that the dependent variable be a measurable characteristic quantified on an interval or ratio scale. Both procedures can be used to test hypotheses concerning significance of the distinction between two populations or subgroups of a population. Of the two, analysis of variance is more powerful and more versatile.

Correlation measures the strength and direction of interrelationships between two characteristics of a population. These procedures lead to a coefficient of correlation which must itself be tested for significance, using the *t*-test. There are two correlation methods. One is the Pearson product-moment correlation procedure, for use when the two characteristics to be correlated are both quantified on an interval or ratio scale. The other, the Spearman rank order correlation procedure, is for use when at least one correlated characteristic is quantified on an ordinal scale.

NOTES

1   This is valid provided we are interested only in geographical location, not in 'Africanness' as a concept. I believe it is likely that North Americans, at least, consider sub-Saharan African countries more African than the countries in North Africa.

2   The mean is often symbolized by $\overline{X}$; for example, $\overline{X}$=2.41 means 'the mean is 2.41'.

3   The standard deviation is calculated by the following procedure. First, the mean is computed. Then the difference between each score and the mean is calculated (these differences will be some positive and some negative; they will all add up to zero). Each difference is squared, and the squares added up. This total is then divided by the number of scores minus 1. Finally, the square root of that result is taken.

4   Opinion polls, of course, are based on samples, not total populations. This is why poll results are usually published with an error range associated with them; this error range is similar to the statement given here. Suppose there is an election poll that shows that Senator Smith will beat Governor Jones in a presidential election by three percentage points, but there is a 5 per cent error range. In the actual election, Governor Jones wins by two percentage points. The poll was accurate, since the result is within its error range.

5   For a more technical discussion of the two kinds of hypothesis, see Hatch and Farhady (1982:3, 4) or Shavelson (1981:271–5). For an illustration by extended example, see Anshen (1978:19–27).

6   Notice that one characteristic is namable (fertilizer treatment – either special fertilizer or cow manure) and one is measurable (weight of tomatoes).

7   See Fishman (1968a) for details of the criteria on which these designations were made.

8   The chance distribution for each cell is calculated by multiplying the row and column sums for that cell and dividing by the total count for the whole table. For instance, for the upper left-hand cell of table 4.1, we sum 27 and 15, getting 42; then sum 27 and 25, getting 52. Multiplying 52 by 42 gives 2,184, which, when divided by the total of 114 nations, gives 19.2, the chance number of homogeneous countries with very high or medium GNP, given that there are 42 countries with very high or medium GNP and 52 homogeneous countries.

9   Chi square (χ^2) is calculated by subtracting the hypothetical value (those in table 4.2) from the observed value (those in table 4.1) for each cell, squaring the result, and dividing by the hypothetical value. The final figure is obtained by summing these values for the four cells. If the chi square table has four cells in a two-by-two arrangement, as in this example, an adjustment called 'Yates' correction for continuity' must be applied. This is done by adding 0.5 to the *observed* value if it is less than the corresponding *expected* value, and subtracting 0.5 from the observed

value if it is greater than the corresponding expected value. The chi square calculation is then carried out as usual.

10 To find the significance of a chi square value from the tables that appear in statistics books, 'degrees of freedom' has to be known. For chi square, degrees of freedom is calculated by multiplying the number of rows minus one by the number of columns minus one. In our example, degrees of freedom is:

$$(2-1)(2-1) = (1)(1) = 1.$$

11 In volume II of this text, there is a field research chapter in which students are directed to conduct a similar experiment.

12 Further discussion of the chi square test is to be found in Hatch and Farhady (1982:165–173) or in Shavelson (1981:517–547). For another explanation of the chi square test with an example, see Anshen (1978:23–25).

13 The first pronunciation is more or less the way the vowel is generally pronounced by English speakers. The other pronunciation would sound roughly like 'hawt' in the word "hut". See Milroy (1980:118–20) for further details.

14 The t value is actually a ratio between the observed difference in the means and a statistic called the standard error of the difference between means. It is calculated by finding the difference between the means observed ($52.0 - 34.7 = 17.3$, in our example) and dividing it by the standard error of the difference between means, an estimate of what the difference for these data would be if only random factors were involved. Our t value indicates that the observed difference is over three times as great as the expected random difference, a magnitude that would crop up only once in a hundred times by chance. Degrees of freedom must also be used in the interpretation of a t table. For 'uncorrelated' or 'unmatched' data, where there is not a one-to-one match between the members of the two samples, degrees of freedom is equal to the number of members of each sample minus two. For correlated data, degrees of freedom is the number of members in the samples (the number is the same for each sample) minus one.

15 Milroy does not herself use the t-test, but rather a one-way analysis of variance, a procedure I will explain next.

16 Hatch and Farhady (1982:108–21) provide a more technical, but clear explanation of the t-test, including other uses than the one described here. Shavelson (1981:403–40) presents two detailed chapters on various applications of the t-test. Anshen (1978:26-7) describes the use of the z-score for testing the difference between means but this should only be done with large samples.

17 The actual calculation of F-ratios is too complicated to be explained in a footnote. The details of the calculation and interpretation of one-way analysis of variance are given in Hatch and Farhady (1982:128-50) and in Shavelson (1981:442-7).

18 Milroy is almost certainly correct in rejecting the null hypothesis in this particular case. The results for the 'hut' class vowel are consistent with the results for several other phonological variables in Belfast, as well as with the general pattern for gender differences in speech in numerous other studies.

19 The calculation of factorial analysis of variance is very complex, as are the fine details of its interpretation. Hatch and Farhady (1982:128-49) deal with these complexities with great clarity as does Shavelson (1981:448-547). Although our example of two-way analysis of variance may look like the chi square example at first, remember that *all* characteristics in a chi square test hypothesis must be namable. Analysis of variance requires that one characteristic, the dependent variable, be measurable.

20 For more detail on interpreting correlations – and the pitfalls to be avoided – see Shavelson (1981:210-8) and Hatch and Farhady (1982:201-3, 208-10).

21 It is important to emphasize at this point that I am describing only very small parts

of sociolinguistic research in connection with particular statistical procedures only for illustrative purposes. For instance, no one would (and Milroy does not) stop with the analysis of just one vowel and only speakers of one sex. This particular result, like all the illustrations used, is only part of a much more comprehensive research project.

OBJECTIVES

1 Be able to recognize a description of the purpose of inferential statistics.
2 Be able to distinguish 'population' from 'sample'.
3 Given an example, be able to distinguish the two kinds of variables (characteristics) in statistics.
4 Be able to distinguish examples of *namable* characteristics from *measurable* one
5 Be able to distinguish examples of *nominal, interval* or *ratio* and *ordinal*-scale quantifications.
6 Be able to identify an example of a reliability check and an example of a validity check.
7 Be able to recognize definitions of the terms 'mean' and 'standard deviation'.
8 Given a sample research hypothesis, be able to identify the corresponding null hypothesis.
9 Be able to state what an expression like $p < 0.01$ means.
10 Given a data description and a research hypothesis, be able to state whether or not a chi square test would be appropriate.
11 Given a data description and a research hypothesis, be able to state whether or not a *t*-test or one-way analysis of variance would be appropriate.
12 Given a data description and a research hypothesis, be able to state whether or not factorial analysis of variance would be appropriate.
13. Given a data description and a research hypothesis, be able to state whether or not correlation would be appropriate.

5

Quantitative Analysis

In chapter 3, we examined systematic attempts to account for the qualitative aspects of societal multilingualism. The approach was to try to discover what functions are fulfilled by language in society and to determine what qualifications a language must have in order to fulfill each function. Occasionally quantification came into play, as in Stewart's six language classes or Ferguson's major, minor and special status categories, but it is possible to take greater advantage of quantitative methods in the study of multilingualism in society. We will look at quantitative analysis in three steps: (1) the data sources that are used, mainly censuses, but also other surveys; (2) the Greenberg–Lieberson method for measuring linguistic diversity; and (3) the application of quantitative methods to issues in the sociolinguistics of language.

CENSUSES AND SURVEYS

Shortcomings

To collect the amount of data needed to measure multilingualism at the national level, enormous resources are required. Therefore, the only data of this magnitude that are available have been gathered under national government auspices. This usually means data in national decennial censuses.[1] Since no quantitative analysis can be better than the data it is based on, it is important to understand the kinds of shortcomings that are common in census data. Four common problems in censuses concern questions, responses, geography and data handling.

Questions. It is not such a simple matter as it may seem to ask people what language or languages they know. Mackey and Cartwright (1979:69–70), McConnell (1979:30), and Lieberson (1967:139) each give a separate classification of the kinds of language questions that are asked on censuses, but they all can be reduced to three general types: mother tongue, use, and ability. The mother-tongue type of question attempts to get at the first language acquired by the respondent. But as McConnell (1979:34) points out, exactly how the mother tongue is defined can vary from one nation to another. The use type of question asks for the language habitually or most often used. The question can be context-free, or contextual, as when respondents are asked for the language most often used at home, at work, with family members, or the like. Ability questions call for the respondent to evaluate her skill in speaking, under-standing, reading, or writing a language, or some combination of these skills. Problems arise when comparable questions are asked differently from one country to another, or from one census to another in the same country.

It is difficult to compare the figures from a country that asks a mother-tongue type question from one that asks a use type question, for example. Kirk (1946, cited in Lieberson 1967:139–140) pointed out that when a language shift is occurring, mother-tongue type questions make it appear that the shift is less advanced than use type questions do. Imagine you are studying the switch to national languages from vernaculars in two different countries. One asks a mother-tongue question in its census and another asks a use question. Let's say both countries have experienced a shift to about the same degree. A person in the first country who has given up the vernacular in favor of the national language during his lifetime – that is, he learned the vernacular first, but now usually uses the national language – will report the vernacular as 'his language'. A person in the other country who has had the same experience, having been asked what language he usually uses, will report the national language. When this pattern is multiplied by hundreds of thousands of people, it will make it look as if the second country is more advanced in promoting the national language than the first country is, but that would only be the result of the difference in question types.

Even when censuses ask the same kind of question, differences in wording can damage comparability. In 1940, the Brazilian census asked: 'Do you speak the national language fluently?' whereas Mexico, in the same year, asked: 'Do you speak the national language?' (Lieberson 1967:140). Both are ability questions, but it seems clear that more people would be willing to say they 'speak the national language' than that they speak it 'fluently'. Other questions might simply be unreliable because they aren't specific enough. A question such as 'What language do you know?' is too vague to elicit reliable information (Mackey and Cartwright 1979:70).

Scholars attempting longitudinal studies are hampered when censuses change the wording of questions from one census to another in the same country. In Paraguay, the language question changed from an ability-type question to a habitual-use type between the 1950 and 1962 censuses. In 1950, Paraguayans were asked what language or languages they were *able* to speak. In 1962, the question was about what language or languages they *habitually* spoke (Rubin 1968a:486, footnote 1). If a person knew both Spanish and

Guaraní, but usually used only Guaraní, she would presumably report herself as bilingual in 1950, but as using only Guaraní in 1962. The proportion of the population of Asunción which reported itself to be bilingual rose from 76 per cent in 1950 to 79 per cent in 1962 (Rona 1966:284, Rubin 1968a:486, footnote 1), but because of the difference in question type, bilingualism probably actually increased more than that. According to McConnell (1979:34), speakers reporting themselves bilingual in a 'standard' mother tongue and a related 'dialect' were not considered bilingual in the 1961 census of India. In 1971, this stipulation was removed, with the probable result that people would be counted as bilingual in 1971 who would not have been in 1961. Lieberson (1967:140) reports the damaging effects for comparability that resulted from the difference in the definition of mother tongue between 1920 and 1940 in the United States census. In 1910 and 1920, the second-generation immigrant was classified by the mother tongue of his foreign born parents, whereas in 1940 it was the language spoken at home in earliest childhood by the respondent himself. Consequently, in the earlier censuses, the second-generation immigrant could not be classified as having English as his mother tongue unless his foreign-born parents used English at home before coming to the United States. By contrast, the limitations were lessened in 1940, when mother tongue referred solely to the linguistic characteristics of the second generation themselves.

Question changes of the sort I have just described are motivated by a desire to improve the quality of data over the quality in previous censuses. Another source of difficulty in census questions is the tendency of governments to ask questions in such a way that national-language policy is supported. It is not unusual for language questions to discriminate against vernaculars. Languages other than officially recognized ones may not be mentioned at all or may be simply lumped together as 'native languages'. When questions on bilingualism are asked, they are often phrased so that only bilingualism involving at least one officially recognized language is counted. For example, in Mexico, an Amerindian who speaks Spanish as well as his ethnic language would be counted as a bilingual; one who speaks two Amerindian languages would not be (McConnell 1979:36). Sometimes colonial languages are also prejudicially treated. From 1931 to 1951, English was not listed as a possible second language in the Indian censuses, although this was corrected in 1961 (Weinreich 1957:231).[2] Sometimes the ambiguity between 'language' and 'dialect' has been exploited, either to increase or dilute the numerical strengths of parts of a population (Lieberson 1967:139; McConnell 1979:43). In old Austrian censuses, speakers of Yiddish were counted as speaking German so as to increase the numbers of German speakers in certain provinces. On the other hand, in Hungary, South Slav minorities were counted by local dialect names so as to reduce the total number of Serbo-Croats (Kirk 1946:225, cited in Lieberson 1967:139).

Although the last-given examples seem blatant and cynical, usually bias in census questions results from the national desire of governments to gather information from the official point of view. Censuses cannot ask everything, so the questions that are asked call for information that seems of greatest importance to the nation (McConnell 1979:36). The bilingualism question on the Mexican census is less motivated by a desire to suppress information on indigenous-language bilingualism than by the belief that bilingualism in Spanish is what is most important to the nation.

Responses.   In earlier chapters, we have seen that it is often difficult to decide if one speech variety is a dialect of another or a separate language in its own right. In the case of second languages, there is a whole range of knowledge of a language, from full fluency to the knowledge of a few words. Given these two continua, together with the necessity for constructing questions in short-answer format, it is not always clear just what it means when an individual tells a census enumerator that he knows a particular language. We said in chapter 1 that the fluidity in languages in northern India creates a chronic problem with what varieties should be considered languages as opposed to dialects. When an Indian citizen is asked to declare her mother tongue and second language, it is up to her to decide what name to give. According to Khubchandani (1978:570) 'declarations keep fluctuating in every census, representing constant shifts in ... M[other] T[ongue] allegiance.' Some speakers of languages such as Bihari and Rajasthani consider their languages substandard varieties of Hindi and may declare their mother tongue as Hindi or not, depending on the political climate at the time of the census (Khubchandani 1978:565). Other speakers seem not to know what an appropriate answer would be and give mother-tongue language names that Davidson (1969:178) finds 'ridiculous'. Similar problems in reporting language names have occurred in recent censuses in Israel and Turkey (McConnell 1979:43).

Almost everyone who has addressed the use of census data has mentioned the wide variety of language ability a person reporting himself as bilingual might have in the second language (Mackey and Cartwright 1979:71; McConnell 1979:35; Lieberson 1967:141; Davidson 1969:179; Weinreich 1957:206, Rona 1966:283). According to Rona (1966:283), Paraguayans might be counted as Spanish speakers if they have only picked up a few words of Spanish in school, or even if they attended school as children but have forgotten all the Spanish they ever knew. Mackey and Cartwright (1979:70–1) suspect that bilinguals who do not regularly interact with native speakers of their second languages might be more generous in assessing their own ability than those who do. Because respondents are given so much latitude, it can be expected that they will often report themselves as speakers of languages it is considered desirable to know, even though their ability is extremely limited.

If we know what languages are considered desirable, we can use this information as a partial corrective device in interpreting census results. In Paraguay, for example, since knowledge of Spanish as a second language confers status, we can assume that almost anyone with the slightest claim to knowledge of Spanish will report himself as knowing Spanish. As a result, census figures for monolingual speakers of Guaraní can be regarded as conservative; they include practically every actual Guaraní monolingual plus some who say they also know Spanish. Conversely, the figures for Spanish–Guaraní bilinguals are no doubt somewhat inflated. They include almost everyone who has a reasonable ability in Spanish along with some with little more than a very vague knowledge of the language. A similar technique is more difficult to apply in India, where the desirability of reporting knowledge of Hindi, for instance, varies from one region to another and from census to census.

This problem concerning extent of second language ability may not be too severe, however. In the first place, it is significant to know what languages people are willing to report that they know, regardless of actual ability. Secondly, as Lieberson (1967:141) points out: 'It seems most reasonable, nonetheless, to assume that the population reporting themselves able to speak a given language have a far higher degree of fluency than the segment of the population reporting themselves unable to speak the language.' Weinreich (1957:206) furthermore believes that the tendency to overestimate ability in a language is not stronger in one part of the country than another, at least in India. But if Mackey and Cartwright are right about the sobering effect of interaction with native speakers of the second language on an estimate of bilingual ability, it could have an important geographical effect in a country like Canada. Citizens living far from the French-speaking areas of eastern Canada might be willing to report bilingualism in French on the basis of less ability than would English mother tongue speakers who hear French spoken every day (Mackey and Cartwright 1979:70–1).

Occasionally there is evidence that language questions have been misunderstood. A limited follow-up research project on the 1961 Canadian census indicates that mother-tongue speakers of English, who answered the question 'Can you speak French?' positively, took it to mean the ability to *understand* French (Mackey and Cartwright 1979:70). A more complicated example is given by Khubchandani (1978:572). In Bombay Province, India, in 1951, a substantial number of native speakers of Sindhi were counted as bilingual in Panjabi. This bilingualism report seems to be based on the learning of a second script for writing Sindhi, not learning another language. Sindhi is normally written in Arabic script. Some Sindhi-speaking Hindus learn to read and write Sindhi in another script, called Gurumukhi. Learning Gurumukhi script is thought of as learning a language called Gurumukhi. As it happens, Gurumukhi script is also the usual script used for writing Panjabi. The end result is that Sindhi speakers who have learned to write their native language in a second script were counted as being bilingual in Sindhi and Panjabi!

Geography. Geographical factors can affect census data in two very different ways, due to the effects of physical geography and geopolitical boundaries. In some countries, there are areas that are isolated because of mountains, jungles, or other physical impediments to transportation. People who live in these areas might not be reached by census-takers at all. We have already seen how this can affect the bilingualism picture in Paraguay. The two areas that were most isolated at the time of the 1950 census are almost entirely Guaraní monolingual. With a large area of Guaraní monolingualism uncounted, the official figures inevitably indicate a higher proportion of bilingualism for the whole country than there actually was (Rona 1966:285). Improved roads to these areas may have made them more accessible to the census-taking enterprise and may partially account for the apparent increase in rural Guaraní monolingualism between 1950 and 1962 (Rubin 1978:189). The problem was made worse, of course, by the change in question type from an ability-type question to a use-type question between the two censuses, making it harder to report bilingualism in Spanish. How much of the apparent increase in rural monolingualism is real and how much is an artifact of increased geographical accessibility and the change of question type is hard to judge. Geographical isolation, together with the possibility of improved transportation between censuses, affects both the accuracy and comparability of census data.

Much more subtle in its effects is the necessity of tabulating census data by geopolitical boundaries. We saw in chapter 1 that the assignment of territories formerly belonging to one nation to another nation after a war can affect the level of multilingualism in both countries. Similarly, countries can reorganize their internal provincial boundaries. If either kind of boundary change occurs between censuses, comparability will be made more difficult (Davidson 1969:193).

Geopolitical boundaries are also significant in the measurement of linguistic diversity. A measurement of the degree of societal multilingualism, based on a political unit that is too large, usually makes multilingualism appear more extensive than it actually is, at least in people's daily lives. If a nation has 200 languages, it would seem that people would have a hard time communicating, as indeed they would if speakers of all 200 languages were uniformly distributed throughout the country. This is never the case of course; speakers of the same language tend to be concentrated in one geographical area, where they interact with each other far more than with people from other parts of the country. As a result, compared with whole countries, small subareas are much more linguistically uniform (Lieberson, Dalto, and Johnston 1975:42; cf. Greenberg 1956:113).

Weinreich (1957:227) gives a dramatic example of this very phenomenon. According to the 1951 census figures, the Trivandrum district of the former Indian state of Travancore-Cochin has a Greenberg Formula A diversity index of 0.48.[3] We will examine this index in our study of the Greenberg–Lieberson diversity measures later in the chapter, but for now it is enough to know it means there is about 1 chance in 2 that two speakers drawn at random from the district would not speak the same language. Thus it would seem that almost every other potential pair of speakers would not be able to understand each other. In actual fact, the eastern half of the district was almost entirely monolingual in Tamil and the western half equally monolingual in Malayalam. In daily life, since people from each half of the district would interact only with people from the same area, it wouldn't matter that they didn't know the language of the other half. Normally, *nobody* would encounter anyone who didn't speak the same language. Measuring the level of diversity for Trivandrum district as a whole gave a result that was almost completely irrelevant to the everyday lives of the people who lived there.[4]

We may now have a partial explanation for the surprisingly low level of bilingualism in India reported by Khubchandani (1978). Compared to the high degree of societal multilingualism in India, the fact that only 9.7 per cent of India's population was bilingual according to the 1961 census is rather surprising. Since bilingualism is only *necessary* when people need to interact regularly with other people who do not know their language, it could well be that the low bilingualism figure is a consequence of a relatively low degree of *local* diversity coexisting with a high degree of *national* diversity. It would seem that the smaller the geopolitical unit for which census data are examined, the easier it is to interpret the results. We will return to a statistical comparison of bilingualism and diversity after diversity measures have been introduced.

Data handling. Further difficulties arise in the collecting, compiling, and computing of census results. Quite a lot of responsibility is frequently placed on the fieldworker in deciding how to assign responses to the slots in the census questionnaire (Mackey and Cartwright 1979:72). One example of this sort of problem arose in the 1961 Indian census. The instructions to the enumerator required that he list only two languages for each respondent in addition to the mother tongue. Furthermore, no second language was to be recorded if it was a dialect of the mother tongue. Since there were no instructions on how to tell if a language named was a dialect or not, what was and was not recorded was up to the individual fieldworker (Khubchandani 1978:554–5, Davidson 1969:179). When the data were eventually ready for tabulation, although two languages other than the mother tongue had been recorded, only the first of the two that the fieldworker had written down was actually counted.

The sheer magnitude of the task of census-collecting practically guarantees that many citizens will be overlooked. In the US census of 1960, apparently well over half a million people were omitted entirely (Lieberson 1967:144). During and after the collection of data for the 1980 census in the United States, news reports were filled with complaints from cities and other jurisdictions that their areas were undercounted and that they would therefore lose out in government aid and political representation. One can only assume that the problem would be worse in less wealthy countries.

Using census data

The discussion of the shortcomings of census data may leave the impression that there is no point in attempting to use them at all. Census data are flawed, but not fatally so, especially if researchers and people who read their results know where the dangers lie. Lieberson (1967:134–5) gives three reasons why census data are indispensable for serious work on the sociolinguistics of society. First, they are practically the only data of the kind collected on such a large scale. Second, they are the only data of such magnitude which are collected at set time intervals, allowing long-range trends to be revealed. Finally, census data are the only large-scale data available that allow comparison between one part of the world and another. Even if a researcher were able to collect census-type data for a certain political subdivision of a country, she could never hope to do so for all comparable subdivisions for the same country, let alone other entire nations.

Validity checks.   It is sometimes possible to perform certain manipulations that give an indication of how valid census data are even before a sociolinguistic study is begun. Lieberson (1967:144–50) describes two kinds of such checks: *external verification* and *internal consistency*. External-verification checks are more convincing, since they compare quantitative data from sources other than the census with similar data in the census itself. If the data are in alignment, it can be assumed that they are accurate, since it is unlikely that both sources would independently make exactly the same errors. In internal consistency, different parts of a census are compared with each other, or a census taken at one time is compared with one taken at another. Internal-consistency checks should be relied on less than external-verification checks, as Lieberson makes clear: 'If the census data prove to be highly inconsistent, then serious doubt is raised about their validity. On the other hand, internal consistency does not "prove" validity as much as show that we are unable to find any evidence of error' (Lieberson 1967:146). It is entirely possible that the same census-taking procedure has an error built into it in some way and that that error is consistently made throughout. A consistent error of this sort would not show up in an internal-consistency check.[5]

A particularly good example of an external-verification check is given by Lieberson (1967:145) in connection with census data from the Canadian province of Quebec. The census includes figures for those whose mother tongue is French and those who speak English as their first language. It happens that there are other data available that can be used to verify the census mother-tongue data. In Quebec, there are Roman Catholic and Protestant school systems. Almost all Protestant schools use English as the medium of instruction and the majority of the Catholic schools use French. Presumably, French mother-tongue children go to the Catholic schools and English-speaking children attend Protestant schools. If so, then the enrollment figures for the two school systems should be close to the mother-tongue figures for the school-age children from the respective mother-tongue groups. When the school enrollment figures are compared with the mother-tongue

Table 5.1   Comparison of school system enrollment and census data
for children 10–14 years old, Quebec, 1957–58

School enrollment	Percentage	Mother tongue	Percentage
Roman Catholic	89.6	French	85.9
Protestant	10.4	English	11.3
		Other	2.8

Source: adapted from Lieberson (1967:145, table 2)

declarations for school-age children in the census, the match is very close indeed.[6] The data are presented in table 5.1.

The slightly higher percentage of Catholic school enrollment over French mother-tongue speakers, with the corresponding discrepancy in the other direction for Protestant enrollment and English mother-tongue declarations, is easily explained. There are probably more English schools in the Catholic system than schools which use French in the Protestant system. As a result, a larger number of English mother-tongue children are enrolled in Catholic schools than there are French-speaking children in Protestant schools. There is no reason to believe that school enrollment figures are not accurate and even less reason to think that, even if there were errors, they would be exactly the same ones that might exist in the census data. The agreement of the census figures with the independent school enrollment figures is powerful evidence in favor of the reliability of the census data.

An internal-consistency check that can be carried out with almost any census that has been taken twice or more involves age cohorts. If a given percentage of a particular age-group report a certain mother tongue in one census, then the age-group ten years older ought to report the same mother tongue at the same percentage level in a census taken ten years later. In order for this assumption to be valid, it has to be true that: (1) the mortality rates in each mother-tongue group are about the same during the ten years; (2) a disproportionate number of one mother-tongue group did not leave the country during the ten years; and (3) a disproportionate number of speakers of one of the mother tongues did not immigrate during the ten years.

The third item can be controlled if the census data allow immigrant responses to be identified and removed from the calculations; Lieberson (1967:146–7) did this in his example. Taking the data from seven age-groups on the 1951 Canadian census on French and English mother tongue,

Lieberson compared them with the data for age-groups ten years older. For example, in 1951, 57.0 per cent of the 10 to 14-year-old age-group reported English as the mother tongue and 33.8 per cent, French. In 1961, in the 20 to 24-year-old age-group, 56.8 per cent reported English and 34.1 per cent reported French. For all seven age-groups, the average difference between age cohorts reporting English is only 0.8 per cent and for those reporting French, the average difference is 0.1 per cent. These values are very close and speak well for the consistency of the Canadian census from one census to the next, at least where mother-tongue information is concerned. Lieberson cautions his readers that such a result does not prove that the census is valid, just consistent. For example, if there had been a biased wording to the mother tongue question that produced distorted responses and the same question were used on both censuses, then the distortion would show up consistently both times. The data would then have been consistent, but not valid. However, in the absence of evidence of persistent errors, a positive result to an internal-consistency check is very reassuring.

Extracting further data from censuses.   With a bit of ingenuity and creativity, it is often possible to get statistical data from censuses that are not direct tabulations of responses. Examples of this are given by McConnell (1979:37–9) and by Lieberson (1967:136–8). McConnell's examples involve straight-forward calculations of total speakers of a language in a country. For example, if mother-tongue speakers of some language X are given and the numbers of mother-tongue speakers of each of the other languages in the country who have learned language X as a second language are also given, obviously the total speakers of Language X can be found by adding the mother-tongue speakers to the second-language speakers. Lieberson's examples are a little more complicated. In one of them, he estimates the proportion of English mother-tongue speakers who have learned French, even though there are no such data listed in the Canadian census. The data he *does* have are:

1   Those whose mother tongue is English.
2   Those who speak English, but do not speak French.

By subtracting the second number from the first, we get (a conservative estimate of) the mother-tongue speakers of English who *do* speak French. Dividing this figure by the first number, we are left with the proportion of the English mother-tongue population that has learned French. To show how this would work, let us imagine an area of Quebec City that has 500 mother-tongue speakers of English. Let us further assume that 190 of these respondents report that they speak English, but not French. If we subtract these from the total mother-tongue speakers of English (500 – 190 = 310), we get 310 mother-tongue speakers who also know French. By dividing 310 by 500, the total number of mother-tongue English speakers, we get 0.62 (=62 per cent), the proportion of mother-tongue English speakers who have learned French.

Another, more risky, way of getting extra language data from census reports is to use what McConnell (1979:24–5) calls 'paralinguistic data'. Paralinguistic data, in his sense, are data on ethnic group membership, which are sometimes available when direct language data are not. If a given ethnic group is sufficiently monolithic with respect to language – for example, if at least 80 per cent of them speak the same language – ethnic-group data are *language interpretable*. This means that ethnic-group membership data can be used with a fair amount of reliability in the absence of language data. Similarly, immigrants from monolingual countries can be assumed to be mother-tongue speakers of the dominant languages of their countries. For instance, immigrants to Canada from the United States or Australia can be assumed to be English speakers with a high degree of reliability (McConnell 1979:25). Needless to say, such indirect data should be used with extreme care (Cf. Mackey and Cartwright 1979:71).

Inferences. If enough background information is known, it is sometimes possible to make inferences from census data. For example, McConnell (1979:31) makes an inferential suggestion based on data in the Turkish census of 1965. Turkish is the official language, but there is a large minority population of Kurds. Given the numerical and political superiority of Turkish speakers, it is not surprising to notice that about 40 per cent of the Kurds speak Turkish as a second language. It is surprising to notice that 400,000 native speakers of Turkish have listed Kurdish as a second language. It is hard to imagine what would induce a Turkish speaker to learn Kurdish, unless he were an ethnic Kurd who had switched linguistic allegiance to Turkish. If this inference is correct, it could give clues about the direction and magnitude of language shift among Kurds in Turkey.

A similar inference from the 1961 Indian census was made by Davidson (1969:194–5). The 1961 census lists about 224,000 mother tongue speakers of English. Davidson was curious to know how many of them were Anglo-Indians. Anglo-Indians were counted as such in the 1951 census, but not in 1961. If one assumes that the population of Anglo-Indians grew at the same rate as the Indian population in general (it probably grew more slowly), there would be up to 135,000 Anglo-Indians in 1961. If this figure is subtracted from the number of mother-tongue English speakers, it means that there were at least 89,000 native speakers of English in India in 1961 who were *not* Anglo-Indians. These details are of little interest except to people with a special interest in the countries involved, but they do illustrate how inferencing can be used to eke out extra information from census data.

Sources. There are a few publications of compiled language statistics from many countries in the same volume. In Kloss and McConnell (1977), there are statistics on the world's written languages. The same two scholars have begun a monumental project to assemble language statistics in a series of volumes which will cover the entire globe. The first volume, on central and western South Asia (Kloss and McConnell 1974), has been published, and the second, on North America, had just been released at the time of this writing. Another valuable source, with a special emphasis on vernacular languages, is Grimes (1978).

Other surveys

Sometimes other surveys of language are conducted on a national scale. Several of the contributions to Ohannessian, Ferguson, and Polomé (1975) describe the techniques, problems, and results of such surveys. If the surveys are conducted by sociolinguists, some improvement in language questions over census questionnaires might be expected. Nevertheless, host countries may place restrictions on just what information may be sought. Polomé (1975:32) says that in a survey in which he participated in Tanzania, it was not permitted to question the status of Swahili as a national language, and systematic study of local vernaculars was discouraged. Most of the other advantages and disadvantages of census data also apply to other large-scale survey data. Of interest is one technique used by Bender, Cooper, and Ferguson (1972), called the *transaction count*. As part of their language survey of Ethiopia, they conducted a market survey in the following manner:

The market surveys were carried out in twenty-three markets in eight towns. . . . Enumerators, drawn from among the students at the local high school, tallied the number of market transactions observed in various languages on a single market day. A number of commodities and services was chosen (for example, cloth, onions, salt, tailoring), and each enumerator observed language usage in each of these items. Thus, for each item, each enumerator noted the number of transactions between buyer and seller carried out in Amharic, the number carried out in Galla, etc. This technique permitted highly reliable estimates to be made of the relative importance of various languages in the market because representative items were chosen for observation and because large numbers of observations were made. (Bender, Cooper, and Ferguson 1972:226)

A technique like this, which would never be used in census-taking, avoids the problem of self-reported data and provides a means of external verification for the more traditional kind of survey data, as well as providing valuable data in its own right.

THE GREENBERG–LIEBERSON FORMULAS

The backbone of the quantitative analysis of the sociolinguistics of society is the measurement of linguistic diversity, the extent of societal multilingualism. The most elegant technique for the measurement of linguistic diversity is the one proposed by Joseph Greenberg (1956) and later extended by Stanley

Lieberson (1964). We will now turn to the description of the Greenberg–
Lieberson method.

Greenberg's diversity measures

Greenberg uses the same basic method to develop eight different formulas,
seven of which are measures of linguistic diversity. The eighth is what he calls
an 'index of communication'. Each of the seven diversity measures is more
refined than the last. The most advanced formula, the seventh, is the most
accurate, but also quite complicated. For our purposes, we will be satisfied
with the first and simplest of the diversity formulas, and the eighth, the index
of communication. There are two reasons we will not concern ourselves with
the more advanced diversity formulas: first, they are too complex to be
covered in an introductory text and second, they demand data that are usually
not available.

To make the task manageable, Greenberg starts out with the following
somewhat unrealistic assumption. Given a geopolitical unit (for example, a
city, district, state, or country), he asks us to imagine that we can put all the
speakers within that unit into a bag, shake them up and pull out two speakers
at random. We assume that these two speakers will want to talk to each other.
What we want to discover is whether they share a language so that they can. As
we have seen, this assumption is more valid in small areas, such as cities, than
in larger units, for example, whole countries. It is more realistic to assume that
two people drawn at random from the same city will actually want to speak to
each other than two speakers drawn from a whole country. Two speakers, if
they happen to be from two distant parts of the same country, may never need
to talk to each other and, in real life, it would not matter much if they do not
happen to share a language.

The totally uniform state. In order to arrive at a workable formula, we will
have to live with the assumption that any two speakers drawn from a
geopolitical unit are equally likely to want or need to communicate. To show
how this works, let us imagine the two extreme cases, the totally monolingual
state and the totally diverse state. First, imagine that we have a political unit –
a 'bag' of 100,000 speakers of language X and no speakers of any other
languages. To calculate the probability that we will draw a speaker of
language X, we divide the number of speakers of language X (100,000) by the
total number of speakers in the bag (also 100,000). That is, we have 100,000
chances out of 100,000 of getting an X-speaker. The fraction 100,000/100,000
= 1, or certainty, that we will get a speaker of X. But we always draw two
speakers so that the first speaker will have someone to talk to. Actually, of
course, there are now only 99,999 speakers left in the bag, since we have
already drawn one, but the fact that there is one less speaker left in the bag at
the second drawing is negligible. Assuming that we still have virtually 100,000

speakers of X, our chances of drawing a speaker of X the second time is also 100,000/100,000 = 1, or certainty. To calculate the probability that we will draw two speakers who share language X, we multiply the probability of drawing one X-speaker by the probability of drawing a second X-speaker. In this case, the answer is 1 x 1 = 1, or still certainty. This roundabout calculation tells us what we knew from the beginning, that we are certain to get two speakers who share the same language in a monolingual state, but the method of calculation will be necessary in less simple cases.

The totally diverse state.   Let us now take the opposite case, the totally diverse state. Now we have a bag of 100,000 speakers of 100,000 separate languages, each speaker knowing a different language (a sort of biblical Tower of Babel case). Assuming that language X is one of the 100,000 languages, our chances of getting a speaker of X (in fact, the *only* speaker of X) on the first draw is 1 in 100,000. But having drawn the only X-speaker on the first try, our chances of drawing a second one is 0/100,000 or 0. Therefore, our chances of drawing two speakers of X is 1/100,000 x 0/100,000 = 0, or no chance at all. Now let us see what our chances would be of finding two speakers who share another of the 100,000 languages, language Y. Putting the two speakers we have already drawn back into the bag, our chances of getting a Y-speaker the first time is again 1/100,000. Having drawn the only Y-speaker the first time, we have no chance of drawing a second one. So the possibility of getting two people who can communicate using language Y is also 0. We could go on trying the remaining 99,998 languages, but we would get exactly the same result each time. Our chances of getting two speakers who can communicate using *any* of the languages in the country is the sum of our chances of getting two speakers who share *each* of the 100,000 languages. In this case, it is the sum of 100,000 zeros, or no chance at all. Again, the calculation is a complex way of showing what we really knew all along, that there is no chance of communication in a totally diverse state.

Greenberg's example.   To get a more realistic case, let us go through Greenberg's (1956:109) own hypothetical example. We assume a trilingual polity speaking language M (by 1/8 of the population), N (by 3/8 of the population), and O (1/2 of the population). First, we imagine that we put all of these speakers in one bag, shake them up, and draw. Our probability of pulling out a speaker of M on the very first try is 1 in 8, the exact proportion of speakers of M to the total population. Our chance of getting a second M-speaker is also 1 in 8 (ignoring the fact that we have reduced the pool of M-speakers slightly by drawing the first speaker). The probability of drawing *two* speakers of language M is the product of these two probabilities, or 1/8 x 1/8 = 1/64. The result is that we have 1 chance in 64 of finding two speakers in our sample polity who can communicate using language M.

Trying the same procedure for language N, the probability of drawing an

N-speaker the first time is 3/8; the probability of getting a second speaker of N is also 3/8. Multiplying these two probabilities, we get 3/8 x 3/8 = 9/64, or 9 chances in 64 of getting two speakers who can use language N to communicate. The result for language O is 1/2 x 1/2 or 1/4. The probability of getting two speakers who can communicate by using *any* language is the sum of these three probabilities: 1/64 + 9/64 + 1/4. This works out to 26/64.

Linguistic diversity.   At this point , we need to recall that our ultimate goal is the measure of linguistic *diversity*. The meaning of linguistic diversity will be the probability that, if we draw two speakers at random, they will speak two *different* languages. But this is just the opposite of what we have been doing so far. It would be possible to compute diversity defined in this way by a direct method, but, given the way raw data come to us, it is most convenient to use a somewhat indirect method. This way is to compute the probability that, if we draw two speakers at random, they will speak the same language, just as in our illustrations so far. Then this probability is subtracted from 1, which gives the diversity measure we want. In the last example, we ended up with 26 chances out of 64 that the two speakers we draw at random will speak the *same* language. Obviously the left-over probability is the probability that the two speakers drawn will speak different languages. How do we find the left-over probability? If there are a total of 64 out of 64 chances in the first place (64/64 = 1, of course) and 26 of these chances are the probability of getting two speakers with the same language, then the remaining 38 chances out of the 64 represents the probability of drawing speakers who speak different languages. Arithmetically, this is the calculation: 64/64 – 26/64 = 38/64. Converting the fraction to its decimal equivalent, we get a value of 0.594.

Another way to view this is to assume that every area we analyze is completely diverse unless we can prove otherwise. This means that we assign to every unit a value of 1, which we specify as meaning totally *diverse* (it is certain that we will get two speakers who do *not* share a language). Then we calculate the probability that we will draw two speakers who *do* share a language. Subtracting this value from the assumed total diversity, we are left with the actual diversity value for that nation, or other geopolitical unit.

Let us return, for a moment, to the two extreme examples we started with. The totally uniform country had a certainty value (that is, 1) that two speakers drawn would speak the same language. To convert this value to a diversity value, we subtract from 1 : 1 – 1 = 0. The diversity value of 0 is just what we want; a totally uniform country is not diverse at all. In the completely diverse country, our chances of drawing two speakers with the same language was 0. Subtracting from 1 in this case, we get 1 (1 – 0 = 1). The value of 1 is exactly appropriate for a totally diverse country. The third case had a diversity value of 0.594. We can now see that this represents a level of diversity somewhat more than halfway between no diversity and total diversity.

Expression of Formula A.   Going back over our calculations, we can see that we calculated the probability of communication for each individual language by multiplying the proportion of the population speaking that language by itself. This is the mathematical equivalent of squaring each proportion. For example, 1/8 x 1/8 is the same as $(1/8)^2$. If we let i stand successively for each of the three proportions in the third example, the probability is the sum of the squares of each of these proportions, that is, i^2. Using the symbol capital sigma (Σ) to mean 'sum of', this can be represented by:

$$\Sigma \; i(i^2)$$

Subtracting this from 1 gives Greenberg's simplest formula, Formula A. The formula is:

$$A = 1 - \Sigma \; i(i^2)$$

Assumptions in Formula A.   The calculation of Formula A makes the somewhat unrealistic assumption that two speakers drawn from anywhere in a geopolitical unit are equally likely to need to communicate with each other. This assumption is made in all eight of Greenberg's formulae. Two further unrealistic assumptions are made in Formula A that are corrected in his more advanced formulas. The first is that every language is totally unintelligible to a speaker of any other language. We have already seen that there are languages in Paraguay and India that can be understood to one degree or another by speakers of other related languages, and this phenomenon is not too uncommon around the world. The second assumption is that there are no multilingual speakers. Formula A implicitly assumes that every individual speaks only one language. Formulas B to G represent Greenberg's attempt to avoid making these undesirable suppositions. The data needed to calculate partial intelligibility between languages is extremely hard to come by. Data on bilingualism are available in some censuses, but in relatively few of them, and the data there are of questionable quality.[7] For all practical purposes, then, Formula A is the only one of Greenberg's measures of diversity that it is possible to use.

Index of communication.   Greenberg's eighth formula, Formula H, is a measure of communication rather than diversity. Because of this, there is no subtraction from 1 involved in Formula H. It differs from Formula A in another way; it requires and takes into account data on multilingual speakers. Basically, H is calculated by: (1) drawing pairs of speakers at random, as in calculating Formula A; (2) taking note of those pairs that can communicate because they share at least one language; (3) calculating the probability of drawing each of these 'good' pairs; and 4) summing these probabilities.

The best way to see how Formula H works is to apply it to an example. Take the following hypothetical data:

In a given country, there are three languages, M, N, and O. Of the total population, 0.15 are M monolinguals, 0.20 are N monolinguals, 0.05 are O monolinguals, 0.25 are MN bilinguals, 0.30 are NO bilinguals, and 0.05 are MNO trilinguals. There are no MO bilinguals.

One way to carry out the first step would be to list each possible pair of speakers: M and M, M and N, M and O, M and MN, etc. This would be a tedious process, however, and it is much simpler to accomplish the same thing by constructing a table.[8] The table is constructed by listing each language and the proportion of the total population that speaks it at the head of the columns and rows of the table. To fill each cell, one multiplies the value at the head of the column by the value at the end of the row. This gives the probability of drawing two speakers with the designated linguistic abilities, since the column value indicates the probability of drawing one speaker, and the row value the probability of drawing the other. This is illustrated in table 5.2. The probability of drawing an M-speaker first and an MN-speaker second is .0375, the result of multiplying 0.15 (the M-speaker probability) by 0.25 (the MN-speaker probability). Notice that probabilities are only entered in cells if the head of the column and the end of the row each have at least one language in common. For instance, no value is entered in the cell calling for an M monolingual and an N monolingual. These two speakers cannot understand each other and drawing that pair contributes nothing to communication in the polity. The index of communication for this country is found by adding all the values in Table 5.2.[9] The sum in our example is .8350, meaning there is an 83.5 per cent chance that two speakers drawn at random from this country will have at least one language in common.

Table 5.2   Table for the calculation of
Greenberg's index of communication (Formula H)

	M (0.15)	N (0.20)	O (0.05)	MN (0.25)	MO (0.00)	NO (0.30)	MNO (0.05)
M (0.15)	0.0225			0.0375	0.0000		0.0075
N (0.20)		0.0400		0.0500		0.0600	0.0100
O (0.05)			0.0025		0.0000	0.0150	0.0025
MN (0.25)	0.0375	0.5000		0.0625	0.0000	0.0750	0.0125
MO (0.00)	0.0000		0.0000	0.0000	0.0000	0.0000	0.0000
NO (0.30)	0.0450	0.0600	0.0150	0.0750	0.0000	0.0900	0.0150
MNO (0.05)	0.0075	0.0100	0.0025	0.0125	0.0000	0.0150	0.0025

Index of communication = 0.8350

As a final note on Formula H, it may seem strange that unlike pairs of speakers appear twice in table 5.2. The pair involving an M-speaker and an MN-speaker, for example, appears once in row M and column MN, and once in row MN and column M. It may seem that only one of these is necessary.

Actually, both are. In one case, we have the probability of getting an M-speaker on the *first* draw and the MN-speaker on the *second*. In the other case, the MN-speaker is drawn first and the M-speaker second. Both possibilities must be considered.

Lieberson's extensions

Formula H. The use of Greenberg's formulas was extended by Stanley Lieberson (1964/1968). Lieberson made two general observations about Greenberg's formulas. First, although Greenberg only talks about his formulas in terms of geographic areas, for example, nations, states, and cities, there is no reason why the index of diversity or communication could not be computed for any definable population. Geography need not be a defining factor at all. For example, a computation of Formula H for Roman Catholics all over the world would give the likelihood that any two selected at random anywhere in the world would be able to communicate in a common language. Lieberson's more important observation is that Greenberg's formulae only give communication or diversity *within* a population. It says nothing about communication *between* two spatially delineated populations. To illustrate the problem, Lieberson uses data from Algeria in 1948. This information appears in table 5.3, from Lieberson's table 1.

Table 5.3   Language distribution in the population of Algeria aged 10 years or over, in 1948

	Arabic	Berber	French and Arabic	French, Arabic, and Berber	French and Berber	French
Total population	0.676	0.097	0.064	0.041	0.006	0.116
Muslim	0.780	0.112	0.053	0.047	0.007	0.001
European			0.135	0.003	0.001	0.860

Source: Lieberson (1968:547)

An ordinary calculation of an H index shows that the index of communication for Algeria as a whole is 0.669, a fairly high figure. This means that if two Algerians were selected at random, the chances are about two out of three that they would share a language. But the index of communication for the whole country gives no information about what the prospects for communication would be if a European were selected at random, and then a Muslim were selected. In cases like this, the conventional index leaves out important information. To use Lieberson's illustration of the extreme case (1968:548), suppose that a nation is composed of two groups, A and B. All members of A are monolingual in language X and all members of B are monolingual in Y. Calculating H for the whole population would give an index of communication which could not be less than 0.500 and could be much higher if one of the two groups were substantially larger than the other. However, it would fail entirely to indicate the sociolinguistically important fact that there would be no communication at all between the two groups.

Fortunately, as Lieberson shows, it is a fairly simple matter to adapt Greenberg's Formula H to reveal such information. To do this, instead of selecting just *any* two speakers from the population, we limit ourselves, in the Algerian case, to selecting one European and one Muslim. Then we observe the probability that they will share a common language. The technique illustrated in table 5.2 can be applied here. Instead of placing the proportions of the entire population that speak the various combinations of languages across the columns and the down the rows, we need to do something a little different. Across one axis, say across the columns, we put the proportions of the Muslim population that speak the various combinations of languages. The same is done down the rows for the European population (omitting Arabic and Berber monolinguals for this population because, as table 5.3 tells us, there are none). The cells are filled by multiplying the proportion at the head of the defining columns and rows, provided that there is a shared language. The probabilities in the cells are added, as before. This is illustrated in table 5.4, using the data from table 5.3.[10] The result clearly shows that the prospects for successful inter-ethnic communication between Europeans and Muslims is far lower than the index of communication for Algeria as a whole might indicate.

Table 5.4   Table for the calculation of the index of communication extended to measure interethnic communication within the Algerian population, in 1948

Europeans	Muslims					
	Arabic (0.780)	*Berber (0.112)*	*French and Arabic (0.053)*	*French, Arabic, and Berber (0.047)*	*French and Berber (0.007)*	*French (0.001)*
French and Arabic (0.135)	0.105		0.007	0.006	0.001	0.000
French, Arabic and Berber (0.003)	0.002	0.000	0.000	0.000	0.000	0.000
French and Berber (0.001)		0.000	0.000	0.000	0.000	0.000
French (0.860)			0.046	0.040	0.006	0.001

Total: 0.214
Source: data from Lieberson (1968)

Formula A.   The same can be done with Greenberg's Formula A for linguistic diversity. Lieberson's example here is taken from the data on the mother tongue of Norwegian foreign white stock in the United States in 1940 (Lieberson 1967:551). These data appear in table 5.5, adapted from Lieberson's table 3.

Table 5.5   *Mother tongue distribution of Norwegian foreign white stock in USA, 1940*

	Mother tongues		
	Norwegian	*English*	*Swedish*
Foreign born	0.924	0.051	0.012
Second generation	0.502	0.477	0.008

Source: adapted from Lieberson (1968:551)

If we wish to look at the linguistic diversity between the generations, we have to change the formula somewhat. Instead of:

$$A = 1 - \Sigma \; _i(i^2)$$

we use:

$$A = 1 - \Sigma \; _i(i_1)(i_2)$$

where i_1 is the proportion of the foreign-born generation that speaks a given language and i_2 is the proportion of the second generation that speaks the same language. Applying the formula to the data in table 5.5, we get:

$$1 - [(0.924)(0.502) + (0.051)(0.477) + (0.012)(0.008)] = 1 - 0.488 = 0.512$$

This diversity measure suggests that there is a better than 50 : 50 chance that randomly selected members from the two generations would *not* share the same mother tongue. It would not be accurate, of course, to suppose that the actual linguistic diversity between the generations is as high as 0.512. Many members of the foreign-born generation no doubt have English as a second language, if it is not their first language. This is probably even more true of the second-generation population that has Norwegian or Swedish as a mother tongue. In addition, some of the second-generation population that has English as a mother tongue may well know Norwegian or Swedish as a second language. The fact that this kind of data apparently was not readily available to Lieberson illustrates the problem with Greenberg's more sophisticated diversity formulae. The data necessary for a truly accurate picture is often not to be had.

Index of communicativity

A further extension of the Greenberg–Lieberson technique was proposed by

Kuo (1979). His index of communicativity is designed to measure the potential of a particular *language* to act as the means of communication in a society. Whereas the Greenberg and Lieberson methods measure diversity or communication, regardless of what languages are involved, Kuo's index measures communication with respect to a given language. The formula Kuo (1979:329) gives is:

$$I_{am} = (P_{am})^2$$

In this formula, P_{am} is the proportion of some population m who can understand some language a. In Kuo's illustrative example, the index of communicativity for English for the adult population of Singapore in 1978 is calculated by taking the percentage of Singaporians who can understand English (61.7 per cent), converting it to a decimal (0.617), and squaring it, giving 0.381. This means that there are almost 2 chances in 5 that two randomly drawn Singapore adults would be able to communicate *in English*. Greenberg's index of communication (Formula H) would be higher, because it would take into account pairs of speakers who could communicate in *any* language.

To extend the index of communicativity in the way Lieberson extended the original Greenberg formulas, Kuo suggests that the index can measure the value of a given language as a medium for *interethnic* communication by adjusting the formula to:

$$I_{amn} = (P_{am})(P_{an})$$

In this formula, P_{am} is the proportion of people in group m who know language a, and P_{an} is the proportion of people in group n who know the same language. If 56.1 per cent of the Chinese in Singapore know English and 0.670 per cent of the Indians also know it, then the index of communicativity of English between these two groups is equal to 0.561 multiplied by 0.670 or 0.376. This means that there is a probability of 0.376 'that a randomly selected Indian and a randomly selected Chinese in Singapore can understand each other in English' (Kuo 1979:329). Kuo's index is a valuable measure of the wider communication function which we encountered in chapter 3. It can also be used as a rough measure of the status of a language as a full-fledged national language.

APPLICATIONS

Typical applications of quantitative methods in the sociolinguistics of society are made in the study of diversity itself, in the study of language maintenance and shift, and in the study of language attitudes. We will encounter quantitative methods in maintenance and shift and in attitude studies in later chapters. Here, we will look at some of the things to be learned about linguistic diversity using quantitative tools. Three aspects of diversity that lend themselves to quantitative analysis are: (1) the developmental issue; (2) communicativity; and (3) bilingualism as compensation for diversity.

The developmental issue

In chapter 1, we saw how Jonathan Pool (1972) presented evidence that national development seemed to be associated with low linguistic diversity.[11] Although Pool was very careful to interpret his results conservatively, it did seem that there might be a causal relationship such that linguistic diversity impedes national development or that national development reduces linguistic diversity. The relationship between linguistic diversity and various measures of development was examined in detail by Lieberson and Hansen (1974), using Greenberg's Formula A diversity measure as a tool. Lieberson and Hansen are disturbed about the temptation to draw causal conclusions from static data. To put the issue briefly, just because there is an association between linguistic uniformity and national development that can be observed at the present time, it does not follow that one of these factors *caused* the other. To demonstrate causation, it would be necessary to use longitudinal data to show that reductions in diversity are accompanied by increases in development.

Lieberson and Hansen (1974:524–5) begin by showing that it indeed *is* the case that diversity is inversely related to development. They do it by a somewhat more sophisticated method than Pool used. Instead of drawing inferences directly from a scatterplot, like figure 1.1, based on diversity versus a measure of development, they use one of the statistical techniques introduced in chapter 4 – correlation. As we know, product–moment correlation techniques require at least interval data for two different characteristics of the same population. Lieberson and Hansen used the Formula A index as a measure of diversity in a number of nations and correlated it with several measures of development for the same nations. One of these was per-capita gross national product, a measure similar to the per-capita gross domestic product measure of development used by Pool. Using data from 77 nations, Lieberson and Hansen found that the coefficient of correlation between A and GNP was $r=-0.35$. This indicates a small tendency for nations with low diversity to have a high per-capita GNP. Two other measures of development showed a stronger relationship to diversity: urbanization ($r=-0.52$) and illiteracy ($r=0.49$). This means that there is a moderate tendency for less diverse nations to be more urbanized and for more diverse nations to have higher rates of illiteracy. Lieberson and Hansen's results show essentially the same relationship that Pool's did; linguistically diverse nations tend to be less developed and those that are more uniform are more developed.

In an attempt to determine if the relationship is a causal one, Lieberson and

Hansen obtained data on diversity and the two highest-correlated measures of development (urbanization and illiteracy) for 23 European nations between 1930 and 1960. Before examining the development measures, they discovered a very high correlation between diversity in 1930 and diversity in 1960 ($r=0.88$). In other words, if one wanted to be able to predict which of the 23 nations would be relatively more diverse in 1960 and which ones would be less diverse, the most valuable data to have would be the 1930 diversity measures. To determine whether urbanization or illiteracy is associated with the decline in diversity during the 30 years (there was a slight decline), an account must be taken of the diversity level at the beginning of the period. Using a somewhat intricate multiple correlation technique, Lieberson and Hansen were able to determine that only 9 per cent of the 1960 diversity not predicted by the 1930 diversity levels could be attributed to urbanization. The results for illiteracy were even more dismal; only 4 per cent of the 1960 diversity is explained by this measure when 1930 diversity is taken into account. In other words, they could find no support for the hypothesis that the decline in diversity in these 23 nations was connected to either urbanization or literacy.

Nevertheless, there are serious limitations to the 30-year study, largely due to the fact that the time period is too short. In an attempt to correct that difficulty, Lieberson and Hansen conducted a longitudinal study of eight nations for which they could obtain data for time periods ranging up to 100 years.[12] The results of this study also failed to show that there is any connection between development and diversity.

If there is no evidence of a causal relationship between developmental factors and linguistic diversity, we are left with a puzzle. In the absence of a causal relationship, what does account for the correlations between measures of development, such as urbanization or gross national product and diversity? The answer seems to be related to the age of nations. When nations are divided into a group of 'old' nations that became independent before 1945 and a group of 'new' ones that became independent after 1945, statistical analysis shows that the measures of development have only a very small association with linguistic diversity, even in static data. As Lieberson and Hansen (1974:537) put it:

It is as if there are two clusters of nations, with one cluster consisting of pre-World War II nations that are generally more developed and less diverse than the second cluster of post-World War II nations. The correlations between diversity and development are created because these two separate clusters exist, but it is only a slight overstatement to say that within each cluster, there is essentially no association between the developmental characteristics and mother tongue diversity.

A more careful historical analysis than I can provide here would be necessary in order to understand the whole reason why these two clusters of nations exist. It can be pointed out, however, that the more recently independent nations are frequently former colonies whose linguistic diversity was brought about in part by forced federation. At the same time, some of the older nations are those in which the industrial revolution began and they had a monopoly on industrialization before the newer nations gained independence.[13]

Communicativity

Kuo (1979) was able to make use of his index of communicativity to reveal a number of interesting sociolinguistic patterns in Singapore and West Malaysia. Linguistic diversity in both countries involves the same six languages: Malay, English, Mandarin, Tamil, Hokkien, and Cantonese. Table 5.6 shows the indexes of communication for the six languages in the two countries in 1978. Recall that this index represents the probability of drawing two speakers from the general population who know a given language.

Table 5.6   Indexes of communicativity for six languages
in Singapore and West Malaysia, 1978

	Malay	English	Mandarin	Tamil	Hokkien	Cantonese
Singapore	0.453	0.381	0.408	0.004	0.607	0.399
West Malaysia	0.746	0.081	0.060	0.013	0.084	0.066

Source: Kuo (1979)

The difference is quite striking. With the exception of Tamil, there are reasonably high communicativity-index levels for all the languages in Singapore. Communication in Singapore appears to be accomplished to a large extent by members of each ethnic group learning one or more of the languages of their neighbors, rather than by everyone learning a common second language. By contrast, in West Malaysia, Malay is by far and away the strongest language in terms of communicativity. Apparently, it is the language of choice as a second language in that country. From the point of view of nationalism, it appears that no language has a clear advantage as a national language in Singapore. Singapore formally recognizes Malay as a 'national language', and three others – English, Mandarin, and Tamil – as 'official' (Kuo 1979:340, footnote 7). Hokkien has a slight apparent advantage in communicativity, but it is not one of the designated official languages and its communicativity indexes between ethnic groups are very low (Kuo 1979:333). Its high overall index is due to its communicative value within the large Chinese ethnic community. Malay seems clearly to be functioning as a national language in West Malaysia. It is the only designated national and official language, and also has the highest overall index of communicativity in the country. Furthermore, it has by far the highest index of communicativity between ethnic groups.

One further fact about Malay reinforces the conclusion that Malay is serving the nationalist function in West Malaysia and also illustrates how survey data need to be interpreted with caution.[14] Comparing the survey results of 1972 and 1978, there is a *decline* of 3 per cent in the number of respondents who report that they know Malay. At the same time, there is a 5.6 per cent *increase* in the number of people who report English, and the percentages reporting the other four languages remain about the same (Kuo 1979:334). At first glance, this would appear to run counter to the idea that Malay is growing as a national language. But Malay surely *is* expanding in its nationalist function as both Kuo (1979:336) and Platt (1977:374) assure us. Kuo (1979:336–7) explains this apparent loss for Malay as being the result of the *success* of the promotion of Bahasa Malaysia as a national language. Recall from the discussion of polyglossia in Malaysia in chapter 2, that there are two forms of Malay, the low-prestige 'bazaar' form and the standardized form. Individuals who might have claimed to understand Malay because they knew Bazaar Malay in 1972 may have become increasingly aware of the standardization of the national language in the ensuing six years. In 1978, realizing that they had problems using the standard language, some fluent speakers of Bazaar Malay may have reported that they did not know Malay. The 3 per cent difference, then, would be a decline in the willingness to *report* a knowledge of Malay, rather than any change in linguistic ability.

Kuo's explanation is almost certainly correct. Although 3 per cent seems a small percentage, it represents an extraordinarily rapid rate in language shift by worldwide standards. Lieberson, Dalto, and Johnston (1975) give data on the proportions of the populations who speak the language of the largest mother-tongue groups in 35 countries over time. The largest average annual change in this proportion is an increase of 0.0041 for Romania between 1930 and 1966. Most of this change took place between 1930 and 1956, a period during which Romania was forced to give up territories to the Soviet Union and Bulgaria. Usually, a nation that gives up part of its territory experiences an increase in the proportion of its population that speaks the major language because areas inhabited by linguistic minorities are most likely to be lost. The next largest average annual changes are in the range of 0.0020–0.0025. Since West Malaysia did not undergo any boundary shifts between 1972 and 1978, one would expect the average annual change in the proportion of the population that knows Malay to be no more than 0.0025. But a 3 per cent change over six years works out to an average annual decrease of 0.0050. This is even larger than the increase in Romania, during a period when it experienced major boundary shifts. In short, it is most unlikely that the 3 per cent decline is an actual language shift, but is rather to be explained along the lines offered by Kuo.[15]

Kuo's index of communicativity gives us a tool for the analysis of national languages and languages of wider communication. If we use the index to compare the communicativity of Hindi-Urdu and English in India, Hindi-Urdu fares better. Using Khubchandani's (1978) data taken from the 1961 Indian census, we find that Hindi-Urdu has a higher index of communicativity in all states but two, Tamilnadu and Kerala. In these two Dravidian-language states, *neither* language has a very high index. In Tamilnadu there is only

Table 5.7   Indexes of communicativity for Hindi-Urdu and
English in the states of India, 1961

State	Region	State language	Communicativity indexes Hindi-Urdu	English
Andhra Pradesh	South	Telegu	0.0083	0.0006
Kerala	South	Malayalam	0.0000	0.0016
Mysore	South	Kannada	0.0105	0.0003
Tamilnadu	South	Tamil	0.0005	0.0013
Assam	East	Assamese	0.0046	0.0006
Orissa	East	Oriya	0.0010	0.0002
West Bengal	East	Bengali	0.0080	0.0018
Gujarat	West	Gujerati	0.0044	0.0002
Maharashtra	West	Marathi	0.0255	0.0007
Bihar	North Central	Hindi	0.3178	0.0003
Jammu and Kashmir	North-Central	Urdu	0.0089	0.0000
Madhya Pradesh	North-Central	Hindi	0.7120	0.0001
Punjab	North-Central	Hindi	0.3614	0.0013
Rajasthan	North-Central	Hindi	0.1333	0.0002
Uttar Pradesh	North-Central	Hindi	0.9350	0.0006
Delhi (union territory)	North-Central	Hindi	0.7518	0.0241

Source: data from Khubchandani (1978)

about 1 chance in a 1,000 of drawing two English speakers; the probability of drawing two Hindi-Urdu speakers is less than half that. The English index in Kerala is about the same as in Tamilnadu and the Hindi-Urdu index is vanishingly small. In fact, the English index is no greater than .0018 in *any* Indian state.[16] Outside the states that have either Hindi or Urdu as official languages, the highest index for Hindi-Urdu is .0255. The full data are presented in table 5.7.

It is also possible to compute indexes of communicativity among the four linguistic regions which Khubchandani divides India into. This will give some idea of how well English and Hindi serve as link languages between one region and another. The data are given in table 5.8. Hindi serves better than English on this criterion as well, but the probability of drawing two speakers of Hindi-Urdu, one each from any two regions, is never even as high as 1 in 10. No other language can compete with Hindi-Urdu as a link language for the whole country. The conclusion we are forced to accept is that there is no language in India that serves the nationalist function, if communicativity is a critical criterion.

By contrast, when the communicativity index for Guaraní in Paraguay is computed using Rona's (1966:284) data from the 1950 census, we find that it exceeds 0.9000 in 11 of the 16 departments. Only in the linguistically diverse department of Boquerón does it fall below 0.5000. The indexes for Spanish are also comparatively high, ranging from 0.1584 to 0.5027 in the departments (0.7030 in Asunción). To get an idea of interregional communicativity for

Table 5.8 Indexes of communicativity for Hindi-Urdu and
English between linguistic regions of India, 1961

| Region | Communicativity indexes | |
	Hindi-Urdu	English
South/East	0.0039	0.0009
South/West	0.0074	0.0006
South/North-Central	0.0430	0.0006
East/West	0.0086	0.0006
East/North-Central	0.0492	0.0007
North-Central/West	0.0936	0.0005

Source: data from Khubchandani (1978)

Spanish and Guaraní, indexes of communicativity were computed between the two departments with the lowest proportion of Guaraní speakers, and also for the department of Olimpo and the city of Asunción, the two jurisdictions with the highest proportion of Spanish speakers. Between Itapuá and Boquerón, where there is the lowest proportionate number of Guaraní speakers, the index for Guaraní is 0.539 and for Spanish is 0.363. Between Olimpo and Asunción, the Guaraní index is 0.818 and the Spanish index is 0.632. Guaraní functions better as a language of wider communication than Spanish both under worst-case conditions for Guaraní and under best case conditions for Spanish. The index of communicativity confirms what less formal indications have shown, that Guaraní is in a very strong position as a national language of Paraguay.

A high index of communicativity is a necessary, but certainly not a sufficient, criterion for the successful function of a nationalist language in the fullest sense. A lingua franca that is used only as a trade language may have high communicativity, but lack the symbolic power required of a language fulfilling the nationalist function. Still, it is probably no accident that some of the most successful promotions of new nationalist languages have occurred in Tanzania, Malaysia, and Indonesia, where lingua francas which already had high communicativity were adopted, standardized, and developed.

Compensation through bilingualism

On of the problems with the use of the simplest diversity index, Formula A, is that it takes no account of multilingualism. This flaw is in principle corrected in Formula H, as well as in some of Greenberg's more complex diversity measures and in Kuo's index of communicativity. Another way to measure the extent to which diversity is compensated for by bilingualism was suggested by Weinreich (1957:228–9). Weinreich reasoned that the amount of bilingualism in a polity could be expected to be proportional to diversity. That is, there should be a tendency for bilingualism to be higher where diversity is high; people will take the trouble to learn second languages in those areas where there are many other people who speak different languages. Davidson (1969:183–8) attempted to verify Weinreich's hypothesis by constructing a list of Indian states, giving the proportion of the population that was bilingual, and Weinreich's diversity measure D for each. Weinreich's D, as it turns out, is similar to Greenberg's Formula A (see note 3). If Weinreich is correct, one would expect that states with high diversity would be the same ones that have high bilingualism. Davidson found the results somewhat disappointing, and the deviations from the expected pattern were difficult to explain. Davidson did not use formal statistical methods, but a coefficient of correlation can easily be computed with the bilingualism proportion and diversity as the two variables. The r value is a rather low 0.286.[17]

Weinreich dealt with the hypothesis constructing a k index. He used the formula

$$k=B/D$$

where B is the proportion of the population that is bilingual and D is his measure of diversity. He also computed k on the basis of district, not state, statistics, data which Davidson did not have from the 1961 census (Weinreich used the 1951 figures). He found the results 'truly striking' (Weinreich 1957:229). For a large number of districts, the value of k was very close to 1, indicating roughly that diversity is just compensated for by bilingualism in that district. Furthermore, the areas where k was markedly below 1 were mountainous and desert regions, the type of terrain where communication would be difficult.

A similar way of measuring the compensation for diversity by bilingualism can be constructed using the Formula A figures. The A-index, as we know, is the probability of drawing two speakers who do not share a mother tongue. The bilingualism proportion is the same as the probability of drawing one bilingual speaker out of the population (if there are two people in a room and one of them is bilingual, the chance of choosing the bilingual at random is 1 in 2). In order for communication to take place, only *one* of a pair of speakers with different mother tongues needs to be bilingual. Therefore, diversity would be exactly compensated for by bilingualism, if the chance of drawing a bilingual is exactly the same as the chance of drawing one bilingual for every pair of linguistically diverse speakers. The ratio we want is the bilingualism proportion divided by half the Formula A diversity measure. If both are identical, the index we are constructing equals 1 and means that our chance of drawing a bilingual from the population is exactly the same as our chance of drawing one member of a diverse pair of speakers. The formula can be expressed as:

$$C = B/(A/2)$$

or, equivalently and more conveniently:

$$C = 2B/A$$

where C stands for the index of compensation, B is the bilingualism proportion, and A is the value of the Formula A index. As it turns out, C is always slightly larger than Weinreich's k, for the same data.

C is a rather crude measure and it is important to examine the ways in which it is unrealistic. First, we are comparing the probability of drawing a bilingual speaker with the probability of drawing a diverse pair of speakers *on the average*. Suppose we draw one set of speakers of different mother tongues and both are bilingual. A second pair of diverse speakers are drawn, neither of whom are bilingual. On the average, there is one bilingual speaker per diverse pair, but only one pair can understand each other. Second, we are using *overall* bilingualism figures. We get a value of 1 for C if there is one bilingual for every diverse pair of speakers whether she is bilingual in the right language or not. If one member of a pair of speakers is a native of Marathi and also can speak Hindi and the second speaker is monolingual in Telegu, the bilingualism of the first speaker satisfies the statistics, but the pair still can't communicate. On the other hand, the assumption that Formula A makes, that we draw two speakers from *anywhere* in the polity, tends to magnify diversity. Applied to India as a whole, for example, a middle-level government worker in Delhi is just as likely to be paired with an agricultural worker from Kerala as he is to his nearest neighbor. In real life, diverse pairs of speakers who need to and do talk to each other are likely to include at least one member who is bilingual in the right language. It is also easy to see that Formula A, and hence our C index, becomes more accurate the smaller the population grouping it is applied to.

We are now in a position to understand more clearly why the bilingualism percentage reported by Khubchandani (1978) for India seems such a poor compensation for India's high diversity. Part of the explanation, as we saw in chapter 1, is to be found in the linguistic fluidity in northern India, but another important factor is that we are looking at the whole country. Khubchandani reports a bilingualism rate of 9.7 per cent for India as a whole, on the basis of the 1961 census. Lieberson, Dalto, and Johnston (1975:37) compute a Formula A diversity measure of 0.837 for India in 1961. Using these figures in the bilingual-compensation formula, we find that the value of C is 0.2318. This means that diversity is not nearly compensated for by bilingualism in the Indian population as a whole.

If we use Davidson's figures for the Indian states plus the union territory of Delhi, we obtain the results in table 5.9. For all but four states, the bilingual-compensation index is close to or greater than 1. For most of the states, the bilingual-compensation index indicates that diversity is adequately counter-acted by bilingualism. In the four states in which there seems not to be 'enough' bilingualism, the C-value is still higher than it is for India as a whole. When Weinreich applied his k-index, whose value is close to C, to district-level statistics, he found good compensation except in mountainous and desert districts. It appears that the closer we get to the level of day-to-day interaction, the better diversity is cancelled out by bilingualism.

On the other hand, as Weinreich (1957:230) noticed, there are few areas where bilingual compensation is *greater* than 1. That is, bilingualism is enough to compensate for diversity, but usually only just enough.[18] In other words, people most often become bilingual for purposes of communication only, not for symbolic, nationalist reasons. As Weinreich (1957:230) puts it: 'High values of k would probably be found in countries with strongly developed national consciousness.'

Table 5.9   Diversity, bilingualism, and bilingual compensation in the Indian states and Delhi, 1961

State	A	B	C
Delhi (union territory)	0.0396	0.2411	12.1768
Punjab	0.0199	0.1002	10.0704
Uttar Pradesh	0.0591	0.0442	1.4958
Kerala	0.0784	0.0568	1.4490
Tamilnadu	0.2256	0.1561	1.3839
Mysore	0.3600	0.2202	1.2233
Madhya Pradesh	0.1351	0.0815	1.2065
Maharashtra	0.2604	0.1510	1.1598
Bihar	0.1351	0.0731	1.0822
AndhrāPradesh	0.2079	0.1094	1.0524
Assam	0.4071	0.2073	1.0184
Gujarat	0.1351	0.0643	0.9519
Orissa	0.2431	0.0871	0.7166
West Bengal	0.3916	0.0854	0.4362
Jammu and Kashmir	0.5239	0.1030	0.3936
Rajasthan	0.1536	0.0253	0.3294

Source: data from Davidson (1969)

In highly diverse countries, the measurement of bilingual compensation can serve as a way of determining the extent to which diversity problems are solved by bilingualism. Further, where C is much greater than 1, we may have evidence that language is serving a symbolic function in nationalism. This measure works better in linguistically diverse countries with a newly developing national consciousness, where the nationalist language has to be learned as a second language, than in countries in which the national language is the mother tongue of most of the population. Paraguay is an example of the latter type of nation. It in fact *has* a high C (over 9), but this reflects a great deal of acquisition (or at least reported acquisition) of the *official* language, rather than learning of the national language as a second language.

SUMMARY

The sociolinguistics of society benefits from the application of quantitative methods, as well as from qualitative analysis. The numerical data required for large-scale quantitative analysis come from major survey projects, most often government decennial censuses. Although there are numerous problems with the collection and handling of these data, perhaps especially those due to the vagaries of self-reporting, census and other survey data are extremely valuable. Their value is enhanced when they are used with care, when they are checked for validity where possible, and when extra information is extracted from them by creative analytical methods and inferencing.

The Greenberg–Lieberson diversity and communication indexing methods are the most sophisticated tools for the measurement of societal multi-lingualism and communication yet available, and their value was extended by Kuo's 'index of communicativity'. The Greenberg–Lieberson indexes can be modified to take multilingualism and partial interlanguage intelligibility into account, but usually data required by these modifications are not available. The assumption of random drawing of two speakers from anywhere in the population under study make the Greenberg–Lieberson formulas less realistic when they are applied to large populations, such as whole countries, than when they are applied to provinces and their subdivisions. The use of quantitative methods based on diversity formulas was illustrated by their application to the question of the relationship between diversity and national development, the statistical evaluation of the communicativity of languages in a country using Kuo's method, and the study of the compensation for linguistic diversity by bilingualism. Further use of quantitative methods will be seen in the chapters on language attitudes and language maintenance and shift.

BIBLIOGRAPHICAL NOTES

There are a number of other recent studies using quantitative analyses of census or survey data, in addition to those cited in this chapter. B. Kachru (1977) and Thompson (1974) mention problems with census data as they utilize and evaluate them. Meisel (1978) and Vallee and de Vries (1978) use census statistics to analyze language issues in Canadian society. Le Page (1972) and Le Page et al. (1974) illustrate what can be done with data from smaller-scale surveys. Other examples are to be found in Ohannessian, Ferguson, and Polomé (1975).

NOTES

1 Sometimes governments sponsor language surveys outside the normal census process. Most notable among these surveys are the monumental Linguistic Survey of India, conducted by Sir George Grierson in the late nineteenth and early twentieth centuries, and the recent linguistic surveys conducted in eastern Africa, reported on in Ohannessian, Ferguson, and Polomé (1975).
2 Notice that English was so treated both before and after independence. As Weinreich (1957:231) points out: 'Curiously, imperial and national politics coincided in giving the English language discriminatory treatment in the census.'
3 Weinreich gives his own '*D*' diversity measure for Trivandrum. Weinreich's

method is similar to Greenberg's and Greenberg's A index can readily be derived from D by the formula $A = D(2-D)$.

4   When India's linguistic states were established, Trivandrum was bisected and assigned to two different states on linguistic criteria.

5   External verification and internal consistency are really special cases of *validity* and *reliability*, respectively. Validity and reliability were concepts introduced in chapter 4, in connection with measuring instruments.

6   The most recent school-enrolment data available to Lieberson at the time were for 1957–58. To get comparable census figures, he used a linear interpolation procedure between the 1951 and 1961 censuses.

7   The scarcity of bilingualism figures in censuses is a nearly universal complaint. Statements of the following sort are common: 'we have learned that it is difficult enough to obtain mother tongue figures, without hoping for the luxury of bilingual figures' (McConnell 1979:36), 'The linguist . . . is lucky to have any information on bilingualism at all' (Davidson 1969:178), 'Strange as it may seem, statistics on bilingualism are quite scarce, since most countries provide census figures on MT groups only' (Weinreich 1957:203).

8   I am indebted to a former student, Wally G. Astor, who developed this method and brought it to my attention.

9   Since there are no MO bilinguals, both the column and the row designated MO contain only blanks and zeros. The MO column and row could therefore have been left out of the table.

10   An empty cell in table 5.4 means that there is no shared language. A value of 0.000 means that there is at least one shared language, but the probability is so small that it becomes 0.000 when taken to three decimal places.

11   Fishman's (1968c) research on the same issue was mentioned in chapter 1 and used as an example of the chi-square test in chapter 4.

12   The eight nations were: Bulgaria, Canada, Finland, Hungary, India, Switzerland, Turkey, and the Soviet Union.

13   It also might be possible to argue that the developed (mostly 'older') nations also have a monopoly on defining 'development'.

14   Kuo's data come from surveys conducted by market-research organizations (Kuo 1979:330).

15   The even larger increase for English also requires an explanation. Could it be the mirror image of the explanation for Malay? Since there are standard and colloquial forms of English, perhaps a de-emphasis on English in Malaysia makes people *more* willing to report knowledge of English on the basis of knowledge of colloquial English only.

16   The English communicativity index in Delhi (a union territory) is higher, but does not compare to the index for Hindi-Urdu.

17   Weinreich's D was converted to an A-value before the correlation coefficient was computed. Even the Spearman's ρ-value, for rank difference correlation, is only 0.370.

18   Delhi and Punjab are two exceptions. Davidson (1969:188) seeks an explanation in the fact that both are in economically advanced areas of the country and that Delhi has an above-average literacy rate.

OBJECTIVES

1   Be able to identify language questions on a hypothetical census as (1) mother tongue; (2) use; or (3) ability.

2   Be able to state whether or not the wording of a question eliciting the same sort of

information (such as languages a person knows) may affect the data that is based on it.

3 Once it is understood that responses to language questions cannot always be taken at face value, it may be possible to make inferences about the direction of the error. As an example, be able to identify the direction of the error in data on speakers of Spanish or Guaraní in Paraguay (is the number likely to be too high or too low).

4 Given an example of suspicious data in a national census that could be related to geography, be able to state if the problem might be due to: (1) physical geography; or (2) geopolitical boundaries.

5 Be able to state the three major features of census data which favor their use in spite of inherent problems (p.120).

6 Be able to distinguish a definition of an external verification check from a definition of an internal consistency check.

7 Given numbers similar to the ones in the hypothetical example about Quebec City (p. 122), be able to state the number (not the proportion) of speakers of one language that have learned another, in the same way that the example in the text gives the number of English speakers who have learned French.

8 Be able to identify the 'somewhat unrealistic assumption' (p. 125) that is made in the Greenberg diversity formulas.

9 Given the proportion of the total population of some politico-geographical unit that speaks language X, be able to recognize how you would determine the probability of randomly drawing one speaker of language X.

10 Be able to recognize the reason Formula A involves subtracting from 1.

11 Be able to explain why the probability of finding two speakers who can communicate using Language M in a polity in which 1/8 of the population speaks Language M, is $(1/8)^2$.

12 Be able to identify the meaning of the term $\Sigma \; _i(i)^2$ in Formula A.

13 Be able to identify the correct answer to the application of Formula A to a simple example.

14 Be able to state a second way in which Formula H is different from Formula A, besides being a measure of communication rather than of diversity.

15 Be able to recognize a statement of the meaning of a Formula H value such as 0.3461 or 0.7639.

16 Be able to identify the correct answer to a simple example of Lieberson's extension to Formula H. To meet this objective, you will have to show that you can use a table of the form of table 5.4. For example:

Given a society in which there are two ethnic groups, group 1 and group 2, and three languages, A, B, and C. The two groups use the three languages as indicated in table A:

Table A   Data given in the example to objective 16

	A	B	AB	AC	BC
Group 1	7/10	—	1/10	2/10	—
Group 2	—	5/10	2/10	—	3/10

Construct a table to show the probability of the correct index of communication (II) between group 1 and group 2 – 1, 66/100, 34/100, or 0.

Solution

Step 1.   Label the axes of the table – group 1 along one axis and group 2 along the other.

Step 2. Calculate the probabilities of communication based on each language combination by multiplying the proportion at the end of each row by the proportion at the head of each column, provided that there is at least one language in common. The result would be table B.

Table B   Table for the calculation of the index of communication for the example in objective 16

Group 2	Group 1		
	A (7/10)	AB (1/10)	AC (2/10)
B (5/10)	–	5/100	–
AB (2/10)	14/100	2/100	4/100
BC (3/10)	–	3/100	6/100

Step 3. Add the proportions in the table. The result is 34/100.
Step 4. Select the correct answer from the choices given.

17 Be able to recognize a correct statement of what Kuo's index of communicativity measures.
18 Be able to recognize what Lieberson and Hansen's correlational study showed about the relationship between diversity, as measured by Formula A, and development.
19 Be able to recognize the general patterns of communicativity indices in Singapore and West Malaysia, and their significance for the status of the national language in each country.
20 Be able to recognize the conclusion that an analysis of the indices of communicativity for Hindi-Urdu and English in India leads to.
21 Be able to state what Fasold's *C* value measures.
22 Be able to recognize the significance of the fact that *C*-values are higher at the state and district levels in India than they are at the national level.

6

Language Attitudes

LANGUAGE ATTITUDES: WHY AND WHAT?

Much of the earlier part of this book has been focused on society as a whole. Societies, however, are composed of individuals; whatever people do with language in a society happens when somebody talks to somebody else. In this chapter and the next, we are going to concentrate on individuals and what they do with language. Our attention will be drawn to the methods and theories of a social science we have not encountered yet, social psychology. One of the subjects social psychologists have found useful to study is language attitudes.

The study of attitudes in general begins with a decision between two competing theories about the nature of attitudes. Most language-attitude work is based on a *mentalist* view of attitude as a state of readiness; an intervening variable between a stimulus affecting a person and that person's response (Agheyisi and Fishman 1970:138, Cooper and Fishman 1974:7). A person's attitude, in this view, prepares her to react to a given stimulus in one way rather than in another. A typical mentalist definition of attitude is given by Williams (1974:21): 'Attitude is considered as an internal state aroused by stimulation of some type and which may mediate the organism's subsequent response.' This view poses problems for experimental method, because if an attitude is an internal state of readiness, rather than an observable response, we must depend on the person's reports of what their attitudes are, or infer attitudes indirectly from behavior patterns. As we know, self-reported data are often of questionable validity, and inferences from behavior take the researcher one step away from what he has actually observed. A great deal of effort in language-attitude research has gone into devising ingenious experiments designed to reveal attitudes without making subjects overly conscious of the process.

The other view of attitudes is the *behaviorist* view. On this theory, attitudes are to be found simply in the responses people make to social situations. This viewpoint makes research easier to undertake, since it requires no self-reports or indirect inferences. It is only necessary to observe, tabulate, and analyze overt behavior. Attitudes of this sort, however, would not be quite as interesting as they would be if they were defined mentalistically, because they cannot be used to predict other behavior (Agheyisi and Fishman 1970:138). Nevertheless, the more straightforward behaviorist approach, in which attitudes are just one kind of response to a stimulus, certainly can not be ruled out.

Another issue that arises in the consideration of attitudes is whether or not attitudes have identifiable subcomponents. Generally speaking, social psychologists who accept the behaviorist definition view attitudes as single units. Mentalists usually consider attitudes to have subparts, such as *cognitive* (knowledge), *affective* (feeling), and *conative* (action) components (Agheyisi and Fishman 1970:139, Cooper and Fishman 1974:7). More or less complex componential models of attitude have been constructed by various scholars, but we don't have to go into the details here (cf. Agheyisi and Fishman 1970:140).

Our interest, of course, is in *language* attitudes, rather than attitudes in general. Language attitudes are distinguished from other attitudes by the fact that they are precisely about language. Some language-attitude studies are strictly limited to attitudes toward language itself. Subjects in these studies are asked if they think a given language variety is 'rich', 'poor', 'beautiful', 'ugly', 'sweet sounding', 'harsh' and the like. Most often, however, the definition of language attitude is broadened to include attitudes towards speakers of a particular language or dialect. An even further broadening of the definition allows all sorts of behavior concerning language to be treated, including attitudes toward language maintenance and planning efforts. The research we will summarize in this chapter deals with language attitudes from the middle viewpoint; including attitudes towards *speakers* of language varieties and not just the language itself.

If the mentalist conception of language attitude turns out to be right, then, if we know a person's attitudes, we would be able to make predictions about her behavior related to those attitudes, with some degree of accuracy. Cooper and Fishman (1974:5) cite several phenomena that may be influenced by language attitudes. The course of sound change is apparently influenced by whether the change is favored or disfavored by the speech community (Bailey 1973), and one definition of 'speech community' hinges on collective language attitudes (Labov 1966).[1] Attitudes toward language are often the reflection of attitudes towards members of various ethnic groups. There is some evidence that language attitudes may influence how teachers deal with pupils (Frender and Lambert 1973; Seligman, Tucker, and Lambert 1972); and the work of Frederick Williams and his associates – (for example, Williams 1974), and employers' hiring practices (Rey 1977). Other evidence suggests that attitudes about language affect second-language learning (for example, Lambert et al. 1968). It even appears to be the case that language attitudes can have an effect on whether or not a language variety is intelligible (Wolff 1959). Given two closely related language varieties, speakers of the higher-status variety may not be able to understand the other one, but can be understood by the speakers of the lower-status variety. If these connections between attitudes and other social phenomena are real, then the study of language attitudes has an important place in sociolinguistics.

METHODS OF LANGUAGE-ATTITUDE RESEARCH

Direct and indirect

Methods for determining attitudes about language can be either direct or indirect. A totally direct method would require subjects to respond to a questionnaire or interview questions that simply ask their opinions about one or another language. A totally indirect method would be designed to keep the subject from knowing that her language attitudes were being investigated. One example of this kind of approach is described by Cooper and Fishman (1974:16–17). They were interested in testing the hypothesis that attitudes towards Hebrew in Israel make it more effective as a language for scientific arguments. Arabic, on the other hand, would be more effective for conveying traditional Islamic arguments. To test the hypothesis, a group of Muslim adults who were bilingual in Arabic and Hebrew were asked to listen to four one-minute passages recorded by a fluent speaker of both languages. One passage decried the evils of tobacco and gave scientific evidence in support of that position. It was recorded once in each language. The other passage, also recorded once in each language, argued against the use of liquor, and used traditional Islamic arguments for support. The respondents were divided into two groups, one of which listened to the tobacco passage in Hebrew and the liquor passage in Arabic, and the other group listened to the reverse combination. Respondents were then asked if they would support increased taxes on tobacco or liquor to discourage their use.

The differences were dramatic. The respondents who had heard the scientific tobacco passage in Hebrew said they supported the tax on tobacco by a two-to-one ratio over those who had heard the same kind of argument in Arabic. The reverse results were obtained in the case of the traditional arguments against liquor; twice as many of the respondents who heard the argument in Arabic said they supported the tax increase than those who heard it in Hebrew. The hypothesis appears to be supported, but the subjects had no idea that their language attitudes were being investigated at all. Their attention had been diverted to the issues of the evils of tobacco and liquor.

The matched-guise technique

An experimental method that has become virtually standard in language attitude research, in either original or modified form, is the matched-guise technique developed by Wallace Lambert and his associates (Lambert et al. 1960; Lambert 1967). The pure matched-guise technique aims at total control of all variables except language. To achieve this, a number of bilingual speakers fluent in the languages under investigation are recruited. These speakers are tape-recorded reading exactly the same passage, once in one language and once in the other. The recorded passages are arranged on a tape-recording in such a way that it appears that each passage has been recorded by a different speaker. If speakers have been recorded once in French and once in English, for example, the recording might begin with one speaker's French performance. The next voice heard might be another speaker's English guise. The third voice might be a third speaker speaking in English. Perhaps the fourth voice will be the first speaker in her English guise. By this time, listeners will presumably have forgotten the voice quality of the first speaker and will take it that the fourth speaker is someone they haven't heard before. The two guises of the several speakers who have been recorded are all interspersed in this way, so that it sounds to the listener that each passage they hear is from a totally new speaker. In the end, then, they assume that they have heard twice as many people as they actually have heard.

A sample of bilingual listeners from the same speech community is then asked to listen to the recordings and rate the speakers on various characteristics, such as intelligence, social class, and likability. If the same person is rated differently in different 'guises', it has to be the difference in language that accounts for it. Since the same person has provided both samples, it cannot be voice quality differences that the listeners are reacting to. Content is eliminated as a variable by having translated versions of the same passage read in each language.

It turns out, of course, that there are several degrees of directness and indirectness in language-attitude research, with various aspects of the experiment being concealed from the subjects. The matched-guise technique is direct in the sense that the listeners are explicitly asked to give their opinions of the speaker's characteristics. It is indirect in the sense that listeners are asked to react to *speakers*, not languages, and they are not aware that they are hearing the same person in each guise.

Semantic differential scales

The format for listener responses that is very often used with the matched-guise technique involves semantic differential scales (Osgood, Suci, and Tannenbaum 1957). These scales designate opposite extremes of a trait at either end and leave a number of blank spaces between them. A typical semantic differential scale item appears in figure 6.1. If the speaker on tape sounds extremely unfriendly, the listener would place a mark on the line closest to the word 'unfriendly'. If he sounds extremely friendly, the mark goes at the other end of the scale. If the speaker seems just average in friendliness, the middle space should be used, and so on. Similar scales are constructed for other characteristics. In this way, each listener has the opportunity to indicate just where on a scale of a particular trait a speaker falls.

friendly _____ _____ _____ _____ _____ _____ unfriendly

Figure 6.1   Typical seven-point semantic differential scale

The following procedure is used in scoring semantic-differential scales. After the responses have been collected, numbers are assigned to each of the spaces in the scale. In a seven-point scale such as the one in figure 6.1, a 7 might be assigned to the space nearest to the word 'friendly', a 6 to the next space, and so on. As the responses are tabulated, a tick mark is made on the blank at each space on the scale for each listener who placed his evaluation of that speaker at that space. For example, suppose a speaker in a particular guise is judged 7 for 'intelligence' by five listeners, 6 by thirteen, 5 by twenty, 4 by eleven, 3 by two, and 2 by one. The initial tabulation would look like figure 6.2.

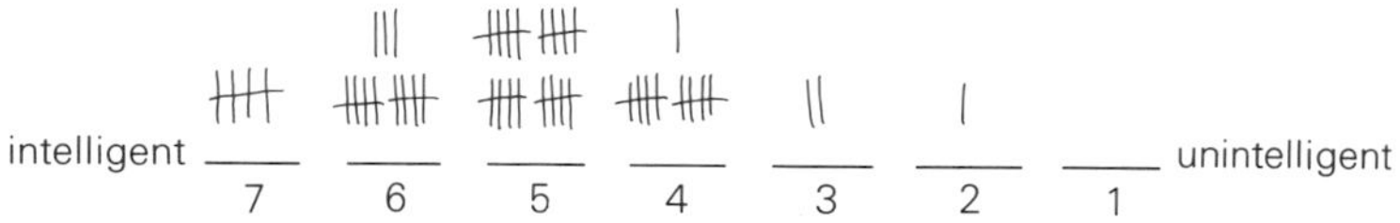

intelligent _____ _____ _____ _____ _____ _____ _____ unintelligent
              7   6   5   4   3   2   1

Figure 6.2   Hypothetical initial tabulation for
semantic differential scale for intelligence

Next the number of marks at each space is multiplied by the value for that space. The results are then totalled. In our example, the calculation would be:

$$(7 \times 5) + (13 \times 6) + (20 \times 5) + (11 \times 4) + (2 \times 3) + (1 \times 2)$$
$$= 35 + 78 + 100 + 44 + 6 + 2 = 265.$$

This value is divided by the total number of listeners (the same as the total number of tick marks in figure 6.2); in this case, 52. The result is 5.10, the value that would be reported and subjected to statistical analysis. This number is the mean evaluation for this speaker on the intelligence scale. It is to be interpreted as indicating that, on the average, this speaker in this guise is judged to be intelligent to the degree of a bit more than 5 on a seven-point scale.[2]

Other methods

Although matched-guise-cum-semantic-differential research is something of a standard in language-attitude research, other direct methods are possible. Agheyisi and Fishman (1970:147–50) mention three other techniques: questionnaires, interviews, and observation.

Questionnaires. These can have one of two types of questions: *open* or *closed*. Open questions give the respondent maximum freedom to present her views, but also allow her to stray from the subject and are very difficult to score. In an open-question questionnaire, respondents may be asked: 'Describe your reactions to this speaker' after they have heard a taped sample. In a closed-question, the respondent is given a particular format to use in recording responses. Apart from the semantic differential, other closed-question formats involve yes–no answers, multiple choice, or ranking schemes. Closed questions are much easier for respondents to deal with and are easy to score, but they force respondents to answer in the researcher's terms instead of their own. Perhaps the ideal compromise is to conduct pilot research with open questions and use these results to construct a closed-question questionnaire. We will see later how such a procedure was masterfully executed by Frederick Williams.

Interviews. Interviews are like open-question questionnaires without the questionnaire. A fieldworker personally asks attitude questions and records the responses in written (or tape-recorded) form as the subject responds orally. The burden of recording open questions is removed from the subject, making it easier to elicit open responses, and the interviewer can guide the conversation if the subject tends to stray from the point. The major disadvantage in interviewing is that it is extremely time-consuming and expensive. It takes a fieldworker longer to conduct one interview than to administer 50 or 100 questionnaires in a group session.

Observation. This is the least obtrusive method and the one designed to collect the most naturalistic data. A favored method for anthropological or ethnographic research, observation refers to the recording of people's activities by the researcher as he watches them. Since people rarely talk about their mental processes unless asked, observation would be most appropriate for a behaviorist view of attitudes. A mentalist who used the observation technique would have to *infer* what the attitudes were on the basis of the observed behavior. In other words, attitudes must either be assumed to be the same thing as overt behavior, or be inferred from observed behavior. Agheyisi and Fishman (1970:150) fault observation for its 'excessive subjectivity and privacy', but believe that 'such data can be subjected to the same rigorous standards of scoring, counting and rating as data collected through more formal methods'.

Matched-guise: problems and modifications

In spite of the successful use of the matched-guise technique in many language-attitude experiments, there are a number of problems inherent in it. In order to control the content of the language samples, the purest application of the matched-guise technique requires that the same passage be read by each speaker in each language (in translated form). But this introduces one variable as it controls another; the speakers may be judged as performers of readings, and not on the basis of the language variety they are using. A modification that has been used in some research (for example, d'Anglejan and Tucker 1973; El-Dash and Tucker 1975; Wölck 1973; Shuy, Baratz, and Wolfram 1969) is to have speakers discussing the same general topic, but not saying precisely the same thing. Speakers are then clearly just talking, not reading, but some control over the subject matter is still retained. Topics chosen in this modification should be of a non-controversial nature so that it does not intrude into the evaluations. For example, d'Anglejan and Tucker (1973) had speakers talk about an exceptionally severe blizzard, and El-Dash and Tucker (1975) use the Giza pyramids as the topic in their language-attitude research in Egypt.

The attempt to control content can lead to a related difficulty: the possible incongruity between language variety and topic. If the two 'guises' happen to be the High and Low forms in a diglossic community, it is easy to see that a topic that is appropriate in one variety might be completely wrong for the other. Respondents might then give low evaluations to one guise, not because they have a negative opinion of the language form itself, but because they think that language form should not be used to discuss that particular topic. Agheyisi and Fishman (1970:146–7) report on a study by Kimple (1968) in which he used a 'mirror-image' technique to deal with this problem. Briefly, the research involved reactions to recorded conversations among bilingual individuals. In one recording, one language was used in some role relationships and the second language in others. In the other recording, the mirror image of the first was used; the languages and the roles they were used in were switched. Different sets of judges were asked to listen to the two conversations, then to answer an attitude questionnaire based on them. The results showed that the impressions speakers gave did not depend just on what language they were speaking, but also on whether they were using the right language in the right situation.

Another difficulty with attitude studies using questionnaire formats, including the matched-guise and semantic-differential method, is the question of *validity* (Agheyisi and Fishman 1970:150). A measure is valid, as we know, only if it measures what it is supposed to measure. Demonstrating validity in the case of cognitive and affective attitudes is nearly impossible. One would have to compare the results of the attitude experiment data with what people are *really* thinking and feeling, as discovered in some independent way. The problem is easier to solve in the case of conative attitudes, the ones that are concerned with behavior. If an attitude questionnaire shows that people have a predisposition to behave in a certain way, then all that must be done is to place them in a situation where that particular behavior is a possibility and see what they do. Fishman has used a technique he calls a *commitment measure* to test validity (Fishman 1968d; Cooper and Fishman 1974:15). In his 1968 research, Fishman not only asked questions involving the attitudes of Puerto Ricans in the New York City area about their ethnicity, but also invited them to an evening of Puerto Rican dances and other cultural activity. It was then possible to compare the responses to the questionnaires with whether or not a respondent answered the invitation, said she would attend, and actually did. If a person answered the questionnaire in a way that indicated pride in being Puerto Rican and then attended the evening's activities, her attendance would be an indication that her answers to the questionnaire were valid.

A simpler design is reported by Giles and Bourhis (1976). In their experiment, two psychologists were introduced to a class of high-school students. One of them told the students that there was concern about erroneous ideas people had about psychology. Using one of two accent guises, he asked them to write down what they thought psychology was about so that steps could be taken to correct any misconceptions that might be discovered. After they had begun writing, this psychologist left and did not return. The other member of the team told the students that there was a plan being considered to have someone address students in high schools about psychology as a way of combating misconceptions. Furthermore, she told them, her colleague who had just left was being considered for the job. When they had finished the open question, they were given a rating-scale questionnaire consisting of closed questions. The same procedure was repeated with another matched group of students, but this time the first psychologist used another accent guise. Of course, the primary interest was in language attitudes to the two guises, not in the students' concepts about psychology. A simple behavioral index was built into the experiment: the *amount* the students wrote in answer to the open questions about the field of psychology and about the experimenter's qualifications to lecture students could be compared in each of the two guises. It turned out that the students wrote more when they were addressed in one guise than when they were addressed in the other, and this result reinforced what had been found in earlier, more traditional matched-guise research. Furthermore, the amount written in response to the two guises was consistent with the attitudes reported on the closed-question rating scales. Giles and Bourhis's experiment tends to indicate that conative attitudes revealed by the matched-guise technique can be valid. Nevertheless, Agheyisi and Fishman (1970:150) refer to 'the familiar problem of the low degree of consistency between attitude measures and overt behavior', an issue that has been addressed by social psychologists for some time (for example, Linn 1965; Fishbein 1965). It remains to be determined just what sort of attitude measuring instruments are likely to be valid.

A final difficulty with the ordinary matched-guise technique is connected with its artificiality (Giles and Bourhis 1976; Bourhis and Giles 1976). Asking listeners to judge people by their voices only, though it does provide maximum control over other variables, is a bit far removed from real-life contexts. Since the pure matched-guise procedure requires that every taped sample has the same content, it could easily be the case that listeners, after becoming bored with the repetition, might begin to pay more than normal attention to vocal variations. Finally, judges in a matched-guise experiment are provided with an *evaluative set*. They are given a rating sheet and told to make judgements about the people they are going to hear. As a result, they are set up to make evaluative judgements in a way that doesn't happen in ordinary interactive settings. The experiment about the two psychologists and the high-school students was designed to overcome these objections to some extent. The speaker was present at the time of the experiment, rather than being a disembodied voice on a tape-recording. There was no repeated content and an evaluative set did not intrude until after the subjects had had the chance to write what they wanted to say about psychology.

Bourhis and Giles (1976) devised an even more ingenious and naturalistic matched-guise experiment, in which the subjects had no idea that they had participated in language attitude research. The guises involved in this experiment were four language varieties relevant to the sociolinguistic situation in Wales. These were: (1) the highest-status pronunciation pattern for British English, called RP ('received pronunciation'); (2) English with a mild South Welsh accent; (3) English with a broad South Welsh accent; and (4) standard Welsh. The 'subjects' were theatergoers, and the experiment took the form of a public-address announcement made during the intermission at a performance. As you have probably guessed, there were four forms of the message, one for each guise. The content was a request for patrons to obtain a questionnaire form in the foyer to fill out in order to help the theater plan future programs. Two kinds of audience 'participated' in the experiment. An Anglo-Welsh audience consisted of those people who attended the theater during five evenings on which two films in English were presented. It was assumed that most of these audiences were Welsh people who spoke only English. The bilingual Welsh audience were those who attended during four evenings when a play in Welsh was presented. The Anglo-Welsh audiences heard the announcement in the three kinds of English, with one variety presented on a given evening (the RP and broad-accent English versions were presented on two evenings each). The bilingual Welsh audiences heard all four guises, one per evening. The behavior that was measured was the number of questionnaires submitted by members of each of the two kinds of audiences when the request was made in the various language guises.

Since the data are nominal (questionnaires either submitted or not submitted), the chi square test was used in the analysis. Tables 6.1 and 6.2 and figure 6.3 show the results. The chi square test for the data in table 6.1 allows the rejection of the null hypothesis that questionnaire completers and non-completers are randomly distributed among the audiences who heard the three language guises. Strictly speaking, this allows the establishment only of the rather bland research hypothesis that there is something in the distribution that is not due to chance, but it is easy to see what that 'something' is. The Anglo-Welsh population is equally responsive to the message in RP and mildly Welsh-accented English, but far *less* responsive when the message is in broadly Welsh-accented English. The results for the bilingual Welsh audiences are quite different.

Table 6.1   Behavioral results to matched-guise experiment
for Anglo-Welsh audiences

Questionnaire completed	Guise		
	RP	*bEW*	*mEW*
Yes	118	53	66
	22.5%	8.25%	25.0%
No	406	599	198
	77.5%	91.8%	75.0%

$\chi2=60.9$; $p<0.001$
RP=received pronunciation
bEW=broadly Welsh-accented English
mEW=mildly Welsh-accented English
Source: data from Bourhis and Giles 1976:14

Table 6.2   Behavioral results to matched-guise experiment
for bilingual Welsh audiences

Questionnaire completed	Guise	
	mEW	*W*
Yes		
	9.2%	26.5%
No	109	48

$\chi^2= 8.20$; $p<0.005$
mEW=mildly Welsh-accented English
W=Welsh
Source: data from Bourhis and Giles (1976:15)

The data for the bilingual Welsh audience are presented in bar graph form in figure 6.3. It appears that the bilingual Welsh population is most responsive to requests in Welsh and least responsive to RP, with the two varieties of Welsh-accented English in the middle. Bourhis and Giles used chi-square to test the difference in distribution between Welsh and mildly Welsh-accented English, and the difference between RP and broadly Welsh-accented English (the difference between the two kinds of Welsh-accented English are clearly not significant). The difference in response between the message in RP and in Welsh-accented English was not significant.[3] The chi-square test of the difference between responses to mildly Welsh-accented English and Welsh is presented in table 6.2. The null hypothesis, that table 6.2 represents randomly distributed data, can be rejected. It is clear that significantly more members of a bilingual Welsh audience will complete the questionnaire when asked to do so in Welsh than when asked in English, even if it is Welsh-accented.

Apart from the results, the Bourhis and Giles experiment shows how the usual objections to matched-guise research based on artificiality can be overcome. Although no speaker was physically present, the context was a totally normal one; undoubtedly the subjects had no idea that their language attitudes had been investigated. No one audience had to listen to the same content more than once, and no evaluative set was introduced. The measure was of unmonitored behavior, and not of scaled evaluations of speakers. On the other hand, some control is lost by not having the same subjects respond to all the guises theater audiences heard the request in different guises). The same was true of the experiment with the high-school students. It is assumed that each set of subjects is the equivalent of every other set of its type, for the purposes of the attitudes being measured. That is, each evening's Anglo-Welsh audience, for example, is taken to have the same predilection to respond to the various language guises as any other evening's Anglo-Welsh audience. There seems to be no reason to doubt that this is a safe assumption, in the experiments I have described. But if artificiality is diminished at the cost

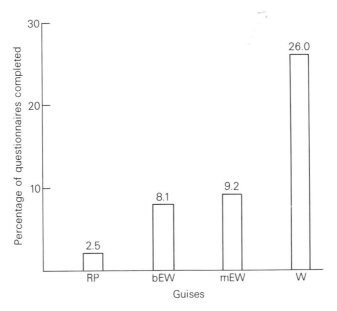

Figure 6.3 Bar graph of behavioral results to matched-guise experiment for bilingual Welsh audiences.
Source: adapted from Bourhis and Giles (1976:15, figure 2)

of using more than one sample of a population, the experimenter should be careful that all the samples are equivalent and representative. Otherwise, uncontrolled variables can unintentionally be introduced.

APPLICATIONS

Social structure

The study of language attitudes is instructive in its own right, but it is even more valuable as a tool in illuminating the social importance of language. In this section, we are going to examine language attitudes as one way of understanding how language is used as a symbol of group membership. We will also see how attitudes serve as a clue for identifying diglossic relationships.

Group identity.   In chapter 1, we saw that language served unifying and separatist functions for sociocultural groups. You might think that attitude studies would show that any language serving these two functions would be highly evaluated by its speakers. It turns out that this is a little too simple. Where a society has linguistic varieties in diglossic relationship, the usual attitude is that the High language is a purer and better language than the Low language. Of course, the unifying and separatist functions are most likely to be fulfilled by the *Low* language. If High language varieties are generally more highly valued than Low varieties, you might be led to exactly the opposite conclusion; a linguistic symbol of contrastive self-identification is likely to be *poorly* evaluated by its speakers.

Perhaps there are some kinds of questions that would elicit higher evaluations for Low varieties. If so, then they could be built into a matched-guise experiment. If the associated semantic differential scales included both affective and status items, it might be predicted that speakers using the High guise would be rated higher on the status scales, but the same speaker would be rated higher on the affective scales in the Low guise. A speaker using a higher-status guise might be rated higher in intelligence, say, or occupational status, but would get higher ratings for friendliness and trustworthiness in his in his lower-status linguistic guise. Researchers who have tested this hypothesis, however, have obtained unexpected results. For example, d'Anglejan and Tucker, conducting attitude research involving European French and two varieties of Canadian French in Quebec, found that the European French speaker was rated not only more intelligent and better educated, but more likeable than Canadian French speakers; the likeability result was unexpected (d'Anglejan and Tucker 1973:22). Similarly, the results of attitude research with Mexican Americans conducted by Carranza and Ryan (1975:99) were that both Anglo and Mexican Americans rated English higher than Spanish on status scales, as expected, but also on solidarity scales, an unexpected outcome for the Mexican Americans. Attitudes of black Americans towards standard English and Vernacular Black English must be closely analyzed in order to discover indications of positive attitudes toward the vernacular (Hoover 1978). El-Dash and Tucker (1975:46) cite three studies, including their own, in which superposed language varieties were preferred over mother tongues, according to the results of attitude research.

On the other hand, attitude research proved a valuable tool in the analysis of Albanian as a possible language of group identity among a sociocultural group in Greece called the Arvanites (ar-van-ee-tess). Using a closed-question questionnaire rather than the matched-guise technique, Trudgill and Tzavaras (1977) were able to trace the declining status of Arvanitika (the Albanian dialect) as a language of group identity. The responses they obtained revealed a clear pattern according to age, as table 6.3 shows.

Table 6.3   Percentage responses to these questions, by age-group:
'Do you like to speak Arvanitika?', 'Do you think speaking
Arvanitika is a good thing to do?', 'Is it an
advantage to speak Arvanitika?'

	Yes			Indifferent			No		
Age	Like to speak?	Good thing?	Advan-tage?	Like to speak?	Good thing?	Advan-tage?	Like to speak?	Good thing?	Advan-tage?
5–9	1	1	1	10	10	17	89	89	82
10–14	16	17	12	17	73	38	67	10	50
15–24	17	18	34	41	48	50	42	35	16
25–34	30	32	40	67	66	49	3	3	11
35–49	46	64	56	53	35	36	2	1	8
50–59	67	95	67	31	4	33	1	1	0
60+	79	86	97	21	14	3	0	0	0

Source: data from Trudgill and Tzavaras (1977)

Table 6.4   Percentage answering 'Yes' and 'No' to the question:
'Is it necessary to speak Arvanitika to be an Arvanitis?', by age-group

Age	Yes	No
10–14	67	33
15–24	42	58
25–34	24	76
35–49	28	72
50–59	33	67
60+	17	83

Source: data from Trudgill and Tzavaras (1977)

The answers to the question 'Is necessary to speak Arvanitika to be an Arvanitis?' seem at first glance to be inconsistent with the general pattern of table 6.3. The answers to this question are tabulated in table 6.4. A majority in every age group thinks that it is *not* necessary to speak Arvanitika to be an Arvanitis, except the *youngest.* As Trudgill and Tzavaras (1977:180–181) explain this result, most members of the older age-groups realize that Arvanitika is dying out, but hope that their ethnic identity can be preserved none the less.[4] As a result, they are obliged to make room for Arvanites who don't speak Arvanitika. The youngest speakers, far from being more hopeful about the future of Arvanitika, seem to foresee the demise of both the language and the ethnic distinctiveness. Their attitude seems to be that it *is* necessary to speak Arvanitika to be an Arvanitis, there are fewer Arvanitika speakers than there once were and therefore fewer Arvanites, but this is no particular cause for concern. As Trudgill and Tzavaras (1977:181) put it:

They are prepared to concede that it is necessary to speak Arvanitika to be an Arvanitis because, although they are aware that Arvanitika is dying out, they do not regard the loss of the language or of the ethnic identity as undesirable. It seems, that is, that with younger people conflicts of this type are being resolved in favour of a Greek identity and the Greek language.

Trudgill and Tzavaras's direct open-question attitude questionnaire appears to give a more accurate picture of the function of a language as an indicator of group identity than more sophisticated matched-guise research does. It would be reckless to speculate about why this might be so, given the multitude of differences between the Greek study and the others. A few factors might be pointed out, however. First, the Trudgill and Tzavaras research was carried out by the oral-interview technique in which the interviewer was known to be an Arvanitis. Matched-guise research involves written responses on printed forms. Second, due to the fact that they are easiest to recruit, teachers and students usually end up being the subjects in matched-guise research. Teachers are responsible for transmitting the prevailing cultural values about language, and so might be more inclined than the general population to report 'official' attitudes. Students, working in a test-like situation, often in school buildings, might be inadvertently led by the setting to report the 'official' viewpoint. The Trudgill–Tzavaras research was not conducted in a school building. Although some of the younger respondents might have been students, they were not in their student roles when they were interviewed. Finally, the very nature of the matched-guise technique requires the comparison of two or more language varieties. Trudgill and Tzavaras's questionnaire did not ask for comparisons between Arvanitika and Greek, but only for attitudes about Arvanitika.

There is evidence that matched-guise research *can* give reliable clues about language as a marker of group identity, but that it has to be done in a somewhat subtle manner. To understand what is involved, it will be useful to introduce the notions *convergence* and *divergence*, terms used by the social psychologist, Howard Giles (for example, in Giles 1973; Giles and Bourhis 1976; Giles, Bourhis, and Taylor 1977). According to Giles's theory, which we will explore in the next chapter, an individual's linguistic behavior may either converge with or diverge from the speech of whoever he is talking with. In a sense, convergence is an expression of a feeling of unity between people engaged in conversation. Divergence is an expression of separation, or a withdrawal away from the person someone is talking to, and into one's own ingroup. Convergence is related to Garvin and Mathiot's (1956) unifying function, and divergence to their separatist function, but there are important differences. The functions of Garvin and Mathiot are more or less permanent, and should be seen as societal phenomena. Convergence and divergence are phenomena that exist only during conversations, and they are individual phenomena. For example, a Paraguayan may have strong feelings about the symbolic nationalist value of Guaraní as a force uniting him to his fellow citizens and separating him from other Latin Americans, yet may accommodate a citizen of a neighboring country by switching to Spanish in a given conversation.

One way in which it is possible to discover a person's sense of group identity through language is through the investigation of *long-range* convergence. If an individual adjusts his speech to match the linguistic patterns of a new group, so that those patterns become his normal means of linguistic expression, it indicates a profound orientation toward membership in that group. An example of this is in a study of West Indian immigrants to Britain (Giles and Bourhis MS; Bourhis and Giles 1977). In the earlier study, 24 white adolescents were asked to judge the tape-recorded speech of a group of 21-year-old working-class men. Among other things, the subjects were asked to determine the ethnicity of the speakers. The majority of the tape-recordings were of third-generation West Indian immigrants to Cardiff, Wales, where the adolescent subjects lived. Nevertheless, 80 per cent of these West Indian speakers were judged to be white by the listeners.

The second study used as speakers 32 male children of about 11 years of age, all but nine of them third-generation West Indian immigrants (the nine exceptions were white). Another group of white Cardiff secondary-school youngsters were asked to listen to and make judgements about these speakers. Bourhis and Giles avoided giving the subjects an 'ethnic set', by making ethnicity only one of several kinds of judgements they were asked to make. Subjects were asked to paraphrase the content of the speech sample, to judge the 'broadness' of the speaker's Cardiff accent, to rate speakers on a few semantic-differential scales, and to judge age, social class, and religion, as well as ethnicity. The reason for the paraphrase was to direct the listeners' attention to the content of the speech samples as well as the form, approximating the normal use of language a bit more closely. The results for ethnic identity were nearly identical to the results when the speakers were older; West Indian speakers were identified as white in 78 per cent of the judgements.[5] Two of them were judged as white by *all* of the judges, and all but five of them were judged to be white significantly more often than they would have been if the listeners were only guessing ($p<0.001$ for most speakers).[6] It seems clear that the West Indian immigrants in Cardiff are identifying with the local community, at least as far as language as a marker of ethnic identity is concerned. As Bourhis and Giles point out (1977:90), their demonstrated linguistic assimilation is the opposite of what happens in the United States. American blacks, especially those in the working or lower classes, use Black English as a symbol of sociocultural identification.[7]

In another study, the same two researchers, in collaboration with Wallace Lambert (Bourhis, Giles, and Lambert 1975), devised a more subtle experiment involving the notions of convergence and divergence. In this research, listeners heard examples of someone actually practicing convergence, divergence, or neither, and were then asked to rate that person on a typical set of seven-point semantic-differential scales. In addition, they were asked if they themselves would converge or diverge in the same situation.

The stimulus tape-recording took the following form. The listeners, a group of twelfth-grade high-school students (aged about 18 years) in a French-language school in Montreal, were told that they would hear recordings of two radio interviews with a French Canadian woman athlete who had placed seventh in a Pan-American diving competition. In one interview, a male sports commentator from France conducted the interview, and a female commentator from Quebec conducted the other. The interviews were fictitious; the 'athlete' was selected for her ability to control European French as well as both formal and informal Canadian French, and the interview texts were carefully constructed to control for content, duration, and grammar. The woman who took the role of the athlete always spoke formal Canadian French with the speaker playing the role of the commentator from Quebec. But when speaking to the 'commentator from France', she used one of three varieties. She either made no change and also used formal Canadian French with him, or she converged by changing to European French, or she diverged by using informal Canadian French.

Thus, a given group of subjects would have heard one of three pairs of interviews: (1) the athlete speaking formal Canadian French with the Canadian commentator and the same kind of French with the French commentator; (2) the athlete speaking formal Canadian French with the Canadian commentator and European French with the French commentator; or (3) the athlete speaking formal Canadian French with the Canadian commentator and informal Canadian French with the French commentator.[8] No one group of high-school students heard more than one of these pairs of interviews.[9]

An analysis of variance was used to test the significance of the semantic-differential ratings by students who heard one of the three pairs of interviews. The only two scales that were significantly different were the ones for intelligence and education. Table 6.5 shows the results, using a format typical of this sort of research. As we know, the significant F-values mean that the variation between groups of judges who heard interviews exemplifying different shift conditions was significantly greater than the variation within each group of judges. In particular, they mean the fact that the athlete was rated most intelligent and educated when she shifted to European French, less so when she did not shift, and least intelligent and educated when she shifted to informal Canadian French cannot be attributed to random marking of the different scales.

Table 6.5   F-values and mean ratings for two traits

Shift	Mean ratings	
	Intelligence	Education
To European French	5.14	5.26
None	4.64	4.95
To Informal Canadian French	4.35	3.75
F-values	3.89*	8.58†

*p<0.02
†p<0.0001
Source: adapted from Bourhis, Giles, and Lambert (1975:62, Table 1)

It is not surprising that the higher-status kinds of French would improve the speaker's rating on scales like intelligence and education. If Canadian French were a strongly-felt marker of ethnic identity, however, you might expect that the students would give the speaker higher ratings on some of the *affective* scales, if she used one of the Canadian French styles when she was being interviewed by the French interviewer. That is, we would not be surprised if the athlete were considered more trustworthy or likable when she refused to switch away from Canadian French, but instead either maintained the formal Canadian style she used in the first interview or switched to informal Canadian French. There was no such result; the ratings on the affective scales were not significantly different, regardless of the shift conditions.

As it turned out, some of the student listeners didn't hear the shifts as they were intended, although 65 per cent of them did. All the listeners were asked if they would have shifted as the speaker on the tape did, and the answers from those who *could* hear the shifts accurately were tabulated. Of those who heard the interviews involving the shift to European French and who recognized what had happened, 86 per cent said they would not have shifted that way themselves under the same circumstances. Of those listeners who said they wouldn't shift 90 per cent said they wouldn't shift because they would lose their Quebecois identity. Of those who heard the no-shift interviews accurately, 63 per cent said they would *not* have shifted to accommodate the French interviewer – that is, they would have behaved as the athlete on the tape had. It is important to remember that these are the same youngsters who rated the speaker as more educated and intelligent when she switched than when she did not.

Of those who heard and recognized a shift to informal Canadian French, 67 per cent said they would *not* make such a shift themselves. The majority opinion that emerged under direct questioning seems to be that one ought to emphasize one's Quebecois identity by resisting any inclination to shift to European French to accommodate a European speaker, but not to overdo it by diverging into informal style. More indirect evidence of this, in the form of higher ratings on affective scales for someone who actually behaved that way, did not show up. If it is true that matched-guise research (and this experiment is a sort of matched-guise procedure) taps more covert attitudes than direct questioning does, it could be that there is a lag between overt and covert attitudes. That is, on a more surface level, the growing independence movement in Quebec has led to an emphasis on language as a symbol of group identity, but the old ideas about European French as a 'better' dialect, persist at deeper levels.

The same research team conducted a similar experiment in Wales, with RP British English replacing European French, mildly Welsh-accented English corresponding to formal Canadian French, and broadly Welsh-accented English in the place of informal Canadian French. The subjects were pupils at a secondary school in South Wales. The same format, involving a supposed athlete and two sports commentators, one speaking RP and one speaking English with a mild Welsh accent, was used. As in Quebec, the speaker was rated significantly more intelligent when he shifted to RP during the interview with the RP-speaking interviewer. Unlike the results in the Quebec study, there were significant main effects on two of the affective scales. The speaker was judged more trustworthy and more kind-hearted when he maintained a mild Welsh accent when talking to the RP-speaking commentator than when he shifted to RP, and even higher on both scales when he shifted to a broad Welsh accent. It appears that Welsh-accented English is better-developed as a symbol of group identity in Wales than Canadian French is in Quebec, since the expected reactions in a matched-guise experiment show up to some degree.[10]

Attitude research sheds light on the status of language varieties as indicators of group identity, but not always in the most straightforward way. In particular, the classic matched-guise experiment, in which listeners are asked to judge speakers one by one on the basis of tape-recorded monologues, often does not lead to predicted results. On the other hand, the Trudgill and Tzavaras results and the direct-question part of the Bourhis, Giles and Lambert research in Quebec appear to give results that are easier to interpret, but may tap only surface reactions. More sophisticated applications of the matched-guise technique, such as the one used by Bourhis and his associates in Quebec and Wales, show promise of probing covert attitudes more accurately than the simpler applications do.[11]

Diglossia. In Ferguson's original description of diglossia, community attitudes toward the High and Low varieties were an important component. High varieties have greater prestige and Low varieties are often disparaged. Attitude-study results ought to fall into predictable patterns in communities where diglossia exists. It turns out that they do to a very considerable extent. As examples of this, we will look at two attitude studies conducted in societies with diglossia. One was carried out in Egypt (El-Dash and Tucker 1975) and involves Classical and Colloquial Arabic (one of the four example cases used by Ferguson). Although diglossia is not the focus of El-Dash and Tucker's work, their results reflect diglossia quite clearly. The second study involves Spanish and English in a Mexican American community (Carranza and Ryan 1975). Here we have an example of broad diglossia, since two distinct languages are involved. Unlike El-Dash and Tucker, Carranza and Ryan explicitly set out to find attitude patterns typical of diglossia.

El-Dash and Tucker employed a classic matched-guise model, with the content controlled by having speakers discuss the same topic (the Giza pyramids, an emotionally neutral subject) rather than having them read a standard passage. Two Egyptian speakers were selected who could speak both Classical and Colloquial Arabic, and English. Quite naturally, they had an Egyptian accent when they spoke English.[12] It was not easy to find speakers who could assume both Classical and Colloquial Arabic guises. The reasons that El-Dash and Tucker give for this won't surprise anyone who is familiar with diglossia:

The distinction between Classical and Colloquial Arabic is not completely clear, however, as various gradations exist between the Arabic of the *Koran* and the speech used by the man in the street to discuss daily affairs. Moreover, Classical Arabic ... is not a spoken language, but rather a written form used throughout the Arabic-speaking world. This form may be read orally, but is seldom spoken extemporaneously. It is reported that very few individuals can actually speak Classical Arabic fluently. (El-Dash and Tucker 1975:35)

The speakers they used were self-conscious about attempting to speak Classical Arabic spontaneously. The very task of tape-recording their speech had an effect on their Colloquial Arabic performance as well; they seemed to use a slightly 'elevated' style of the colloquial dialect (El-Dash and Tucker 1975:53). In spite of these problems, the research results give a clear picture of a sort of triglossia situation, with Egyptian English occupying a position between the Classical and Colloquial forms of Arabic. Listeners were asked to evaluate the speakers in all the language guises on four semantic-differential scales, for intelligence, leadership, religiousness, and likability.[13] The results were subjected to analysis of variance. A significant main effect for language variety was found for all four traits.

Unfortunately, the discovery of a language main effect is not very helpful. To see why this is so, consider table 6.6, a slightly simplified reproduction of one line of El-Dash and Tucker's (1975:42) table 2. The significant *F*-ratio simply tells us that somewhere among the six language guises, speakers of some guises are judged significantly more intelligent than speakers in other guises. It does not tell us in *which* guises the differences are significant. Fortunately, there is another statistical test, called the Newman–Keuls multiple-comparison test, which is designed to identify the source of variation in cases such as this. El-Dash and Tucker applied this test and the results are summarized in table 6.7.

An examination of table 6.7 shows that speakers of Classical Arabic and Egyptian English are rated as more intelligent and as having greater leadership ability than speakers of Colloquial Arabic. This is consistent with the diglossia pattern; the average person in the society would think that High-dialect speakers have these traits to a greater degree than Low-dialect speakers. Although Classical Arabic received higher ratings on both traits than Egyptian English did, the difference was not significant in either case. For religiousness, since religious use is generally a High-variety function, speakers of Classical Arabic are rated significantly higher than speakers of each of the other two guises. However, the fact that English is not indigenous to Arab culture is important here. Although English *in general* shows up as a Higher language, this is not relevant where religion is concerned. Colloquial Arabic speakers are judged slightly higher for religiousness than Egyptian English speakers are, but not significantly so.[14] The one affective scale, 'likeability', fails to show an advantage for the Low language, Colloquial Arabic. On the contrary, the judges found speakers of Classical Arabic significantly more likeable than speakers of either of the other two varieties. The expectation that the 'homier' language might rate higher on an affective scale is again not fulfilled.

Table 6.6   Mean ratings for intelligence, according to guise

Trait	Classical Arabic	Colloquial Arabic	Egyptian English	American English	British English	F-ratio	Significance
Intelligence	10.25	8.49	9.59	9.13	8.45	20.33	$p < 0.01$

Source: data from El-Dash and Tucker (1975:42, table 2)

El-Dash and Tucker also asked a number of questions about the suitability of the different language varieties for use in several situations. The answers were given in a semantic-differential scale format, ranging from high to low suitability. The possible scores ranged, as in the matched-guise part of the experiment, from 2 to 12. The subjects were asked to judge the suitability of each guise, as they heard it, for use: (1) at home; (2) at school; (3) at work; (4) on radio and television; and (5) for formal and religious speeches. There were no significant differences among the three guises for the 'at work' situation, but the other four situations gave exactly the results you would predict from a knowledge of diglossia. The results for these four situations are given in table 6.8, using the same format as in table 6.7.

*Table 6.7   Comparison of the mean evaluations of four traits
for speakers in three guises*

Trait	Classical Arabic		Egyptian English		Colloquial Arabic
Intelligence	10.25		*		8.49
	10.25		9.59	†	8.49
Leadership	8.74		*		7.20
	8.74		8.56	*	7.20
Religiousness	9.38		*		7.75
	9.38	*	7.11		7.75
Likeability	9.48		*		8.51
	9.48	*	8.71		8.51

* indicates that the differences between the scores is significant at $p<0.01$.
† indicates that the difference between the scores is significant at $p<0.05$.
Where there is no symbol midway between the guises (for example, for intelligence, between Classical Arabic and Egyptian English), the difference between the scores is not significant.
Source: data from El-Dash and Tucker (1975)

*Table 6.8   Comparison of the mean evaluations of three
guises for suitability in four situations*

Situation	Classical Arabic		Egyptian English		Colloquial Arabic
At home	6.36		*		8.70
	6.36	†	6.69	*	8.70
At school	9.11		*		8.19
	9.11	*	8.16		8.19
On radio and television	9.79		*		7.78
	9.79	*	8.84	*	7.78
Formal speeches	9.13		*		5.39
	9.13	*	6.60	*	5.39

* indicates that the difference between the scores is significant at $p<0.001$.
† indicates that the difference between the scores is significant at $p<0.05$.
Where there is no symbol midway between the guises (for example, at school, between Egyptian English and Colloquial Arabic), the difference between the scores is not significant.
Source: data from El-Dash and Tucker (1975)

Colloquial Arabic is by far the most suitable variety for use at home, and Classical Arabic is least suitable, ranking significantly lower (at $p<0.05$) than Egyptian English. At school, on the other hand, Classical Arabic is the most suitable variety, with no difference between Egyptian English and Colloquial Arabic. For use on radio and television and in formal speeches, there is a three-way distinction. Classical Arabic is significantly more suitable than either of the other two, and Egyptian English is significantly more suitable than Colloquial Arabic.

The two parts of El-Dash and Tucker's research design combine to paint a rather clear picture of diglossia being reflected in community language attitudes. Speakers of Classical Arabic and Egyptian English are seen as having greater leadership ability and higher intelligence than speakers of Colloquial Arabic, and their way of speaking is perceived as most suitable for use on radio and television and in formal and religious speeches. Classical Arabic is significantly more suitable for use in the same two situations than Egyptian English is, but there is no significant difference between the two for intelligence and leadership ability. Classical Arabic speakers are judged more religious than speakers of either of the other two language varieties and it is considered more suitable for use at school. For use at home, Colloquial Arabic is by far the most suitable, and Classical Arabic is judged the least suitable.

The only result that doesn't seem to come out the way we might expect is the judgements on likeability. Speakers of the High dialect, Classical Arabic, were judged most likeable, whereas we might have expected speakers of Colloquial Arabic to get this evaluation. But El-Dash and Tucker's study is not unusual in this respect; the superiority of prestige languages on affective scales is a fairly common result in attitude studies.

The study of attitudes about Spanish and English in a Mexican American community in Chicago (Carranza and Ryan 1975) was designed explicitly with diglossia in mind. Two specially developed sets of semantic-differential scales were used: a *status-stressing* set and a *solidarity-stressing* set. The design included the mirror-image feature in the stimulus tapes. (Recall that a mirror-image design means that each linguistic guise in the experiment will appear in each of two or more situations.) Carranza and Ryan's application involved four paragraphs: (1) a narrative about a mother preparing breakfast in the kitchen in Spanish; (2) a paragraph on the same topic matched for style in English; (3) a paragraph about a teacher giving a history lesson in school in English; and (4) a matched paragraph in Spanish. This gave four passages: English–Home, Spanish–Home, English–School and Spanish–School. The status-stressing scales were scales for education, intelligence, successfulness, and wealth. The four solidarity-stressing scales were for friendliness, goodness, kindness, and trustworthiness. The stimulus tape contained four readings of each of the four passages by a different freshman student at the University of Notre Dame. Each reader was a native speaker of the language she was reading. As a result, the tape contained sixteen readings by sixteen different speakers.[15]

The subjects were anglo and Mexican American high-school students at a

Catholic high school in Chicago. The Mexican American students were native speakers of Spanish and studied and used English in school. The anglo students were native speakers of English, but had studied Spanish in high school.[16] The Mexican American students, of course, were the only ones who were members of the diglossic English–Spanish community; the anglo subjects were a sort of control group. Carranza and Ryan began the research with the following four hypotheses (Carranza and Ryan 1975:89).

1 Mexican American ratings will be higher for Spanish in the home domain, but higher for English in the school domain.
2 Anglo ratings will be more favorable for English than Spanish in both domains.
3 Mexican American ratings will be higher for Spanish on the solidarity scales but higher for English on status scales.
4 Anglo ratings will not differ for the two scale types.

The results were analyzed by a four-factor analysis of variance: group (anglo or Mexican American) x scale type (status scales or solidarity scales) x context (home or school) x language (English or Spanish). There were no group effects at all, either as main effects or interactions, which simply means that the anglos were marking their scales no differently, as a group, than the Mexican Americans were. This is a surprising result, but might possibly be explained if we assume that the anglo speakers were taking the point of view of Spanish speakers. This is plausible, if several facts are considered.

First, the research was carried out in mixed classes, with anglo and Mexican American students listening to the tapes and marking the scales at the same time. Second, the anglo students were all students of Spanish and were learning something about the language and culture of Spanish speakers. Perhaps most important, most of the anglos no doubt realized that the comparison of Spanish and English in context was not relevant to them. There could be no question of Spanish being appropriate in *their* homes. The only way to make sense of the procedure would be to adopt the perspective of their Mexican American classmates, which they seem to have done very successfully.

On the other hand, there *were* other significant effects. There was a significant main effect for language ($F = 9.10$, $p<0.01$), with English having a mean rating on all scales of 4.77 and Spanish of 4.62 (on seven-point scales, with favorable adjectives assigned the value 7). Overall, then, both the Mexican Americans and the anglos, possibly taking the Mexican American perspective, evaluated English more highly than Spanish, a typical result for High languages in diglossia. Much more interesting were two of the significant interaction effects, for context by language ($F = 14.46$, $p<0.001$) and scale type by language ($F = 6.80$, $p<0.05$). This means, for the context by language interaction, that English and Spanish were rated significantly differently, depending on whether they were heard in the home context or in the school context. Similarly, the ratings for the two languages were significantly different, depending on whether a solidarity or a status scale was being marked.

The mean ratings showing these interactions are displayed in table 6.9. By context, we can see that Spanish is rated higher than English, on the average, in the home context, and English is higher in the school context. This is precisely the sort of result one would expect in a diglossic community. As Carranza and Ryan (1975:99) point out: 'The results confirm the significance of the manipulation of the context. If context were to be ignored, the results would have indicated only an overall preference for English.' The results for scale type are not quite so clear, in the sense that English is rated higher on both scales. The difference on the solidarity scales, however, is very small; it is more substantial on the status scales. The fact that there is a significant interaction means that this pattern is meaningful. In other words, on balance, the subjects seem to recognize the distinction between the two languages with respect to the concepts of status and solidarity. The distinction is in the direction that would be predicted from an understanding of diglossia.

Table 6.9   Mean ratings for Spanish and English by context and by scale type

	Context		Scale type	
	Home	*School*	*Solidarity*	*Status*
English	4.60	4.94	4.82	4.72
Spanish	4.73	4.51	4.77	4.47
Difference	−0.13	0.43	0.05	0.25

A negative difference indicates that the difference is in favor of Spanish.
Source: data from Carranza and Ryan (1975)

The results in Egypt and in a Mexican American community in the United States indicate that diglossia is transparent to confirmation by matched-guise language-attitude research.

Education

Perhaps the most useful application for language-attitude research beyond the understanding of social structure is in education. Attitude studies conducted in education have been of two types: (1) language attitudes of teachers; and (2) language attitudes of second-language learners. The second type of study is usually set up to find out if learners' attitudes toward the language they are learning affect their progress. We will not take up this kind of research here, but some references are given in the bibliographical notes to this chapter. In volume II, the importance of teacher attitudes in general education is discussed. Here, we will examine how the attitudes of teachers are measured and what sort of results emerge.

Of all the social psychologists, educators, and psycholinguists who have done research on language attitudes in education, none has done better work than Frederick Williams.[17] Based on a number of research projects conducted in the mid-1970s (Williams, Whitehead, and Miller 1971, 1972; Williams 1973; Shuy and Williams 1973; Williams 1974; Williams and associates 1976), Williams's painstaking research design and statistical procedures have been rewarded with particularly clear and replicable results. It is worth our while to review his methods and results in some detail.

Williams's research design. Williams's fundamental method is to have subjects evaluate recorded speech samples (audiotaped and videotaped) according to the familiar semantic-differential scale format. His stimulus recordings do not use the matched-guise technique, except in the very loosest sense. There is no attempt to have the same speaker speak in more than one guise, but there are samples of different children of the same age, who are matched for ethnicity and social status – the two independent variables Williams is most interested in. The recordings involve relatively free conversation, and there is no attempt to control content. Although some researchers would find the lack of control distressing, the kind of recordings Williams uses avoid the repetition and lack of spontaneity that sometimes plague more tightly controlled research.

In Williams's research, very special care went into the development of the semantic differential scales themselves. Whereas many attitude research designs simply use scale-defining adjectives that seem reasonable to the researcher, Williams (1974:23) went through a four-step procedure leading up to the main research effort. First, a pilot study was conducted in which a small group of teachers listened to speech samples and evaluated speakers in an open question format in which they were asked to describe the speakers in their own terms. Second, a variety of adjectives was taken from these open-question responses and put into a set of prototype scales. This procedure gave some assurance that the scale-defining adjectives were appropriate to teachers, since teachers had spontaneously used them in describing how children talk. Third, these prototype scales were used by another group of respondents to evaluate language samples. Fourth, a statistical technique called *factor analysis* was used to find out whether the various scales revealed more basic response dimensions.

The last step requires some explanation of factor analysis. Factor analysis is a complex procedure, so I won't try to explain exactly how it works. Instead, we will just look at the kind of results it gives. The basic idea is this: sometimes two scales measure much the same thing. Imagine a semantic-differential questionnaire with the following two scales:

The speaker is:

1 intelligent ——— —— —— —— —— —— —— unintelligent
2   bright ——— —— —— —— —— —— —— dull

Probably the same speakers who rank high on the 'intelligence' scale would also rank high on the 'brightness' scale, and vice versa. That is, you would expect that a speaker who seemed to be a 6 on the intelligence scale would also be a 6 on the brightness scale, or in any case a 7 or a 5. Factor analysis is a procedure that tells the researcher to what extent an expectation like this is correct. If a questionnaire were used that contained the two scales above, and our guess is correct, the two items would receive a high 'loading' in factor analysis. (For our purposes, 'loading' simply refers to a relatively large number.)

The example we used is deliberately artificial to make the point clear. Probably no one would use too such closely-related adjectives, unless the researcher wanted to use each to check the *validity* of the other.[18] Further-more, factor analysis can reveal relatedness among a set of *several* items, not just two. For example, in Williams's research, the following set of scales formed a 'cluster', according to the results of factor analysis: unsure-confident, active–passive, hesitant–eager, like–dislike talking. In other words, teachers had pretty much the same quality in mind when they marked any one of these scales.

The cluster of scales I have just listed was one of only two that Williams discovered. Labelled *confidence–eagerness*, these scales measured teachers' global attitudes based on a child's fluency and enthusiasm. The second cluster was called *ethnicity–nonstandardness*. These scales seemed to tap the teachers' attitudes toward speech features associated with lower versus higher social status and white versus non-white ethnicities. Scales associated with these dimensions were then established as the appropriate ones to use.

Two dimensions may seem to be very few for capturing the entire array of teacher attitudes; how confident can we be that they are adequate? Williams (1974:24) points out a number of indications that the two dimensions are both valid and reliable. Validity is indicated in two ways. First, features found in the actual speech samples could be used to 'predict' the results on the two kinds of scales, in a statistical sense. Using a procedure known as linear regression analysis, Williams discovered that the frequency of various nonstandard grammatical and phonological features – such as a *d* sound for voiced *th* or clause fragments – could predict ratings on the ethnicity-nonstandardness scales to a large degree. In other words, a child who used a lot of pronunciations like *dem* and *dose* and a lot of clause fragments would be likely to get high scores for being 'ethnic' (in the context of Williams's research this meant black or Mexican American) and 'nonstandard'. Similarly, the frequency of 'hesitation phenomena' like *uh* and *uhm* was successful in predicting the results on the confidence–eagerness scale. The second reason for accepting the validity of the two-dimensional model is best explained by Williams himself (1974:24): 'The two factor model was found in almost exactly the same interpretable dimensions in separate Chicago and Texas studies, where scale development in both began with selection of adjectives from teachers' discussions.' In other words, two pilot studies in separate communities, involving teachers who did not know each other, gave the same two-factor result. Reliability was established in a technical statistical sense by the calculation of 'reliability coefficients' (Williams 1974:24). In addition, one indication of reliability emerged from those experiments that involved repeated evaluations of the same speech samples by the same teachers. Even when the ratings were done almost three weeks apart, the results were essentially identical.

In a less technical sense, the two dimensions have considerable plausibility when we try to discover what they mean in real life. It appears that the teachers are responding to the *form* in which the children express themselves (ethnicity-nonstandardness), and the *manner* in which they deliver their talk (confidence-eagerness). Furthermore, the youngsters received high and low ratings on the scales in an easily interpretable pattern, as figure 6.4 shows. Notice that higher-status children, for example, tend to be rated non-ethnic and standard (and also confident and eager), whereas lower-status children received the opposite ratings. As far as ethnicity goes, there is relatively little difference on either scale between black and white middle-status children, although the white youngsters are rated a little less confident and eager and a little more non-ethnic and standard than the black youngsters. The lower-status black children are rated very much more ethnic and nonstandard than white lower-status children, and also somewhat less confident and eager.

Williams's results. Perhaps the major result of the research carried out by Williams and his colleagues is the discovery of the two-factor model that reliably and validly captures at least two major dimensions of teacher attitudes. Beyond this, there were other fascinating results. For example, when the ratings of white versus black children by white teachers and black teachers were compared, it was discovered that black teachers rated black children substantially more *non*-ethnic and *standard* than white teachers did (Williams 1973:122-3). In the ratings of white children, both black and white teachers evaluated high-status white children about the same for ethnicity-nonstandardness, but black teachers found low-status white children more *ethnic* and *non*standard than white teachers did. In other words, where there were differences between the two groups, teachers tended to rate children of their own ethnicities more non-ethnic and standard than teachers of the other ethnicity did. The ratings on the confidence–eagerness dimension between black and white teachers were very similar.

Another key result found by Williams was the role of *stereotypes* in the evaluation of speech (Williams 1973:117–23). Williams found it easy to elicit

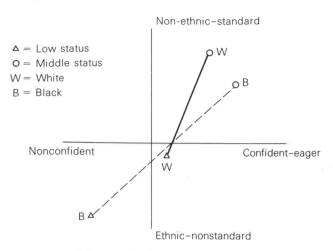

Figure 6.4   Graphic display of the two-factor model
Source: adapted from Williams (1974:25, figure 1)

evaluations of speech, using the same semantic-differential scales, when *no* speech samples were presented, but subjects were simply presented with ethnic labels. For example, a teacher would be told to rate the speech qualities of an 'anglo', 'black' or 'Mexican American' child, based on her experiences – real or anticipated – with such children. Stereotypes elicited in this way were differentiated by the ethnicity of the child. The stereotype for anglo children is that they are far more confident and eager and non-ethnic and standard than children from either of the other two groups. Black and Mexican American children were rated close to each other toward the ethnic–nonstandard end of the ethnicity–nonstandardness scale. They were distinguished on the confidence–eagerness scale, however, with black children stereotypically rated substantially more confident and eager than Mexican American children (but still not as confident and eager as anglo children). Not only was it possible to elicit stereotypes, but there was evidence that the results were highly reliable (Williams 1973:118–20).

An interesting question occurred to the researchers: what role did stereotypical attitudes play in teachers' evaluations of real speech samples? Would a child be evaluated largely on the basis of the stereotype, regardless of what she sounded like? Or did stereotypes come into play only when no speech samples were presented? Would teachers respond only to the characteristics of the speech sample, regardless of the ethnicity of the child who was talking? Or was there perhaps some sort of interplay between stereotype and speech-sample characteristics? Williams and his associates developed an ingenious method for answering this question (Williams, Whitehead, and Miller 1971; Williams 1973). Special videotapes were carefully prepared, involving the visual image of children of all three ethnicities talking. In each instance, the children were filmed from a side view so that their lips could not be read. This was important, because the *same* audio track was dubbed onto *all* of the videotapes. Furthermore, this audio track contained a *standard* English passage. The result was that the subjects (this time white student teachers) viewed black, anglo, and Mexican American children, all seeming to speak standard English.[19] Figure 6.5 displays the results.

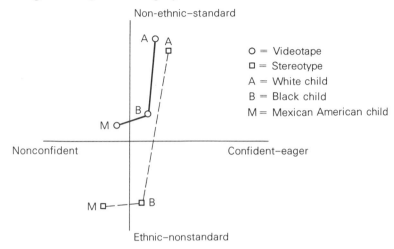

Figure 6.5   *Ratings of the same standard English audio samples with anglo,*
black, and Mexican American video images
Source: from Williams (1973:126, figure 7)

Notice first that the stereotype and videotape ratings for the anglo child are very close. The evaluations of the black and Mexican American children are in markedly different positions, in spite of the fact that the actual speech is the same as was heard with the anglo child's videotape. If speech characteristics were the only thing the subjects were responding to, all three circles should be in the same place, that is, where the circle for the anglo child is. On the other hand, if the stereotypes alone were relevant, then the circles for the black and Mexican American children ought to be as close to their stereotype ratings as the anglo child's videotape rating is to his stereotype rating. What appears to be happening is that the stereotypes are a sort of 'anchor point', used by the evaluators when evaluating a speech sample. This anchor point keeps the actual speech sample, no matter how standard it in fact is, from being evaluated too far from the stereotype. Nevertheless, the speech characteristics *are* taken into account, with the evaluations of the black and Mexican American children's standard English moving away from the stereotype 'anchors' toward the non-ethnic–standard end of the ethnicity-nonstandardness scale. Since the anglo child spoke the way the subjects expected, the videotape and stereotype ratings are almost identical. Although Williams (1973:126) cautions that these results are not necessarily definitive, because the experiment involved a relatively small group of subjects and a limited number of stimuli, if they prove to be representative, the significance could be important. It appears that expectations might lead teachers to hear a non-white child as sounding somewhat ethnic and nonstandard, regardless of how standard her speech actually is.[20]

Williams and his colleagues have not taken the next step yet and attempted to show that the attitudes which their research reveals actually influence how teachers act toward students. Other researchers, however, have made attempts to investigate this problem, Seligman, Tucker, and Lambert (1972) found that 'voice' was just as significant as composition-writing and picture-drawing as a basis for judging a schoolboy intelligent, a good student and self-confident. Frender and Lambert (1973) found some evidence that speech characteristics had an influence on the grades students got in school. There were problems in both experiments, however, and it cannot be said that we can prove that the language attitudes of teachers have an effect on teacher behavior, although it seems reasonable to expect that they do.

SUMMARY

There are two major views of the nature of attitudes. According to the mentalist view, an attitude is an intervening variable between a stimulus and a response; behaviorists consider attitudes to be a behavioral response in themselves. Most of the research on language attitudes takes the mentalist point of view. There is a variety of experimental methods for studying language attitudes, some rather direct, others more indirect. One technique that has become almost a standard in the field is the matched-guise procedure coupled with a semantic-differential response format; this method appears in a large number of research projects with various modifications. We have seen how attitude research has illuminated the study of social structure, including language as a marker of ethnicity and diglossia, and the role of language in contributing to teachers' attitudes toward students. There are numerous applications of language-attitude research, including the role of attitudes in second-language acquisition, language attitudes in the practice of law and medicine, the study of attitudes toward foreign accents, and the study of attitudes toward speech involving acoustic measurements. References to work in these areas are found in the bibliographical notes to this chapter.

BIBLIOGRAPHICAL NOTES

The book by Ryan and Giles (1982) is a comprehensive overview of language attitudes with numerous case studies taken from North America. Besides the works cited in this chapter, other studies of language attitudes related to ethnic identity include Cohen (1974, Lambert, Giles, and Picard (1975), Lewis (1975), James (1976) and Ryan and Carranza (1977). Studies of language attitudes as they relate to second-language learning include Lambert et al. (1968), Gould (1977), Gardner (1979), and Taylor, Meynard, and Rheault (1977). Lind and O'Barr (1979) and Scherer (1979) have studied the relationship of language attitudes to the practice of law, and Shuy (1977) has investigated how language is important to medical interviews. There are several anthologies of articles on language attitudes, among which are Shuy and Fasold (1973), Cooper (1974, 1975), Giles and Powesland (1975), Giles (1977), Giles and St Clair (1979), and Williams and associates (1976).

NOTES

1 These two issues are discussed in more detail in volume II (*The Sociolinguistics of Language*).

2 Recalling our discussion of scale types in chapter 4, it is not clear just what sort of scale a semantic differential is. It is at least an ordinal scale, but can it be considered an interval scale? If so, we assume that the difference between, say, a 7 and a 6 on an intelligence scale is the same in the mind of the listeners as the difference between a 4 and a 5. But suppose a speaker reserves a 7 for speakers who sound like geniuses, whereas a 5 might go to a person who sounds just slightly more intelligent than average. For this respondent, the difference between a 7 and a 6 might be much greater than the difference between a 5 and a 4, and the scale loses its interval properties. The decision as to whether a semantic-differential scale is an interval or an ordinal scale is crucial to the researcher, who must decide whether parametric or non-parametric statistical tests are appropriate. There are further complications, of course, because the scale values themselves are not statistically analyzed, but rather the *mean* values derived from them. These means *are* points on an interval scale, but it is one derived from a scale whose status is murky. In actual practice, parametric statistics are commonly used to analyze semantic-differential scale results, usually analysis of variance.

3 Bourhis and Giles report significance at $p < 0.10$, a level generally considered not sufficient for rejection of the null hypothesis.

4 Trudgill and Tzavaras think that this view is unrealistic.

5 The experiment was done with children to test the hypothesis that younger children would be less concerned about gaining acceptance by the host community than adults and would therefore be easier to identify as West Indian by voice cues. Bourhis and Giles (1977:90) speculate that this hypothesis was not confirmed for one (or both) of the two following reasons: (1) the children were acquiring community speech patterns before the age of 11, and (2) their parents (second-generation immigrants) had already acquired the linguistic patterns of the Cardiff community. Both reasons, but especially the first, probably account for the results of the second study.

6 The statistical test used to test for significance, the binomial test, was not described in chapter 4, but is clearly explained in Anshen (1978).

7 Here I am referring to standard Black English as well as Vernacular Black English.

8 The effect of this last pair of interviews is roughly comparable to the effect in the United States if a black American were to speak standard American English with an American interviewer and change to Vernacular Black English when interviewed by an English interviewer with an RP British accent.

9 The order in which these interviews were presented was originally counter-balanced. That is, the interview with the 'French' commentator was played first in each pair for one group of listeners and the one with the 'Quebec' interviewer was

first for another group. When this order proved to make no difference, the results were combined to give only three conditions.

10   Apparently, direct questioning was not used in the Welsh experiment. It is possible that Canadian French has advanced as a marker of group identity since the mid-1970s, when these experiments were done. If so, the matched-guise results would be more like the results of the experiment in Wales, with significantly higher scores on affective scales when the speaker does not switch to the high-prestige variety. The direct-question results in the Canadian experiment might be an early indication of such a development as this.

11   For further general discussion of the relationship between language attitudes and group identity, see Lambert (1979).

12   American and British speakers were also included, so that reactions to these two native English dialects could be measured. The strict matched-guise technique had to be modified to allow *different* speakers to supply these two guises.

13   The semantic-differential scales each had six points on them. There were two speakers for each guise, so that each guise could have a total score between 2 and 12, after the scores for the two speakers were added together.

14   Although it is a little removed from the point I am making here, it is interesting to note that all three Egyptian guises, the two kinds of Arabic and Egyptian English, were rated significantly higher for religiousness than either British or American English. El-Dash and Tucker speculate that Egyptians may see themselves as more religious than English-speaking foreigners in general, or take 'religious' to mean 'Muslim', which they expect Americans or Britons not to be.

15   Strictly speaking, of course, this isn't a matched-guise design at all, since we don't have the same speakers speaking in each of two guises. It is obviously inspired by matched-guise attitude study research, however, and the design is of the same general type.

16   Three students in the 'Anglo' group spoke English, but were *native* speakers of languages other than English or Spanish.

17   Williams is also the author of one of the sources underlying the discussion of statistics in chapter 4.

18   The concept 'validity' was discussed in the chapter 4.

19   Note that this experiment is a kind of reverse matched-guise technique. Instead of having the same speaker using different language varieties, different kinds of speakers appeared to be using the same language variety.

20   It is important to note that the subjects were: (1) student teachers (that is, they had little actual classroom experience); and (2) white. Given the evidence that there are differences between black and white teachers' stereotypes, important differences are to be expected if this experiment were repeated with black or Mexican American teachers.

OBJECTIVES

1   Be able to distinguish *mentalist* and *behaviorist* theories of language attitudes, and to tell which one forms the basis of most work on language attitudes.

2   Be able to state the three increasingly wider-scope subjects that can be studied as 'language attitudes' (p. 148).

3   Be able to assign the terms 'direct method' and 'indirect method' to descriptions of language-attitude research.

4   Be able to recognize a description of a *matched-guise* experiment.

5   Given a sample *semantic-differential* scale, be able to show how you would mark a given attitude on it.

6   Be able to state the three general techniques for studying language attitudes given by Agheyisi and Fishman (described on p. 152), if you are given their descriptions.

7   In matched-guise research in which the same reading passage is read (in translated form) by every speaker in every guise, speakers may be judged as oral readers, not as speakers of a particular language variety. Be able to state how some researchers have attempted to avoid this problem (p.153).

8   Be able to tell if a given hypothetical research procedure is a valid example of a *commitment measure* or not (pp. 153-4).

9   Be able to recognize the definition of the term 'evaluative set'.

10 Be able to tell whether matched-guise research has generally shown that lower-status languages are rated higher for such traits as 'friendliness' and 'trust-worthiness' than superposed language varieties (pp. 158-9).

11 Be able to recognize the age pattern of attitudes toward Arvanitika (table 6.3), and what Trudgill and Tzavaras say it means.

12 Be able to cite the evidence that West Indian immigrants to Cardiff have identified with the local community.

13 Be able to identify a statement of the inherent contradiction in the results of the 'interviews' with the Canadian French 'athlete'.

14 Be able to recognize the difference in the Welsh and Quebec versions of the 'athlete' experiment that indicate that Welsh-accented English was a better-developed symbol of group identity than Canadian French was.

15 Be able to identify the two problems faced by El-Dash and Tucker in eliciting speech samples (pp.165-6).

16 Of Classical Arabic, Colloquial Arabic, and Egyptian English, speakers of two varieties were judged more intelligent and having more leadership ability than speakers of the third. Be able to state which two these are.

17 Be able to state which two of the three Egyptian language varieties mentioned in objective 16 made their speakers seem more religious than the third.

18 Be able to identify which of the Egyptian language varieties made its speakers seem most likeable.

19 Be able to name the language variety in Egypt judged *most* suitable for use at home, *least* suitable for use at home, and *most* suitable for use at school.

20 Be able to recognize the difference in the ratings for Spanish and English by *context* in Carranza and Ryan's research (p. 169).

21 Be able to recognize the difference in the ratings for Spanish and English by *scale* type.

22 Be able to recognize the particular piece of evidence that Williams's two-scale dimensions are *valid* that was 'best explained by Williams himself' (p.173).

23 Be able to state what it was that Williams was able to elicit when he asked teachers to rate speech when they were given only ethnic labels, but didn't hear any children speaking.

24 Be able to recognize Williams's discovery about the role of stereotypes in teachers' evaluations of children's speech (pp.175-6).

7

Language Choice

A moment's thought will make it clear that sociolinguistics only exists as a field of study because there are choices in using language. The very term 'societal multilingualism' (the title of chapter 1) refers to the fact that there can be several languages in a society. There couldn't be a second chapter on diglossia, if there were no High and Low varieties. If we think about the subject matter of each of the chapters in this book so far, we will realize that each is centered on the possibility that there are choices that can be made in a society among language varieties. Even statistics would not be necessary, if there was no variety in language use and choices among the varieties.

In this chapter, we will investigate what makes people in a society choose to use one language rather than another in a given instance. We will distinguish three kinds of language choice, then discuss how sociologists, social psychologists, and anthropologists approach language choice.[1] Finally, we will try to put together the results of the three approaches and see how they contribute to a better understanding of how people choose which language to speak.

KINDS OF CHOICE

The first thing that comes to mind when we think of language choice is 'whole languages'. We imagine a person who speaks two or more languages and has to choose which one to use. This is, in fact, one of the major kinds of choice we have to deal with, and is sometimes called *code-switching* (Laosa 1975; Greenfield 1972; Herman 1968; Rubin 1968b; Sankoff 1980). More subtle than this is *code-mixing,* where pieces of one language are used while a speaker is basically using another language. The language 'pieces' taken from another language are often words, but they can also be phrases or larger units (Gumperz 1977; Parasher 1980; Hill and Hill 1980). When they are words, the phenomenon is called borrowing. Finally, there is *variation within the same language* (Blom and Gumperz 1972; Thelander 1976; Coupland 1980). This is the kind of language choice that often becomes the focus of attitude studies, such as the studies of the variation among RP and mildly and heavily Welsh-accented English, or European and formal and informal Quebec French of chapter 6. In these cases, a speaker must choose which set of variants to use within a single language in any given situation. When we consider within-language variation to be a kind of language-choice problem, then language choice is a possibility for monolingual speakers as well as bilinguals.[2]

Of course, it is often the case that these three kinds of choice cannot be cleanly separated from each other. As we so often find in the study of sociolinguistics, the continuum concept serves us best. The three kinds of choice are best viewed as points on a continuum from relatively large-scale to relatively small-scale choices. The middle category, code-mixing, is very difficult to distinguish from the other two. Hill and Hill (1980:122), in their study of language choice between Spanish and Nahuatl in a Mexican Indian group, found it hopeless to try to distinguish between code-mixing and code-switching:

This index counts the first occurrence of each Spanish item for a speaker, regardless of whether it is a hispanism within an otherwise thoroughly Nahuatl context or is a Spanish vocabulary item in what might be judged a switch from Nahuatl into Spanish: we find there is no satisfactory way to draw a neat boundary between the two phenomena.

On the other hand, code-mixing or switching is often hard to distinguish from intra-language variation. After describing the difference between code-switching and variation within a single language, Thelander (1976:103) concludes: 'linguistic situations are now gradually emerging for which neither of these two models for description can be automatically accepted.'

To see how this can be, consider the phenomenon of borrowing of vocabulary. If a speaker of English, for example, uses a foreign word or phrase in an otherwise English sentence, it might be said that he has mixed a word from the other language with his English. However, words from one language that are repeatedly used in another language eventually become indistinguishable from the native vocabulary. Many speakers of American English may not be aware that *thug* is a borrowing (from Hindi), and so are *stucco* (from Italian) and *patio* (from Spanish). For all practical purposes, they have become English words. Other words are used, usually without awareness that they come from other languages, but can be identified as such with a little reflection; for example, *bouquet* (from French). Still others are consciously imported from other languages; when written, they are often underlined or printed in italics, and any diacritical marks that would appear in the orthography of the lending language are retained. One case of this is *raison d'être* (from French); another would be *gemütlichkeit* (from German). When borrowings of this class are used in the spoken language, some attempt is usually made to imitate the pronunciation of the original language. These orthographic and pronunciation conventions might be used as criteria for separating the last class of borrowings from the rest and calling them the only true examples of switching. What, then, would we do with cases in which some sounds are pronounced as they would be in the foreign language, but others are not? An example might be the not uncommon pronunciation of Mozart's name in which the German *ts* sound is given to the printed *z*, but an American English constricted *r* sound is used in the second syllable.

Similar problems arise in longer stretches of mixed language. Let's study an excerpt from the example of mixed Spanish and English given by Labov (1971:457):

y　cuando estoy con　gente　yo me... borracha porque　me siento
and when　I am　with　people I　get　drunk　because　I　feel

mas　happy, mas　free, you know, pero si yo estoy con　mucha
more　happy, more free, you know, but　if I　am　with a lot of

gente　yo　no estoy, you know, high, more or less, I couldn't get along
people I'm not

with anybody.

One criterion that is sometimes offered to distinguish switching from mixing is that the grammar of the clause determines the language. By this criterion, if a person uses a word or a phrase from another language, he has mixed, not switched. But if one clause has the grammatical structure of one language and the next is constructed according to the grammar of another, a switch has occurred. On this criterion, everything up to *'pero'* in the excerpt is Spanish; the words 'happy', 'free', and 'you know' are borrowed from English. The if-clause that follows is fundamentally Spanish, in spite of the fact that the expressions 'high' and 'more or less' are English. The consequent clause is entirely English, both in grammar and vocabulary. Adhering to this criterion, we would have to say that the antecedent if-clause is Spanish mixed with English as far as the words 'more or less'. The switch to English does not begin until the following 'I', in spite of the fact that four English words have preceded it.

Verma (1976:158) gives another example involving Hindi–English contact.

Vinod:　mãĩ to kahũũgaa ki　yah one of the best novels of the year hai.
　　　　I　　would say that it　　　　　　　　　　　　　　is.

Mira:　That's right. It is decidedly one of the best novels of the year.

Vinod's utterance has two clauses in it: one meaning 'I would say' and the one meaning 'It is one of the best novels of the year'. Although most of the words in the second clause are English, the clause is grammatically Hindi (it begins with the Hindi pronoun *'yah'* and has the Hindi word *'hai'* ('is') in clause-final position, as Hindi grammar demands). Even though the sentence contains a long phrase in English, if switches are said to occur only when whole clauses are switched, we would have to say that Vinod's sentence is entirely in Hindi, with a borrowed phrase from English. Mira's contribution, of course, represents a switch to English in the discourse, though by a different speaker. This way of distinguishing between language switching and language mixing may be technically satisfactory, but it seems to me that it violates common sense in these two examples. It is perhaps better to say that the two phenomena are points on a continuum from the sociolinguistics point of view.[3]

THREE DISCIPLINES – THREE APPROACHES

Sociology: domain analysis

One way of examining language choice from the sociologist's point of view was introduced by Joshua Fishman (1964, 1965, 1968e). Fishman proposed that there were certain institutional contexts, called *domains,* in which one language variety is more likely to be appropriate than another. Domains are taken to be constellations of factors such as location, topic, and participants. A typical domain, for example, would be the *family* domain. If a speaker is at home talking to another member of her family about an everyday topic, that speaker is said to be in the family domain. Domain analysis is related to diglossia, and some domains are more formal than others. In a community with diglossia, the Low language is the one that will be selected in the family domain, whereas the High language will most often be used in a more formal domain, perhaps education.

One study of language choice that utilized domain analysis is Greenfield's research (1972) on the choice between Spanish and at least three congruent components: persons, places, and topics. In order to test whether a combination of these three factors were actually associated in the minds of members of the community, Greenfield distributed a questionnaire in which subjects were given two congruent factors and asked to select the third, and also the language that they would use in that combination of circumstances. For example, subjects were told to think of a conversation with a parent on a family matter and asked to select the place from among 'home', 'beach', 'church', 'school', and 'work-place'. In this particular case, 100 per cent of the subjects selected the expected 'home' location. With one exception (selection of 'beach' as the appropriate location for the friendship domain), the expected congruent third component was selected by at least 81 per cent of the subjects. This result tended to confirm the validity of the five domains as real in the minds of the subjects.

After they had selected the appropriate third component, the subjects were asked to indicate which language went with that domain on a five-point scale very similar to the semantic-differential scales used in language-attitude research. A 1 on the scale indicated all Spanish, 2 meant more Spanish than English, 3 was used for equal amounts of Spanish and English, 4 for more

English than Spanish, and 5 for all English. The results were averaged in exactly the same way as semantic-differential scales are scored. This means that a low average number indicates more Spanish and a higher number favors English. Greenfield's results are displayed in table 7.1. There is a clear difference in favor of Spanish in the 'intimate' domains. An analysis of variance with language selection as the dependent variable showed that the difference by domain category shown in table 7.1 was significant at $p < 0.01$. A reasonable interpretation would be that Spanish is significantly more likely to be chosen in situations when intimacy is salient, and English where a status difference is involved. In short, there is evidence that the New York City Puerto Rican community tends to be diglossic, with Spanish as the Low language and English as the High.

Table 7.1   Language selection scale averages in two domain categories by New York City Puerto Rican subjects

Components given	Domains	
	Intimate (family & friendship)	*Status (religion, education & employment)*
Place, topic	3.27	4.81
Person, topic	2.60	4.27
Place, person	2.64	4.38

Source: data from Greenfield (1972:25)

A similar pattern was found by Parasher (1980) among 350 educated people in two cities in India. Like Greenfield, Parasher used self-reported questionnaire data and attempted to determine people's language use in domains, in Fishman's sense. He asked about language use in seven domains: (1) family; (2) friendship; (3) neighborhood; (4) transactions; (5) education; (6) government; and (7) employment. Parasher's domains, instead of being explicitly composed of persons, places, and topics as Greenfield's are, are simply the total of a set of similar *situations.* The friendship domain, for instance is composed of the following five situations:

conversing with friends and acquaintances;
conversing with people at clubs and social gatherings;
introducing friends to others;
discussing personal problems with friends/colleagues;
arguing with friends/colleagues in heated discussions.

Parasher's situations, as you can see, also vary persons, places, and topics, but not quite so systematically as Greenfield's system does.

The subjects who answered Parasher's questionnaire were asked to state which language of five languages or language types they would use in each situation. These five were: (1) English; (2) mother tongue or first language; (3)

the regional language; (4) Hindi; or (5) other language. For each language, they were asked to mark a five-point scale indicating that they would use that language in that situation always, usually, often, sometimes, or never. The five points were given these values: always = 40, usually = 30, often = 20, sometimes = 10, never = 0. If a respondent reported usual use of her mother tongue when introducing her friends to others, but that she sometimes used English, that would result in 'mother tongue' getting 30 points in that situation and 'English' getting 10. For comparative purposes, Parasher used the totals for all respondents for each language in each situation. His results for the family domain were summarized as follows (where the points represent the average for the family domain 'situations'):

English	Mother tongue	Regional language	Hindi	Other
3,007	9,855**	115	134	88

Not surprisingly, mother tongues received the highest score; in fact, the mother tongues had more points in this domain than all the other languages put together. When this happens, Parasher says that the language or language type 'dominates' in that domain; he indicates dominance in a domain with double asterisks (Parasher 1980:153).

Of Parasher's seven domains, it would appear that family, friendship, and neighborhood might be Low domains, and that education, government, and (at least for these highly educated individuals) employment might be High domains. The transaction domain might be rather Low or rather High, depending on the kind of transaction. Thus we might expect the mother tongue to be dominant in the three Low domains and English, Hindi, or the regional language to be dominant in the High domains. In the first place, it turns out that very little use of Hindi, the regional languages, or 'other' languages was reported.[4] More important, the family domain was the *only* domain where the mother tongue, or any language other than English, dominated. English dominated in the friendship domain, and had the highest rating in the neighborhood domain, although it did not 'dominate'. It is not too surprising that English should score so high in the education, government, and employment domains', especially among highly educated Indians and perhaps especially in the southern part of the country, where the research was conducted and where English tends to be favored. It *is* surprising, however, that English should appear so strong in the friendship and neighborhood domains. The answer turns out to be quite simple; most of the educated bilinguals in the sample did not share a mother tongue with their friends. In the second place, any discussion with friends concerning a topic from a more formal domain, such as education, science, or technology, is likely to trigger the selection of English no matter what the setting or how close the speaker is to the people he is talking to. Both of these factors caused English to be used in this Low domain. The strength of English in the neighborhood domain is explained by Parasher (1980:157) in this way:

Where the neighbours do not share the mother tongue, for example, people living in houses on the premises of the institution/organization where they work, they prefer to use English. The regional language or Hindi was also reported to be used, particularly when the neighbours do not share the mother tongue and/or any one of the interlocutors does not understand English. This evidence leads us to the generalization that an important factor governing the subjects' language choice in this domain is whether or not the interlocutors have a common mother tongue.

The language understood by participants, not surprisingly, is a crucial factor in language choice.

Figure 7.1 shows the ratings for 'mother tongue/first language' in descending order by domains. Mother tongues are used most, as expected, in the Low domains and least in the normally High domains. The fact that English is rated *higher* than the mother tongues in all but the family domain, is to be explained for the most part by the fact that the subjects were from the best-educated segment of the Indian population and also by the fact that the location in which the research was done was in the southern part of the country.

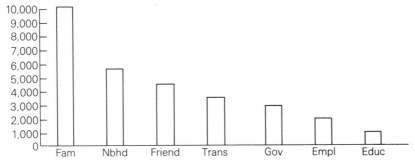

Figure 7.1   Use ratings for mother tongues in seven domains by educated Indians
Source: data from Parasher (1980)

Another study that shows a diglossia-like pattern of language choice was conducted by Laosa (1975). Using a research design that is a model of excellence for this type of investigation, Laosa examined the language used by elementary-school children from three Spanish-speaking communities in the United States – Cuban Americans in Miami; Mexican Americans in Austin, Texas; and, like Greenfield, New York City Puerto Ricans. Examining language selection between Spanish and English in three contexts – within the family, in the classroom, and in recreation activities at school – Laosa found that the use of Spanish was most often reported in the family context, less often in the recreation context, and least often in the classroom, in all three communities. The difference between the family and the two school contexts was greater than the difference between classroom and recreation at school. There were important differences among the three communities in their language-choice patterns, but all three show the same tendency toward diglossia that Greenfield and Parasher discovered.[5]

Social psychology

Sociologists typically approach a problem like language choice by searching for a social structure, such as domains, conducting a survey of a sample of the target population relating to the proposed social structure, and doing a statistical analysis of the results. Social psychologists, as you might expect, are more interested in people's psychological processes than in large societal categories. They, too, often use surveys, samples, and statistics, but they search for individual motivations rather than social structures. In other words, social psychological research on language choice is more person-centered than society-centered. Important work on the social psychology of language choice has been carried out by Simon Herman (1968) and by Howard Giles and his associates (Giles 1973; Giles, Bourhis and Taylor 1977).

Simon Herman – overlapping situations. As Herman sees the problem of language choice, a bilingual speaker finds himself in more than one psychological situation simultaneously. Herman talks about three kinds of situation: one concerned with the speaker's personal needs and the other two connected with social groupings. In a given situation, then, a speaker may feel herself pulled in different directions by her personal desire to speak the language she knows best and the language expected of her by the social group. The group may be the immediate one, that is, the people who are actually there at the time. More subtle is the 'background' group, which Herman describes as 'groups in the wider social milieu that are not directly involved in the immediate situation but yet may influence the behaviour – "hidden commit-tees", so to speak' (Herman 1968:494–5). That is, a speaker may want to be seen as a member of some social group that is not present, or may want to dissociate himself from that group. A black American in a group of white Americans, for example, will obviously be racially black, but can linguistically reveal his *ethnic* orientation at the moment by shifting his speech toward Vernacular Black English or toward standard American English. In the one case, he is emphasizing his membership in the absent group, in the other, he is minimizing it.[6] The three psychological situations Herman speaks of are personal needs, background situation, and immediate situation.

Since these situations overlap, and since each might incline an individual toward the choice of a different language, Herman is led to a consideration of the circumstances that cause one of the three situations to gain *salience* at the expense of the other two. The situation with salience is the most prominent one at a particular time and the one that the speaker will respond to.

Based in large measure on empirical data on language choice in Israel, Herman suggests that certain circumstances will increase the salience of one of the three situations. The circumstances and the situations that they promote are listed in table 7.2. For example, some Israeli immigrants reported that they would use their native language at home (private setting), but Hebrew on a

Table 7.2   *Circumstances causing an increase in salience
for one of three psychological situations*

Situation	Circumstances
Personal needs	1 Setting is private rather than public. 2 The situation provokes insecurity, high tension, or frustration. 3 The situation touches the central rather than the peripheral layers of the personality.
Background situation	1 The activity takes place in a public rather than a private setting. 2 The behavior in the situation may be interpreted as providing cues to group identifications. 3 The person involved in the activity wishes to identify with a particular group or be dissociated from it.
Immediate situation	1 The person is not concerned about group identifications. 2 The behavior is task oriented. 3 Well-established patterns of behavior characterize a relationship.

Source: Herman (1968:495–6)

bus (public setting). A purely instrumental function, like asking a fellow worker to pass a tool, will cause the immediate situation to gain salience and the speaker will use whatever language he normally uses in that situation, without worrying about what group associations that language has, or what language he personally feels most comfortable with (task orientation). If two people always use a particular language between themselves, then that language will be selected whenever they talk to each other; the immediate situation takes precedence over background and personal considerations (established relationships). Herman's central idea, however, seems to be the potential conflict between choosing a language that is most comfortable for the speaker, that allows her to 'be herself' and choosing a language that identifies her with one or another of the society's sociocultural groups.

Giles's accommodation theory.   Starting with the same basic concept, Giles has developed the notion of *accommodation* in linguistic behavior. Normally, accommodation takes the form of *convergence,* in which a speaker will choose a language or language variety that seems to suit the needs of the person being spoken to.[7] Under some conditions, though, a speaker may fail to converge or he may even *diverge.* In other words, a person might make no effort at all to adjust his speech for the benefit of the other person and might even deliberately make his speech maximally unlike the other person's. This will happen when the speaker wants to emphasize his loyalty to his own group and dissociate himself from his interlocutors' group. This phenomenon served as the basis for one of the attitude research projects discussed in the last chapter; the hypothetical behavior of a black American who might deliberately use features of Black English when speaking to white people is another example. Giles, Bourhis, and Taylor (1977:323) give yet another example: the first time the Arab nations issued an oil communique in Arabic instead of English during the mid-1970s.

Convergence and divergence do not require the selection of one choice (that is, convergence, nonconvergence, and divergence). It is possible to make numerous combinations of choices among the variants within a language, as well as to use strategies such as translating portions of one's discourse or slowing down the rate of speech. Table 7.3 shows some possible degrees of accommodation in terms of a speaker's interaction with an outgroup member (someone from a different sociocultural group). The most convergent behavior would be to use the other person's language and to make every effort to pronounce it the way its native speakers do. Less convergent would be to use the other language, but with a relatively heavy accent (for example, an English-speaking Canadian speaking French to a French-speaking Canadian, but with a heavy English accent). The next step has the speaker using his own language, but speaking slowly out of deference to the other person, who may not understand it well. The most divergent of the four strategies has a speaker speaking his own language at a normal rate of speed, leaving the other person on her own to understand as best she can.

Table 7.3   Some increasing variants of convergence and divergence

Linguistic dimensions	Increasing convergence	Increasing divergence
1 Outgroup language with native-like pronunciation		
2 Outgroup language with features of ingroup pronunciation		
3 Ingroup language with slow speech rate		
4 Ingroup language with normal speech rate		

Source: Giles, Bourhis, and Taylor (1977:324, table 2)

Speakers can adjust their linguistic behavior in reaction to the person they are talking to by changing to a different language (or not), using words or larger units from another language (or not), selecting among within-language variants in one direction or another; and using strategies such as short-passage translation, modifying rate of speech, and maximizing or minimizing their accent. Is it possible, however, to say anything about *when* a speaker is likely to use convergent strategies and when nonconvergent or divergent strategies will be the choice? Giles, Bourhis, and Taylor (1977:332–5) have tried to answer this question on the basis of whether the speaker is a member of a dominant or subordinate sociocultural group in the society and whether or not he thinks social change (in terms of improving the position of subordinate groups) is possible.[8] Their analysis is summarized in table 7.4.

Table 7.4   Expected linguistic accommodation behavior by dominant and subordinate groups under various perceptions of social change

	Response	
Perception of social change	Dominant group	Subordinate group
No possibility of social change perceived	Nonconvergence	Convergence
Possibility of social change perceived (favorably)	'Downward' convergence	Divergence
Possibility of social change perceived (unfavorably)	Divergence	—

Source: Giles, Bourhis, and Taylor (1977)

If the dominant group expects to remain dominant, then its members will assume, without even thinking about it, that subordinate-group members will make any necessary linguistic adjustments. As a result, they will speak their own prestige language or dialect in the normal fashion without attempting any convergence. The way I have described this situation makes it seem that the dominant group is arrogantly demanding its right to domination, but, under a static social order, 'downward' convergence is scarcely possible. It is a well-known phenomenon that attitudes toward 'correct' or 'good' language are often more widespread within a speech community than its use is. We have already seen this in connection with diglossia, where Low languages are typically disparaged and High languages revered, even though everyone knows the Low language and very few speak the High. As a result, if a native speaker of a 'correct' variety or a 'good' language were to deliberately give up his natural linguistic practices in favor of a usage with less prestige when speaking to people from subordinate groups, there is a real danger of offending the subordinate-group member. It might seem that the dominant-group member was mocking him. Imagine the impact, for example, if a white American doctor were to try to use Vernacular Black English with a black working-class patient, to attempt a Spanish accent when speaking to a Chicano patient, or try to sound like a blue-collar worker when talking to a patient who works in a steel mill!

On the other hand, if the subordinate group sees no possibility of social change, then the only chance for social improvement in the society beyond his own sociocultural group lies in the direction of acceptance by the dominant group. Acceptance, then, is to be gained by any possible expedient, including linguistic convergence. Subordinate group members can be expected to converge when dealing with the dominant group, if social change seems unlikely. I should point out that the convergent strategy would be used by those members of the subordinate group who consider it desirable and possible to make social gains in the larger society. Others, who see no possibility or desirability in trying to 'move up' through the indulgence of the dominant group, may well withdraw into their own ingroup, seldom dealing with the dominant group and making a minimal attempt at convergence when they must.

When social change does seem possible and a member of the dominant group considers it desirable (perhaps for reasons of conscience), Giles, Bourhis, and Taylor see the possibility of downward convergence, that is, the dominant-group member may attempt to show sympathy by convergence with the lower-prestige linguistic variety. The example they give is the case of some upper-middle-class students in Britain in the early 1970s who adopted liberal ideals and demonstrated it by rejecting the speech and dress styles expected of their class. It seems to me, though, that the acceptance of 'downward' convergence by subordinate groups depends partially on the sociolinguistic status of the subordinate language variety. If it is considered a *language,* then the subordinate group might accept or even demand its use by the dominant group during the process of social change. The awakening nationalism in Quebec is one example of this. If the subordinate group's linguistic system is thought of as a substandard variety of the dominant group's language, downward convergence is much less likely to be acceptable. Part of the reason is that attempted use of the ethnic variety by non-members might be seen as mockery, but during a time of social change, an attempt to converge is likely to be seen as a claim to membership in the subordinate group. The subordinate group will not be inclined to accept such a claim by a member of the oppressor group, however sympathetic the individual might seem to be.

Finally, if it seems that the status of a subordinate group has a real chance of improving, and the dominant group takes an unfavorable view of that development, Giles, Bourhis and, Taylor hypothesize that the dominant group would diverge, in order to emphasize the linguistic differences between them and the threatening group. Language use would be one way of holding the 'upstart' group at a distance. Apparently Giles and his associates do not consider it likely that a subordinate group would take a negative point of view of a social change that involved an advantage to their own group. But there are probably always some members of subordinate groups who consider the risks involved in trying to improve their position greater than the likely benefits, and so would not be in favor of the change. These individuals, it seems to me, are likely to reveal their point of view by linguistic convergence in periods of change; and in that way they would show the dominant group that they are content with the existing social order. Of course, this behavior is likely to cost them the respect of the more progressive members of their own group.[9]

Anthropology

Comparison with other social sciences. Where social psychology looks at language choice from the point of view of an individual dealing with the structure of his society, and sociology attempts to explain it in terms of abstract social constructs, anthropology has a different orientation. Anthropologists are most interested in discovering the *values* of a sociocultural group, and the cultural rules of behavior that reveal those values. Like the social psychologist, the anthropologist is interested in how the individual speaker is dealing with the structure of his society, but not in terms of his own psychological needs so much as how that person is using his language choices to reveal his cultural values. Since an individual can make different selections among the values allowed her by her culture at different times, anthropologists are interested in the minute analysis of particular interactions. Anthropologists, to a greater extent than sociologists and social psychologists, pay close attention to code-mixing and inherent variation, as well as to large-scale code-switches. To an anthropologist, each of these variations represents a change in the expression of cultural values, and this is what it is important to understand.

Methodology. In addition to general orientation, there is a noticeable difference in methodology between anthropologists and the other two kinds of social scientist. Sociologists and social psychologists are likely to rely on questionnaire data or the observation of people's behavior under controlled experimental conditions. The results are collected as numerical data and statistical analysis is applied to discover if there are significant tendencies. Anthropologists place the highest value on normal, uncontrolled behavior. This leads them to apply a research methodology seldom used in sociology or social psychology – 'participant observation'.

For example, to collect data for her superb study of language choice and shift in Oberwart in Eastern Austria, Gal (1979) spent a year living in the town with a local family. Blom and Gumperz (1972), Gillian Sankoff (1980) and Rubin (1968b) spent similar long periods of residence in the communities they were studying, and Dorian (1981) spent over a decade working on language change in East Sutherland, in the Scottish Highlands. Although subjects may be interviewed and questionnaire data collected, these data are considered strictly supplementary; the main core of data consists of the observation of people's behavior as they carry on their everyday lives. Gal (1979:120) collected well-patterned interview data in which people reported what their language choices would be, depending on who they were talking to, but she was only willing to use it after she had demonstrated that it was corroborated by her records of actual observations. The two sources of language-choice data were highly consistent, providing strong support for the *validity* of both, in the sense discussed in chapter 5. On the other hand, Dorian (1981:97–8) found the results of the questionnaire she distributed in East Sutherland so problematical compared with what she knew of the linguistic situation from her long period of participant observation, that she 'banished' all discussion of the questionnaire to an appendix.

Statistical analysis, beyond raw data tabulations and averages, is usually not used (Gal's work is an exception to this; she makes some use of Spearman's ρ for rank-order correlation). Rather, anthropologists feel that their intensive involvement with the societies they are studying allows them to discern what is and what is not important without resorting to formal numerical analysis. In fact, this difference in methodology is a source of some disagreement between the social sciences; anthropologists take the viewpoint that work in sociology lacks a certain degree of depth, and sociologists find work in anthropology to be lacking in rigor.

Community structure.   Anthropological work on language choice has thrown considerable light on the phenomenon of community structure. We will concentrate on one major insight, one that derives largely from the work of Blom and Gumperz (1972) and Gal (1978b, 1979). Recall one of Fishman's categories of diglossia – 'diglossia without bilingualism'. The criteria for this category are the existence of two separate communities in the same society, one a ruling elite and one the governed group. The two use different languages and there is relatively little communication between them except perhaps by means of a pidgin. In its pure form, 'diglossia without bilingualism' is difficult to find, but there are societies that *approach* the social structure Fishman had in mind. In such a society, the governed group would acquiesce to the rule of the elite, but would not consider themselves part of the same speech community. They would not feel any particular need to learn the dominant group's language, except the minimum required for interacting with them. Fundamentally, this means that there are *two separate* communities in the same society, related by the power the one group has over the other, but with neither considering themselves at all *part* of the other group.[10]

A contrasting social arrangement has two groups within the same society; one with more prestige and power than the other, just as in the first case. But in this case, members of the lower-status group see the more prestigious group as a wider category that *includes* them. They have a kind of 'dual group membership'. Like the acquisition of High and Low language varieties, this dual membership is sequentially ordered within a person's lifetime; he first becomes a member of the lower-status group, whose values are most relevant to his home and neighborhood. As he grows older, he realizes that he also owes some allegiance to another social grouping which is somewhat foreign, but which, in a sense, includes his own. The dual allegiances set up in this way cause some degree of conflict, and members of the lower-status group will resolve these conflicts in various ways – with interesting linguistic consequences. Figure 7.2 is an illustration of the two kinds of social structure.

194 *Language Choice*

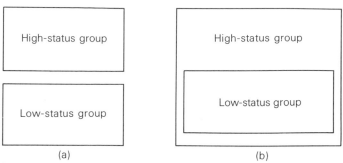

*Figure 7.2 Schematic representation of two kinds of social structure:
(a) high- and low-status groups as members of separate communities;
(b) the low-status group simultaneously part of the high-status group*

Blom and Gumperz's work (1972) in the Norwegian village of Hemnesberget is illustrative of a society that is apparently in the process of transition
between the two social structures illustrated in figure 7.2. Hemnesberget
citizens recognize two linguistic varieties: (1) Ranamål, the local variety used
for everyday conversation; and (2) Bokmål, a standard Norwegian variety.
For most of the people who live in Hemnesberget, the linguistic situation is a
case of broad diglossia between two varieties of the same linguistic system,
with Ranamål linguistic forms associated with the typical Low language
functions, and Bokmål forms with the usual High functions. Their language-
choice behavior is characterized by what Blom and Gumperz call 'situational
switching'. If the situation is considered rather formal and relatively remote
from local and personal concerns, then Bokmål forms will predominate. If the
situation is one of closeness and is part of the specifically Hemnesberget
community (as opposed to the Norwegian scene as a whole), then there will
be a greater concentration of Ranamål forms. Blom and Gumperz (1972:
424–5) illustrate situational switching in the following way:

when, on the one hand, we speak of someone giving a classroom lecture or performing
a Lutheran church service or talking to a tourist, we can safely assume that he is using
[Bokmål] grammatical forms. On the other hand, two locals having a heart-to-heart
talk will presumably speak [Ranamål]. If instead they are found speaking in [Bokmål],
we conclude either that they do not identify with the values of the local team or that
they are not having a heart-to-heart talk.[11]

The other kind of switching that Blom and Gumperz discovered is called
'metaphorical switching'. In metaphorical switching, the linguistic choice
becomes a symbol or 'metaphor' for the relationship being enacted *regardless*
of the situation. Official community affairs are considered nonlocal and
therefore demand the use of Bokmål. But many of the individuals who have
government jobs are friends with many of the citizens who have to deal with
them in their official capacities, creating something of a conflict. A common
solution is for a resident to approach a clerk's desk and extend greetings and
ask about family affairs using Ranamål forms, but to increase their use of

Bokmål forms when conducting the official business. In this way, Ranamål symbolizes or serves as a metaphor for the friendship role that exists between two members of the same community and Bokmål for the citizen–government official role.

The distinction between the two kinds of switching is crucial in situations that are *purely* local, where no other status besides membership in the Hemnesberget community is relevant. To make it easy to observe this kind of situation, Blom and Gumperz set up a series of 'experiments'.[12] They asked people in the community who had become their friends (Blom and Gumperz had lived in the community for some time) to arrange small social gatherings and allow them to be tape-recorded. They succeeded in arranging three of these gatherings. The third group consisted of young men and women who had grown up in Hemnesberget and were proud of their home town and its local dialect, but who had all been away at universities in other Norwegian cities and had absorbed pan-Norwegian identities and values to some extent. The first two groups did not have any returned university students in them. Accordingly, in the first two groups, there are no instances of metaphorical switching or any use of Bokmål at all, except when someone is quoting what someone else said in Bokmål or in speech directed to Blom or Gumperz themselves. In a gathering of that sort, there are no relationships to enact except local ones, and consequently, only Ranamål is appropriate. This was true no matter what the topic under discussion was; even government affairs were discussed in Ranamål. This was not true of the group of returned students. When a topic arose in which a speaker would benefit from an appeal to her status as an intellectual, for example, Bokmål forms would be used, even in this gathering of friends who had all grown up in Hemnesberget. What this means is that for this group, being a member of the Hemnesberget community and of the larger Norwegian community both remained relevant, even in a situation that was purely local for the other two groups.

We would want to say that members of all three groups would see themselves as represented in figure 7.2(b). All of them demonstrate by their use of metaphorical switching that, even at a rather deep psychological level, they think of themselves as both Hemnesberget residents and as Norwegians. The more traditional members, however, have reserved their 'Norwegian' identities for certain designated relationships; relationships that are peripheral to their most intimate concerns. In an intimate social setting with their own local friends, they are, to use Blom and Gumperz's term, 'local team' members exclusively. For the young people in the third group, their 'Norwegian' identity has become so much a part of them that it coexists with their 'local team' identity, even in an intimate social setting.[13]

Gal's work (1978b, 1979) in Oberwart, Austria shows the distinction even more clearly. In this community, near the Hungarian border, there are many bilinguals in Hungarian and German. Hungarian, the traditional ingroup language of one segment of the society, is the Low variety. German, the national language of Austria as well as the language of education and of the professional class, is the High language. Hungarian is associated with traditional rural peasant values: hard work, ownership of farm animals, and land ownership as a source of status. German symbolizes the more 'Austrian' and urban values that have moved into the community since the Second World War. To an even more striking degree than in Hemnesberget, there are individual differences in the acceptance or rejection of national and urban values associated with the use of German.

A very powerful clue to a person's sociolinguistic self-identity is his behavior toward monolinguals, which in Oberwart means monolingual in German, since virtually all adult Hungarian speakers are bilingual. As a general rule, it is expected that members of the Hungarian-speaking community will switch to German in the presence of German monolinguals. Gal (1979:166) relates the following story to show how this might work:

> Several monolingual construction workers, strangers to Oberwart, had been repairing the street in front of the inn. At lunch time they entered and sat down near the table of four bilinguals who were conversing in Hungarian. The monolinguals jokingly but insistently told the bilinguals to stop. 'Let us hear what you are saying. We live in Austria. We are all Austrians. Don't you know how to talk German?' were among the comments made. The bilinguals switched to German.

Even though the bilingual men were not talking *to* the construction workers, they were responsive to appeals to their status as 'Austrians' to use the national language even within earshot of their 'fellow citizens' in a public place. Obviously, this group of local men were willing to acknowledge their identity as 'Austrians' as well as members of their own subgroup in this setting.[14]

Gal emphasizes that this was not always so, and is not the way *all* Oberwart Hungarian speakers would respond. In another incident, an old Hungarian peasant couple invited a monolingual German neighbor to help with a pig-killing. The neighbor was with them for three or four hours, not only helping them with the work, but staying on for a meal. None the less, all conversation was in Hungarian, except for a few instructions about the butchering job that were given to the monolingual neighbor in German. Gal (1979:165) points out that this cannot be explained as deliberate rudeness (or divergence, in Giles's terms), since the neighbor had been helping them, was there at their invitation, and shared a meal with them. Apparently, they simply reserved the right to use their own language in their own home and believed the 'foreigner' would not expect them to do otherwise. Their behavior was not impolite in their eyes, simply normal. To this old couple, Hungarian and German represented 'parallel and coordinate social groups' (Gal 1979:161), not a small group nested inside a larger one. This was, in fact, the general conception of the relationship of the two languages and their speakers before the 1940s.

Even more striking is the contrasting behavior towards women from other

Austrian villages, who had married Oberwart Hungarian community men and gone to live with their in-laws. Gal (1979:142–3) interviewed twelve married women who had been monolingual in German and married into the community in this manner. Of the twelve, six had learned Hungarian and six had not. All six who *had* learned the language had had similar experiences. Scarcely anyone but their husbands would speak German with them. Other family members would speak only Hungarian and the new bride was more or less forced to learn it. This was true, in spite of the fact that everyone who spoke Hungarian also knew German. If we realize that these families no doubt were operating with the 'parallel social group' conception of figure 7.2(a), their behavior becomes clear. Anyone who was a family member could not possibly remain a 'foreigner'. The young women had to become members of their husband's communities and that could not be done without learning the community language. The wives who did not learn Hungarian were able to find people they could speak to in German, and their relatives were not able to control their language choices to the same extent. This lack of ability to control the language environment on the part of a woman's in-laws is no doubt important, but it is interesting to note that the wives who remained monolingual were married after the Second World War or had husbands who held non-agricultural jobs (or they had such jobs themselves). These younger, more urban people would be more likely to think of the local social structure more in the manner illustrated in figure 7.2(b). Even if a woman was not a member of the local community in the fullest sense, because she could not speak Hungarian, there was some community in Oberwart that she could function in. As a result, the new bride could survive socially without learning Hungarian.

Another consideration to be found in Gal's study is the degree of fluency in the Higher language. A century ago, peasants in Oberwart (then known by its Hungarian name 'Felsöör') only spoke German 'well enough to get by at markets in neighboring villages' (Gal 1979:155). By the 1970s, the goal was not only to learn German fluently, but to speak German so free of any trace of a Hungarian accent that one is 'able to pass as a monolingual' (Gal 1979:107). This increased concern with the quality of a person's ability to speak German is another subtle reflection of the growing 'dual membership' concept.

Language choice as a concomitant of one's concept of group membership comes out most clearly when we get an understanding of the language-choice model Gal finds most revealing. She discovered orderly patterns of language choice when individual selection patterns were placed on an 'implicational-scale' table with speakers represented by rows and interlocutors by columns.[15] The implicational scale for women (the scale for men is almost identical) appears as table 7.5.[16] The use of German with any particular interlocutor *implies* or predicts that German will be used with all interlocutors to the right. Similarly, if Hungarian is used with any interlocutor, it will also be used with all interlocutors to the left on the scale. Use of both German and Hungarian to the same interlocutor will appear *between* the use of only Hungarian and the use of only German.

Table 7.5   Implicational scale for language choice by women speakers in Oberwart

Speaker's age	1	2	3	4	5	6	7	8	9	10	11	12
						Interlocutor						
14	H	GH		G	G	G	G			G		G
15	H	GH		G	G	G	G			G		G
25	H	GH	GH	GH	G	G	G	G	G	G		G
27	H	H		GH	G	G	G			G		G
17	H	H	H	GH	G	G				G		G
13	H	H		GH	GH	GH	GH			G		G
43	H	H		GH	GH		G*	GH	GH	G		G
39	H	H		H	GH	GH	G	G	G	G		G
23	H	H		H	GH	H*	G		GH*	G		G
40	H	H		H	GH		GH	G	G	G		G
50	H	H		H	H	GH	GH	GH	G	G	G	G
52	H	H	H	GH*	H		H	GH	G	G	G	G
60	H	H	H	H	H	H	H	GH	GH	G	G	H*
40	H	H	H	H	H	H	H	GH	GH	GH		G
35	H	H		H	H	H	H	H	GH	H*		G
61	H	H		H	H	H	H	H	GH*	H		G
50	H	H	H	H	H	H	H	H	H	H		G
66	H	H		H	H	H	H	H	H	H	GH	G
60	H	H		H	H	H	H	H	H	H	GH	G
53	H	H		H	H	H	H	H	GH*	H	GH	G
71	H	H		H	H	H	H	H	H	H	GH	G
54	H	H	H	H	H	H	H	H	H	H		G
69	H	H		H	H	H	H	H	H	H	GH	G
63	H	H		H	H	H	H	H	H	H	GH	H*
59	H	H	H	H	H	H	H	H	H	H		H
60	H	H	H	H	H	H	H	H	H	H		H
64	H	H		H	H	H	H	H	H	H	H	H
71	H	H		H	H	H	H	H	H	H	H	H

Interlocutors: 1 = God; 2 = grandparents and their generation; 3 = black market clients; 4 = parents and their generation; 5 = age-mate pals, neighbors; 6 = brothers and sisters; 7 = salespeople; 8 = spouse; 9 = children and that generation; 10 = government Languages: G = German; H = Hungarian.
*These cells fail to conform to perfect scalability.
Source: Gal (1979:121, table 4.3)

Bearing in mind that left-to-right order of the interlocutors at the top of table 7.5 was determined by an attempt to make the scale as nearly perfect as possible, it is interesting to see just what order that procedure gives. First of all, it is clear that older friends and relatives are the ones most likely to be addressed in Hungarian and younger ones in German. This is to be expected, since younger people are the most likely to have the newer concept of the social order. Of non-relatives, apart from speech addressed to God in prayers and hymns, the most likely people to be addressed in Hungarian are 'black-market clients'. 'Black market' activity in Oberwart is not nearly as sinister as it sounds; it merely represents the community attempt to maintain their tradition of mutual exchange of services in the face of the strict Austrian regulations for the licensing of skilled labor. A Hungarian-speaking carpenter, for instance, who does some work for a neighbor that can legally only be done by a licensed (and expensive) contractor, is engaging in 'black market' activity. Note that this kind of arrangement represents the maintenance of traditional peasant values, requires a high degree of mutual trust, and is in defiance of 'Austrian' law. It is no wonder that 'black market clients' are so likely to be addressed in the small community language. By contrast, 'government officials' are part of the larger society establishment and so are likely to be addressed in German. The same language is used with the doctor, who represents a prestigious profession.

Alert readers may be surprised that speech addressed to God (prayers and hymns) are the *most* likely speech events to be carried out in Hungarian; yet religion is typically a High domain and Hungarian is the Low language in this society. In other societies we have looked at, the Highest language is the most suitable for religious activity. In Egypt, for example, Classical Arabic was the language judged to be most suitable for religion. The answer is that religious speech activity will be carried out in the Highest language variety relevant to the speech community in which the religion is situated. In Oberwart, almost all members of the Hungarian-speaking community are Calvinists; German is considered the language of other people's religions, for the most part Lutherans and Catholics. Hungarian is the only possible language for use in the Calvinist churches, but church Hungarian is the most prestigious *style* of Hungarian in use in the community. Islam, by contrast, is not only the religion of all Egyptian Muslims, but in one form or other of *all* Arab Muslims. Classical Arabic is, of course, the Highest language of that speech community.[17]

Just reading across the top of table 7.5 tells us a lot about what is behind language choice in Oberwart. It is equally informative to read down the left side of table 7.5. It's easy to see that younger speakers tend to cluster toward the top and older ones are located near the bottom. Speakers near the top, of course, are the ones who use German with the most interlocutors and those near the bottom are most likely to choose to speak Hungarian with most other people. This age distribution tendency can be measured by one of the statistical tests described in chapter 4, Spearman's rank-order correlation test. The value for Spearman's rho between age-ranks and the rank-order from the top to bottom of the implicational scale was a very high 0.82 for a table that combined table 7.5 with the equivalent table for male speakers. This correlation is consistent with the fact that younger people are more likely to have absorbed the urban, pan-Austrian values associated with the use of German.

Once we can establish a language-choice ranking on some basis such as table 7.5, this rank-order can be used in correlation measurements with other factors. We are working with the idea that a greater use of Hungarian means that a speaker tends to think of the Hungarian-speaking and wider Austrian communities more as parallel than as overlapping. Therefore, it might be expected that the implicational scale rank-order would correlate with the tendency to have intensive interaction with other members of the Hungarian-speaking community. All we need is a measure of community interaction.

Gal (1979:140–1) developed the following method to measure the 'peasant-ness' of an individual's contacts, since commitment to a peasant life-style entails a commitment to the traditional Hungarian community values. The measure is based on a binary assignment of 'peasantness', in which an individual is a 'peasant' if he lives in a household where cows or pigs or both are owned, and is not a 'peasant' if neither of these larger farm animals is owned. This criterion is a bit crude, but is consistent with the way involvement in an agricultural life-style is evaluated in Oberwart. Gal was able to find out, after she had lived in Oberwart for a while, who each of her list of contacts spoke with over a period of weeks and how often. The interaction measure was simply the percentage of contacts with 'peasants'. Individuals could be rank-ordered by these percentages and this order correlated with the implicational scale ordering. The result was a healthy Spearman's ρ value of 0.78, showing a strong relationship between a dense communications network with traditional members of the Hungarian-speaking community and the tendency to choose Hungarian. This result is not as circular as it may seem, since everybody in the Hungarian community is bilingual and it is possible to use German to speak to anyone. In fact, some members of the community actually *do* use German with the same people that others address in Hungarian. What Gal's measure gives us is an indication of the extent to which the smaller community, and particularly its more traditional members, is sufficient for an individual's social needs.[18] A person with a social life strongly rooted in the smaller community is unlikely to have much allegiance, if any, to the larger one and her language-choice patterns reflect this.

Prediction versus interpretation.   The goal of the study of language choice is to explain it. There are two levels of explanation that have been entertained by scholars involved in language-choice research: first, prediction and, second, explanation.[19] The most ambitious kind of prediction would be to be able to predict just when a bilingual speaker would switch from one language to the other within a conversation. A more limited kind of prediction would be to be able to predict which of three language-choice patterns an individual would use in a certain situation; her first language, her second language, or a combination of both, without trying to predict each and every switch.

Interpretation has a still more modest goal. Rather than trying to predict when a switch will occur, or even which general language choice pattern will be used, the goal is to take a particular language choice as given and to understand the interactive work it is accomplishing for the speaker. There is a general consensus that it is unrealistic to attempt to try to predict, or even interpret, the social meaning of every single switch. Some scholars, however, have tried to discover elements in a speech event that would make it possible to predict the broad choice of one language or the other, or the use of a combination of both.

A broad-category prediction technique sometimes used in the analysis of language choice is the 'decision tree'.[20] A decision tree is reminiscent of domain analysis, since some of the nodes of the 'tree' are the same as the components of domains. For example, Rubin (1968b:526) uses a decision tree in her analysis of language choice in a country we are already familiar with – Paraguay. From her observations and questionnaire data in a larger and a smaller Paraguayan town, Rubin found that, by and large, a Paraguayan's decision to speak Spanish or Guaraní was based on an ordered series of situational considerations, as represented in figure 7.3. The chart is meant to

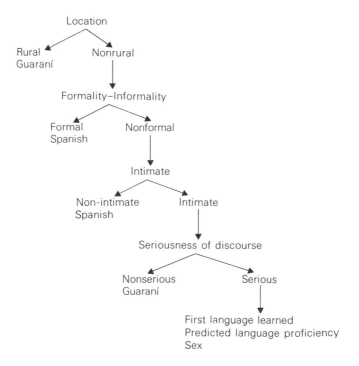

Figure 7.3   Decision tree for language choice between Spanish and
Guaraní in Paraguay
Source: Rubin (1968b:526)

indicate that the first thing a bilingual Paraguayan considers is whether or not he is in a rural location. If he is, then he will choose Guaraní; if not, he considers the formality of the situation. If it is formal, then Spanish is the choice; if it is informal, then intimacy comes into play. If the situation is not intimate, then Spanish will be spoken; if it is, then one must consider whether or not the discourse is serious. If it is not serious, then Guaraní is the automatic choice; if it is, then the choice is influenced by minor factors. For instance, one such factor is a speaker's first language (presumably the speaker will choose his first language, if the major influences are indecisive). Predicted language proficiency is another (Guaraní will be chosen, if the other person doesn't seem to be the sort who would know Spanish). A third is sex (bilingual men will select Guaraní when speaking to other men with whom they share a high degree of solidarity, but Spanish with solitary women; bilingual women are more likely to choose Spanish with both men and women, even when it is someone they are close to). A similar decision tree is given by Sankoff (1980:36) for the choice among three languages in New Guinea, but her tree contains a good deal more indeterminacy.

Both decision-tree analysis and domain analysis propose certain aspects of social situations as ones to watch if broad language-choice predictions are the goal. Four factors that are mentioned in several studies are: (1) location or setting (Rubin 1968b; Herman 1968; Blom and Gumperz 1972; Greenfield 1972; Dorian 1981); (2) situation (Rubin 1968b – especially her 'formality' category; Herman 1968; Blom and Gumperz 1972; Sankoff 1980); (3) topic (Rubin 1968b – with respect to 'seriousness of discourse'; Greenfield 1972; Sankoff 1980; Parasher 1980; Dorian 1981); and (4) participants (Rubin 1968b – 'intimacy' and some of her minor factors; Herman 1968; Greenfield 1972; Giles, Bourhis, and Taylor 1977; Gal 1978b, 1979; Sankoff 1980; Parasher 1980; and implicitly in Blom and Gumperz 1972). A short list like this that seems to be endorsed by a number of scholars might make it appear that a great deal of progress has been made in discovering the determinants of language choice. This would be a mistaken conclusion for at least two reasons. First of all, although many scholars use the same *terms*, there may be little in common in what they mean by them. For example, location to Rubin means the broad contrast between urban and rural areas of Paraguay; to Herman it means the distinction between public and private settings; Blom and Gumperz refer mainly to the kind of activity that normally takes place at a particular location, such as a government office or a church; and Greenfield is mostly concerned with congruency among location, topics, and participants within a domain. Secondly, almost all these scholars stop short of saying that they know how to use these factors to make reliable predictions about language choice. Rubin qualifies the predictive power of her decision-tree analysis when she mentions the fact that the rules for language choice are changing and that educated Paraguayans often use Spanish where her analysis would lead one to expect Guaraní.

An exception to this is Gal (1979:119). Gal's analysis allows her to predict language choice on the basis of participants alone:

The meaning conveyed by the invariable choice of one language between speakers can best be explicated by first returning to the question of how people choose between G, H, and GH. *For any informant, the choice of language can be predicted if one knows the identity of the informant and of the interlocutor.*(My italics)

Predictions can be made, if we know who the participants are, by using the language choice implicational scales. Gal goes on to emphasize that the identity of the participants is virtually the only thing that needs to be known. She explicitly excludes location, with the exception of school (where German is by law the only language of instruction), as a possible influence on language choice. Topic also, in so far as it is the same thing as 'occasion or purpose of the interaction' (Gal 1979:125), is said to 'make little difference'. There is one minor influence on language choice, apart from the actual participants and school location, and that is whether or not there are German monolinguals present, as we have seen.

Probably no sociologist and very few anthropologists would be satisfied with a prediction scheme that required the analyst to know the identity of a specific individual and his position on an implicational scale. But Gal seems to be only one short step away from being able to say, for the community she studied, that a person with x degree of commitment to the values of the small, or Low, language community will make y language choice when speaking to z interlocutor. All that is missing is a reliable measure of 'x'. If a way can be found to measure community involvement on a continuous scale, it would appear that a rather highly reliable method of language-choice prediction would be possible for Oberwart. A similar technique might well apply to other speech communities, too.

The interpretive study of code-mixing or 'conversational code-switching' (Gumperz 1977) reveals some fascinating similarities in situations from around the world. Although predicting every switch seems to be out of the question, in some cases there is striking agreement on how to interpret switches between High and Low languages within single conversations. Fundamentally, of course, using the High language means the speaker is invoking the values and status of the wider community; choosing the Low language similarly calls up the cultural patterns of the small community. It is possible, however, to find similarities in detail in how the general principle is applied. Three particular applications show striking parallels in widely separated speech communities around the world. These three are: (1) use of the High language to make an utterance more authoritative; (2) using the High language to give the 'point' or reason for telling a story that had been narrated mostly in the Low language; and (3) using the High language to impress a child with the seriousness of a command. The following quotations illustrate these cases.

(1) Appeal to authority.

The expression or assertion of expertise and knowledgeability either about an issue or in an area of activity, a skill or craft, was often accomplished by the speaker through a switch to German when giving a judgement or opinion. (Gal 1979:117 on German/ Hungarian bilingualism in Oberwart, Austria)

Our analysis ... revealed that when an argument required that the speaker validate his status as an intellectual, he would again tend to use standard forms. (Blom and Gumperz 1972:430 on the Bokmål/Ranamål contrast in Hemnesberget, Norway)

Three distinct lines of evidence ... all suggest that much Spanish usage in Nahuatl is a metaphorical switch, evoking the power and prestige of the Spanish-speaking world. (Hill and Hill 1980:130 on Spanish/Nahuatl bilingualism in the states of Tlaxala and Puebla, Mexico)

Here B disputes A's statement and A counters in German, as if to lend his statement more authority. (Gumperz 1977:19, commenting on an example of German/Slovenian switching in an unnamed Austrian village)

(2) Giving the point of a narrative.

Yet another use of language switching was what might be called emphasis or 'validation'. In a narrative of personal experience, the phrase that summed up the moral, or reason for the telling of the narrative was said twice, once in each language. (Gal 1979:117)

In narration, hispanisms tend to be highly concentrated in the most 'evaluative' sections of the discourse, where the speaker is showing why his story is worth hearing. (Hill and Hill 1980:125)

(3) Commands to children.   So striking is the similarity of three cases of switches in giving commands to children that I have chosen to quote the examples in full. The High language parts of each utterance are printed in boldface. In the first example, a grandfather is reprimanding his three-year-old granddaughter and her cousin, who have just scattered a pile of firewood (Gal 1979:112).

Grandfather: Szo!   ide dzsüni! (pause) jeszt jerámunyi mind
        Well, come here!   put all this away, both

e kettüötök, no hát akkor! (pause) **Kum her!** (pause)
of you, well now!   **Come here!**

Ném koapsz vacsorat!
You don't get supper!

In the second example, an Indian adult is warning a ten-year-old who is practicing swimming to stay near the side of the pool (Gumperz 1977:28).

Baaju-mẽ, beTa, baaju-mẽ! **Stay on the side!**
On the side, son, on the side!

The third example is taken from a Mexican American professional family's interaction (Gumperz 1977:28).

Ven acá!   Ven acá! **Come here, you!**
Come here! Come here!

In the first example, notice that the grandfather has given two commands in Hungarian that were not obeyed and that he paused after each. The command in German counts as an escalation in seriousness and is all the more striking because the little girl had not yet learned any German. Maybe that is one reason why she doesn't obey even the German order, and the grandfather has to escalate further, to an explicit threat. When the Spanish/English and Hindi/English cases were discussed with members of the appropriate speech communities, in both cases there was agreement that, like the Austrian case, the switch to the High language suggested a warning or mild threat (Gumperz 1977:28).[21]

Apart from these instances in which speakers appeal to qualities associated with the language they switch to, students of language choice have noticed two other uses of language switches: quotations and addressee specification. Gal (1979:100), Hill and Hill (1980:124), and Gumperz (1977:14) have all noticed that there is some tendency in bilingual settings to quote people in the language of the original utterance. For example, one of Gal's contacts, while narrating the story of his father's death in Hungarian, switched to German when he quoted what the doctor had said. However, Gal does not consider quotations to be fully genuine instances of switching. Gumperz (1977:21), on the other hand, points out that bilinguals do not *always* quote in the original language and their decision whether or not to do so probably has communicative significance.

Both Gal (1979:122) and Gumperz (1977:15) give examples of a language switch being used to select the person a remark is directed to, when there is more than one potential addressee. It is not necessarily a person who understands one language, but not the other. An addressee can sometimes be identified because the language the speaker has just switched to is the one she usually uses with that particular person, who may well be bilingual.

In spite of similarities in the way language choice is interpreted around the world, it is not the case that every single switch can be unambiguously interpreted, even within one community. Gal's framework for the analysis of conversational language-switching accounted for only half of the 40 cases she examined in detail (Gal 1979:117). According to Gumperz (1977:30), we should not expect to be able to assign a single interpretation to each switch because 'what is generated are preferred or possible interpretations, not clear and uncontestable meanings.' Sankoff (1980:44), after examining numerous cases of switching be tween Tok Pisin (H) and Buang (L) in New Guinea, concludes that it is not possible or even important to interpret individual switches: 'That the speaker use both languages in this context is important – he keeps in touch with all segments of his audience by constant alternation. But exactly what he says in one language or the other is not in itself important.' Perhaps an investigator would have to be a mind reader to know exactly why a person chooses one language or another at a particular point in a speech event. On the other hand, it is sometimes reasonably clear and recent research has at least given us a good idea of the kinds of communicative significance that can be attached to conversational switching.

Choosing without a choice.   Before we end our discussion of the anthropological study of language choice, it is important to report another peculiar phenomenon noticed by several of the language-choice researchers. Conversational language switching patterns, in particular, seem to be beyond the conscious control of individual speakers and often even *contrary* to their expressed language attitudes. Furthermore, switching of the metaphorical type seems to be almost universally deplored by bilinguals as 'language mixture'. Nevertheless, no matter how profound the prejudice against it, metaphorical switching is common among the very people who are most critical of it (Gumperz 1977:3, summarizing a portion of the Blom and Gumperz 1972 results; Hill and Hill 1980:131). The following exchange reported by Verma (1976:160) is a self-explanatory example:

> kyõ saheb! Hindii-mẽ English-ke expressions kyõ prayog hone
> why sir   Hindi-in English-of expressions why usage   has
>
> lage hãĩ
> become

Why have so many English expressions found their way into Hindi?

> hãã. yah to baRii hii   unnatural lagtii hai. merii
> yes This   very indeed unnatural seems   Of-me
>
> to is-topic-par scholars-se   kaafii   frank discussions
> this-topic-on   scholars-with numerous frank discussions
>
> hui   hãĩ.
> have been.

Yes. It seems very unnatural. I have had numerous frank discussions with scholars on this topic.

Conversational switching is such a powerful interactive resource that in practice it completely displaces a person's feelings for language purity. Like other sociolinguistic phenomena that most people do not have much regard for, such as pidgin and creole languages, nonstandard dialects, and diglossia, metaphorical switching is too useful a communicative tool to be easily given up.

TOWARD A SYNTHESIS

It is no doubt reasonably clear by this time that I am most impressed with the anthropological approach to language choice. Although anthropological linguists don't practice the same standards of research design and statistical validation that the other two social sciences require, it seems to me that their insights into what makes code-switching and mixing occur go deeper than the sociological and social psychological research we have reviewed. This is not to say that the anthropological results contradict or replace the findings from the other two disciplines. Domain analysis, with its emphasis on language choice as determined by the kind of communicative event that is in progress, has a great deal in common with the anthropologist's approach. It seems to me, though, that an analysis like Gal's goes a step deeper by explaining why some community members make different choices than others in the very same domains. By remaining content with a statistically significant relationship between language choices and the domains in which they are made, the sociological work on domain analysis appears to imply that variation in language choice cannot be or does not need to be explained. The domain-analysis concept of the congruence of factors like topic, location, and participants as components of a higher-level structure contrasts with Gal's evidence that language choice in one community can be explained on the basis of participants alone. Whether a complex domain concept is necessary or whether it is generally true that the social positions and self-concepts of the participants are enough to explain language choice is an empirical question.

The work of Herman and Giles and his associates on the desire for an individual to emphasize or de-emphasize his ties to social groups is also consistent with the discoveries of the anthropological linguists. Giles's notion of accommodation lends itself particularly well to the anthropological framework. Whether a person thinks of herself as a member of the same community as the person she is talking to, whether the other person is thought of as a visitor in the speaker's community or vice versa, and the presence or absence of conflict between their communities all work together to determine the degree and direction of accommodation. Gal's story of the old peasant couple who invited their German-speaking neighbor to help with farm work, but who did not use convergent accommodation is one example. They no doubt considered the neighbor to be a visitor from another community, who therefore should expect to be the one to make the adjustment. The Hungarian-speaking men in the inn, on the other hand, who 'converged' by switching to German simply because monolingual German speakers could overhear them, is the opposite kind of case. In their eyes, the monolinguals were members of the same (wider) community and therefore were entitled to convergent accommodation. Deliberate and self-conscious divergence probably only happens when speaker and interlocutor are not only from different communities, but there is hostility between the communities as well.

SUMMARY

Sociolinguistic variation implies that speakers have a choice among language varieties. This choice may be between one language or another, depending on the situation (code-switching), whether or not to use elements from one language while speaking another (code-mixing), or among the myriad variants within a single-language system.

The sociolinguistic aspects of language choice have been studied by sociologists, social psychologists, and anthropologists. This chapter included discussions of domain analysis from the sociological research on language choice, the work of Herman on 'overlapping psychological situations', and Giles and associates' 'accommodation theory' from social psychology, as well as the work of several anthropological linguists. The anthropological perspective looks for explanations for language choice in the speaker's perception of himself as a member of only one community, or as a concurrent member in two or more. Language choice at a particular moment is seen as evidence of a person's desire to be associated with the values of one speech community or another.

In seeking explanations for language choice, anthropologists have considered whether prediction or interpretation is the appropriate goal. Prediction, for example, by means of a decision-tree, might be possible with respect to choosing between languages, or deciding to use more than one language in the same speech event. It is generally agreed, however, that there is little hope of being able to predict every language switch a bilingual makes. Gal (1979), for example, is willing to make large-scale predictions for the community she studied in Oberwart, Austria, on the basis of the implicational-scale analysis of individual speakers. Although the prediction of switches within a single conversation seems to be out of reach, it is often possible to interpret conversational switches once they are observed. In fact, there are some surprisingly similar interpretations for metaphorical switches between High and Low languages from geographically and culturally diverse speech communities. But although the interactive task that a speaker wants to accomplish by means of a metaphorical language choice can often be understood, we cannot expect to assign an unambiguous interpretation to every observed switch.

The communicative power that a speaker derives from the use of two languages in the same situation is very often not appreciated by bilinguals themselves. None the less, although it is common for bilinguals to criticize 'language mixing' and support 'language purity', these attitudes have almost no effect on the actual use of language; these same speakers continue to practice metaphorical switching without being fully aware of it.

The contributions of the three social science disciplines all provide valuable insights into the phenomenon of language choice. Anthropology seems to provide the greatest explanatory depth of the three, in spite of methodological practices that are not sufficiently rigorous from the point of view of sociology or social psychology. The most thorough understanding of language choice as a sociolinguistic phenomenon seems to come from incorporating the insights of sociology and social psychology into an anthropological framework.

BIBLIOGRAPHICAL NOTES

Language choice between English and Hindi is not the only such phenomenon to be found in India. Similar relationships exist between English and Kannada (Sridhar 1978) and Malayalam (Kola 1977). Other studies of language choice include Heller (1978, Montreal), Ros and Giles (1979, Valencia) and Scotton and Ury (1977). The Ros and Giles article is written from the perspective of accommodation theory.

NOTES

1   The linguistic issues that arise in the study of language choice are the subject of a chapter on code-switching and inherent variability in volume II. Here we are concerned with language choice as a social phenomenon. Gumperz (1977) discusses some of the syntactic and pragmatic constraints on code-mixing.

2   In one of the most thorough studies of language choice and language shift, Gal (1979) deals with all three kinds of language choice; as does Dorian (1981), in another fine study of these issues. Gumperz (1977) mentions some differences between language variation and language choice involving separate languages.

3   The *linguistic* difference between switching and within-language variation is theoretically important, but it is very often hard to tell which is going on in a particular case. In any event, the distinction is not so important *sociolinguistically*, and I take it that the choice from among variants of the same language is fundamentally the same sociolinguistic phenomenon as switching and mixing.

4   This is a bit misleading, since Hindi-Urdu was the mother tongue of over a quarter of the respondents and Telegu, the regional (state) language of Andhra Pradesh, was the mother tongue of 28 per cent (Andhra Pradesh was the research site.) If a language was counted as mother tongue, it would not also count under 'Hindi' or 'regional language'.

5   Among the interesting differences is that the most Spanish usage is reported by the Miami Cuban Americans and the most use of mixed Spanish and English by the Austin Mexican Americans.

6   At this point, Herman's analysis touches on the same issues as Giles's accommodation theory, as we will soon see.

7   I was able to observe a particularly dramatic example of this on a trip to Europe

with my father, who had emigrated to the United States from Germany thirty years earlier. Since he seldom used German in the US, it required some effort to speak German fluently without lapsing into English at the beginning of a trip to Europe. In making arrangements with a hotel clerk on our arrival in Luxembourg, he began in German, switched to English, caught himself, and spoke German again; this occurred several times during the conversation. The hotel clerk converged perfectly, answering in whichever language he had last been addressed in.

8   To anticipate our later discussion, we are here examining a *predictive* analysis of language choice. As we will soon see, a more modest goal would be an *interpretive* analysis, in which no attempt is made to say what a speaker will do in advance, but instead to understand her motivations once we know what language-choice decision she has made.

9   We have been concentrating on accommodation of various kinds within particular interactions, but accommodation can occur over the long run as well. We saw in the chapter 6 that West Indians in Wales accommodated to the local speech community to the extent that their ethnic origin could not be detected in their speech. An excellent study of the same phenomenon was carried out by Wolfram (1973, 1974), in which he was able to show that some Puerto Ricans in New York City accommodated, in a long-range linguistic sense, to Vernacular Black English rather than any other variety. These turned out to be the same young men who had the most black peers in their communications networks and knew most about black cultural values and institutions.

10   In the terms associated with address forms in chapter 1 of volume II, there is a 'power' relationship, but no 'solidarity' between the two groups.

11   Blom and Gumperz use the expression 'local team' to express the concept of membership in the local, as opposed to the wider, community. In this article, they take an interpretive, rather than a predictive, stance on language-choice analysis. We will discuss this controversy next.

12   Notice that this kind of 'experiment' is strictly an anthropologist's experiment. Apart from bringing about a gathering of people who already belonged to the same social network and giving a little help in getting conversations started, Blom and Gumperz did nothing to intervene. In most social psychology experiments, the experimenter does something to control the circumstances the subjects find themselves in.

13   We are now in a better position to understand the educated Indians of Parasher's study who report extensive use of English even in such typically 'Low' domains as friendship and neighborhood. Their self-identities as members of the English-educated stratum of society are allowed to coexist with and even exceed their self-identities as members of their mother-tongue groups in these as well as 'Higher' domains. Only in the most intimate family domain does self-identity as a member of one's mother-tongue group predominate.

14   Gumperz (1977:12) reports a parallel case in another Austrian bilingual community, this time on the Yugoslavian border with Slovenian as the Low language. In this village, speaking Slovenian in the presence of monolingual speakers of German is so strictly avoided that it is possible to stay there for weeks and not even realize that any language but German is spoken. Dorian (1981:79–80) reports a very slightly different treatment of monolinguals in the area of the Scottish Highlands where she worked. Here, bilinguals will switch from Gaelic to English if even one monolingual English speaker *joins* the group, but will not switch just because they can be overheard by monolinguals.

15   Implicational scales prove to be a very useful analytical tool in the discussion of several of the topics in volume II.

16   The 'cells' that fail to conform to perfect scalability, marked with an asterisk in table 7.5, are sometimes arbitrarily chosen. The correct *number* of cells are marked; it is often not possible to be sure *which* cells should be considered deviant.

17   A situation very similar to the one in Oberwart recently existed in East Sutherland, an area in the northern Scottish Highlands (Dorian 1981:90, 93–94). There, English can be considered the High language in much the sense that German is in Oberwart, yet Gaelic, the Low language, was used in church services by the fishing community, which is the counterpart of the Oberwart Hungarian-speaking peasants. The variety of Gaelic, though, was somewhat archaic and had much higher status than the variety used for everyday speech. I should point out that Dorian denies that diglossia is applicable to the community she studied, partly because the Low-language candidate was used in religion, a typically High domain. The situation as she describes nevertheless seems to fit comfortably into the extended idea of diglossia presented in chapter 2.

18   Milroy (1980) made the parallel finding within the varieties of English used in Belfast. Those with the densest local communications networks used the most local dialect variants. Hill and Hill (1980) come to a similar conclusion in their work, finding that Indians with the deepest commitment to Nahuatl community values are the ones who borrow from and switch to Spanish the least.

19   Prediction and interpretation as goals of language-choice study are thoroughly discussed in Sankoff (1980).

20   This is a term used by Gal (1979:100), although she does not use the technique.

21   We have been assuming that the 'wider community' would be the one that spoke the language with higher status and the 'small community' was the one with the lower-status language. This is true for all the cases we have studied, *except* the case of educated Indians. Here, the speech community that uses English is far smaller than the Hindi-speaking community, as we already know. Yet English in this situation is the prestige language and functions as a High language.

OBJECTIVES

1   Be able to list the three kinds of language choice mentioned on p.180.

2   Be able to state whether or not the three kinds of language choice can be readily distinguished.

3   Be able to recognize the definition of *domain*.

4   Be able to identify how the concept 'domain' is related to the concept 'diglossia'.

5   Be able to identify the similarities and differences in the results obtained by Greenfield in a New York Puerto Rican community and by Parasher among educated Indians in the south of India.

6   Be able to write an explanation of the reason for the unexpected result that Parasher obtained in India.

7   Be able to name the two factors mentioned by Simon Herman that are concerned with social groupings, and the third factor that is not.

8   Be able to recognize Herman's 'central idea' (p. 188).

9   Be able to define the three kinds of accommodation in Giles's theory.

10   Be able to state whether or not 'accommodation" is only a matter of language choice (pp. 189-90).

11   Given one of the three patterns of the perception of social change in table 7.4, be able to identify the prediction that Giles, Bourhis, and Taylor would make about the linguistic behavior of dominant and subordinate groups. For example, given that there is no perception of the possibility of social change, you would state that

the dominant group would practice *nonconvergence* and the subordinate group would *converge*.

12   During periods when a subordinate group is asserting its rights with respect to a dominant group, linguistic convergence by members of the dominant group might not be accepted. Be able to identify the reason for this phenomenon (pp. 190-1).

13   Be able to identify the main interest of anthropologists in studying language choice, as opposed to sociologists and social psychologists.

14   Be able to identify a description of the anthropologist's technique of *participant observation*.

15   Given a description of the two community structures illustrated in figure 7.2, be able to recognize the resulting implications for language choice.

16   Be able to distinguish *metaphorical* and *situational* switching.

17   Be able to describe the contrasting linguistic behavior of the Oberwart Hungarian men in the tavern and the old Hungarian peasant couple, and what their behavior signified about their sense of social identity.

18   Understand the meaning of Gal's use of *implicational scaling* well enough to do the following. Given an Oberwart interlocutor and the language(s) a speaker will use with him, and also given a second interlocutor, be able to state the language that the speaker will choose with the second interlocutor, assuming a perfect scale. For example, if you are told that German is used with 'salespeople', you should know that German will be used with everyone to the right of 'salespeople' in table 7.5. Therefore, if asked what language would be used by that same speaker to a 'government official', assuming a perfect scale, you would be able to answer 'German'. Hint: to meet this objective, you will not have to memorize table 7.5, but only have a general idea of how interlocutors are ordered on the basis of age and social status.

19   The choice of a language of religion in a bilingual community is often different from the language choice in other 'High' domains. Be able to identify the general rule for selection of the language of religion (p.199).

20   Be able to read a *decision tree* well enough so that, if you are given figure 7.3, and one of the 'nodes' on the tree, you could state the next step in the language-choice decision. For example, if you are told that a speaker is in a nonrural location, you should be able to say that formality or informality will be inspected as the next step in a language choice.

21   Given their definitions, be able to supply the stronger and weaker goals in language-choice analysis (pp. 200-1).

22   Be able to name the three applications of language choice between 'higher' and 'lower' languages that have been found at widely separated locations around the world.

23   Be able to recognize the extent to which language-choice determination has been successful, according to the prominent scholars cited on p. 202.

24   Be able to recognize an explanation of what Fasold means by 'choosing without a choice' (pp. 206-7).

8

Language Maintenance and Shift

SHIFT AND CHOICE

Language shift and, the other side of the coin, language maintenance are really the long-term, collective results of language choice. Language *shift* simply means that a community gives up a language completely in favor of another one. The members of the community, when the shift has taken place, have collectively chosen a new language where an old one used to be used. In language *maintenance*, the community collectively decides to continue using the language or languages it has traditionally used. When a speech community begins to choose a new language in domains formerly reserved for the old one, it may be a sign that language shift is in progress. If the members of a speech community are monolingual and are not collectively acquiring another language, then they are obviously maintaining their language-use pattern. Maintenance, however, is often a characteristic of *bilingual* or *multilingual* communities as well. Ths only happens, as we will see in detail, when the community is diglossic, in the expanded sense of chapter 2. Another way of saying the same thing is that language-maintaining multilingual communities reserve each language for certain domains with very little encroachment of one language on the domains of the others.[1]

Language shift is sometimes referred to, somewhat dramatically, as *language death*. Language death occurs when a community shifts to a new language totally so that the old language is no longer used. There is a small controversy about whether language death should apply only when the shifting speech community consists of the last surviving speakers of the language, or whether it can be applied to a total shift in a given community, whether or not there are other people in the world who still use the language. No one would doubt that when the last surviving speaker of 'tribal Guaraní' in Paraguay dies, probably early in the twenty-first century, tribal Guaraní will be 'dead'. But if the Hungarian bilingual community in Oberwart shifts entirely to German, there will still be plenty of Hungarian speakers left in Hungary (although not of the Oberwart dialect). Hungarian would be 'dead' in Oberwart, but certainly not worldwide. Dorian (1978:647) is one scholar who takes the point of view that language death can properly be used of total shift in one community only, provided that the shift is from one *language* to another, rather than from one variety of a language to another variety of that same language. That is, the 'dying' language must be succumbing to competition from another language, not a prestige form of the same linguistic system. Referring to language shift in East Sutherland, a region in the Scottish Highlands, and to Pennsylvania Dutch (actually a variety of German), Dorian says: 'Thus, although the Gaelic language will not itself wholly disappear when its East Sutherland variety becomes extinct, and the German language will obviously survive the demise of Berks County Dutch, the Gaelic language is dying in East Sutherland and the German language in Berks County.' Denison (1977:15) expresses the opposite point of view in the following tongue-in-cheek fashion: 'though the disappearance without trace of all Basque speakers would signal the "death" of a language, if all Viennese dialect speakers were to be carried off by Hong Kong flu, it would mean scarcely more than a headache to "the German language".' It isn't too important to decide whether the term 'language death' should be allowed its broad interpretation or be restricted to the narrower one, as long as we are aware that it is used in both these ways.

There are two aspects to language death that have interested linguists: the linguistic aspect and the sociolinguistic aspect. Languages that are in the last stages of use in a community undergo interesting alterations in their pronunciation and grammar systems, in some respects reminiscent of pidginization (Dressler 1972).[2] The sociolinguistic aspect, the subject of this chapter, is the search for the set of conditions that cause people to give up a language in favor of another.

Methodology

Like the study of language choice, language maintenance and shift are studied by different methods, depending on the academic discipline of the scholar. Anthropologists and anthropological linguists use the same methods, particularly participant-observation, as they use in the study of language choice. In fact, anthropologically oriented investigators usually study language choice and maintenance and shift simultaneously as part of the same phenomenon. The traditional interest of anthropologists in the intensive study of individual communities makes this a reasonable approach. The choices made by the members of a particular speech community, reflecting their cultural values, add up to shift or maintenance in that community. The search for general or universal causes for maintenance and shift would be drawn from a study of a number of intensive investigations of individual communities.

In sociology, the approach is quite different. Sociologists are likely to take a much broader view of the whole issue. Rather than intensively studying a particular community to find an explanation for why it did or did not shift, they often prefer to examine survey data from as many communities as possible. Their data are not like the observation notes of an anthropologist, but are likely to be the returns from censuses or other survey questionnaires. There are two ways in which shift can show up in survey data. If there are data available from the same population for more than one time (usually census data), and there is a significant decline in the number of respondents reporting a given language, that might signal a shift. If census data are inadequate or not available, a one-shot survey may have to do. The thing to look for is age-distribution numbers. If older speakers report more use of one language and younger speakers more use of another one, this can be an indication of shift. The dangers of jumping to conclusions on the basis of this kind of data, though, are often pointed out (Lieberson 1980, Mackey and Cartwright 1979). Two of the major problems in interpreting one-time survey results are connected with *age-grading* and *migration*.

If there is a genuine shift taking place, it would certainly show up in the larger proportions of older speakers using the declining language than younger speakers. Language shift, however, is not the only way that age-related differences can arise. It is often the case that different language behavior is expected of people in a society at different ages. In a community with diglossia, young children learn the Low language first. As a result, almost all small children might be monolingual in that language. As they grow older, some will acquire the High language. Survey data that indicate a high level of monolingualism among young children and a high level of bilingualism among adults could not be taken to mean that the High language is necessarily dying out. Many of the monolingual children will probably learn it as they enter school and begin to function in High domains. In short, the young speakers may be monolingual early in life, but it would be foolish to assume that they will remain so all their lives. Lieberson (1972, 1980:14–15) reports a case from French–English bilingualism in Montreal that shows how age-correlated data on bilingualism can be misleading, even within the adult portion of a life-span. We will be looking at this case in detail later in this chapter.

Migration is another confounding factor in survey data. To the extent that people have moved into or out of a given region between censuses, the results for that area do not show whether individual speakers are giving up or keeping languages, since the data will be about partially different populations in the two censuses. Of course, a geographical *area* can be said to be undergoing language shift if a large number of speakers of some other language move in, even if none of the older residents learn the new language. Substantial in-migration can put pressure on older residents to learn the language of the incoming group, especially if they gain control of the economic and social institutions. But it could be that the regional data are really a conflation of data on two speech communities who happen to live in the same geographical area. One community might be maintaining two languages and the other only one, with neither *community* having shifted at all. Of course, even without migration, survey data can easily mix data from more than one speech community.

We have already seen two of the more general problems that plague survey data. Survey data are almost always self-reported, which makes them somewhat suspect, but, like weather forecasts, self-reported data are not always wrong either. Recall that Gal (1979) found this when her survey results correlated highly with her observations. Another problem in using survey data on language shift is connected with the discovery of causes. Unlike anthropological participant-observation, survey data are very unlikely to provide information on cultural values. Therefore it is necessary to look for *measurable* causes, such as urbanization, migration, or shifts in economic indicators. Even a correlation between such measurable values and statistical evidence in the decline in the number of speakers of some language, if it is found, would not establish a cause relationship. In chapter 5, we examined some of the work of Lieberson and his associates that show how misleading such correlations can be (Lieberson and Hansen 1974; Lieberson, Dalto, and Johnston 1975). In spite of all this, the careful use of survey data is a valuable tool in the understanding of maintenance and shift. The supplementary use of survey data by more anthropologically oriented sociolinguists like Gal (1979), Dorian (1981), and Huffines (1980) is indirect evidence that this is true.

There is one other type of sociological research on language maintenance and shift. This is the search for factual and theoretical generalities without direct recourse to specific data. Tabouret-Keller's (1968) comparison of European and African maintenance and shift patterns and Verdoodt's (1972) analysis of three German–French contact situations in Western Europe are two examples. In this type of study, the facts of the case are largely presupposed and the investigator goes on to analyze what is behind them. Although data-based studies tend to be more convincing, these 'step back and take a look' studies can be very well worth doing.

The impetus to shift

Certain conditions tend to be associated with language shift in several studies of the phenomenon. Perhaps the most basic condition is societal bilingualism. It is important to notice that bilingualism is not a sufficient condition for shift, although it may be a necessary one. Almost all cases of societal language shift come about through intergenerational switching (Lieberson 1972, 1980). In other words, a substantial proportion of the individuals in a society seldom completely give up the use of one language and substitute another one within their own lifetime. In the typical case, one generation is bilingual, but only passes on one of the two languages to the next. Since intergenerational switching requires the earlier generation to be bilingual, the proportion of a population that is bilingual constitutes an 'exposure to risk' that one of the languages might eventually be lost (Lieberson 1972:242). The language of a monolingual community is virtually certain to be maintained as long as the monolingualism persists. Many bilingual communities remain bilingual for decades or centuries, so the existence of societal bilingualism does not mean that shift will take place. In addition to bilingualism, other factors have to be present.

There is a strong tendency for language shift to be attributed to the same causes in study after study. Among the most frequently-cited causes are: *migration*, either by members of small groups who migrate to an area where their language no longer serves them, or by large groups who 'swamp' the local population with a new language (Tabouret-Keller 1968, 1972; Lewis 1972a, 1978; Dressler and Wodak-Leodolter 1977; Lieberson and McCabe 1978; Gal 1979; Dorian 1980; Timm 1980); *industrialization* and other economic changes (Tabouret-Keller 1968, 1972; Dressler and Wodak-Leodolter 1977; Gal 1979; Huffines 1980; Timm 1980; Dorian 1981); *school language* and other government pressures (Dressler and Wodak-Leodolter 1977; Gal 1979; Kahane and Kahane 1979; Dorian 1980; Huffines 1980; Timm 1980); *urbanization* (Tabouret-Keller 1968; Gal 1979; Timm 1980; Dorian 1981); higher *prestige* for the language being shifted to (Denison 1977; Gal 1979; Kahane and Kahane 1979; Dorian 1981); and a *smaller population* of speakers of the language being shifted from (Lieberson and McCabe 1978; Kahane and Kahane 1979; Dorian 1980; Huffines 1980). Just as we saw in the case of language choice, however, where the same factors were cited independently by many scholars, there has been very little success in using any combination of them to predict when language shift will occur. In fact, there is considerable consensus that we do not know how to predict shift (Kloss 1966:209–12; Denison 1977:16; Gal 1979:3; Dorian 1981:4; to mention only a few). Although many of the most often-cited sociological factors are present when a shift does occur, it is all too easy to find cases in which some speech community is exposed to the very same factors, but has maintained its language.

Most discussion of language shift concerns the shift of small, lower-status linguistic groups who shift to the language of a larger, higher-status group. None the less, there are a few fascinating cases in which the more powerful group has assimilated linguistically to the people they control politically. Perhaps the most commonly cited example of this is the ultimate shift to English by the Norman conquerors of England in the eleventh century (Kahane and Kahane 1979, Denison 1977). Another example is one we are familiar with, the spread of Guaraní among the descendants of the Spanish colonists in Paraguay, although not to the extent that Spanish disappeared, as Norman French did in England. It would be worth the effort to try to find out what made these two conquering groups give up their original languages in favor of the languages of the subject populations.

CASES OF MAINTENANCE AND SHIFT
Developing nations

Although Fishman (1964) called attention to language maintenance and shift as phenomena worthy of study nearly twenty years ago, the topic has inspired relatively few studies.[3] Gal (1979) and Dorian (1981) are the first widely available monograph-length investigations of language shift in a specific community. A number of shorter reports of maintenance and shift research have appeared recently, but European and North American cases have received most of the attention. It would be of great interest to have in-depth studies of the phenomena in developing countries, to see what similarities and differences there are compared with the western nation cases. On the basis of a broad overview of European and African instances, Tabouret-Keller (1968:117) concluded that there were more differences than similarities when present-day Europe is compared with present-day Africa. A historical view, though, would show 'more analogies than differences, provided we compare the present transformations in Africa with the transformations that began toward the end of the nineteenth century in Europe'. Among the available studies in developing nations are a general review of maintenance and shift in the Philippines (Asuncion-Landé and Pascasio 1979), another set in Singapore (Chong 1977), and Lieberson and McCabe's (1978) survey research in Nairobi. In addition, there is a lot to learn about maintenance and shift in reports on developing nations that are focused on other topics; Abdulaziz Mkilifi's (1978) research in Tanzania, and Kuo's (1979) and Platt's (1977) work in Malaysia are examples we have already encountered. None the less, for the time being we have to be content with the available in-depth studies from Europe and North America.

Developed nations

Cases of shift – Oberwart.   To get a feel for what language shift is like, we will look at a profile of two cases of language shift, a case of language maintenance, and one instance where the data are ambiguous. We are already familiar with Gal's (1978b, 1979) research in Oberwart, Austria as a study of language choice; we will now examine it as an instance of language shift (see map 8.1).

German–Hungarian bilingualism has existed in Oberwart (Felsöör in Hungarian) probably since before 1500; by the nineteenth century, the majority of peasants in Oberwart were bilingual. During that century, Oberwart changed from being a peasant village to a socially and culturally diverse town.

Map 8.1   Location of the bilingual community of Oberwart, Austria

Monolingual German-speaking immigrants arrived and formed a prestigious class of merchants, artisans, and government officials. The original peasant population found itself in the lowest social and economic stratum of the local society. They were the only bilinguals and the only ones who spoke Hungarian. All this occurred while Burgenland, the province where Oberwart is located, was still part of Hungary; the transfer of Burgenland from Hungary to Austria in 1921 added to the prestige of German by making it the official national language as well. In spite of the high prestige of German, the low social status of the peasant class, and their widespread individual bilingualism, there was no shift: Hungarian was the linguistic symbol of group identity for the Oberwart peasants and German was merely a language to be used for dealing with outsiders. Economically, subsistence agriculture was feasible, although it was sometimes necessary to supplement income by working part-time for the merchants and artisans, and German was necessary for this. This kind of work was not lucrative enough to replace agriculture and, as a result, it was neither possible nor considered desirable to become a member of the social groups who were monolingual in German. Religion was another unifying and separating factor; the bilingual peasants were Calvinists, whereas the monolingual German speakers were Lutherans or Catholics.

This state of affairs began to change after the Second World War II. The local industrial and commercial economy, and the attendant increase in government employment, developed to the point where nonagricultural employment became an attractive possibility. To take advantage of these new opportunities, it was necessary to become a real Austrian, rather than to remain a local peasant who speaks Hungarian primarily, but happens to live in Austria. As a result, the social identity associated with the German language became desirable. Although bilingualism persisted, the use of German began to expand into formerly Hungarian domains, Hungarian became a marker of the increasingly disparaged peasant class, and the signs of language shift became more and more apparent.

Before the Second World War, then, the two language groups in Oberwart were parallel rather than competing. Each language had its own kind of prestige and each group considered the other to be outsiders. More recently, the two languages have become symbols of two ethnic identities, *both* of which are possible for an Oberwart peasant. The two identities coexist and compete; so do the two languages. As a result, to the extent that an individual thinks of himself as a member of the Austrian social and economic system, to that extent his use of German increases at the expense of Hungarian. An individual who conceives of himself as a peasant will maintain Hungarian to a greater extent.

As we know, Gal found that the use of the two languages by bilinguals can be predicted on the basis of interlocutor only, and she found a more complex domain analysis unnecessary. We have seen how the implicational scale in table 7.5 shows the sequence of the spread of German to situations where Hungarian would have previously been used and where more conservative individuals still use it. By glancing across the top of table 7.5, you can see that, although the interlocutors specified are a heterogeneous set, they are, as Gal (1979:126) points out, 'ranked according to their degree of "urbanization" or "Austrianness".' Since these qualities have the higher prestige, German is used in high-status settings first and by the most people.

We are already familiar with the age distribution of speakers compared with the relative strengths of German and Hungarian. By and large, it is the youngest speakers who use German in the most situations and the older ones who best preserve Hungarian. This pattern suggests that German is gaining at the expense of Hungarian as time goes on. But, as Lieberson warns us, it can be dangerous to interpret age correlations uncritically as evidence of change. Gal (1979:154–6) is well aware of this trap and has produced historical evidence that shows that in Oberwart the correlation of language use with age *is* to be interpreted as an indication of change through time. As we will see more clearly when we examine the other two cases of shift, another important piece of evidence, together with age correlation, is the language passed on to children. Apparently, most Oberwart peasant children are still growing up bilingual.[4] For the most part, parents are not passing on the higher status language to the exclusion of the lower. There is one important exception to this. Where there is intermarriage between a German monolingual and a German-Hungarian bilingual, the children will grow up monolingual in German, no matter which parent speaks only German (Gal 1979:107). Usually, it will be the mother who speaks only German, since local bilingual young women are increasingly reluctant to marry peasant men and commit themselves to the hard life that that would mean. This makes exogamous marriages more and more often the only alternative for young men who want to continue in the peasant tradition. In general, peasant families are the most likely to preserve Hungarian, but only if both parents speak it. The developing marriage pattern bodes ill for the preservation of Hungarian.[5]

Institutional support for a language can have a bearing on whether or not it will be maintained. Two of the most important institutions are schools and the church. In Oberwart, German is the language of education in the state schools, but the Austrian government officially guarantees minority-language rights. Immediately after the Second World War, a government-supported Hungarian language school was established, but it was eventually closed due to lack of support in the community. German is seen, even by bilinguals, as the only proper language of education. Church services have traditionally been conducted in Hungarian in the Oberwart Calvinist church, but a German service had recently been instituted when Gal began her research. None the less, the Hungarian service is much preferred:

They prefer to pray and sing hymns in Hungarian and even prefer to hear the sermon in Hungarian although this is always delivered in standard by the Hungarian-born minister. They explain that this is the way they are used to it and that it is the Lutherans and Catholics who do it in German; 'we' do it in Hungarian. Gal (1979:106).

In the Hungarian-speaking group, the church is a small-community institution and it would not be appropriate to use the language of the larger community there. Notice, however, that it is the highest variety of the Low language that is used in church.

Finally, there are two somewhat more linguistic aspects that may have a bearing on language shift. First of all, in addition to the prestige differences between German and Hungarian, a better *kind* of Hungarian is recognized. There is a 'proper' Hungarian associated with writing, and with educated speakers from Hungary. The local dialect is noticeably different and believed to be not as good. It can be difficult for a speaker of standard Hungarian to understand a speaker of Oberwart Hungarian, but Oberwart residents who travel to Hungary report that they can overcome this. On the other hand, if an Oberwart speaker were to attempt to use standard Hungarian speech in everyday situations, she would be immediately censured. This ambivalent attitude toward the styles of Hungarian was summed up by one of Gal's Oberwart contacts who 'expressed regret that she could not speak more beautiful Hungarian, but then added that if she ever did people would laugh at her' (Gal 1979:106). The other linguistic phenomenon is borrowing: Hungarian forms are rarely used when a person is speaking German, but German words are freely used in Hungarian.

Cases of shift – East Sutherland.   Another case of language shift is in progress in East Sutherland, a region in the northern Highlands of Scotland (Dorian 1981, see map 8.2). Like Oberwart, East Sutherland, as well as the rest of the Highlands, has had a long history of bilingualism. The languages are English and Gaelic. Like Hungarian in Oberwart, Gaelic is the language with the longer history, but lower status. Since the fourteenth century, the Scottish court, based in the Lowlands, has used English. Over the years, English was associated with the 'civilized' Lowland population, and Gaelic with the 'savage' Highlanders. The 1707 Act of Union which united the English and Scottish parliaments brought the Highlands under another layer of rule by English speakers. Nevertheless, geographical distance and the lack of roads kept the Highlands isolated until the early nineteenth century. At that time, an English-speaking elite population moved into northern Scotland. English 'pressed in from the top of the social hierarchy and spread steadily downward', until Gaelic moved from majority to minority language status (Dorian 1981:53).

    In another striking parallel with Oberwart, the next-to-last group to retain Gaelic were the 'crofters', people with small land holdings who live by subsistence agriculture and are the closest equivalent to a peasant class (Dorian 1981:6). Dorian arrived too late to study shift among the crofters, since their shift to English was virtually complete by the early 1960s, when she began her work. In East Sutherland, there was one more group who still spoke Gaelic, the fishing community. These fisherfolk acquired their occupation and status in an amazing way. In the early nineteenth century, agriculture as it was then practiced was unprofitable for the large landholders. At the same time, a potentially lucrative sheep-herding industry developed, but this required large tracts of land. In order to open up the land for the sheep, tenants who were working small plots of land had to be 'cleared'. It seemed to the landlords that there was an unrealized potential fishing industry that might support displaced tenants. Accordingly, the tenants were summarily moved to coastal locations, where, by no choice of their own and with

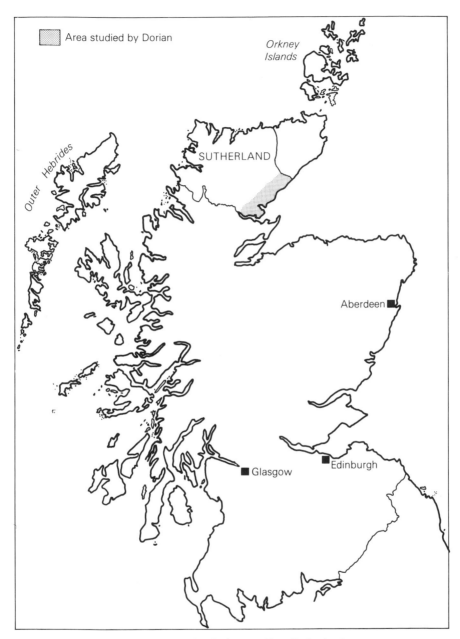

Map 8.2   Scotland, showing East Sutherland

considerable suffering, they eventually learned to support themselves by fishing.

These fishing communities immediately became a separate sociocultural group (Dorian 1981:54–5). They lived in their own tight residential areas, sometimes called 'Fishertown' by their neighbors. They were socially ostracized, had no choice but to marry within their group, and became characterized as the people who spoke Gaelic (although they eventually became bilingual in English). To a greater degree than in Oberwart, the lower social status of the East Sutherland fishing communities was forced on them by the refusal of other members of the wider communities to accept them. Almost paradoxically, the very fact that speaking Gaelic came to be known as a characteristic of the fishing communities both made possible its maintenance and guaranteed its eventual doom (Dorian 1981:67). As long as the fisherfolk remained members of a distinct sociocultural group with Gaelic as its linguistic symbol, the language would continue to be learned and used. But since the fisherfolk were thought of and, indeed, thought of themselves as a less worthy group of people, the moment social mobility became possible, the group would dissolve itself and its linguistic symbol would be abandoned in the process. This process began in the decades after the First World War when the fishing industry, marginal as it had always been, entered into a serious decline. Gaelic-speaking fishing people had to find other jobs and prejudice against them began, although painfully slowly, to weaken. Intermarriage became possible. The process of acceptance was speeded up to some extent by a further influx of people from other areas, who didn't know that they weren't supposed to like the people in the fishing community. Slowly, and to the degree allowed them, people gave up their fisher identity and Gaelic with it.

Since Gaelic had become one of the behaviors which allowed the labeling of individuals as fishers, there was a tendency to abandon Gaelic along with other 'fisher' behaviors. As the same woman said: 'I think, myself, as the children from Lower Brora got older, they . . . were ashamed to speak the Gaelic, in case they would be classed as a – a fisher.' (Dorian 1981:67)

The use of Gaelic and English within the East Sutherland fishing community depended on how closely the speech event was associated with the smaller community. In the early twentieth century, home, work, and religion were domains that demanded or favored the use of Gaelic, whereas national secular institutions (schools, political parties, courts, military, police), local public life, and written uses demanded or favored English (Dorian 1981:75). Dorian's description indicates that the domains in which Gaelic and English would be used could be set up along a continuum, something like the column headings of table 7.5, such that domains on the left would be ones where only Gaelic would be used, ones on the right would guarantee the use of English, and middle ones would show the use of both languages. For example, at that time only Gaelic would be used at home and only English would be used in the national secular institutions. In other domains, such as work, either language might be chosen, depending on other factors. Dorian (1981:75–8) mentions setting, interlocutor, and function in addition to domain as determining factors. (Unlike Greenfield 1972, she apparently takes 'domain' to be a unitary factor, rather than a constellation of other ones.) The person being talked to, the interlocutor, seems to be the most important. It is fairly obvious that outgroup members are addressed in English, as are ingroup members if an English monolingual is considered part of the conversation.[6] Even within the community, some individuals, but not all, are always addressed in Gaelic.[7]

The age-correlated patterns are similar to the situation in Oberwart; the oldest speakers are the ones who are the most comfortable with Gaelic and younger speakers are better in English (Dorian 1981:4–5) The use of the two languages within the family is strongly influenced by the age of the addressee. Grandparents would use and expect Gaelic; parents would use Gaelic with other people of their own and the ascending generation, but use English with their children and expect it in return (Dorian 1981:76). For these parents, English coexists with Gaelic in the home domain, which once absolutely required Gaelic. At the present time, this is the most common pattern. Parents speak Gaelic to each other at home, but not to their children. The result is that the children grow up able to understand Gaelic, but not to speak it. In such families, Gaelic is almost sure to die out in the next generation, when the children of these passive bilinguals grow up totally monolingual in English.

The home is the last bastion of a subordinate language in competition with a dominant official language of wider currency. An impending shift has in effect arrived, even though a fairly sizeable number of speakers may be left, if those speakers have failed to transmit the language to their children, so that no replacement generation is available when the parent generation dies away. (Dorian 1981:105)

Ever since the middle of the nineteenth century, the language of education has been English. In the nineteenth century, children could be beaten for using Gaelic within hearing of the headmaster.[8] Over the years, the anti-Gaelic education policy was moderated in the direction of tolerance for and then promotion of Gaelic. But these changes came in very small steps, sometimes with decades intervening between them, and the new policies were only half-heartedly implemented. Within the memory of many people living in East Sutherland, there were two services in the Free Presbyterian churches, one in Gaelic attended only by fisherfolk and one in English for everyone else (Dorian 1981:64). Currently, no Gaelic is used in church services. The variety of Gaelic that was used was a conservative, high-prestige variety that was not used in everyday speech, or for any other purpose except religion (Dorian 1981:90).

The linguistic facts about variation within the Low or small-community language and about borrowing are similar to what was found in Oberwart. East Sutherland Gaelic speakers apologize for their 'bad' local Gaelic and often say that speakers from other areas speak a better form of the language (Dorian 1981:86–93). 'Good' Gaelic seems to be particularly likely to be attributed to people from the Outer Hebrides, islands off the northwest coast of Scotland. Gaelic is declining before English roughly from the south and east toward the north and west, so the Hebrides are the main area where Gaelic is most widely used (and perhaps the closest equivalent to the position of Hungary for Oberwart Hungarian speakers). People from East Sutherland report considerable difficulty in understanding people from other dialect areas such as the Hebrides. There is also something of a written standard for Gaelic which does not quite correspond to any of the spoken dialects, but apparently differs from East Sutherland Gaelic more than it does from some of the others. It also enjoys more prestige than the local spoken form of the language. As in Oberwart, speaking the local form of the dialect is a symbol of group loyalty, and no one actually tries to speak a 'better' kind of Gaelic. In fact, when local classes in written Gaelic are offered and the teacher insists too strongly on standard pronunciations, East Sutherland natives have been known to leave the class rather than conform (Dorian 1981:88–9). The borrowing patterns are similar to the ones in Oberwart; there is relatively little use of Gaelic words when people speak English, but English words are freely incorporated into Gaelic, where they are made to conform to Gaelic rules of word-formation and pronunciation.

A comparison of the two situations reveals a great deal in common. In both cases, the small-community language had coexisted with a higher-status language for decades without a substantial shift away from it. In both, social and economic changes had brought more speakers of the dominant language into the areas and had increased the possibility and desirability of identifying oneself as a member of the majority sociocultural group. This led to the steadily increasing use of the majority language by small-community speakers in two ways; more and more individuals use it and its use spreads into more and more small-community, or Low, domains.[9] The High language is used first and most frequently in circumstances, and to speakers, associated with the large-community culture, and the Low language in small-community-based situations. In both communities, older members are the ones who are strongest in their use of the Low language. In Oberwart, where the Low language is still apparently being transmitted to children, this 'strength' refers primarily to the use of Hungarian in most situations. In East Sutherland, it also means that more old people are able to speak Gaelic than young people and that they speak it more fluently. In Oberwart, children and young people generally are the ones with the most widespread use of the High language; in East Sutherland, many younger people have spoken ability only in the High.

In both communities, the language of education is the High language. In Scotland, the opportunity to use Gaelic in schools has been extended unenthusiastically at best. In Austria, provision for minority-language use in education is made, but the Oberwart Hungarian-speaking community has chosen to use German for educational purposes. It is not clear whether the use of the High language in the education domain is a cause or effect of language shift. Gal (1979:162) thinks it is both; Dorian (1981:27) agrees that the educational policy was no help in maintaining Gaelic, but she is quick to point out that languages can sometimes survive quite nicely while being excluded from the schools, as in German-speaking Switzerland. In East Sutherland, the school policy was fundamentally one more manifestation of the low prestige of Gaelic, albeit an important one. In both communities, the religious domain is one of the last ones in which the Low dialect was maintained. In both cases, religion was associated with the small community. In Oberwart, the small community is characteristically Calvinist, whereas almost everyone else is either Lutheran or Catholic. In East Sutherland, both the larger and smaller communities are largely Free Presbyterian, but in at least one town, the two groups attended separate church services, in different languages, in the same building. Further more, it was common for fisherfolk to have daily family worship at home in Gaelic (Dorian 1981:90). The two cases are different in that Hungarian is still the language of religion in Oberwart, but the language used in the domain of religion has recently shifted from Gaelic to English in East Sutherland. This is no doubt partly due to the fact that both the large and small communities have the same religion in East Sutherland and not in Oberwart, but it is also true that language shift is generally more advanced in East Sutherland.[10]

In both communities, the local variety of the Low language is at once a source of embarrassment and a strong symbol of ethnic loyalty. Speakers readily admit that users of the language in other communities are 'better' speakers, and that the written standard form is both different from and better than the local spoken dialect. Furthermore, speakers in both communities have a certain amount of difficulty understanding, and being understood by, speakers of more prestigious dialects of the Low language. In neither case, however, is any serious attempt made to learn and speak a 'better' nonlocal form of the community's language; on the contrary, prestige varieties are actively resisted in actual practice. As for borrowing, use of Low-language forms in speaking the High language is substantially less frequent than the opposite. High forms are readily used when people are speaking in the Low language, but they are generally made to conform to Low language grammar and pronunciation rules.

A case of maintenance – Montreal. Except in the case of immigrant groups (for example, the studies in Fishman 1966, Hofman and Fisherman 1972), language shift has held more fascination for scholars than language maintenance has. Consequently, it is harder to find research that is focused on language maintenance as such in a sedentary population. None the less we will look at some data on one bilingual community that has a history of maintenance of both languages, and one that is an interesting example of both maintenance and shift. The first community is the French-speaking population of Montreal, and the second is the Tiwa Indians, a pueblo-dwelling group in New Mexico.

The maintenance of French in Montreal was studied by Stanley Lieberson

(1972), on the basis of data from the Canadian census. As a result, we are not relying on participant-observer data as we did in the language-shift cases, but rather on survey data. The figures that Lieberson used are those from the answers to questions about mother tongue, and which of the two official languages of Canada – English and French – the respondent knew. Compared to the intimate look at a culture that an ethnographer can gain through months or years of participant-observation and in-depth individual interviewing, data like these seem sparse indeed. But the census data have two great advantages that cannot be easily duplicated in ethnographic research. First, the data represent not scores or hundreds of people from a small village, but hundreds of thousands of people in a major city; and second, the data cover a period of thirty years. In the hands of an investigator with Lieberson's skill and experience, data of this sort become the source of considerable insight.

At first glance, it would seem that a major prerequisite for shift from French to English is present – widespread bilingualism. As we saw in East Sutherland, where bilingual parents pass only one language on to their children, bilingualism can precede language shift. This potential pre-condition existed in Montreal in 1961. Of the male French mother tongue population, an estimated 48 per cent were bilingual, with a somewhat lower percentage for women. By contrast, only 28 per cent of the English mother tongue males were bilingual by the same estimate (Lieberson 1972:240–1).

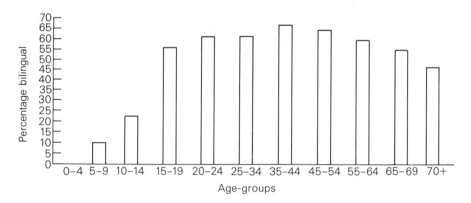

Figure 8.1   Age-correlation with bilingualism in Montreal, 1961
Source: data from Lieberson (1972:249)

The data on the correlation between age and bilingualism for male speakers, based on the 1961 census for Montreal, appear in figure 8.1. If the data in the table are interpreted mechanically as reflecting what is happening over time, you would have to say that bilingualism increased from substantial levels to even higher levels, but then decreased sharply, over the last fifty years or so. If we are more careful, and assume that many of the young people under 20 years old may yet become bilingual, we would not necessarily have to interpret figure 8.1 as an indication of a recent decline. But the data for young adults through to old age indicates an increase in bilingualism, and therefore a possible increase in the 'exposure to risk' of a shift.[11] We might, then, conclude that a shift to English is in progress. This conclusion would be quite wrong.

To begin with, the data on the mother tongues of small children show that French is, if anything, gaining strength. Lieberson (1972:243–4) compared the data on the mother tongues of women of child-bearing age with the mother tongue data for children under 5 years old, with this result:

> we find that the higher degree of bilingualism among the F[rench] M[other] T[ongue] population has not led to a net switch to English among the children. In all periods, a larger proportion of small children than of women in the child-bearing ages have French as their mother tongue . . . The net results of our intergenerational analysis indicate that French is not merely holding its own but is actually gaining between generations.

It is clear that the pattern in figure 8.1 does not indicate a shift in progress. In fact, it is doubtful that it even reflects an increase in stable bilingualism over time. What, then, *does* it indicate? To answer this question, Lieberson performed an analysis of 'age cohorts'. The idea of age cohorts is simple; it assumes that people who were, say, 25 at the time of the 1951 census would have been 35 when the 1961 census was done. By comparing the bilingualism data for each age-group with the data for the group ten years older in the next decennial census, the patterns of reported bilingualism emerge. These patterns, reported separately for men and women, appear in figure 8.2.

The trends are extremely interesting. We find a rapid increase in bilingualism from early childhood to young adulthood, and a further incremental increase into middle age. Beginning in the forties, people report progressively

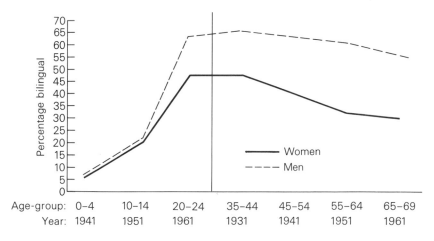

Figure 8.2   *Percentage of the population bilingual in Montreal,*
by age cohorts and sex, 1931-1961
Source: Lieberson (1972:249)

less bilingualism and this trend continues into old age. In addition, there is no difference between male and female speakers until early adulthood, when the women's pattern runs roughly parallel to that of the men, but at a lower frequency of bilingualism. It should be mentioned at this point that we are not looking at the same people all the way across the graph. The percentages reported to the left of the vertical line in figure 8.2 are true cohorts; the people who were between birth and 4 years old in 1941, in the 10 to 14-year-old age-range in 1951, and were aged 20–24 in 1961. Similarly, the percentages in the right side of the figure represent true age cohorts.[12] The 35-44 age-group, however, are not the cohorts of the 20-24 group. From the data in figure 8.2 alone, we can't be sure that people represented by the 20-24 age group will follow the pattern on the right side of the figure as they grow older. However, the data in figure 8.2 is only a sample of the figures that Lieberson gives. Using a whole range of overlapping age-groups, he is able to show that the increase and decrease pattern, and the difference between men and women, is fairly consistent throughout. For example, 68.8 per cent of the men who were aged 25–34 in 1941 were bilingual; in 1951, when they were aged 35–44, there was a slight drop to 68.1 per cent and a further decrease to 63.6 per cent in 1961, when they were aged 45–54. The comparable figures for women speakers were 48.1 per cent, 45.2 per cent and 42.6 per cent (Lieberson 1972:249, table 4). It seems safe to take the pattern in figure 8.2 to be representative of bilingualism self-reports through the phases of people's lives.

The interpretation Lieberson gives is fascinating and quite convincing. If we start with the fact that English is something of a High language in French-speaking Canada, especially with respect to the employment domain, the patterns begin to make sense. Clearly, French Canadian children are learning only French at home. English is taught as a subject in schools, where French is the medium of instruction (as it is in the schools that almost all French-speaking children attend), and it appears that English is acquired by an increasing number of young people as they move through school. Of course, not all second-language learning takes place in school. A lot of competence in English will be gained as young people find it necessary to participate in the wider society. Recall that English mother-tongue residents, who similarly must study French as a subject in their English-medium schools, become bilingual far less frequently. As people move into their careers, many of them have traditionally found that a knowledge of English was essential. Thus, reports of bilingualism increase slightly and then level off through the middle years. As people grow older and leave the workforce, English is no longer needed for employment and, as a result, less bilingualism is reported.[13] This interpretation is reinforced by the fact that fewer women than men are bilingual after childhood. If we assume that most women take on the traditional female occupations of homemaking and child-rearing, rather than working in employment institutions that require English, fewer women will need English and so won't learn it.

If we attempt to view all this in the light of our expanded concept of diglossia, we can see that it all points toward the continued maintenance of French, even if considerable bilingualism in English continues. Although we do not have data that allow us to infer the distribution in other domains, if Lieberson is correct, then English is used in the employment domain (for some jobs) – a High domain. In the home domain – the prototypical Low domain – French is the only language. Furthermore, English seems to be acquired only by those who really need it and not before they need it. The willingness to report the knowledge of English, if not the knowledge itself, is given up as soon as possible by a great many people. It appears reasonable to infer that English is not leaking into French domains at all; if anything the current upsurge of nationalism in Quebec might propel French into traditional English domains.

One last fact Lieberson points out is that, since fewer women than men are bilingual, a large number of families will include a bilingual husband and a wife who is monolingual in French. French, the only language in common, will be passed on to the children, further strengthening its maintenance. The same phenomenon is working *against* the Low language in Oberwart. There, many families include one parent who is bilingual in Hungarian and German and one who is monolingual in German, but virtually none where Hungarian is the only common language. Tabouret-Keller (1968:112) reports that the same pattern is working in favor of the spread of Wolof over other languages in Senegal.

Maintenance and shift – the Tiwa.   The final example is based on a small study that I carried out in the Tiwa Indian community of Taos, New Mexico by means of a questionnaire.[14] The Tiwa are a pueblo-dwelling group of about 2,000 individuals, most of whom still live in their ancestral pueblo homes. Bilingualism has been a fact of life for the Tiwa for generations, with Spanish giving way to English as the second language over the years. The Tiwa are remarkable for the fact that they have maintained their indigenous language for centuries, despite being under the hegemony first of Mexico and more recently of the United States, and in spite of the fact that the group is very small.

The data from the Tiwa are not all that could be desired. There was no opportunity for extensive observation and, as a result, the self-reported language-use data could not be checked against observations, as Gal and Dorian were able to do. The 48 questionnaires which were collected is a very small number, although it represents a larger percentage of the population than it would in a larger community.[15] The data were not evenly distributed by age, and the youngest speakers were overrepresented. Nevertheless, the results lead to some interpretations that are compatible with the history of the community and with what we know about maintenance and shift. Although a more extensive and better-designed research effort might lead to different conclusions, the data we do have can be used to illustrate the conclusions we would draw if they were representative.

The first aspect of Tiwa bilingualism we will explore is the evidence that they have experienced a massive shift in the High language, while maintaining Tiwa. The subjects were asked which of the three languages in local use (Tiwa, Spanish, and English) they spoke themselves and understood.[16] They were also asked which of the languages their parents and grandparents spoke. The question about the language of the grandparents was divided into separate questions about maternal and paternal grandparents, so that the second ascending generation has more responses than the other generations (not all respondents were able to answer for both sets of grandparents, however). When these data are arranged by the age-groups of the respondents, a decline of Spanish as a second language and an increase in English becomes fairly clear. The data appear in table 8.1. The respondents themselves were divided into four unequal age-groups: 50–75, 30–45, 16–25 and 11–14 (these seemed to be more or less natural divisions in the data). Taking the data reported by the respondents about themselves and their parents and grandparents, four general patterns of bilingualism seemed to emerge, according to age. Individuals were divided into 'generations' on the basis of these apparent patterns. These 'generations' had the following composition:

Generation 1:   Parents and grandparents of the age-group aged 50-75 years old and grandparents of the age-group aged 30-45 years old.

Generation 2:   Grandparents of the age-groups aged 16-25 and 11-14 years old and parents of the age-group aged 30-45 years old.

Generation 3:   The age-groups aged 50-75, 30-45, and 16-25 years old and the parents of the age-groups aged 16-25 and 11-14 years old.

Generation 4:   The age-group aged 11-14 years old.

The dominant pattern in the first generation is Tiwa–Spanish bilingualism, with a few people who report knowledge of English and a few monolinguals in Tiwa. No one is monolingual in English. In the second generation, Spanish has lost ground to English to a considerable degree. Most people who know Tiwa and Spanish also know English, and there are nearly as many Tiwa–English bilinguals as there are people who can speak Tiwa and Spanish. There are a few Tiwa monolinguals, but only one person shows up as monolingual in English. By the third generation, the overwhelmingly dominant pattern is Tiwa–English bilingualism. Everyone who knows Spanish also knows English. There are two individuals who are monolingual, one in Tiwa and one in English. In the fourth generation, no one at all claims to know Spanish; there are no Tiwa monolinguals, but several English monolinguals.

It is not possible to prove beyond a doubt that the data in table 8.1 are to be interpreted as representing a change through time. However, it seems unlikely that the pattern involving the loss of Spanish is to be interpreted in any other way. The alternative would be to suppose that the data represent the changing

Table 8.1   *Patterns of bilingualism through four 'generations'
in the Tiwa community*

Generation		Languages				
		TS	TES	TE	T	E
1	Number	20	2	2	4	0
	Percentage	71.4	7.1	7.1	14.3	0
2	Number	6	27	29	10	1
	Percentage	8.2	37.0	39.7	13.7	1.4
3	Number	0	6	51	1	1
	Percentage	0	10.2	86.4	1.7	1.7
4	Number	0	0	18	0	6
	Percentage	0	0	75	0	25

TS = Tiwa, and Spanish; TES = Tiwa, English and Spanish; TE = Tiwa and English; T = Tiwa only; E = English only

use of languages associated with the periods of a person's life. This would imply that the members of the younger generations will forget English and learn Spanish as they grow older! It is somewhat more reasonable to suppose that some of the younger people who now report bilingualism in Tiwa and English might claim to be monolingual in Tiwa when they get older, as Montreal French Canadians apparently do. However, there are not many who report being monolingual in Tiwa even in the older generations. It seems most likely that table 8.1 represents language maintenance (of Tiwa) and shift (Spanish to English) over the past 125 years or so. This dramatic second-language exchange is illustrated in graphic form in figure 8.3.

Figure 8.3 indicates that Tiwa was learned by virtually everyone in the community in the first three generations, when English was gradually replacing Spanish. In the youngest age-group, however, there is a sudden downturn in reported knowledge of Tiwa. Since this reduction in the proportion of Tiwa speakers is based on only 24 speakers, it is possible that it is due to a sampling error, or a flaw in the division into age-groups. There is at least some indication, though, that we ought to look for signs that English might eventually displace Tiwa – something Spanish never did. As we know by now, there are certain indications of language shift to look for. One of these is the advance of one language into the domains of the other.

An implicational table similar to Gal's was constructed for 42 of the Tiwa respondents (omitting the six monolingual speakers and two respondents whose data had been misplaced). The result appears as table 8.2.[17] It appears that the data scale fairly well; there are only a modest number of deviant cells (marked with an asterisk). In fact, the percentage scalability is 91.7 per cent, a respectable figure.[18] As in Oberwart, there is a tendency for the small-

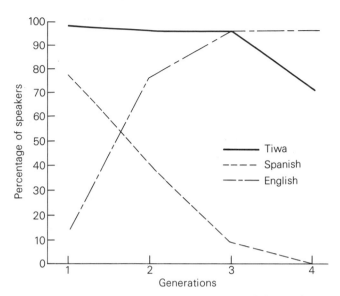

*Figure 8.3   Language maintenance and shift in the
Tiwa community in apparent time*

community language to be selected more often with grandparents than with parents, and with parents more often than with brothers and sisters. This lessening of the use of Tiwa with younger interlocutors is similar to the Oberwart pattern, where it apparently indicates the beginnings of a shift. There seems to be a small tendency for older speakers to appear toward the top of the table, where the more conservative patterns are located, and for younger speakers to appear at the bottom. But there are a number of young people reporting conservative patterns and some middle-aged speakers fairly far down on the table. There were 25 speakers with no scaling deviations and their reports were tested for correlation with age. (Speakers with deviations were omitted because it is not totally clear where they where should be placed.) The test used was the Spearman's ρ rank-order correlation test, using age and position in table 8.2 as the variables. The result was a small and not significant positive ρ value.[19] Besides, there are a great many young speakers, and speakers in this group may well change their use habits as they grow older. It is therefore not possible to say with any confidence that young people are leading a shift to English.

Turning to the order across the columns, the first thing to notice is that for most speakers, the scale works better if language used with Indian friends in the pueblo and in town (situations 3 and 4) are both placed to the left of with brothers and sisters (situation 5). This seems a little strange, since family members are usually considered intimates who can be expected to be addressed in the Low language.[20] It is here that the lack of familiarity with the community is a serious drawback. It is possible that there is a value placed on

Table 8.2 *Implicational scale for language choice by Tiwa speakers*

Speaker number	Speaker's age	Interlocutor						
		1	2	3	4	5	6	7
1	65	T	T	T	T	T	TE	E
2	43	T	T	T	T	T	TE	E
3	20	T	TE*	T	T	T	TE	E
4	18	T	TE*	T	T	T	TE	E
5	25	T	T	T	T	T	E	E
6	12	T	T	T	T	T	E	E
7	75	T	T	T	T	TE	TE	E
8	65	T	T	T	T	TE	E	E
9	52	T	T	T	T	TE	E	E
10	14	T	T	T	T	TE	E	E
11	13	T	T	T	T	TE	E	E
12	13	T	T	T	T	TE	E	E
13	25	T	T	T	T	E	E	E
14	12	TE*	T	T	T	TE	E	E
15	35	T	TE*	T	T	TE	E	E
16	20	T	TE*	T	T	TE	E	E
17	19	T	TE*	T	T	TE	E	E
18	41	T	T	T	TE	TE	TE	E
19	65	T	T	T	TE	TE	E	E
20	16	T	TE*	T	TE	T*	TE	E
21	43	T	T	TE	TE	TE	TE	E
22	43	T	T	TE	TE	TE	E	E
23	44	T	T	TE	TE	TE	E	E
24	17	T	T	TE	TE	T*	E	E
25	14	T	T	E*	TE	TE	E	E
26	14	T	TE	TE	TE	TE	E	E
27	13	T	TE	TE	TE	TE	E	E
28	21	T	TE	TE	TE	TE	E	E
29	17	T	TE	TE	TE	T*	TE	E
30	13	T	TE	TE	TE	T*	TE	E
31	12	TE	TE	TE	TE	TE	TE	E
32	17	TE	TE	TE	TE	TE	TE	E
33	18	TE	TE	T*	TE	TE	TE	E
34	14	TE	TE	TE	TE	TE	E	E
35	14	TE	TE	TE	TE	TE	E	E
36	13	TE	TE	TE	TE	TE	E	E
37	11	TE	TE	TE	TE	TE	E	E
38	13	TE	E*	TE	TE	TE	E	E
39	31	TE	TE	T*	TE	T*	E	E
40	13	TE	TE	T*	T*	TE	E	—
41	14	TE	TE	T*	TE	T*	E	E
42	13	TE	TE	TE	T*	TE	T*	E

Interlocutors: 1 = grandparents; 2 = parents; 3 = Indian friends in the pueblo; 4 = Indian friends in town; 5 = brothers and sisters; 6 = Indian friends when anglo and Chicano friends are around; 7 = anglo and Chicano friends

Languages: T = Tiwan; E = English

*These cells fail to conform to perfect scalability

using Tiwa with other members of the community in public, but that it's considered alright to use English sometimes in private settings, where family members are likely to be. Another possibility is that interlocutor situations 3 and 4 were interpreted by some respondents as situations where they would just greet the other person, whereas speaking with brothers and sisters would involve longer conversations. It is possible that some speakers would greet their friends only in Tiwa, but some conversations with brothers and sisters would be in English. There may be other possibilities as well, and it would not be wise to speculate on the basis of the questionnaire data alone. The position of Indian friends in the order of interlocutors doesn't give us any real clues on whether or not there may be a shift going on.

The position of relatives of ascending generations on the Tiwa side of table 8.2 involves two considerations. Remember that older speakers are more often the ones who don't know English. The reason that old people are addressed in Tiwa may in some cases simply be due to the fact that they don't understand English. The other possibility is that old people have a greater commitment to small-community values and so expect to be spoken to in Tiwa. If people address their elders in Tiwa because they don't understand English, it would mean that choice was motivated by the sheer need to be understood and may not mean that there is a cultural value involved. However, there is some indication that it is culturally appropriate to address older people in Tiwa. Two respondents, in answering the 'Indian friends' questions, added notes to the effect that it would depend on age. Tiwa would be selected if the other Indian were older; English if she were younger.

It is clear that English is the only language to be used with outgroup interlocutors. Most, but by no means all, Tiwa Indians report that only English would be used with Indian friends if anglo or Chicano friends are around. In Oberwart, and to some extent in East Sutherland, this indicated that the speaker saw himself as a member of the High-language-speaking group as well as his smaller group. This shared membership entitled members of the larger group to have the common language used in their presence. However, two respondents who reported Tiwa and English in this situation explicitly stated that they would use Tiwa to prevent anglos and Chicanos from understanding them. This kind of behavior would be, in Giles's terms, fairly divergent, emphasizing membership in the small group to the exclusion of members of the wider community. The fact that a substantial number of speakers would use Tiwa in the presence of Anglos and Chicanos, some apparently explicitly to exclude them, makes the data in column 6 very unclear as far as an indication of shift is concerned.

All the 'deviations' marked with asterisks in table 8.2 are responses that are technically out of place. Many of them are probably not failures to conform in any sense, but evidence of patterns other than the dominant one. One of the most startling is the number of respondents who use both languages with their parents, but only *Tiwa* with their brothers and sisters. This is reported by the speakers numbered 3, 4, 20, 29, 30, 39, and 41. Speaker 38 would use both languages with her brothers and sisters, but only English with her parents. Five of the eight also use only Tiwa with their Indian friends in the pueblo, and speaker 38 uses both languages with her friends as she does with her brothers and sisters. Besides this, five of the eight are among the minority who use both Tiwa and English with their Indian friends, even when outsiders are present.

Five of these eight speakers are between the ages of 16 and 35; the other three are slightly younger at ages 13 and 14. If the speakers are divided into three age-groups – those over 40; young adolescents 12–14; and young people aged between 16 and 35 – we discover an interesting fact. The oldest group fits on the scale in table 8.2 perfectly – there is not a single scaling deviation. The middle age-group, however, fits better on the scale in table 8.3.[21] There is a total of four fewer deviations; six speakers have fewer deviations in table 8.3 than they had in table 8.2, whereas only two have more. Five of the six had one deviation in the earlier table, but scale perfectly on table 8.3. (The 12-14 year old adolescents fit about as well in table 8.3 as they do in table 8.2.)

Table 8.3   Implicational scale for language choice by Tiwa speakers aged 16-35

Speaker number	Speaker's age	Interlocutor						
		1	3	4	5	2	6	7
5	25	T	T	T	T	T	E	E
13	25	T	T	T	E*	T	E	E
3	20	T	T	T	T	TE	TE	E
4	18	T	T	T	T	TE	TE	E
39	31	TE*	T	TE*	T	TE	E	E
15	35	T	T	T	TE	TE	E	E
16	20	T	T	T	TE	TE	E	E
17	19	T	T	T	TE	TE	E	E
20	16	T	T	TE*	T	TE	TE	E
24	17	T	TE	TE	T*	T*	E	E
28	21	T	TE	TE	TE	TE	E	E
29	17	T	TE	TE	T*	TE	TE	E
32	17	TE	TE	TE	TE	TE	TE	E
33	18	TE	T*	TE	TE	TE	TE	E

Interlocutors: 1 = grandparents; 2 = parents; 3 = Indian friends in the pueblo; 4 = Indian friends in town; 5 = brothers and sisters; 6 = Indian friends when Anglo and Chicano friends are around; 7 = Anglo and Chicano friends
Languages: T = Tiwa; E = English
*These cells fail to conform to perfect scalability

The difference in the interlocutor order between the two tables is that parents have been moved to the right to a position just before Indian friends when anglo and Chicano friends are around. That is, for this age group parents are more likely to be addressed in English than any kind of interlocutor when outsiders are not involved. In other words, this age-group scales better if we assume that Tiwa is more favored when you are talking to a person of the same age (either brothers and sisters or Indian friends), than it is when you are talking to parents. Grandparents are the most likely to be addressed in Tiwa, but that may be either because many old people do not speak English or because of a strong cultural value that it is appropriate to address old people in the traditional community language.

Taking these facts together, we may have evidence that there is a group of young people who are moving away from large-group identity towards an emphasis on their identity as Tiwa Indians. Their parents may have been part of an earlier trend toward English and may expect to be addressed in English some of the time. However, the number of speakers involved is small and we can't put too much confidence in this interpretation without a deeper knowledge of the community.

An unmistakable sign of shift is when bilingual parents pass on only one language to their children. (This has no doubt happened in the case of the six monolingual youngsters.) There were twelve parents in the sample who were young enough to have children at home, or to have had them at home recently. The questionnaire asked for the language spoken with spouses as well as the language used with children. Of the twelve, six used Tiwa only or both Tiwa and English with their spouses and also with their children. These six are apparently not involved in intergenerational language shift. Three reported using both languages with each other, but only English with their children. This would be possible evidence for a shift toward English. Two of the other three, however, used only English with their husband or wife and Tiwa and English with the children, and the third reported bilingual use with the other parent and only Tiwa to the children. Their pattern could serve as evidence for a shift toward Tiwa. The small amount of evidence that there is shows the intergenerational trend toward English, counterbalanced by a trend toward Tiwa.

All the respondents were asked what languages they would want their children to know. Only one person said they would want their children to know only English. Most of the rest said they wanted their children to know both Tiwa and English, and quite a few said they would want their children to be monolingual in Tiwa, or to know Tiwa, English, and Spanish. These last two kinds of response show that answers to a question of this sort may not be too realistic. There are hardly any Tiwa monolinguals nowadays and almost none are learning Spanish.

Another indication of shift is a feeling that the language being shifted from is not a very good language. When asked which of the three languages was the most beautiful, over 80 per cent said Tiwa was. Only a single respondent said that English was the most beautiful, with the rest choosing either Tiwa and English or Tiwa and Spanish. These attitudes are shared by the monolingual children. None of the six said they would want their children to be monolingual in English. Two said they would like their children to be bilingual, two would want them to know Spanish in addition to Tiwa and English, and two marked only Tiwa for this question. Four of the six said that Tiwa was the most beautiful language and a fifth marked both Tiwa and English. The sixth monolingual child was the one respondent who said English was the most beautiful. Besides this, three of the six children who said they spoke only English said that they could *understand* Tiwa.

In sum, the evidence from the questionnaire results is really quite ambiguous. The possibility of a shift toward English is indicated by: (1) the fact that six of the 24 children in the youngest age-group sample were monolingual in English; (2) the fact that table 8.2 shows that younger interlocutors are more likely to be addressed in English than older ones; (3) the small tendency for younger speakers to use both languages with more interlocutors than older speakers do; and (4) the majority tendency to use English only with other Tiwa Indians if outsiders are present. On the other hand, the correlation between age and position in table 8.2 is not substantial and is not statistically significant. Furthermore, the patterns for many of the speakers from late adolescence to young adulthood are at least consistent with the hypothesis that there is a trend among younger speakers to strengthen their use of Tiwa at the expense of English. With two exceptions, which may be mistakes in marking the questionnaire, there are no bilingual respondents who use only English except when speaking to, or in the presence of, outsiders. There is no evidence of a general trend for parents to pass on only English to their offspring; on the contrary, all but one respondent say they want their children to know Tiwa. The great majority say that Tiwa is the most beautiful local language and all but one of the rest think it is at least one of the most beautiful. Even the monolingual children say they want their children to learn Tiwa and all but one think Tiwa is more beautiful than English, or at least as beautiful. We would do well not to attach too much importance to the answers to these last two questions since it is not too unusual for people's professed attitudes to be different from their behavior. But the more indirect evidence is ambiguous and the data we have on the Tiwa Indians are an example of how difficult it can be to predict maintenance or shift.

SUMMARY AND CONCLUSIONS

Language maintenance and shift are the long-term, collective consequences of consistent patterns of language choice. Language shift is sometimes also called language death, especially if the shifting group consisted of the only people in the world who spoke that language. Language maintenance and shift are most often studied with the methods of either anthropology or sociology. Participant-observation, sometimes supplemented by questionnaire survey data, is the technique used by anthropologists or anthropological linguists. Sociologists and sociolinguists are more likely to use censuses or other survey data. Caution must be used in interpreting this kind of numerical data; two common problems are migration and age-grading.

There is a sense in which it is possible to answer 'yes' to the question of whether it is possible to predict language maintenance or shift. Language shift will occur only if, and to the extent that, a community desires to give up its identity as an identifiable sociocultural group in favor of an identity as a part of some other community. Very often the other community is the larger social group which controls a society where the first group is a minority. This is really not much help, however, because it simply postpones the problem. Now we have to be able to predict when a community will be likely to want this kind of change in identity. *This* prediction is probably impossible, at least at the present time. There are groups who maintain their language and ethnic identity under the very same social and economic conditions that induce another group to shift identity and language. Even if we could identify communities who are in the process of changing their self-concept, long-range predictions of language shift would still be hazardous, because there would be no guarantee that their sense of identity would not reverse itself (a possibility in the Tiwa community).

Nevertheless, we can at least point to a number of signs that a community is in the process of language shift at a given moment. A prevalent tendency to maintain a distinction between 'us' and 'them', that is, the ingroup and a particular outgroup, is one sign that shift is not in progress. Language is often a focus for an 'us–them' concept. For example, Old Order Amish people in Pennsylvania and elsewhere, who have maintained Pennsylvania German in the United States for centuries, are likely to refer to their monolingual English-speaking neighbors as 'English people'. A teacher in an Amish parochial school wrote on a language-use questionnaire that she only used English in school and when talking to 'English people'; Huffines (1980:47) reports the use of the same terminology. Of course, citizens of England are not being referred to, simply Americans who can be characterized as speaking English. A similar use of the label 'German' is used by Hungarian-speaking peasants in Oberwart (Gal 1979:107):

Peasant parents often say of their grown children who are employed in bureaucratic or commercial work and who go to cafes and shop downtown: **Ü má egisz nímet** 'He-she is already totally German.' This does not refer to their nationality which is always given as Austrian, or to their language abilities, as they are recognized to be bilingual and often speak Hungarian at home. Rather, it indicates the close symbolic relationship between the children's occupation, status, and the German language.

A virtual *prerequisite* for language shift is bilingualism, but many bilingual communities are perfectly stable. Probably the earliest sign of shift is the movement of one language into domains that used to be reserved to the old. This would show up, for example, in an implicational scale such as the one Gal constructed. A scale in a shifting community will have interlocutors or domains most closely identified with the traditional community at the end where most use of the traditional language is to be found and interlocutors or domains associated with the other community at the other end. Older speakers will use the traditional language in the most circumstances and younger speakers will have advanced the new language into the most domains. A pattern like this has to be carefully interpreted. First, there may be 'deviant' patterns that indicate a contrary trend and, second, the age distribution may not be a symptom of change, but rather a reflection of the changes in language use from one period of a person's life to another.

The late stages of shift have several characteristics. First, the language being shifted from will probably be considered inferior to the incoming language. Not only that, but it may also be considered inferior to one or more varieties of the same language – either the written standard, or varieties spoken in communities where the language is being maintained, or both. There will also be an imbalance in borrowing; words from the incoming language are freely borrowed into the traditional language, but borrowing in the other direction is much less common. If religion is one of the ways in which the shifting group contrasts with the other community, then the shift will be nearly complete when religious activity is conducted in the new language. Of course, an unmistakable sign of the final stages of shift is when bilingual parents pass on only the new language to their children.[22]

Taking the wider view, there are certain large-scale socioeconomic conditions that favor shift, but do not guarantee it. People who live in urban, industrial or commercial centers, if they speak a small-group language, are more likely than others to shift to a language of wider currency. People who live in isolated geographical regions, or who practice agriculture, have a better chance of maintaining a minority language.[23] Improved means of transportation and communication with the centers of culture associated with the incoming language also seem to promote shift, as does an influx of people from the larger group, but these large factors are only conditions that *may* cause a community to identify with a new or larger group. Community-by-community ethnographic research is the best way to discover whether language shift actually *is* going on.

Lieberson's (1972) demographic study of French–English bilingualism in Montreal is a clear case of stable bilingualism. In spite of the fact that there is patterned variation in the numbers of speakers who are bilingual according to age, these patterns are not evidence of change through time, but are a case of age-grading. French Canadians in Montreal use English only when it is demanded by a particular domain, such as employment, and evidently give up its use as soon as they no longer function in that domain, for example, after retirement. In any case, there is no tendency at all to pass on English to the children, on the contrary, young children under school age are over-whelmingly monolingual in French.

A study of the Tiwa Indians of New Mexico on the basis of imperfect questionnaire data indicates that the Tiwa language has been maintained over the past century or so while the community's High language has shifted from Spanish to English. The data in some ways suggest that a shift from Tiwa to English may have begun, but other indications suggest that there is no shift going on, or even that there is currently a reversal from a shift pattern back to maintenance. In any case, without deeper knowledge of a community's language-values, or at least better survey data, it is impossible to say whether language maintenance or language shift is to be expected in the future.

BIBLIOGRAPHICAL NOTES

Apart from the references cited in this chapter, other recent studies of language maintenance and shift include Adler (1977) and Jones (1979) (in addition to Lewis 1978) on Welsh, Agnew (1981) on the three Celtic languages of the British Isles (Gaelic, Welsh and Irish), Jaakkola (1976) on Swedish in Finland, Knab and Hasson de Knab (1979) on a native American group, Perez-Alonso (1979) on Catalan in Spain, and Wood (1980) on the French Flemings. Wexler (1981) is, in part, a study of maintenance and shift in Jewish minority populations. Fishman (1976) and Fishman et al. (1977) are both studies of the worldwide spread of English as a case of language shift. Cooper (1982) is a collection of articles on language spread as a worldwide phenomenon.

NOTES

1   Domain analysis is 'another way of saying the same thing' as diglossia implies that domains are always organized on a High to Low continuum. This seems to me to be true, but I realize that other sociolinguists are likely to disagree.

2   Pidginization, the formation of 'simple' languages under certain sociolinguistic conditions, is discussed in Volume II.

3   Fishman's (1966) collection of studies of language loyalty among immigrant groups in the United States is an early classic in the field. Many of the earlier studies of language maintenance and shift dealt with immigrants.

4   Although some of the adults represented in table 7.5 report the exclusive use of German with 'children and their generation', even the youngest subjects report the exclusive use of Hungarian at least in prayers and hymns, and the use of both languages at least with grandparents and other old people. The same is true of the corresponding table for male speakers (Gal 1979:122). It follows that they must know Hungarian as well as German.

5   I highly recommend Gal (1978a) to readers interested in sex-related differences in language choice or to those who just enjoy reading a good ethnography of communication. Gal presents a thorough and entirely convincing analysis of why women in Oberwart are leading the shift toward German and the 'worker' life-style. Although it is not obvious that her analysis will extend to other cases, it is by far the most convincing explanation for linguistic differences by sex that I am aware of.

6   This does not happen if an English monolingual is merely in a position to overhear. This is in contrast with the cultural rule in Oberwart, as we saw in chapter 7.

7   Dorian does not attempt to characterize what sort of ingroup member is most likely to use or be addressed in Gaelic, but it is not unlikely that they would be the

ones with the greatest commitment to the fishing community, analogous to the Oberwart situation.

8   A system that was used was to hand a piece of wood called a tessera from one child to another as they were heard to speak Gaelic. At the end of the day, the tessera was handed back through the ranks with each child being flogged in the process. Timm (1980:30) reports that a very similar system was used in Brittany against children heard speaking Breton in school.

9   In other words, diglossia begins to leak. In communities experiencing language shift, the leak increases from a drip to a torrent.

10   Like East Sutherland, religion was a small community domain in Brittany and, until recently, the Low language, Breton, was used (Dressler and Wodak-Leodolter 1977, Timm 1980). The small community has the same religion – Catholicism – as the majority religion of the wider French community. If space allowed, it would be easy to show that the shift from Breton to French in Brittany runs parallel to the East Sutherland and Oberwart cases.

11   Several assumptions are being made in the interpretations of the data in figure 8.1. It is assumed that all the bilinguals are French mother-tongue speakers and that the only second language is English. The second assumption is valid as far as the census data are concerned, since only questions about bilingualism in the two official languages were asked. For a French mother-tongue speaker to be listed as bilingual, he would have to know English. The first assumption is further from being strictly accurate, but since the French mother-tongue population is a large majority in Montreal and since French mother-tongue speakers are more likely to be bilingual than English mother-tongue speakers, any trends in the French-speaking population would surely show up in the data for the city as a whole.

12   Care must also be taken in interpreting what we call 'true age cohorts'. What is really meant is that the percentage for the cohort aged 0–4 represents Montreal residents in that age-group in 1941 and the percentage for the cohort aged 10–14 represents a sample of whoever of that age was living in Montreal in 1951. It may not have been the same people. But it would not have to be the very same individuals as long as both samples were drawn from groups with the same demographic characteristics. After careful examination of the data, Lieberson is satisfied that the interpretation we are giving the age cohorts is valid. (For details, see Lieberson 1972: 251–2.)

13   Lieberson (1972:250) thinks that bilinguals forget English when they no longer use it, as people forget algebra after they leave school if they no longer use it. Language learning, however, is more like learning to ride a bicycle than learning algebra, and it is my opinion that the emphasis should be on the tendency to *report* bilingualism, rather on a real 'loss' of bilingual competence. A retired man may still be able to speak English, but since he no longer has the status that requires him to present himself as someone who knows English, he no longer reports it.

14   I am grateful to David and Alice Hull for distributing and collecting the questionnaire, as well as for valuable help in constructing it.

15   Gal (1979:26, 134) also interviewed 48 people out of the Oberwart Hungarian-speaking population of about 1,500. The comparison is not quite just, however, since she observed the whole community for an extended period of time, knew her respondents personally, and conducted in-depth interviews, rather than simply distributing a questionnaire.

16   The Taos area is more similar to the multilingual societies discussed in this book than most areas of the United States are. Besides the Tiwa Indians, there is a Chicano population which uses Spanish extensively. English is the official language and the language of education, as well as the language of the Anglo community and the language of intergroup communication.

17   The few references to the use of Spanish were omitted.
18   Percentage scalability, the percentage of items in the 'proper' position, is a rather crude measure of scalability, but one that is widely used. Percentage scalability was computed for table 8.2 on the basis of columns 1–6 only. There is no variation in column 7, so there was no possibility for a deviation.
19   The validity of the Spearman's ρ statistic in this case is damaged by the gaps between the age-groups. As a result, the difference between the 44-year-old speaker and the 65-year-old speakers, who are the next oldest, is treated the same as the difference between the 13 and 14-year-old speakers. Using the Pearson product-moment test would mean that positions in table 8.2 are being treated as interval data; it would be a serious mistake to treat them as anything other than ordinal.
20   As table 7.5 shows, Gal found the same ordering in Oberwart, where 'brothers and sisters' are nearer to the *German* end of the continuum than 'age-mate pals, neighbors'.
21   I am indebted to Takashi Nagata for this insightful rescaling of the Tiwa data by age.
22   An interesting variation on this pattern is reported for the Pays d'Oc area of France by Tabouret-Keller (1972). There has been a nearly complete shift from the local patois to French. Children learn French first, but many later learn patois. The reason for this is that it is customary to segregate children from adults in some settings (for instance, family meals) until they are about 10 years old. Bilingual adults apparently speak only French to small children, but use both languages with each other. When children begin to be treated as adults, they get the opportunity to learn patois, but even this relatively late learning of the small-group language is declining.
23   Measures of urbanization and similar measures are apparently not very good predictors of language diversity in an entire nation, as Lieberson, Dalto, and Johnston (1975) have pointed out and we saw in chapter 5.

OBJECTIVES

1   Be able to write definitions of *language maintenance* and *language shift*.
2   Be able to recognize the two aspects of *language death* that have interested linguists (p. 214).
3   Be able to recognize the differences in approach to the study of language maintenance and shift by anthropologists compared to sociologists.
4   Be able to explain how *age-grading* can complicate the interpretation of one-time census data in the study of language maintenance and shift.
5   Be able to recognize the only type of cause for maintenance and shift that can come from census and survey data analysis.
6   Be able to identify the relationship of bilingualism and human generations to the possibility of language shift.
7   Be able to list any three of the commonly-cited causes of language shift given on p. 217.
8   Be able to state the extent to which scholars of language shift think they can predict when a shift from one language to another will occur.
9   Be able to indicate whether majority bilingualism in Oberwart existed well before the shift began or only shortly before the onset of the shift.
10   Be able to identify both the surface socioeconomic factor and the resulting social-identity factor that precipitated language shift in Oberwart.

11 Be able to explain how peasant identity and marriage patterns work together against the maintenance of Hungarian (pp.220-1).

12 Be able to identify the language that Oberwart Hungarian community members insist on for education and the language and its variety that they prefer for church services.

13 Be able to recognize the two 'linguistic' factors that have a bearing on shift mentioned on pp.221-2.

14 Be able to name the last socioeconomic group to maintain Gaelic in East Sutherland.

15 Be able to identify aspects of the East Sutherland language shift case that *are* similar to the Oberwart case and those aspects that are *not* similar.

16 Be able to state the source of the data used in Lieberson's study of Montreal language maintenance.

17 Although in some ways less satisfying than the work of Gal and Dorian, Lieberson's method has at least two advantages. Be able to recognize them.

18 Be able to name the prerequisite for a shift to English that is present in Montreal (p.228).

19 Be able to cite the evidence for the maintenance of French based on a comparison of the mother-tongues of women of child-bearing age and of small children (pp.229).

20 Be able to recognize a description of the 'age-cohort' bilingualism pattern in figure 8.2.

21 Be able to identify Lieberson's interpretation of his data with respect to the employment domain.

22 Be able to state the fact that the age-group study revealed about the history of the High language in the Tiwa community.

23 Be able to recognize the implication with respect to the age of the interlocutor that table 8.2 reveals and to state whether or not the pattern is similar to the Oberwart shift pattern.

24 Be able to state the language use pattern based on the age of the *speaker* in the Tiwa community, using the data in table 8.2.

25 Be able to give the possible interpretation of the age of interlocutor pattern which, if correct, would mean that this pattern has no bearing on whether or not the pattern reflects a cultural value (p.236).

26 Be able to identify the apparent 'deviations' from the dominant pattern in table 8.2 that indicate that there might be a group of young Tiwa Indians who are re-emphasizing the Tiwa language as a symbol of group identity.

27 Be able to recognize a description of the evidence on intergenerational language-switching in the Tiwa community (p.238).

28 Be able to identify Fasold's conclusion about whether the Tiwa community is shifting to English or maintaining Tiwa.

9

Language Planning and Standardization

It is a fundamental fact about language that it is constantly in dynamic flux. There is a whole spectrum of linguistic variation in the world, from the most subtle stylistic variants within one dialect to separate languages with substantially different grammatical and pronunciation systems. Not only is there variation in language structure, but in the use of language. Speakers do not use the same varieties for all purposes, as we know. They may shift from the use of one language, dialect, or style in a particular domain to the use of another. A speech community may even decline to pass on one of its traditional community languages to a new generation, allowing it to die out, at least in that community. All of this means that speakers constantly have *alternatives* available to them. They are constantly choosing between linguistic varieties or among variants within a linguistic system. The existence of alternatives makes planning possible. Language planning is usually seen as an explicit choice among alternatives. This, in turn, implies that there has been an evaluation of alternatives with the one that is chosen having been evaluated as the best (Jernudd 1973:17, Haugen 1966b:52). An attempt is then made to see that the chosen alternative wins out over other possibilities.

KINDS OF CHOICES

It is convenient, although a slight oversimplification, to divide the kinds of choices that are made into two large categories. These categories have been labeled in various ways. For example, Neustupný (1970:4) speaks of a *policy* approach and a *cultivation* approach. The policy approach refers, among other things, to the selection of a national language or a dialect to be made the standard, and the solution to problems of orthography. The cultivation approach includes considerations of style and correctness. A similar, but not quite identical, distinction is made by Jernudd (1973:16–17), who speaks of *language determination* and *language development*. Language determination means 'large-chunk' choices of languages to be used for specific purposes. If a nation decides that a particular language is going to serve as its official language, or be used as the medium of instruction in all elementary schools, that is an example of language determination. Language development, by and large, refers to the selection and promotion of variants *within* a language. If a widely respected grammar book states that the present perfect tense in English is properly used with the time adverbs 'already' and 'yet', but the simple past is not, then that is one kind of language-development choice. Whenever you look up a word in a dictionary to find a correct spelling, you are referring to an authority's language-development decision. Roughly speaking, Jernudd's 'language development' means the same thing as the 'language standardization' part of the title to this chapter. His 'language determination' parallels 'language planning', but only in the narrow sense. It is appropriate, at a more inclusive level, to include language standardization, or development, as a kind of language planning.

Language determination

Possibly the most important language determination issue around the world is the choice of national languages. When I say 'national language', I am referring to Fishman's definition of nationalism which we discussed in chapter 1. A national language is more than just the language of government or of education. It is the symbol of people's identity as citizens of that nation. A major problem involved in the selection of a national language is communication (Haugen 1966b:55, Jernudd and Das Gupta 1971:208). If virtually everyone in a country spoke a common language, then the life of the nation would be much easier to carry on. But if communication were the only issue, Ireland would never have gone to such extraordinary lengths, as it has, to restore Irish Gaelic as its national language (a case which we will discuss in detail in the next chapter). It was not the desire to improve communication that motivated Ivar Aasen to try to develop an authentic national language for Norway when the country already had a single linguistic norm in the form of the Dano-Norwegian language called Bokmål (Haugen 1959, 1966a). It would be a mistake to think of national-language determination only in terms of communication.[1]

It would also be a mistake to think of language planning for national languages only with respect to nation-states. All over the world, there are nationalities who do not have political control over their own territories where planning efforts are being made to preserve languages that symbolize their nationalism. Subnational nationalities don't have the power that nation-states do to specify which languages will be used in public education, in the civil service, or in the military. This does not prevent them, however, from using the means they do have on behalf of their national languages. Griffen (1980) documents one example of the complexities that can arise in language-planning efforts by a subnational nationality, in this case, the Welsh.

A national language in some cases might not be enough for the fulfilment of all High functions. National languages serve the *unifying* and *separatist* functions of Garvin and Mathiot (1956); some human activities, however, require what Garvin (1973:30–1) calls the *participatory* function. The participatory function refers to participation in worldwide cultural developments, such as science and technology, international business, and diplomacy. Since the separatist and participatory functions are opposed to each other (the separatist function involves a sense of distinction from other nations of the world; the participatory function involves a degree of international unity), not every nation will be able to use the same language for both. One example might be Tanzania, where Swahili is the emerging national language, but where English seems destined to be retained for participatory purposes, in Garvin's sense.

Language development

If language determination, to use a crude analogy, can be compared to selecting the make and model of a new car, then language development is like making custom modifications to the new car (or maybe an old one you already had). Ferguson (1968) sees three categories of language development: (1) graphization; (2) standardization; and (3) modernization. Graphization means the adoption of a writing system and the establishment of spelling and other orthographic conventions, such as capitalization and punctuation.[2] Standardization, according to Ferguson (1968:31), 'is the process of one variety of a language becoming widely accepted throughout the speech community as a supra-dialectal norm – the "best" form of the language – rated above regional and social dialects'.[3] By modernization, Ferguson means 'the process of ... becoming the equal of other developed languages as a medium of communication' (Ferguson 1968:32).

Modernization, so defined, is a concept that many linguists would be wary of, simply because it implies that there are 'undeveloped' languages that are not the equal of developed languages as media of communication. There has been a consensus in the field of linguistics that the basic grammatical and pronunciation systems of any natural language is adequate to allow any speaker to say anything. Of course, some languages may lack the *vocabulary* to say certain things, but this is fairly easily corrected by adding new vocabulary to the language, either by coinage or by borrowing from other languages. Indeed, vocabulary development is one thing Ferguson has in mind in connection with modernization. To be modernized, a developing language must undergo expansion of the lexicon. But he also refers to 'the development of new styles and forms of discourse' (Ferguson 1968:32). Garvin (1973:27) uses the term *intellectualization*, which he says 'roughly corresponds' to Ferguson's 'modernization'. Intellectualization has both lexical and grammatical aspects. The characteristics of grammatical intellectualization are described as follows: 'In grammar, intellectualization manifests itself by the development of word formation techniques and of syntactic devices allowing for the construction of elaborate, yet tightly knit, compound sentences, as well as the tendency to eliminate elliptic modes of expression by requiring complete constructions.' It is doubtful that there are any languages in which compound sentences are impossible, although they may come out 'loosely knit' in some. In fact, it seems that all languages have not only coordination, but also the natural language analogues of logical operators such as 'and', 'or', and 'if-then', and various syntactic techniques for subordination as well. Garvin's speaks of the 'elimination' of elliptical modes of expression. If elliptical modes of expression can be 'eliminated', then it seems that the alternative fuller modes of expression required by intellectualized language also exist in pre-intellectualized language. They are just not used much.

The examples Ferguson gives of 'new forms of discourse' are 'paragraphing, ordered sequences, transitions, summaries, cross-references, etc.' These items are clearly examples of language-use techniques, not grammatical constructions that need to be added to a language. It appears, to me at least, that modernization, when it does not refer to vocabulary, is about the acquisition of skill in the use of linguistic resources that a language probably already has. To invoke another crude analogy, I have a calculator that is capable of computing sines, cosines, tangents, converting ordinary values into degrees, minutes, and seconds, and carrying out other functions that I have never required it to do and don't know how to do. If I ever need to use these capabilities, I would only need to become more skilled in the use of the machine that I already have; I wouldn't need to modify it or buy a new one. I suspect that the comparison with language modernization holds. At least, I have never seen an example of a language that actually needed its basic grammatical structure strengthened in some way before it could be used for higher functions.[4]

As far as vocabulary expansion goes, it doesn't matter much to the linguist whether the new vocabulary comes from some other language (by borrowing) or whether it is made up of elements already in the language.[5] However, borrowing versus coinage often becomes an emotional issue in actual practice. Not infrequently, a planning agency will attempt to 'purify' the language by replacing borrowings with newly coined words. As long as coinage does not conflict with what members of the society are prepared to do, it works out well. Haugen (1966b:64) reports that the coining of new words for intellectual phenomena was very successful in Estonian and Lithuanian, no doubt because the coinages were readily acceptable to the users of these two languages. When loanwords are already in regular use by speakers and writers, however, an attempt to purge them will probably fail. Attatürk had firm control of the Turkish government and wanted very much to purge Arabic and Persian loanwords from Turkish, but he met with so much resistance that he had to limit his goals in vocabulary planning. The revival of Hebrew in Israel is one of language planning's great success stories, but the attempt to purify Hebrew of loanwords from European languages was not part of the success (Morag 1959).

TWO CONCEPTS OF LANGUAGE PLANNING

The instrumental approach

Most students of language planning take one of two points of view: either the *instrumental* approach or the *socio-linguistic* approach. The instrumental approach (Tauli 1968 is probably the best-known advocate, although Ray 1963 and 1968 takes the same position to some extent) sees language fundamentally as a tool. Just as work is easier for mechanics if mechanical tools are standardized, communication would be easier if language were standardized. The only criteria to be used in the standardization of mechanical tools are concerned with making them more suitable to the task they are used for, and, in this view, the same goes for language standardization. Some languages are better than others in their balance of beauty, clarity, elasticity and economy and these ought to be chosen over less adequate languages where possible. When it is not possible, language planning should be used to improve the quality of the inadequate language. The instrumental approach characteristically considers some languages inherently better than others and places great confidence in conscious efforts to make inadequate languages better. The symbolic value of language and language attitudes are not taken into account.[6]

The socio-linguistic approach

I call the second approach the 'socio-linguistic' approach, with the hyphen explicit, to emphasize that this approach begins with the recognition of a social problem that is connected with language. Scholars with this philosophical orientation don't attempt to improve the esthetic and functional qualities of languages as instrumental tools. Rather, they see language as a resource that can be used in improving social life. This way of practicing language planning would attempt to determine which of the available linguistic alternatives is most likely to improve a problematic situation. Then orderly steps are to be taken that will make the best alternative the one that actually succeeds. Scholars from this tradition are very skeptical about the instrumentalist idea that it is possible to determine what is most efficient in language in the absolute sense and plan for that (Ferguson 1968:28; Jernudd and Das Gupta 1971; Jernudd 1973:14; Rubin 1973:4). As Jernudd (1973:14) puts it: 'if a community lacks a common language it matters [little] if the first effort in bridging that gap is linguistically beautiful (in any absolute sense) or not.' The best solution is the one that works best in alleviating the social problem.

Scholars who work in this frame of reference also take the idea of 'planning' seriously. In dealing with a societal problem connected with language, as in dealing with social problems in general, the facts are to be marshalled, alternatives identified, evaluations of the alternatives made, steps in the implementation of the plan carefully designed and executed, and judgements made about how successful the plan was (Rubin 1971, 1973; Jernudd 1973; Jernudd and Das Gupta 1971). This degree of care in the planning process is sometimes referred to as an ideal that is seldom realized in actual practice.

PRACTICAL CONSIDERATIONS

Who and how

Who. Now that we have seen something of what language planning is about, the kinds of choices that are made in language planning, and the two main philosophical approaches to it, it makes sense to consider who does language planning and how it is done. The answer to the question 'Who does language planning?' is rather surprising; it can be almost anybody (Haugen 1966b; Ray 1968; Jernudd 1973; Rubin 1973). Governments, of course, are in a position to make the most wide-ranging (but not necessarily the most successful) decisions that influence language. The decision by the Roman Catholic Church some twenty years ago to allow the use of vernacular languages in the place of Latin, and the recent revision in liturgical language in the Church of England are examples of language planning in the religious domain. Some countries have language academies, where experts issue decisions about the proper use of their languages. In the English-speaking world, two private citizens who constructed dictionaries had a profound influence on the standardization of the meanings and spellings of words – Samuel Johnson in England and Noah Webster in the United States.

In the early days of printing, individuals who decided how the language was to be used in the first publications set precedents that influenced to a great extent what was considered appropriate in written language for some time thereafter. Luther's translation of the Bible into German, one of the earliest works to be widely published, had a strong influence on the standardization of the German language. In the latter half of the fifteenth century, William Caxton brought one of the early printing presses to England from the Continent and used it to publish numerous manuscripts. In the process, he acted as editor of everything he published and tried to make consistent decisions about the various grammatical forms and spellings in the manuscripts he received. In this way, he had a more powerful influence on the standardization of English than someone else, who lived at a different time would have had (Shaklee 1980:48). In our own century and continuing to this day, missionaries who carry out literacy programs in previously unwritten languages are often the people who decide how these languages will be written and sometimes which dialect will be used for written purposes.[7]

Jernudd (1973:18–19) has given the following short list of language planning agents, in addition to governments:

1   national, but nongovernmental agencies – for example, the Singapore Chamber of Commerce, which constructed and issued language examinations and a style manual for business correspondence in Malay;
2   non-national and nongovernmental agencies – for example, the Shell Company provides its own Malay oil terminology in Malaysia and influences language development in its personnel and training policies;
3   a newspaper's proof-reading function;
4   the individual author, letter-writer, or even after-dinner speaker.

Jernudd goes on to speculate on whether it is appropriate to speak of language planning when an office manager specifies which words can and cannot be used in correspondence in her office, or when a group of university students argue about the correct pronunciation of some word. Ray (1968:764) points out that the efforts of institutional authorities are dependent for success on what 'lesser authorities' of just the type Jernudd is talking about decide to do:

In other words, any formal organized action by an acknowledged authority, such as a State or a Church or a learned society or an author, can be successful in its intention to encourage or discourage linguistic habits only if it correlates maximally to informal unorganized action on the part of numerous locally more accessible authorities.[8]

How.   The question 'How is language planning done?' is connected with the *planning* and *implementation* stages of a larger planning process. Rubin (1971:218–20) outlines the four steps of this larger process.

1   Fact-finding: a substantial amount of background information should be available before any planning decisions are made.
2   Planning: here the actual decisions are made; 'The planner will establish goals, select the means (strategies), and predict the outcome' (Rubin 1971:219).
3   Implementation: the planning decisions are carried out.
4   Feedback: at this step, the planner finds out how well the plan has worked.

Probably the major tool that governments use in implementing language-planning decisions is the educational system. If a language has been selected to be the national language, the government can order it to be taught as a subject to all school children, or even to be used as a medium of instruction for teaching other subjects. If there is an official list of vocabulary innovations, these can be taught in schools, as can orthographical modifications and standard spellings. In extreme cases, school children can be prohibited from speaking disapproved languages in school. We have come across some cases, like the ones involving children speaking Guaraní in Paraguayan schools and Gaelic in Scottish schools, in which children have been physically punished for speaking disapproved languages in school. When a teacher tells a youngster not to say 'ain't', this is a minor instance of the use of the school system to implement language planning, or at least language treatment.[9]

Governments can also require competence in a selected language as a prerequisite for civil service employment. In countries where the civil service is one of the few ways to advance economically and socially, this can be a significant motivating factor. The language that governments use for legislative debate and the language in which laws are written and government documents are issued are also means that can be used to promote a selected language or language variety. The language used in the military can have a profound effect, especially in a country with universal military conscription. If the government is sufficiently authoritarian, it can regulate which languages can be used in the print and broadcast media, and in which languages it is permitted to publish books. Less authoritarian governments can try to influence language use in print and broadcast media by offering subsidies or tax advantages for the use of a favored language. Ray (1968:761) gives a list of specific means a government can use to influence how language is used in published work.

Language-planning agents that are not governments do not have as many means at their disposal. Professional societies can and do issue official terminology lists as guides for their members. Authors of grammar and usage guides have an impact on language use to the extent that their work is consulted. As Jernudd pointed out, businesses and business organizations have an effect on language by their personnel and training practices, especially in countries that are trying to modernize a new national language. Organizations attempting to preserve the national languages of subnational nationalities have options such as offering night courses and presenting theater and other cultural activities in the language under treatment. Politically, they can put pressure on the government of the country they live in to support the use of their language.[10] Individuals also can have an impact. A talented novelist, poet, playwright, or film-maker with a good reputation, if she publishes only in a particular language, obliges her audience to learn that language if they want access to her work. A technique such as this would be the more effective, if a group of talented artists were to follow this kind of practice.

Even individual speakers might take steps on behalf of a certain language. It is apparently the practice of some prominent native French-speaking bilinguals in Switzerland to refuse to use German with a native German-speaking Swiss, on the grounds that the French Swiss have always been the ones who have had to converge linguistically to accommodate their German Swiss compatriots. Giles, Bourhis, and Taylor (1977) report the extreme example of a Welshman who would refuse to speak any other language but

Welsh outside the work domain. If the person he was talking to knew Welsh only slightly, this man would speak slowly, but require the other person to rely on whatever competence in Welsh he had. If the other person was monolingual in English, the Welshman would speak in Welsh, but translate into English as he went, sentence by sentence.

LIMITATIONS IN LANGUAGE PLANNING

Cost–benefit analysis

One limiting factor in language planning is connected with a consideration of costs and benefits. Even if a change that seems worthwhile can be brought about, good planning means that the benefits a society stands to gain will be matched against the costs. Cost–benefit analysis is a technique sometimes used by economists, and Thorburn (1971) and Jernudd (1971) have discussed how it can be applied to language planning. Thorburn (1971:256) defines cost-benefit analysis in language planning this way: 'Cost-benefit analysis in language planning is, in principle, an attempt to state the difference in consequences between two exactly defined alternatives in language planning.' The use of the technique in business is much simpler than in language planning. A typical application in manufacturing would be to calculate the cost of wages, materials, and so on and compare the result with the prices that will be received when the product is sold. Applying the same technique to a public administration problem, such as language planning by a government, is not so straightforward for a number of reasons. First, the results of decisions are not paid for by a fixed price at a fixed time. In fact, many of the costs and most of the consequences of language planning have very little at all to do with money. Second, the consequences of planning decisions in public administration may not be fully apparent for a long time. The further into the future the planning reaches, the more indeterminate are the results. Nevertheless, an adaptation of the technique along the following lines is worth considering.

The first requirement of cost–benefit analysis is to have at least two clear alternative plans under analysis. Cost–benefit analysis is *comparative*; we want to know which of two or more courses of action is going to yield the most benefits for the least cost. Once the alternatives have been established, three steps follow: (1) *identification* of the consequences of choosing one course rather than another; (2) *quantification*; and (3) *evaluation* of those consequences (Thorburn 1971:257). By evaluation in this context, Thorburn means *monetary* evaluation. Here is where one of the two major difficulties comes in; more consequences can be identified than quantified, and others can be identified and quantified, but not monetarily evaluated. For example, suppose part of a plan calls for the commissioning of a book of poems in a new national language. It is a reasonably simple matter to calculate what it will cost to pay the poet's commission, publish the volume, and distribute it. It may even be possible to estimate how many people will read it and to what extent it will be reviewed in literary journals and studied in university courses. These quantities would no doubt be a measure of an increase in the status of the new national language as a vehicle for serious literature. Literary stature for its national language is of considerable value to a nation, but this value is no doubt extremely difficult to translate into *monetary* terms.

Other consequences probably cannot even be quantified. If an indigenous language can be established as a truly functioning national language, this feat would be of immense importance to the unity and stability of the nation. But how qualities such as unity and stability can be expressed numerically, let alone in monetary terms, is hard to imagine. Some consequences can be both quantified and evaluated, at least in principle, but with great uncertainty. A plan, for instance, that called for the promotion of a 'world' language such as English or Russian in the domain of international business would arguably increase a nation's foreign trade. If this plan were compared with an alternative that called for the use of an indigenous language – one that is not spoken outside the country – it is possible that the monetary value of the amount of foreign trade under the two alternatives could be estimated and compared. The problem is that an estimate of this sort would not be very accurate.

I think it is clear that cost–benefit analysis is not a magic formula which will spew out numbers associated with alternatives so that all the analyst has to do is pick the number that indicates the most benefits for the least cost. As Thorburn (1971:257) says, 'a cost–benefit calculation can be more suitable as a supporting analysis than as a sufficient basis for the final decision.' Nevertheless, carrying out language planning with an outline cost–benefit analysis forces the planner, first of all, to clarify the alternatives. Second, it leads the planner to try to specify all the possible consequences of the plan. Finally, the planner will be led to think in terms of costs as well as benefits, and the relationship between the two. A plan that would indisputably bring about considerable benefits might have to be abandoned because of its high cost. Such costs may not only be in money.

Take some of the methods of language planning referred to above. Suppose, for example, a government decrees that an indigenous language must be used in government administration after a certain date. Even if the new language already had an adequate vocabulary, or has been provided with it by language planning, government workers who are used to working in another language, say a former colonial language, might have to spend considerable time looking up new terms in prepared lists or glossaries. Other administrative personnel might have to do the same when they are trying to read and understand written communications in the new language. All of this will slow down efficiency, at least for a while, and impede day-to-day nationist activity. This can be costly, not only in the fact that the government will have to pay workers for more hours to accomplish the same amount of work, but it could cause citizen dissatisfaction, if government services are delayed or never reach them.

More seriously, the same decision can cause severe political problems if the selected official language is the native language of only part of the population. Speakers of other languages may feel they are at an unfair disadvantage if their members have to learn the new national language to deal with or work for the government, whereas the native speakers don't. When a colonial language is used, they may argue, at least everyone is at the same disadvantage. This very problem, of course, is the main cause for the indefinite delay in the institution of Hindi as the exclusive language of government in India. Each of the methods outlined in the earlier section carries with it similar 'costs'. In chapter 11, we will deal with the special costs and benefits that are associated with the alternatives in the selection of a language of education.

Cost–benefit analysis seems to have advantages in spite of its limitations. Nevertheless, there haven't been many published reports of its application to language-planning problems. One scholar who has used the technique is Tadadjeu (1977); he examined the costs and benefits in the selection of languages of education in sub-Saharan Africa. Mackey (1978) uses cost–benefit analysis in the more limited area of language teaching techniques. An interesting variation on cost-benefit analysis is applied by Mackay (1980) in his evaluation of Bodine's (1975) suggestion that 'singular *they*' be used in place of masculine forms of the generic pronoun. Mackay compares 'costs and benefits', not in terms of money or general value to the society, but in terms of whether this language-planning alternative would make communication more efficient or less so.

Acceptance

The acceptability criterion. Haugen (1966b:61–3) has proposed three criteria for language planning. Of the three, two ostensibly deal with the state of the language itself. These two are *efficiency*, or ease of learning and use, and *adequacy*, the ability of a form to convey information with the desired degree of precision. The third criterion is connected with the social status of the language. Haugen calls it *acceptability*. A language, a language variety, a list of approved vocabulary items, or whatever linguistic practice is the object of planning must be accepted by members of the society where the planning is taking place. In particular, Haugen, following Ray (1963), believes that there is a crucial segment of society called the 'lead', who are considered worth imitating and whose usage is most likely to spread. Success in language planning, then, requires the implicit co-operation of the lead. Of the three, it seems to me that acceptability is by far the most important. A language that people have an aversion to will never be 'easy to learn and use', regardless of how straightforward its grammar and pronunciation seem to be in some absolute sense. Adequacy is clearly to be related to some particular purpose; a language that is adequate for family dinner-table conversation may not be adequate for a lecture in chemistry. As a result, there is no reason for people to accept a new language practice when the current ones are adequate for any purpose they can anticipate. Even if the planners can envisage the necessity for a higher degree of 'modernization' for future national development, it doesn't mean too much if the people don't see the same need.

It is far from automatic that the implementation of a language-planning alternative will be successful, even if its benefits justify its costs. As Ray (1968:762) puts it: 'There is no quick way of making the horse drink the water, if it does not want to.' Haugen (1966b:60) adds: 'In any literate community with some tradition behind it there is a whole set of convictions and rationalizations concerning speech and writing, against which the planner may turn out to be powerless'; a statement that probably should not be limited to literate communities. A planning agency can only make it easy and attractive to follow the chosen linguistic practices, or difficult or unattractive not to. Language use is fundamentally such a personal affair that real change is only possible with the consent of the language user.

The naturalist approach.   Since the goal of language planning is to set the direction of a linguistic change of some sort, a reasonable place to start would be to consider what makes natural linguistic change take place, that is, change that happens without conscious language planning. What might be called a *naturalist* approach would advocate harnessing natural forces to bring about a consciously selected outcome. The first step in a naturalist approach to language planning is to specify the domain or domains the plan is designed to apply to, and how large a segment of society is supposed to use the planned alternative. For example, it would be a relatively simple matter for an association of professional chemists to standardize the terminology its members are to use in their research reports. A plan of this sort applies only to vocabulary, only to writing in a particular subject area, and only to a relatively small group of users. An attempt to induce the population of a whole country to shift to a newly instituted national language for all spoken and written purposes would be an example of the opposite type. Here, all domains are involved and all of a country's people are supposed to follow the plan. Needless to say, the second plan would be much harder to implement.

It is a fundamental sociolinguistic fact that some uses of language cause people to attend to *how* they are getting their message across as well as *what* their message is.[11] In other situations, people put almost all their emphasis on the content of their message, leaving its form, so to speak, on automatic pilot. Higher uses of language are the ones where more attention is likely to be paid to message form. As a result, language planning aimed at High uses is far more likely to be successful than planning that includes Low uses. If a language user is paying conscious attention to the form of her message, the planner has the relatively easy job of convincing her that the selected alternative is the one she ought to use. Since her attention is on linguistic form as well as message content, her usage is more likely to conform to what she is consciously convinced of. To influence a person's language use when little monitoring of form is being done is much more difficult. In such cases – and these cases probably constitute the greatest amount of language use – the planner must find a way to get into people's linguistic 'automatic pilots'.

An obvious category of language use in which a lot of attention is paid to form is written use. Writing is slower than talking; writers can take more time to think about how they are going to put their thoughts, and they can revise and rewrite, if they do not like their first attempts. Language planning, then, is often aimed at written usage rather than speech, with the recognition that planned innovations in written use may eventually filter into speech (Haugen 1966b:53, Ferguson 1968:30). As Haugen points out, this reverses the linguist's usual way of looking at language, since linguists, correctly, see spoken language as more fundamental than written language.[12]

The fact that there is a distinction between the *formal* standards that are overtly prescribed and the *informal* standards that people conform to in their everyday spoken usage has often been noticed (for example, Gumperz and Naim 1960; Stewart 1968:534 fn 5; Wolfram and Fasold 1974:18–21; Schmidt and McCreary 1977). Schmidt and McCreary present experimental evidence of a discrepancy between their subjects' written usage when their attention was drawn away from a particular grammatical form and the form they overtly endorse as correct. One such grammatical variable was concerned with the choice between 'is' and 'are' in 'there'-inserted sentences with plural logical subjects, for example, the difference between 'There's two guys in the car' and 'There are two guys in the car'. In a 'performance' experiment, subjects were presented orally with a 'there'-inserted sentence with a *singular* subject, and a plural noun phrase which they were told to place in the original sentence so that it made sense. For example, given the sentence 'There is enough time left', and the noun phrase 'about five minutes', it is clear that the new noun phrase is supposed to replace 'enough time', but no mention is made of the form of the verb 'to be'. After completing this task, the same subjects were asked about which forms they would use themselves and which they thought were correct, and whether they thought they used them or not. Figure 9.1 illustrates the responses of a group of high-school seniors and a group of college freshman English students. In both groups, the form endorsed as correct by the most speakers is the opposite of the one used by most in the performance task. More report that they use the form they say is correct than the form they actually used in the test.[13] It is clear that it isn't so easy to influence linguistic practices that speakers do not consciously monitor.

In order to have any hope of influencing language futures at this level, we will need to look back at what we have learned about what makes people shift their language use. The study of language choice and language maintenance

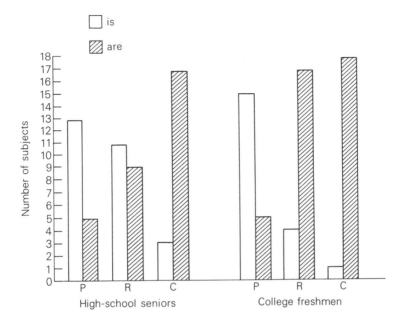

*Figure 9.1   Forms used in a performance test (P), self-reported as most often
used (R), and endorsed as correct (C) by American English-speaking high-
school seniors and college freshmen, in such sentences as
'There (is, are) about five minutes left'*
Source: data from Schmidt and McCreary (1977)

and shift show that a great deal depends on a person's *identity*. When and how
often an Oberwart citizen would use German depended on the degree to which
she thought of herself as an 'Austrian' worker rather than an Oberwart
peasant, and the circumstances under which she would want to claim each
identity. Similarly, the use of Gaelic or English in East Sutherland was
strongly influenced by whether a person wanted to present himself as being
Highland Scots or as a fisher. It appears, then, that to get people to change
their linguistic practice at the lower and unmonitored levels, planners have to
somehow get people to adopt the identity that goes with the new linguistic
forms. This has led to the notion of 'identity planning' (Lamy 1979). In a study
of identity planning, Pool (1979) was able to show a definite relationship
between use of language and willingness to claim a particular identity, using
survey data. Data from Wales and Canada show that people who know Welsh
and French, respectively, are more likely to see themselves as 'Welsh' rather
than 'British', or as 'French' rather than 'English' Canadians. In Canada,
language spoken was much more strongly associated with a willingness to
claim French ethnic identity than residence in Quebec, being a Catholic, or
even having a French surname or being of French ancestry.

Pool's results are far from being the first evidence that links the use of language with social identity. There are numerous instances in the literature in which social groups follow informal standards that have little or no official support. The Tiwa Indians are one case we have already seen, and the Oberwart peasants and the East Sutherland fishing communities were examples until quite recently (some Oberwart peasants still are). An early study by Labov (1972b:255–96) demonstrated how young black men in Harlem conformed most consistently to the informal standards of Vernacular Black English, if they had a strong sense of identification with adolescent peer groups. Black adolescents of the same age and living in the same neighborhoods who had no such connections ('lames') were the ones most likely to have shifted in the direction of formally standard English. Wolfram (1973) showed that Puerto Rican young men who had the most extensive contacts with speakers of Vernacular Black English were acquiring those English features rather than the formal standards taught in school. Poplack (1978) found a similar same trend in the Puerto Rican community in Philadelphia, even though there were few VBE speakers in the neighborhood (there was some evidence that the ones who were there enjoyed considerable prestige). Quite apart from any influence from VBE, the Puerto Rican youngsters Poplack studied treated local Philadelphia pronunciation variants as *prestige* forms. Native Philadelphians, by contrast, move away from local variants toward more formal norms when they monitor their speech. Finally, to repeat an example we used to illustrate the use of statistics, Milroy was able to show convincingly that Belfast residents with strong local network ties were the ones to use the most distinctly local, but officially nonstandard, forms (Milroy 1980; Milroy and Margrain 1980).

The conduct of identity *planning* would seem to involve using available resources to make it attractive to identify with the speakers of a particular language or variety. But students of language maintenance and shift are nearly unanimous in agreeing that the same social and economic conditions that produce shift in one group will not budge another group from their determination to maintain a traditional language.[14] The general conclusion, then, is that the usual language planning methods are not particularly likely to influence speakers' linguistic practices in unmonitored language use – unless they are designed to support the direction in which natural social forces are moving anyway.

LINGUISTIC STRUCTURE AND LANGUAGE PLANNING

Unless one takes the instrumental approach to language planning, there seems to be very little technical linguistics in language planning. The socio-linguistic (or socio-linguistic-cum-naturalistic) orientations advocate the promotion of any linguistic form that will work and make the social situation better. Even the supposed grammatical aspects of 'modernization' or 'intellectualization' seem more like questions of skill in using the existing resources in a language than anything syntacticians deal with. In other words, it seems to be the case that what is considered standard, or worthy of official promotion, depends only on the social position of the people who use that particular variety. One waggish way this idea is sometimes put is to say that a standard language is any language whose speakers have an army and a navy!

Although language planning does seem to me to be far more a sociopolitical matter than a strictly linguistic one, I believe it is possible to go to extremes in playing down the linguistic aspects of language planning and standardization. If social forces are inconclusive, linguistic considerations might some times prove decisive in selecting a planning alternative (cf. Bailey 1975). On the question of whether or not it is possible to characterize standard languages on *linguistic* grounds, it would be wise not to answer 'no' too quickly. Kroch (1978:20) argues that 'non-prestige dialects tend to be articulatorily more economical than the prestige dialect.' This means that standard dialect pronunciations are likely to make more distinctions than are strictly necessary for understanding.[15] If Kroch is correct, it would be interesting to find out if there is a parallel trend in syntax. If so, it would be a trend only. Vernacular Black English, for one example, is a nonprestige dialect in which verb system distinctions can be made more clearly than in standard American English. Nevertheless, I think it is best to treat the question of the linguistic characteristics of standard dialects as an open one.

SUMMARY

The fact that languages vary and change, and are maintained or abandoned, means that linguistic alternatives are constantly available to speakers. The existence of alternatives opens up the possibility that speakers might be influenced to choose some alternatives rather than others. The attempt to exert such conscious influences is what is meant by language planning and standardization.

Within language planning there are two major divisions: language determination and language development. Language determination refers to the choice of larger linguistic units, languages or dialects of languages, for particular purposes. Language development refers to the selection of variants *within* a language or dialect. Ferguson (1968) subdivides language development into three parts: graphization, standardization, and modernization. Modernization (or intellectualization) can be further broken down into vocabulary development and grammar (perhaps more precisely, usage) aspects. Possibly the major language-determination issue in the world is the selection of national languages.

Most scholars who have an interest in language planning take either the instrumentalist or the socio-linguistic approach. Instrumentalists emphasize the function of language as a means of communication, somewhat at the expense of its symbolic social importance. As a result, language planning for them ought to be directed at making languages more efficient and esthetically more pleasing in its communicative role. The socio-linguistic approach takes the point of view that language is a social resource. If this is so, then language planning ought to be directed at using this resource wisely in achieving social goals, even if the planned alternative is not efficient or beautiful by some absolute criterion.

Language planning is usually thought of as being conducted by governments, but efforts to influence language change can be made by religious organizations, organizations promoting the interests of subnational nationalities, business organizations, and even individuals. A thorough language planning project would include the four steps outlined by Rubin (1973). Specific means used in language planning range from the issuing of lists of approved vocabulary items to the designation of a particular linguistic variety as the sole means of instruction in a country's state schools.

There are certain definite limitations on language planning. One important consideration is the cost. The use of cost-benefit analysis can aid in the evaluation of a proposed plan, although cost–benefit analysis cannot be applied in the fullest sense to language planning. One reason that cost–benefit analysis can only have a supplementary function in language planning is that many of the costs and benefits cannot be evaluated in monetary terms and some cannot even be quantified. Another reason is that the consequences of language planning are often to be realized so far into the future that predictions become very unreliable.

A more fundamental limitation is concerned with acceptance. No chosen alternative will be successful unless it is accepted by the population the planning is being done for. Maximizing the chances of acceptance may depend on how well the plan conforms to the natural forces at work in the society. This is especially true of planning that attempts to influence what people do in unmonitored language use. Research indicates that the usual language-planning practices are more successful when they are directed at monitored language use (when people are paying a lot of attention, not only to what they are saying, but how they are saying it). This is one reason why language planning is more often directed at the written language than at the spoken form.

People's linguistic choices, especially unmonitored ones, are likely to symbolize their sense of sociocultural group identity. This fact has led to the concept of 'identity planning'. Consciously taken steps to influence a person's self-identification appear to be at least as difficult as steps to plan languages directly, however.

Linguists usually take the position that languages are structurally equal and that whether a language variety is a standard or prestige variety or not is determined by social forces alone. Kroch (1978), however, argues that prestige dialects tend to preserve more of the underlying phonological distinctions than nonprestige dialects do. Whether or not there is any sense in which prestige dialects tend to maintain more morphological and syntactic distinctions than nonprestige dialects do is an open question. It is clear that there are nonprestige varieties that have some grammatical distinctions which the corresponding socially approved varieties lack.

BIBLIOGRAPHICAL NOTES

Several anthologies have been published on language planning, including Rubin and Jernudd (1971), Rubin and Shuy (1973), Fishman (1974), Rubin (1977), and Rubin et al. (1977). Two case studies of language planning, aside from those cited in this chapter and the next, and those in the volumes cited above, are Shaffer (1978) (on Afrikaans) and Dahlstedt (1977) (on Swedish). Some of the studies on orthography planning include De Francis (1972), Sjoberg (1966), Berry (1968), Dewees (1977) and the articles in Fishman (1977). For terminology standardization, see the articles in Sage (1980).

NOTES

1 Haugen (1966b) has provided one of the clearest, most insightful basic discussions of language planning available. Nevertheless, he has, in my opinion, made the mistake of overemphasizing communication as the only motivation for language planning. He speaks of *primary* speech communities, such as Iceland, where linguistic variation is slight enough so that everyone can understand each other fully; *secondary* speech communities, such as England, where linguistic variation is more substantial and there is only partial understanding; and *tertiary* speech communities, for example, Switzerland, where there may be no understanding between citizens without an interpreter. In his view (Haugen 1966b:55), only a secondary speech community needs a national language. By 'national language' he seems to mean something different from what Fishman means by the term, namely, a national standard to guide choices among variations in the same linguistic system. Primary communities are said not to need language planning at all and tertiary ones to need an 'international or auxiliary' language. Ireland is a reasonable approximation of a primary speech community, but it is still planning for a national language. Most nations that would qualify as tertiary speech communities would hardly be satisfied with an 'international or auxiliary' language to overcome communication problems, or more of the developing countries would adopt the former colonial language for that purpose.
2 Problems of graphization are very important in language planning and a rather extensive literature has developed on the subject. Some of the research on graphization is listed in the bibliographical notes above.
3 It is at this point that language development and language determination tend to blur into each other. The more this 'one variety' is treated as a whole, the more the planning will resemble determination. The more the standard variety is treated as a set of 'correct' features that are selected from the existing variants within a single linguistic system, the more the planning looks like a development effort.
4 Pidgin languages and creoles in the early stages of decreolization might be valid examples.
5 Ray (1968:756) finds the term 'borrowing' misleading since there is no obligation

to pay back, and prefers 'inheritance'. It seems to me that 'lexical copying' would be more accurate to describe what actually happens. When one language 'borrows' a word from another, the 'lending' language doesn't lose the word, the borrowing language simply has a 'copy' of it for its own use. The term 'borrowing', though, is so well established that it makes no sense to try to change it.

6   See Haugen (1971) for a critique of the instrumental approach. Ray differs from Tauli in being somewhat less sanguine about the prospects for successful language planning.

7   A case in which missionary language-planning activity later played a role in a national language-planning controversy is documented by Dewees (1977).

8   In writing this book, I have tried to play the role of a 'lesser authority' language planner. I've tried to use a more colloquial style and less formal syntax than is normally used in a textbook. You may also have noticed that I have switched between masculine and feminine personal pronouns where I needed a singular generic pronoun. By doing that, I am hoping to influence readers in the direction of my favorite solution to the problem of sexism in the use of English pronouns. To the extent my readers find these practices worth adopting in their own usage, I will have had a tiny influence on the English language.

9   Rubin (1973) and Jernudd (1973) distinguish between the orderly process of *planning* and more haphazard efforts to influence language, for which they use the broader term 'language treatment'.

10 In 1982, political pressure by Welsh nationalists contributed to a decision by the British government to fund televison programming in the Welsh language.

11 This aspect of language use is emphasized by Labov (1966, 1972a) and is discussed in volume II.

12 Haugen is also correct in pointing out that Bloomfield's (1933:21) comment that writing is 'merely a way of recording language by means of visible marks' is very much an overstatement, though understandable in the light of Bloomfield's purposes.

13 Some informal standards differ from the corresponding formal ones because the formal prescriptions never thoroughly took hold. Schmidt and McCreary (1977) investigate another case, the use of the objective case of English personal pronouns, in which it appears that a new informal standard is developing which is different from the formal standard, because the formal standard has not yet caught up with changing informal language norms. The fact that language standards change over time is documented for British English by Shaklee (1980) and for American English by Heath (1980).

14 Although a logical alternative would be to get a different language to symbolize an identity that a group already has, in thinking about real cases, this task usually turns out to be absurd. I can't imagine how one would bring it about that German symbolized peasant identity in Oberwart, or English symbolized Quebecois identity in Montreal!

15 In technical terms, prestige-dialect surface pronunciations are likely to preserve more underlying distinctions than pronunciations in nonprestige dialects.

OBJECTIVES

1   Given a hypothetical language-planning objective, be able to state whether it is an example of language *determination* or language *cultivation*.

2   Be able to state whether or not language planning is used only to improve communication.

3   Be able to recognize a definition of Garvin's *participatory* function.

4   Be able to recognize the interpretation of Ferguson's 'modernization' or Garvin's 'intellectualization', besides vocabulary expansion, that Fasold would endorse. Hint: this interpretation is not spelled out in so many words, but found in what is said on pp.248-9.

5   Be able to recognize the linguist's attitude toward coinage versus borrowing as a way of expanding vocabulary as well as a common attitude of language planning agencies (p.249).

6   Be able to recognize a description of the two approaches to language planning discussed on pp. 250 ff.

7   Be able to recognize possible answers to the question of who conducts language planning.

8   Be able to state which of 'formal organized action' or 'informal unorganized action' by 'numerous locally more accessible authorities' is more crucial for the success of language planning according to Ray.

9   Be able to name Rubin's four steps in the language-planning process.

10   Be able to name the major tool that governments have in implementing language planning decisions (p. 252).

11   Be able to identify what a cost-benefit analysis applied to language planning requires and what it ideally would provide (pp. 254-5).

12   Although language-planning decisions cannot be based on cost–benefit analysis alone, attempting this kind of analysis forces the planner to perform three useful tasks. Be able to identify them (p. 255).

13   Be able to name the three criteria for language planning given by Haugen, recognize their definitions, and state which is the most important (p.256).

14   Be able to recognize the most fundamental reason why language planning aimed at High uses is more likely to be successful (pp. 257-8).

15   Be able to identify the relative numbers of Schmidt and McCreary's subjects: that (1) said that 'are' is correct in there-sentences with plural logical subjects; (2) *reported* that they used the form 'are' in this kind of sentence; and (3) actually *placed* 'are' in such sentences in a performance test.

16   Be able to name the deeper social factor that may have to be planned before it is possible to succeed at language planning for Low domain usage (p. 259).

17   Be able to recognize Fasold's view on whether or not standard varieties of languages can be generally characterized on *linguistic* grounds.

10

Language-Planning Cases

In the last chapter we took a general overview of language planning and standardization. Now it will be useful to see how it works out in actual practice. As examples, we will use two cases where the most difficult language planning objective of all was attempted – the institution of a national language. One reason for using the national-language case is that it usually includes more modest language-planning goals. Language determination is the central problem in instituting a new national language, but dialect determination and various types of development are also needed. The particular cases we will investigate include one of the most successful instances of national language institution in the world: Swahili in Tanzania. The other case has run into difficulties throughout its history and has so far fallen considerably short of its goals: planning for Irish Gaelic in Ireland.

TANZANIA

History

The United Republic of Tanzania, composed of what was once the British colony, Tanganyika, and the island of Zanzibar, is an East African nation; it has an area of about 350,000 square miles, a 500-mile coastline bordering the Indian Ocean, and its population numbers about 15 million (see map 10.1). It is primarily an agricultural country, and has no major plans to become industrialized. Linguistically, it is a very diverse nation. Polomé (1980a:3) mentions reasons why it is difficult to list accurately the languages of Tanzania.[1] Two of these reasons are familiar to us – lack of language questions in the post-independence censuses and the difficulty in distinguishing related 'languages' from partly mutually-intelligible 'dialects'.[2] In a later article (Polomé 1982:172), he gives 135 as the number of 'different linguistic units identified as distinct languages by their speakers'. In 1957, 94 per cent of the population spoke one of the languages of the Bantu language family. With so many languages spoken by a relatively small population, there are very few

Map 10.1   Tanzania

languages spoken by large numbers of people. The largest group, the Sukuma, comprise only 12.6 per cent of the population and the next largest group (the Nyamwezi) comprise only 4.2 per cent (Whiteley 1971a:148).

Swahili was apparently first spoken along the coast, probably never by a very large population as a native language. In its early history, the language was spoken by Arabs and Africans of Muslim faith and written in Arabic script. By the mid-nineteenth century, Swahili had become the dominant trade language along the trade routes from the coast into the interior of what is now Tanzania, Kenya, Uganda, and eastern Zaire. The trading activity led to the learning of Swahili as a second language by a substantial number of people living in the interior. This fact was exploited by the Germans, who administered much of what is now Tanzania as German East Africa from about 1890 until the end of the First World War. The German policy was to rule the colony with a minimum of German civilian–military administrators and a cadre of African junior officials. The African administrators were all speakers of both the local language of the area and Swahili. The German colonists would learn only Swahili. A German administrator, then, could learn a single African language, Swahili, that was understood by key people over a wide area instead of a local language that would be of no use elsewhere. When the British took over the colony, renamed Tanganyika, at the end of the First World War, they continued the language policy the Germans had used. Although English gained in importance, both as a language of government and higher education, Swahili was established as a language of national communication. These forces led to the 'triglossia' situation described by Abdulaziz Mkilifi (1978) and discussed in chapter 2.[3]

Swahili was adopted as the language of TANU (Tanganyika African National Union) in its struggle for independence. As Whiteley (1969:65) points out, the ability to speak English enhanced the status of Tanzania's President Julius Nyerere as a leader because it enabled him to negotiate with the British. Swahili, however, was at least as important to him as English. So effective was Swahili as a language of wider communication that Nyerere was obliged to use interpreters on only two occasions during his many pre-independence tours of the country. This is a most impressive fact when we remember that we are talking about a country with some 135 indigenous languages. A few years after achieving formal independence in 1961, Tanzania designated Swahili as its national language. In 1967, it was made the official language of the country as well.

Planning efforts

Determination.   The determination of a national language was less a problem for Tanzania than it is for many developing countries.[4] The history of the language as a trading language and as a language of government by two colonial powers had ensured that it was widely known throughout the country. There was really no competing indigenous language. The one numerically large sociocultural group, the Sukuma, had never been politically ambitious, and their language was not a serious contender as a national language. One further advantage for Swahili was that, as a Bantu language, it is structurally similar to the native languages of around 95 per cent of the population. In fact, Abdulaziz Mkilifi (1978:132) reports that his respondents who knew both a small-group Bantu language and some Swahili before going to school 'did not realize they were speaking (or mixing) two distinct languages' until they started school. The only real alternative, for an official language, if not a national language, was English. As an imperial language and one spoken by relatively few Tanzanians, the selection of English was to be avoided if possible. At independence, Tanzania was in the enviable position of having a candidate for a national language that was: (1) indigenous; (2) not the language of one of several sociocultural groups competing for dominance;

(3) widely known as a second language; (4) linguistically related to the native languages of by far the majority of its citizens; and (5) historically used as a language of initial education and at least the middle echelons of government.

On the other hand, there are numerous dialects of Swahili, and the national language would have to be developed from one of them.[5] It was perhaps fortunate that dialect determination had been accomplished well before independence by the British authorities. In 1930, an organization known as the Inter-Territorial Language (Swahili) Committee, later called the East African Swahili Committee, was established to determine the form of Swahili to be used in education. The committee was supposed to find a unified policy for Kenya and Uganda, as well as Tanganyika. The two leading competitors for the dialect to form the base for the standard language were Kiunguja, the dialect spoken in Zanzibar Town, and Kimvita, the dialect of Mombasa, a Kenyan city near the Kenya–Tanzania border.[6] Two years before the establishment of the Committee, an inter-territorial conference selected Kiunguja over the objections of many of the conferees. Kimvita had the advantage of a strong literary tradition, which Kiunguja lacked. This disadvantage leads Whiteley (1969:329) to call the selection of Kiunguja 'in many ways . . . unfortunate'. On the other hand, the literary tradition in Kimvita was Islamic, a fact that did not impress the colonial language planners, who were western in cultural outlook, if not actually Christian missionaries (Hinnebusch 1979:268). In favor of Kiunguja was the fact that the dialects of Swahili spoken in the interior of Tanganyika were very similar to it, since Kiunguja is native in Zanzibar Town, the origin of the old trading journeys. This advantage was an important reason why the standard language in Tanzania was ultimately so widely accepted.

Standardization.   The Committee and its successors were responsible for the standardization of Swahili throughout the colonial period. The Committee's concern, typical for language-planning agencies, was almost exclusively with the written language. For many years, the granting or withholding of its imprimatur virtually determined whether or not a book would be published. This power was similar to the influence that William Caxton had when he had the only printing press in England. The Committee had little effect on the way people who already spoke Swahili used it, but it did influence how Swahili was taught in mission and government schools. In its early years, the Committee was somewhat heavy-handed in its insistence on the forms it had decided were correct. This caused resentment, and standard written Swahili was sometimes considered stilted and lifeless and an imposition on East Africa by Europeans. Rigid control over the written language was eventually relaxed. The standardization effort was reasonably successful in Tanzania, both because the written standard is close to accepted spoken norms based on Kiunguja, and because most of the controversy connected with standardization had spent itself before independence.

The Language Committee eventually became the Institute of Swahili Research of the University of Dar es Salaam, Tanzania. Swahili language development in Tanzania is largely the concern of the Ministry of Education and the Ministry of Community Development and National Culture, which has an appointed officer called the 'Promoter for Swahili'. Some of the Ministry's plans for the promotion of the national language have had to be shelved for lack of funds.

Orthography and vocabulary.   Swahili was originally written in Arabic script. However, Roman script soon replaced it under the influence of Christian missionaries, who provided most of the formal education and published Bible translations and other printed material in the early days of European contact. There were a few minor controversies in the use of Roman script, such as whether to use a plain c instead of ch and whether or not to separate certain bound morphemes from the roots they were bound to. In all these cases, innovative proposals failed and the older practices are standard today.[7]

Even before official efforts at language planning were begun by the colonial governments, there were dictionaries (and grammars) by missionaries in East Africa. One of the first tasks of the Inter-territorial Language Committee was to produce a Swahili and English dictionary; this was published in 1939. A new dictionary was being developed in the late 1960s by the Committee's successor, the Institute of Swahili Research. According to Hill (1980:383) the English–Swahili and Swahili–English dictionaries were still in preparation in 1979, but a new Swahili–Swahili dictionary was 'said to be at page-proof stage'. Apparently priorities had shifted, so that the Swahili–Swahili dictionary was given precedence over the bilingual ones. The 1939 dictionary was supplemented by word lists that were periodically published by the Language Committee's *Bulletin*, now a journal called *Swahili* which is published by the Institute. Whiteley (1969:92), who was at one time involved with the publication himself, has some doubts about how much impact these official word lists had. Hinnebusch (1979:287–288) has carried out a small study comparing word lists published in *Swahili* and the terms actually used. He found that sometimes the official term is used and sometimes not. He concludes that 'new vocabulary catches on and is used by the general population when it meets a communicative need sometimes coming from above and sometimes from the grass roots' (Hinnebusch 1979:288). The Institute is not the only source of official word lists; any individual government institution can and does propose word lists in its own field. A dictionary of law was published in the mid-1960s and has caused a small controversy (Harries 1968, W. O'Barr 1976a). Much more interesting, at least to the linguist, are innovations in vocabulary that are occurring in Swahili quite apart from overt planning. Hinnebusch (1979) provides an interesting sketch of several of these processes.[8]

Education. Before independence, it was usually the practice for schools operated by missionaries to use the local vernaculars in primary education and English at the higher levels. Official policy under British rule was to use Swahili as the medium of instruction at the primary level and English beyond.

Educational policy in Tanzania after independence was designed to contribute to the national policy, to concentrate on agriculture and to support *ujamaa*, the African concept of socialism which is the nation's designated political and economic system. One implication was that primary education should be self-contained, rather than designed as a preparation for secondary education, which most citizens would *not* receive. As President Nyerere wrote in *Ujamaa: Essays on Socialism:* 'in Tanzania the only justification for secondary education is that it is needed by the few for service to the many' (1968:62). In actual practice, in 1978 there were only 20 per cent as many youngsters in Standard VII (the highest level of primary education) as in Standard I and less than 10 per cent as many in Form I, (the first level of secondary eduation), as in Standard VII (Polomé and Hill 1980:407, appendix 14:B).

Given this general policy, there was in principle no reason to retain English as the medium of instruction in primary schools. Swahili was made the medium of instruction, although English continues to be taught as a school subject. (In the early years, wealthier parents would sometimes send their children to English-medium primary schools, but since 1967 it has been against the law for a Tanzanian citizen to attend an elementary school where the medium is anything but Swahili.) English has remained the medium of instruction to a large degree at the secondary level, although the goal is to replace it with Swahili at this level as well. The effort to extend the use of Swahili in secondary and higher education has been severely hampered by two factors: (1) the lack of technical terminology and printed materials; and (2) the difficulty that teachers face when they have to teach a subject in Swahili that they themselves studied in English.[9] Nevertheless, the Ministry of Education has been developing curricula and examination forms that will allow the use of Swahili as a medium up to the university entrance level. By 1979, it appeared 'fairly clear' to Hill (1980:386) that the widespread use of English as the secondary-school instructional language would be discontinued in the foreseeable future. At the University of Dar es Salaam, instruction is in English, except for a few Swahili language courses, but Swahili is used as the medium in the teacher training colleges, where English is taught only as a subject.

Government. Since Swahili has been declared the official language as well as the national language, it is intended that it should be the language of government. In fact, it *is* the functioning language of the national assembly and the lower courts, as well as the language used for official functions by Tanzania's only political party, TANU. It is also increasingly displacing

English in the civil service, although there is still considerable Swahili–English code-switching. Many written forms used in connection with public services are still printed in English although the language spoken to citizens by the government employees who provide the services is usually Swahili. English, Swahili, and the vernaculars are all used in a complex pattern in the courts (Kavugha and Bobb 1980), with a greater percentage of English used at the higher court levels. The Tanzanian political system is organized hierarchically, from the national legislature to district councils to village councils to neighborhood cells. Swahili is the language to be used in all of these except for the neighborhood cells, where the vernaculars are sometimes used (J. O'Barr 1976b). The policy with respect to the language of government in Tanzania has been very successful, although neither English nor the vernaculars have been completely displaced.

Apart from the actual use of language in government, at least two government policies have made an important contribution to the spread of Swahili in Tanzania (Polomé 1982). One policy was to transfer civil servants, for limited periods of time, to parts of the country other than their own region, so that they would have no choice but to use Swahili on the job (they would not know the vernacular language of the region they were assigned to). The other policy was the establishment of *ujamaa* villages (agricultural communes), in which people from diverse language backgrounds live. The absence of a common vernacular language in the *ujamaa* villages promotes the advance of Swahili for local use.

Success

Criteria. Before we can say how successful the language-planning effort in Tanzania has been, we need to have some idea about what counts as success. One possible criterion would be to say that the result has been satisfactory if Swahili has become *in fact* both the national and official language. This takes us back to Fishman's *nationalist*–nationist distinction. Swahili is a true language of nationalism, if it serves as an effective symbol of Tanzanian citizenship for a large majority of the population. It is a true official language (as opposed to simply having being so declared), if it actually is used in carrying out the nationist tasks of day-to-day administration and education.[10]

I think it is fair to say that Tanzania has achieved an impressive measure of success in both senses. There is no doubt that Swahili symbolizes Tanzanian nationalism. The level of success that has been achieved for Swahili in the nationist area is also impressive. It is true that the language is not used for all official purposes at all levels of government, and that it has proved difficult to extend its use into higher education and technical domains. Nevertheless, Swahili *is* very widely used in government and exclusively at the primary level of education. Furthermore, this has all happened in a very poor country (according to J. O'Barr 1976a:50, Tanzania ranked 123rd in a list of 135 countries). A question we will take up at the end of the chapter is to what extent these good results are actually due to language planning.

Speakers. Whether a language is a country's national language in the fullest sense depends on how many of its citizens can speak it. That is, it is not quite enough that the language be seen as only a symbol, it must be used for communicative purposes as well. Swahili in Tanzania fares very well on this criterion. It is estimated that 80–90 per cent of the Tanzanian population speaks Swahili, the great majority as a second language (J. O'Barr 1976b:70). W. O'Barr gives the following breakdown of the population of the rural village of Usangi by language competence, it is probably fairly typical for town populations (W. O'Barr 1971, quoted in Johnson 1977:62):

Asu monolinguals	5 per cent
Asu-Swahili bilinguals	63 per cent
Asu-Swahili-English trilinguals	32 per cent

The data provided by Polomé (1982:177) show a slightly higher proportion of speakers who know Swahili, English, and at least one vernacular:

Vernacular(s) only	1.8 per cent
Swahili only	1.8 per cent
Vernacular(s)–Swahili only	41.2 per cent
Vernacular(s)–Swahili–English	52.2 per cent

The 274 speakers who provided this information are apparently disproportionately urban or well-educated or both, since Polomé (1980b, 1982) states that rural people in general and farmers in particular are likely to know one or more vernaculars, perhaps Swahili, but *not* English.[11]

There are certain groups who are more likely to be speakers of Swahili than others. We have already seen that Swahili is easier for speakers of Bantu languages to learn than for speakers of other languages. It would be reasonable to expect that a higher percentage of native speakers of Bantu languages will know Swahili than other groups, although I haven't seen any figures to this effect. According to Polomé (1982:175), Swahili is more likely to be spoken along the coast and inland along trade routes and in major towns, by better-educated people, and by people working in the civil service. W. O'Barr (1976a:42–3) found that Swahili is more likely to be found among men than among women (almost all the men in Usangi spoke it), among younger people than older, and more among better-educated citizens than less educated ones. The fact that younger and more educated speakers know the language is no doubt due in part to the Tanzanian language policy. O'Barr attributes the discrepancy by sex to the fact that men may have spent time outside their home regions working in cities or on plantations, or served in the armed forces. Another reason he gives is that education, a Swahili domain as we know, is more available to men than women; Polomé (1975:38) also refers to 'the considerable lag in education for girls and their confinement to the home'). If the egalitarian policies of the Tanzanian government make at least primary education universal and if women are given more equal access to it, the disparities that O'Barr points out will be reduced.

Attitudes.   It is clear that a large and increasing proportion of the Tanzanian population speaks Swahili. It is just as clear that Swahili symbolizes Tanzanian nationality, serving the unifying and separatist functions at the national level in a way that would be impossible for English to do. It remains to be discovered how Tanzanians feel about Swahili compared to the small group vernaculars. Is the symbolic value of Swahili as a nationalist language only valid for the 'detribalized' city dwellers, the better educated, and those involved in national government and politics? Just what is the value of Swahili for a typical individual from one of the sociocultural groups that make up Tanzanian society? Recall that Oberwart peasants were bilingual in Hungarian and German for generations without German serving as any kind of symbol of identity. It was simply a tool for dealing with 'outsiders'. Very much the same seems to be true of English in Quebec. Is this the role that Swahili plays for the majority of Tanzanians?

Scholars who are familiar with Tanzania all agree that there is currently no overall switch taking place from the vernaculars to Swahili (Whiteley 1969:115; W. O'Barr 1976a:42; Scotton 1978: 755, footnote 24; Hinnebusch 1979:292). The triglossic situation in Tanzania that we outlined in chapter 2 is a stable one. It has been very well described by Whiteley (1969:115):

In other words, the United Republic [of Tanzania], with many other countries in the world today, is multi-lingual, with each language fulfilling certain functions. . . . To the extent that modern states participate in supra-national groupings, for example the European or East African Common Market, the Organization of African Unity, the United Nations, etc., then some supra-national language is necessary. In so far as there is a need to establish a national identity for political or cultural reasons, then a national language, in this case Swahili, has an important role to perform. Where local ties are important, to reinforce a sense of continuity with the past, for example, or to affirm the values of a local group at a time when these seem in danger of submersion within a larger unit, then a local language comes to the fore.

One piece of information to look for, as we learned in the study of language maintenance and shift, is the language or languages passed on to children. Scotton (1978:755, footnote 24) reports the following fact about one of the Tanzanian groups, the Chagga, who, according to Whiteley (1969:114), are particularly loyal to their language: 'Many of the Chagga who live on the slopes of Mount Kilimanjaro report they use Swahili in everyday conversation with such relations as brothers or sisters although they still use Kichagga *with children* and elders' (my italics). It is quite possible that Kichagga is used with elders because the old people don't know Swahili very well, perhaps because they acquired their language competence before the rise of nationalism. The use of the local language with children, however, means that the Chagga want their children to identify themselves with their own group, and not to be Tanzanians only. On the other hand, Polomé (1980b:117) reports that some parents who both speak the same vernacular will use it with each other, but Swahili with their children. We saw that this pattern meant that East Sutherland had reached the last stages of the shift from Gaelic to English. Tanzanian families with this language-choice pattern, however, are apparently in the minority. Person-to-person interviews with final-year students in the teacher training colleges in 1970 revealed that 80 per cent of them wanted their children to learn their traditional vernacular as well as Swahili. Two main reasons for this were given: 'The motivation was most often self-identification, the vernacular being the genuine bearer of traditions; important also was the need for the child to be able to communicate adequately with his/her grandparents, whose knowledge of Swahili may have been limited. (Polomé 1980b:131, footnote 21).'

It is easy to establish that the vernaculars are symbolic of small-group membership for most Tanzanians and that most also speak Swahili. It is somewhat less clear whether or not Swahili is considered a tool only or both a tool and a symbol. That is, is it possible to identify yourself as *both* a Chagga, for example, *and* a Tanzanian citizen? It appears to Abdulaziz Mkilifi (1980:161) that the answer to the question is 'yes': 'The attitude toward Swahili is a positive one. At the moment it is the language of prestige and national identity. . . . The attitude to the mother tongue is one of natural sentimental attachment to the language of the "home", and of one's primordial identity and culture.'

There is at least one important reason why this would be so. The independence movement in Tanzania was conducted in Swahili. TANU leaders, such as Julius Nyerere, addressed their audiences in Swahili, as national political leaders still do. Swahili in that way became the language associated with the unity of all the smaller sociocultural groups against a common adversary, the colonial power. If such a sense of dual identity is widespread, it may be that Tanzania has achieved a near-optimum mix of unity and diversity. If so, Swahili has played a central role in its development.

Literature. One serious drawback to the progress of Swahili is a lack of literature in the language. Most of the published work in Swahili, aside from periodical literature, is in the form of school materials. In order to read novels, poems, and drama, even by African writers, it is necessary to learn English. This fact not only damages the status of Swahili in the eyes of the more educated people, but it impedes the advance of the language into higher levels of the educational system, since there isn't too much to read at that level. In order to demonstrate that the language is fully capable of being used for literary work, President Nyerere himself tranlated Shakespeare's *Julius Caesar* into Swahili. An economist named Peter Temu followed this lead with the publication of a textbook in Swahili in his field (W. O'Barr 1976a:47). It is one of the main tasks of the Promoter for Swahili to encourage the literary use of the language. There has been some improvement in recent years with the publication of popular novels such as detective stories and romances. There have also been translations of titles by African authors that had been written in English originally (Hinnebusch 1979:292).)

Comparison with Kenya

It will be instructive to take a brief look at Tanzania's neighbor, Kenya, with respect to the national language issue. Kenya is similar to Tanzania in many ways. It is a multilingual East African country, a former British colony that achieved independence at about the same time, and Swahili is widespread as a language of wider communication. However, Swahili is not the official language of Kenya; English is. KANU (Kenya Africa National Union), Kenya's only political party, has long held that Swahili ought to be the national language, at least the equal of English. For a long time, very little was done to implement that policy. In 1974, Swahili was declared the language of Kenya's parliament. The announcement caused such a storm of protest that parliament had to be closed the next day. Scotton (1978:735) points out that the official use of Swahili in parliament will have little overall effect, if English remains the language of daily government activity, the medium of instruction, and the language of private business. The reason Swahili has not *in fact* been installed as Kenya's national language is that it has not been accepted.

Numerous reasons have been given for the difference between the experiences of the two countries. First, although both nations were British colonies, only Tanzania had been governed by Germany. The German practice of using Swahili-speaking middle-level administrators was taken over by the British. In Kenya, the policy vacillated, sometimes favoring Swahili, sometimes English, sometimes the vernaculars. Part of the reason for this is that Christian missions were somewhat more influential in Kenya than in Tanzania. Typically, missionaries favor the use of the local vernaculars, since they feel that an individual's native language is most appropriate for evangelism. This meant that missionary influence would be exerted in favor of the vernaculars for early education. A second reason that is sometimes given is the differing post-independence political objectives in the two countries (Scotton 1978; J. O'Barr 1976b). Tanzania is following a vigorous policy of *ujamaa* (African socialism) with a heavy egalitarian emphasis. This naturally leads to the use of Swahili, the most widely available language. Kenya's political and economic system is less emphatically egalitarian. The present holders of power have achieved power with the use of English and have a stake in the sociolinguistic status quo.

The third and fourth reasons that are commonly given are more purely sociolinguistic in nature. Recall that the two dialects that competed for regional dialect determination during the colonial period were Kiunguja and Kimvita. Kiunguja was a native dialect in Zanzibar, now part of the United Republic of Tanzania. The up-country dialects in both countries are similar to Kiunguja as a consequence of the nineteenth-century trading activity. Kimvita is the Swahili dialect of the city of Mombasa, which is in Kenya. Although it was not selected as the regional standard, it still has loyal adherents. Although the Kiunguja-based standard is fairly well accepted throughout Tanzania, it is not widely accepted along the southern coast of Kenya. Kimvita, on the other hand, is seen as an inferior kind of Swahili by up-country speakers in Kenya. In short, even if Swahili language determination were to be achieved in Kenya, standard dialect determination would be very much more difficult.

Finally, Kenya has fewer and larger ethnolinguistic groups. According to the 1962 census figures quoted by Whiteley (1971a:147–8), there are 31 language groups as opposed to the 114 he lists for Tanzania (Polomé's figure is 135, based on more recent survey data). Four of these groups comprise more than 10 per cent of the population each, the Kikuyu (19.8 per cent), the Luo (13.8 per cent), the Luyia (13.1 per cent), and the Kamba (11.2 per cent). Each of these four languages has over a million speakers. These larger groups are less likely to learn Swahili for two reasons. From the communication perspective, the more people there are who share a person's native language, the less likely it is that that person will need to learn another language. With respect to the symbolic aspect of language, members of larger groups are likely to feel it is beneath them to have to learn some other language; other people should learn theirs. Swahili has an advantage, even in Kenya, that proposed national languages in other countries do not have. Unlike, say, Hindi in India, Swahili is not the native language of one of the large sociocultural groups. Presumably it would not be as hard to get a speaker of one of the four large groups to learn Swahili as it would be to get him to learn the language of one of the other groups. Nevertheless, there is in general a relationship between group size and hostility to lingua francas (Scotton 1978:723). The prospects for Swahili are further complicated by the fact that fewer of Kenya's citizens speak Bantu languages (60–65 per cent compared with Tanzania's 94 per cent). The second-largest group, the Luo, speak a Nilotic language which makes them even less inclined to accept Swahili, a Bantu language. The comparison of Kenya and Tanzania gives the impression that, if a country is moderately to extremely multilingual, it is better for national-language determination for it to be *more* diverse rather than less.

Whether any or all of these reasons serve as the explanation, Swahili has fared much less well in Kenya than in Tanzania. Although it might be said, and often is, that Swahili has not been accepted because language planning in Kenya has not been vigorous enough, the reverse seems to me to be nearer the truth: language planning has not been vigorous because the national leadership has been politically astute enough to realize that, for very powerful historical and ethnographic reasons, Swahili would not be readily accepted.

IRELAND

History

Ireland is the second largest of the British Isles and is located just west of Great Britain. It is divided politically into the Republic of Ireland, an independent nation, and Northern Ireland, six northern counties under British rule. The Republic of Ireland has an area of 27,000 square miles and a population of three million people (Ó Huallacháin 1970:181).

Several centuries ago, the Irish people spoke Irish Gaelic (now usually called 'Irish'). The Irish language and people once possessed a flourishing culture, and Gaelic literary history goes back more than a thousand years. English rule, which was at times very repressive, was solidly established in the seventeenth century and a gradual language shift from Irish to English continued into the present century. The 1961 Irish census data indicate that somewhere between 2 and 3 per cent of the population of the Republic speaks Irish as a native language.[12] At about the same time, something in the region of 20 per cent of the population claimed to be speakers of Irish; most of them had learned Irish as a second language.[13] The native speakers live in relatively remote regions on the west coast. In contrast to the extreme diversity of Tanzania, Ó Huallacháin (1970:181), himself very much in favor of the restoration of Irish, says 'the nation as a whole is, practically speaking, monolingual (English).'

Another contrast with Tanzania is the fact that the independence movement in Ireland was carried out in English. Nineteenth-century nationalist sentiment was, for the most part, not expressed in Irish. Macnamara (1971:68) feels that the very success of the independence movement sapped strength from the language-restoration effort. People thought that if the Irish had political control of their own territory, working for the language would not be necessary.

Planning efforts

Determination.   Language determination, of course, was not an issue in Ireland. If there was to be language planning, it would have to be on the behalf of Irish. If English were to be the only national language, it would hardly require planning.[14] The Irish constitution designates Irish as the national language and the first official language. English is constitutionally recognized as a second official language. Dialect determination was a slightly larger issue. In spite of the fact that there are few native speakers of Irish, there are three recognized dialects – Munster, Connacht, and Donegal Irish. In his earlier article, Ó Huallacháin (1962:78) speaks of 'a standard grammar which draws on all three dialects'. The Munster dialect at one time was favored by the typical primary-school teacher, but more recently there has been a 'widespread swing to Connacht Irish' (Macnamara (1971:72,74). The Connacht dialect has the advantages of being the dialect with the most native speakers and being intermediate between the other two. Ó Huallacháin and a group of associates were commissioned by the government to make a study of natively spoken Irish and use the results to develop teaching materials. This work was completed in the mid-1960s and includes language-laboratory tapes and materials for Irish language courses that are broadcast on radio and television. According to Macnamara, the Connacht dialect was favored in these materials, ensuring its prominence as a basis for the standard language.

Standardization. Before 1950, a number of simple grammars were available for teacher use. An official standard grammar was published in 1953 and revised in 1958 and has been generally accepted. The materials produced by Ó Huallacháin and his associates, called *Buntús Gaelige* (Foundations and beginnings of Irish), have no doubt had a great impact on the standards for teaching the language in school, although technically they don't constitute an official grammar.

Orthography and vocabulary. Orthography planning proved to be reasonably easy. An early dictionary by Father Patrick Dinneen had the effect of stabilizing the orthography. A simplified spelling system was published by the government in 1945 and was 'well-nigh universally accepted' (Macnamara 1971:73). Vocabulary planning appears to have been equally successful. Dinneen's Irish–English dictionary and an English–Irish dictionary compiled by Father Lambert McKenna, SJ were replaced by an official dictionary published in 1959. The new dictionary had a section for technical terms as well as entries for more commonly needed items. The dictionary was important not only for the entries it has, but for setting up principles for further lexical extension. Basically, the principles were to use words in current use first and turn to the older literary language or neologisms only when necessary. Technical terms tended to be borrowed from Greek and Latin, in the style of most modern European languages. Vocabulary development has succeeded to the extent that there are courses taught in Irish at University College Galway, these include Latin, history, economics, chemistry, experimental and mathematical physics, as well as Irish (Macnamara 1971:89, footnote 24; Ó Huallacháin 1962:77). Of a list of 80 modern terms developed by a Yale University professor as a test for language modernization, Irish lacked only three, the words for 'demography', 'neurosis', and 'regimentation' (Ó Huallacháin 1962:78).

Education. As in Tanzania, much of the language planning in Ireland involves the educational system. In order to get a clearer picture of how language planning in the educational system works, it is important to have an idea of what the system is like. There are three levels of education – primary, secondary, and higher. The primary schools are government controlled. There are two types of secondary schools – vocational and academic. Secondary schools in Ireland are all private institutions; most of them are operated by religious orders. At the third level, there are three kinds of institutions – the university colleges, colleges of advanced technology, and teacher training colleges for primary-school teachers (Ó Huallacháin 1962, Macnamara 1971).

The primary schools are used as an instrument for the restoration of Irish to such an extent that Ó Huallacháin (1962:80) sees them as having 'a double purpose: to give the instruction usually imparted to children up the age of fourteen and to teach Irish'. As soon as independence was achieved, the Irish government decreed that Irish was to be either taught or used as a medium of instruction for at least one hour a day in all primary schools that had a teacher competent to teach it. By 1934, the official policy was that Irish was not only to be taught as a subject, but was to be used as a medium of all work in the 'infant' classes, and in higher classes for the teaching of history, geography, singing, and physical training, if at all possible. It was further advocated that Irish be used as a teaching medium as far as possible in all classes. The extent to which these policies were 'possible' in a particular school was decided by officials of the individual school (Macnamara 1971:70–1). To find teachers who could implement these policies, the government required teachers under the age of 45 to take summer courses and provided for the preferential recruitment of teachers from the *Gaeltacht* (Irish-speaking areas). This was done by reserving for Irish speakers half the state scholarships to 'preparatory colleges'. Students at the preparatory colleges, went on to the teacher training colleges, which were also taught in Irish. When this system was in full operation, it supplied a third of the primary teachers, and these teachers had a good grasp of Irish (Macnamara 1971:71). In 1962, Ó Huallacháin (1962:81), reported that 80 per cent of the primary teachers held certificates of competence to teach bilingually. In the early 1960s, however, these pre-paratory colleges were discontinued.[15] By 1971, the teacher training colleges were conducting only 'a limited amount of their teaching in Irish' (Mac-namara 1971:75).

Ó Huallacháin (1970:181–2) describes the situation in the primary schools in three patterns. First, in 269 primary schools, Irish is the only medium of instruction, although English textbooks have to be used in some subjects at the post-primary level. Most of these school are in the Irish-speaking areas, where most of the students are bilingual, but dominant in Irish. In schools following this pattern outside the Irish speaking areas, some of the students may be monolingual in English. English is taught as a subject.[16] Second, in 427 other primary schools, both Irish and English are used as media of instruction, but no information was available on how much instruction was given in each language. Most of the students come to school monolingual in English, but some may speak Irish. Irish is a compulsory subject at all grade levels. Third, in the remaining schools (about 3,700), the only medium of instruction is

English, although Irish is again a compulsory subject. Only a small minority of students at these schools speak Irish at home.

The government does not directly impose Irish as a teaching medium on the private secondary schools. However, those that receive government support (that is, most of them) must teach Irish as a subject. There are various incentives for using Irish as a medium of instruction. For example, secondary schools that teach all subjects through Irish get larger government per-student grants. Secondary students are given the choice of taking public examinations in Irish or English. Students who choose Irish get a bonus increase in their grades (Macnamara 1971:74–5). In spite of these policies, the use of Irish as a medium in secondary schools is declining. In 1962, Ó Huallacháin (1962:79) reported that 56 per cent of the secondary schools in Ireland did not teach *any* subject through Irish. The data he gave in 1970 (Ó Huallacháin 1970:181–2) indicate that the figure had increased to over 75 per cent. Macnamara (1971:75) similarly documents a decline in the number of academic secondary schools (grammar schools) that teach *all* subjects (except English) through Irish. Part of the reason is no doubt a lack of textbooks in Irish appropriate to the secondary level.

We have already referred to the wide variety of subjects taught in Irish at University College Galway. Although this shows clearly the success in language-development planning for Irish, UCG, the smallest of the university colleges, is not typical of higher education in the nation. Both UCG and UCC (University College Cork) in 1971 required that appointments to certain faculty posts be filled by applicants who could teach their subjects in Irish (Macnamara 1971:75). However, only 'some subjects' were taught through Irish at UCC; the same was true at St. Patrick's College, Maynooth (Ó Huallacháin 1962:78). The use of Irish as a medium at other institutions of higher education is negligible, except for the 'limited amount of teaching in Irish' in the teacher training colleges, which, as we have already seen, represents a sharp decline from what had been the case ten years earlier. Ó Huallacháin (1962:79) finds a partial cause for the small amount of use of Irish in higher education in 'a number of academic and administrative people in positions of great influence who resist bilingualism consistently'. Macnamara (1971:75–6) sees the following complex of causes:

What strikes one as one surveys the educational scene is the reduction in restoration effort as one passses from primary- to secondary-level and again from secondary to higher education. The difference between the levels can be attributed in part to the pedagogical principles of those who planned our education since 1922, in part to the increasing demands on students' time as they grow older, in part to the fact that hitherto the state exercised more control in primary- than in secondary-, and in secondary- than in third-level instruction, and in part to the increasing shortage of textbooks in Irish as one ascends the educational ladder. The arrangement clearly embodies the belief that the time to teach a second language is when children are young. Explanations apart, however, the effect is that the main burden for the restoration of Irish has been placed on the shoulders of that section of the school population that is weakest and is least likely to resist. Furthermore, the educational provision for the restoration calls into question the seriousness of the whole effort to restore Irish.

Government.   In a further contrast with Tanzania, virtually all parliamentary business in Ireland is carried out in English. Legislation is printed in Irish and English. Unlike Tanzania, Ireland has a multi-party political system. Macnamara reported in 1971 that all three major parties supported the restoration effort, although one somewhat less enthusiastically than the other two (Macnamara 1971:77).[17] Civil servants and the officers in the state police force are required to demonstrate a knowledge of Irish when they are employed, but few civil servants use the language in their work and only the police stationed in Irish-speaking areas ever use Irish. Ireland's small army trains its officers mostly in Irish, maintains a 175-man Irish-speaking company, and gives all drill orders in Irish. Lawyers have to show competence in Irish before they are allowed to practice, but courts in English-speaking districts almost never conduct any business in Irish. Local government activities are carried out in English in English-speaking localities.

The state-run broadcast media are required to provide programming in Irish. These programs are quite well received. The booklets accompanying the radio and television programs that grew out of the research conducted by Ó Huallacháin and his associates sold around 200,000 copies (out of a total national population of under three million). Audience research has shown that as many as three out of four persons will watch television news in Irish, if they are in a position to see the program.[18]

Success

Criteria.   As we said in our assessment of language-planning success in Tanzania, the degree of success depends on the criteria used. If we measure what has been accomplished against the goals affirmed in a 'White Paper' issued in 1965, then we would have to conclude that the restoration movement is a failure. According to that document, 'the national aim is to restore the Irish language as a general medium of communication' (Ó Huallacháin 1970:180; Macnamara 1971:83). As we will soon see in detail, this goal is very far from being achieved. In 1962, Ó Huallacháin (1962:77) stated that 'bilingualism is more a feature of the schools than of life outside them.' Eight years later, he saw no need to modify that statement (Ó Huallacháin 1970:180). If the institution of Irish as a nationist (official) language is the goal, our assessment would be equally bleak. Although the Irish constitution declares Irish to be the main official language, it is very little used to carry out nationist functions.

Yet there is a sense in which Irish is something of a *nationalist* language. Of Tanzania, we said that a language can only be a nationalist language 'in the fullest sense', if a substantial proportion of the population speaks it. In this fullest sense, of course, Irish does not qualify. Our discussion of attitudes, however, will show that Irish serves as a *symbolic* (if not communicative) national language to a surprising degree. Furthermore, Irish language planning has succeeded very well at the intermediate goals of dialect determination and language development in the areas of orthography, vocabulary expansion, and standardization.

Speakers. I have already stated that 3 per cent of the population, at the very most, are native speakers of Irish, and that the percentage of the population that claims to speak it as a first or second language is less than 25 per cent (probably closer to 15 per cent). Of the 924-speaker random sample analyzed by Ó Huallacháin (1970), only 2 per cent said that they used the language at home all or much of the time. Only 53 per cent of those who said they spoke or read Irish 'at least occasionally nowadays' thought that the knowledge of the language was of any practical use to them. Those who found it useful generally cited uses that are directly connected to official planning measures: helping children with homework, help towards getting a job, and reading official forms and documents (some also found the language useful in talking to people in Irish 'when necessary').

The self-assessment of their competency in Irish by the sample gives a discouraging picture of the impact of the education system in restoring Irish. Some 50 per cent of the sample said they studied Irish only at the primary level. Only 9 per cent of these rated themselves fluent or fairly fluent. Another 63 per cent said they had 'some knowledge', and an amazing 27 per cent said they had 'no knowledge' of Irish. This figure is quite startling, since it means that over a quarter of the sample was willing to admit 'no knowledge' of something that they had studied every school year to the age of 14, even when given the option of reporting 'some knowledge'! Of those who had gone on to study Irish at the post-primary level, a third said that they were fluent or fairly fluent; most of the remainder reported 'some knowledge', although 6 per cent who had continued the study of Irish still claimed 'no knowledge'.

In Tanzania, there was a relationship between sex, age and education level, and knowledge of the national language. In Ireland, there is an increase in knowledge of Irish associated with higher levels of education, but only if the language was studied at those higher levels. There is virtually no difference by sex.[19] There is an interesting pattern by age, however, which is the one illustrated in figure 10.1. There is a fairly regular pattern consisting of a decreasing claim to fluency and an increasing tendency to report no knowledge as age increases. As with all age patterns, we have to be careful with our interpretation. If figure 10.1 is to be interpreted as a display of 'apparent time', then it looks very encouraging. It appears that knowledge of Irish is taking a firmer hold with each passing decade. However, all the indications are that the pattern is to be interpreted as an 'age-graded' phenomenon, similar to the pattern of bilingualism in Montreal in figure 8.1, and for much the same reason. In their study of language attitudes in Ireland, Brudner and White (1979:65) state: 'In a large proportion of the population, despite stated language preferences for Irish, ability in Irish tends to decay over time, after people leave the school situation in which Irish is learned.' In Montreal, it was not only the education system, but also the occupation system that supported English. As a result, the decrease in reported ability in English did not set in until late middle-age. In Ireland, there is no occupational support for Irish aside from the minimal requirements associated with the civil service. As a result, the decrease in reported ability in Irish begins much sooner.

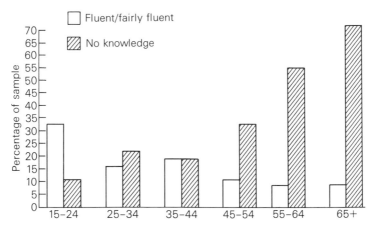

Figure 10.1   Percentage of a sample of the Irish population reporting fluency or no knowledge of Irish, by age
Source: data from Ó Huallacháin (1970:191, table 3)

Attitudes.   In Tanzania, it was not too difficult to establish that Swahili was serving the communicative functions of a nationalist language fairly effectively, and that it was a symbol of a person's identity as a Tanzanian. In Ireland, it is abundantly clear that the communicative function is fulfilled, to an overwhelming degree, by English. The issue of membership in subnational groups scarcely arises in Ireland. Nevertheless, there is considerable evidence that, if we can speak of a national language as being symbolic without being a communicative tool, Irish would be that language.

In a large-scale study of reported attitudes and reported language use, Brudner and White (1979) found that attitudes about Irish were generally positive, highly structured, and internally coherent. However, they found that reported attitudes had little effect on whether or not a person used Irish (a finding that, after our study of language attitudes, should not surprise us). Their statistical tests (in this case, factor analysis, a technique not covered in chapter 4) *did* indicate a close association between attitudes towards Irish nationality, Irish speakers, and Irish as an ethnic symbol (Brudner and White 1979:62–3). They go on to point out that, although attitudes toward Irish may not predict individual *language* behavior, they may have predictive value in political behavior (political support and voting patterns) where language is an issue.

Apparently there is considerable support for continuing the current level of effort for the restoration of the language. Although Ó Huallacháin (1962, 1970) feels that not enough has been done to make the restoration a success, and Macnamara (1971) questions the seriousness of the effort, there is not much indication that people want an overt policy to reduce the emphasis on Irish either. Macnamara reports that when the one political party that supports restoration the least enthusiastically – Fine Gael – raised the issue of dropping the policy of requiring the teaching of Irish as a subject at the secondary level, the issue failed to be taken seriously (Macnamara 1971:77). He further cites survey data showing that 76 per cent of the respondents wanted to see Irish widely spoken as a second language, 53 per cent thought this was not unrealistic, and 76 per cent approved of the teaching of Irish in primary schools (Macnamara 1971:83). Once we decide to look at the communicative and symbolic uses of a national language separately, it is no longer so clear that Irish is in no sense the national language of Ireland.

Literature.   In sharp contrast to the situation in Tanzania, there is a considerable volume of literature in Irish. Not only are there literary works that go back a thousand years, but there is something of a literary revival currently in progress. In contrast to East African writers, who at least until recently chose to write in English rather than Swahili, a number of Ireland's best novelists, short-story writers, and poets write all or part of their work in Irish, even though they have reduced their potential audience by doing so. There is also some periodical literature and a fair-sized book club. 'Taken as a whole, the literary output has been impressive and today anyone who wishes to understand modern Ireland and above all the full range of its literary activity should learn Irish' (Macnamara 1971:82).

ANALYSIS

National language institution

Of the two cases we studied, Swahili has been instituted as the national language of Tanzania with considerable success, but the same cannot be said of Irish in Ireland. It is hard to avoid the conclusion that the differences in success rates have very little to do with language planning. Perhaps Ireland could have done more, but a comparison with Tanzania shows that very much the same techniques were used. Both countries used the proposed national language in the education system to the maximum extent possible. No doubt many children in Tanzania, possibly especially those whose native language is not a Bantu language, are discriminated against because they cannot understand the school language. However, to insist that Irish be the sole medium of instruction in Ireland would be a severe hardship on the vast majority of the school population. Swahili can be used as a language of government because so many civil servants speak it. To increase the role of Irish in government, the language would have to have more speakers. In short, the institution of a national language in Tanzania was successful, not so much because of superior language planning, but because historical and social causes left Swahili virtually poised to become the national language. The failure to make Irish the national language of Ireland in the fullest sense is not due to great failings in language planning. The fundamental reason is that social forces had brought about a near-total shift to English before the language planning ever began.

There is, in my opinion, a vast difference between the power of 'natural' social change, of which language maintenance and shift is one type, and the relative puniness of official planning. Governments and other planning agencies would be well advised to observe the direction in which social forces are guiding language behavior and to consider carefully whether proposed language-planning goals are consistent with them. In the realm of social change of the magnitude of national-language institution, language planners are like rowers in a boat in a fast-flowing river. If they decide to row downstream, the progress of the boat can be smoother, since the rowers can guide it around rocks and shallow places. If they decide to row upstream, the river is so swift that the boat will go downstream anyway and a lot of effort will be wasted in the meantime.

Although the rowing-downstream principle also applies to smaller-scope kinds of language determination and development, the chances of success are better the smaller the scope. Tanzania and Ireland were about equally successful in dialect determination, standardization of grammar, and ortho-graphy planning.[20] In vocabulary planning, Ireland seems to have had more success than Tanzania. Irish is used to such a limited extent in education and government because of a lack of speakers, rather than because of a lack of vocabulary. We can even argue that Ireland has been scarcely less successful than Tanzania in developing a *symbolic* national language. Irish seems to be very much a symbol of national identity in Ireland, even for people who don't speak it. It is in the *communicative* function of its national language that Tanzania has a wide advantage.

The institution of a national language is very complex and exceptions can probably be found to any generalizations I might attempt to make. Nevertheless, a few generalities seem to me to be worth proposing. First, the easiest national language case is to declare as a national language one that is already in use by almost everyone in the society. Japanese in Japan and Portuguese in Portugal are two examples of such 'easy' cases. The situation that appears to me to be next easiest may be a surprise. This would be a nation, similar to Tanzania, with extreme linguistic diversity and no dominant sociocultural groups. In such a country, a language that is not native to a major subgroup can be promoted as a national symbol that transcends the subnational groups. Even though it is a very different case, the institution of Hebrew as a national language in Israel – another success story – had these same features. Immigrants to Israel came with a wide variety of native languages, no ethnolinguistic group was particularly dominant, and Hebrew was the native language of no particular group. These same features, to one degree or another, seem to be true of two other relatively successful instances – the institution of Bahasa Malaysia in Malaysia and Bahasa Indonesia in Indonesia.[21]

Far more difficult is national language planning in a country such as India or the Philippines, where the indigenous languages that were selected were native to a major subgroup. In the Philippines, the proposed national language, Pilipino, is very much based on Tagalog, the language of one of the nation's three largest ethnic groups, and, there have been real difficulties in bringing about its widespread use throughout the country. We have already seen the extent of the resistance to Hindi in parts of India. Even though nations in this category need a language of communication on the national level, it often seems that the citizens would rather put up with communication problems than to adopt someone else's language when they feel that they are just as good as anyone else. Perhaps nothing is so difficult as bringing in another language when communicative needs are being met by an existing one. This is what Ireland is attempting. Given the odds against language planning in a setting like this, it is amazing that Ireland has achieved as much success as it has.

In the difficult cases, it might be best not to try to make language a basis for national identity. The Irish have never thought of themselves as English people, even when they were shifting to the English language. The same solution might be the best alternative for nations such as India. Recall the quotations by Indian scholars in chapter 1 that indicate that linguistic diversity is not necessarily a barrier to nationalism in India. A *national* language might not even be needed. Communicative needs can perhaps be met by some combination of an official language that no one pretends is a symbol of national identity, and bilingualism. In fact, this appears to be what is actually going on in India.

The two cases we have been looking at show that a lot can be done with language planning. However, it is also abundantly clear that some goals are simply out of the reach of available language-planning methods.

BIBLIOGRAPHICAL NOTES

There are so many discussions of language-planning cases in books and journals that it is not possible to cite more than a sample of them. Aside from the articles cited in this chapter, there are several excellent case histories in Rubin and Jernudd (1971), Rubin and Shuy (1973), Fishman (1974), and Fishman, Ferguson, and Das Gupta (1968). Other case histories are book-length treatments or are scattered in journals. Studies of East Africa that were not cited in this chapter include Ladefoged, Glick and Criper (1972), Whiteley (1971b, 1974), Hopkins (1977), and Harries (1976). For Tanzania, in particular, Polomé and Hill (1980) is an especially rich source. Additional studies of the Irish case, all published in Ireland, include Cronin (1978), the papers in Ó Cuív (1969), and *White Paper on the Restoration of the Irish Language* (1965). Southeast Asian cases are found in Alisjahbana (1972, 1976), Noss (1971), DeFrancis (1977), Omar (1975), and Kelz (1981). Language planning in China is the subject of Li and Thompson (1979) and Mills (1956). Eastern Europe and the Soviet Union are treated in Lunt (1959), Byron (1976), Lewis (1972b), and Branko (1980). On the long list of treatments of the fascinating case of Israel are: Cooper and Danet (1980), Fishman (1975), Fishman and Cooper (1976), Fishman and Fellman (1977), Fishman and Fishman (1978), Poll (1980), Nakir (1978), Rabin (1974), Fellman (1973), Morag (1959), Gold (1981), and Nadel, Fishman, and Cooper (1977). Other descriptions of language-planning cases are Neustupný (1977) (Australia) and Haugen (1966a, 1968) (Scandinavia).

NOTES

1   There have been many studies of language planning in Tanzania, and much of the information is repeated in more than one of them. For this reason, I will just list my sources here and not in the text, unless I am citing specific information. My main sources on Tanzania are: Whiteley (1968, 1969, 1971a), Polomé (1975, 1980a, 1980b, 1982), J. O'Barr (1976a, 1976b), W. O'Barr (1976a), Abdulaziz Mkilifi(1978, 1980), Scotton (1978), Hinnebusch (1979), and Hill (1980).
2   The absence of language questions in the Tanzanian censuses is consistent with the national policy of emphasizing Swahili as the national language and reducing emphasis on the various small-group vernaculars.
3   As may be apparent, such a three-language system – consisting of a small-group local language, an indigenous language of wider communication, and a European language – is a common pattern in countries that were once colonies of European powers.
4   For a succinct, but more complete, summary of language-planning efforts in Tanzania than I can give here, see Abdulaziz Mkilifi (1980).
5   For a clear and readable description of the kinds of linguistic differences that exist among Swahili dialects, as well as an excellent short sketch of the language in general, see Hinnebusch (1979).
6   The prefix *ki* in Swahili means 'language' or 'talk'. It is sometimes written together with its root, as I have done here, or hyphenated (*Ki-mvita*), or with the root capitalized (*KiMvita*). The prefix *ki* is commonly used with the word 'Swahili' itself (*Kiswahili*), especially by African writers, to specify that it is the language that is meant, not the people who speak it. The *ki* prefix is used in the words for the kinds of Swahili spoken by European (*Kisettla*) and Asian (*Kihindi*) immigrants (Kisettla is apparently a severely pidginized version of the language). It is also

used in the words for particular styles of the language, such as *kingua*, a kind of 'double-talk' used in rural Tanzanian councils (W. O'Barr 1976b) and *kigazeti*, the Swahili style found in newspapers (Hinnebusch 1979). Kigazeti is heavily influenced by English, due to the necessity of translating rapidly from the English wire services.

7   The variation in the printing of the prefix *ki* mentioned in the previous footnote indicates that this is one area of orthographical practice that is still in flux.

8   One of these processes is 'extension' and one important product of the process is the word '*ujamaa*'. Derived from *jamaa*, a word originally borrowed from Arabic meaning 'family', *ujamaa* primarily means 'familyhood' or 'brotherhood'. It now refers to the particularly African type of socialism, which is the official policy in Tanzania. The more general word for 'socialism', usoshalisti, comes from English.

9   These problems are not unique to Tanzania at all. The very same problems are faced in almost every developing country which is trying to use indigenous languages in education. We will face this issue in more detail in the next chapter.

10 Whiteley (1971a:151) refers to this distinction as the 'ideological' versus the 'technical' aspects of language policy.

11 These figures account for only 97 per cent of the 274 speakers. The remaining speakers did not fit into any of these categories because they reported knowledge of Arabic.

12 Myles Dillon of the Institute for Advanced Studies, Dublin, commenting on Ferguson (1966:316–17), was 'sorry to say that an estimate of 3 per cent of Irish speakers in my opinion would be pretty high – it's nearer 1 per cent.' He also thought that there would be more speakers of Irish in Boston than in Dublin.

13 There is a slight discrepancy in the figures given in Ó Huallacháin (1962) and the census figures from the 1961 census quoted by Macnamara (1971). Ó Huallacháin says that 'half a million have claimed to be Irish speakers, which works out to about 17 per cent of 3 million people. Macnamara quotes the census as reporting 27 per cent of the population 'able to speak Irish' (Macnamara 1971:87, footnote 4). In a later article, Ó Huallacháin (1970) reported that 15 per cent of the respondents in a random sample of 924 Irish citizens said they were 'fluent' or 'fairly fluent' in the language.

14 A solution to the national-language problem in Ireland that has always seemed reasonable to me personally would be to work for the standardization of *Irish English*, that is, English as it is spoken in Ireland. This would involve explicitly declaring that the use of uniquely Irish features (many of which are ultimately traceable to contact with Irish Gaelic) is the correct way to use the language. Vocabulary planning could promote the borrowing of terms for concepts that are particularly strongly associated with Irish culture from Irish Gaelic. This solution is probably not possible in actual practice, since (1) there is considerable variation within Irish English (Ó Huallacháin 1962:75); and (2) it appears that some of the most uniquely Irish aspects of Hiberno-English are socially stigmatized.

15 One reason was connected with a 'string' attached to the scholarships. If a person who had attended a preparatory college under a scholarship ever left the teaching profession, he had to repay all the money that had been spent on him. In effect, this locked almost all preparatory-college students into teaching for life. The moral pressure that this policy placed on people was one reason that the preparatory schools were discontinued. Another reason was a desire to draw teachers from a wider segment of the community (Macnamara 1971:71).

16 I have combined Ó Huallacháin's figures for the pattern in the Irish-speaking areas with the figures for his 'pattern C'. I think this gives an accurate picture, but it is not entirely clear.

17   I have not found any statements on the language used to conduct party business, but there can be little doubt that it is almost always English.
18   These facts are drawn from Macnamara (1971:76–9). Ó Huallacháin (1970:185) also reports a substantial interest in Irish language broadcasts.
19   Some 16 per cent of the male respondents and 13 per cent of the female respondents reported that they were 'fluent' or 'fairly fluent' in Irish (Ó Huallacháin 1970:191).
20   In this, the two countries are not altogether typical. Planning in any of these areas can be extremely controversial and difficult.
21   Both languages are based on Malay, which, like Swahili in East Africa, had been a trade language in the two countries.

OBJECTIVES

1   Be able to recognize the closest approximation to the number of languages spoken in Tanzania, if you are given several.
2   Be able to recognize the major factor contributing to the importance of Swahili in East Africa *before* colonization.
3   Be able to recognize the factor that contributed to the ultimate success of Swahili in Tanzania and had its origin during the colonial period.
4   Be able to recognize the factor that contributed to the success of Swahili and that is associated with the independence period.
5   Be able to cite three of the five reasons that made Swahili the obvious choice as the national language of Tanzania (pp. 268-9).
6   Be able to identify one advantage of the selection of Kiunguja as the dialect on which standard Swahili would be based and one advantage enjoyed by a competing dialect.
7   Be able to cite the power that the pre-independence Inter-Territorial Language (Swahili) Committee had that contributed to its relative success in standardizing the written language.
8   Be able to recognize Hinnebusch's conclusion on the effectiveness of officially published word lists on the use of new vocabulary in Tanzanian Swahili.
9   Be able to recognize the language of education practice at various levels in Tanzania.
10   Be able to identify a description of the degree to which Swahili is the functioning language of government in Tanzania.
11   Be able to recognize an accurate description of the evaluation of Swahili as a nationalist language in Tanzania, based on information about its speakers.
12   Be able to recognize an accurate statement about the attitudes of Tanzanian citizens toward their ethnic languages and toward Swahili.
13   Be able to state whether literature in Swahili is a strength or a weakness for its status as a national language.
14   Be able to recognize the fifth and final reason (given on p.277) for the relative lack of success in promoting Swahili in Kenya, compared to the effort in Tanzania.
15   Be able to recognize a statement about how difficult the language-determination and dialect-determination problems were in Ireland.
16   The issues of standardization, orthography planning, and vocabulary development all had about the same degree of success in Ireland. Be able to recognize that degree of success.
17   Be able to state whether the primary schools in Ireland are used extensively, moderately, or only to a limited extent as an instrument of language planning.

18 Be able to recognize the three patterns of the use of Irish in primary schools (see pp. 280-1) and to state which has the fewest schools that follow it, which has somewhat more and which has by far the most.

19 Be able to state whether Irish is used as the medium of instruction in more or less than half the secondary schools in Ireland, and whether its use is increasing, remaining about the same, or declining.

20 Be able to state where Macnamara says the 'burden' of the Irish restoration effort has been placed, as a result of the decline in the use of Irish as the level of education increases (pp. 281-2).

21 Be able to state whether the use of Irish for nationist purposes in Ireland can most accurately be described as substantial, moderate, or minimal.

22 Be able to recognize the criteria by which Irish language planning has been a failure and the criteria by which it can be called a success.

23 Be able to give the reason why the data illustrated in figure 10.1 cannot be interpreted as indicating an increase in knowledge of Irish over time.

24 Be able to state whether reported attitudes toward Irish are generally positive or negative.

25 Be able to recognize a statement of the relative power of natural social change and conscious language planning that is implied by the 'rowing-downstream principle'.

26 Be able to rank the following four cases in order of ease for the determination of a national language: (1) nations that have a few large and dominant sociocultural groups; (2) nations in which the vast majority speaks a single language; (3) extremely diverse nations with no clearly dominant sociocultural groups; (4) nations attempting to institute a new national language when communicative needs are already being met by an existing language.

11

Vernacular Language Education

One of the most crucial language planning decisions that a country can make is the determination of a language to serve as the medium of instruction in schools. In Ireland and Tanzania, the determination of a language of education was to some extent part of the determination of the national language, but in both countries compromises had to be made. In Ireland, Irish would not be used as a medium of instruction in schools where too few pupils could speak it. In Tanzania, Swahili was judged to be widespread enough to be made the nationwide language of primary education. As we pointed out, though, there probably are Tanzanian children who have difficulty at first because they don't speak Swahili when they come to school. On the other hand, the use of Swahili as a medium of instruction falls off at the secondary level, and it is hardly used at all in higher education. The main reason here is that Swahili doesn't have the necessary vocabulary and it lacks textbooks, literature, and trained teachers at the higher levels. Irish is used less as a medium of instruction at higher levels of education, but this is mainly because there are so few students who speak it. Irish vocabulary is apparently sufficient for the language to serve as a medium in higher education, although it does suffer from a lack of textbooks and teachers.

Even a review of the situation in Ireland and Tanzania as brief as this serves to point to the three main considerations in choosing a language of instruction: (1) do the prospective students know the language well enough to learn effectively through it; (2) would the proposed choice be consistent with overall nationalist aims; and (3) are the language itself, the material written in it, and the number of people able to teach in it adequate for use at the proposed level? Conflicts arise when the three considerations do not all point in the same direction. Swahili would be the choice for higher education in Tanzania on the first two criteria, but is prevented on the third one. Irish would be the universal medium of instruction at the primary level if the second and third criteria had to be considered; it cannot be used universally because of the first consideration.

THE 1951 UNESCO REPORT

The recommendation

In 1951, Unesco (The United Nations Educational, Scientific, and Cultural Organization) convened a Committee of Experts to consider the question of the language of education on a worldwide basis. Its report (Unesco 1953, 1968) has had a profound impact on the discussion of educational linguistic matters ever since.[1] The position the Committee took was that the first of the three main considerations, namely the language that children can effectively use, should be given priority in selecting the medium of instruction. If this is done, then it becomes clear that the choice in virtually every case will be the child's mother tongue:

> It is axiomatic that the best medium for teaching a child is his mother tongue. Psychologically, it is the system of meaningful signs that in his mind works automatically for expression and understanding. Sociologically, it is a means of identification among the members of the community to which he belongs. Educationally, he learns more quickly through it than through an unfamiliar linguistic medium. (Unesco 1953:11)

The Unesco Committee defined *mother tongue* as 'the language which a person acquires in early years and which normally becomes his natural instrument of thought and communication'. The Committee then states that a mother tongue 'need not be the language which his parents use; nor need it be the language he first learns to speak, since special circumstances may cause him to abandon this language more or less completely at an early age' (Unesco 1968:689–90). Another term that the Committee defines is *vernacular language*: 'A language which is the mother tongue of a group which is socially or politically dominated by another group speaking a different language. We do not consider the language of a minority in one country as a vernacular if it is an official language in another country.' (Unesco 1968:689–690).[2] The notion 'vernacular language' is important, because the Unesco recommendation is most controversial if the mother tongue happens to be a vernacular language.

Not only does the Unesco Report recommend that initial education be given through the mother tongue, even if it is a vernacular language, but it also recommends that 'the use of the mother tongue be extended to as late a stage in education as possible'. (Unesco 1968:691). In fact, the Committee is prepared to make very few exceptions to the general rule.

Responses to objections

The Unesco Committee anticipated several objections to its recommendation. Some languages, it may seem, have no grammar or alphabet. To this the Report answers that all languages have a grammar, or they could not be spoken, although some languages do not have a *written* grammar. The grammars of many vernacular languages are as intricate as those of world languages. Similarly, a language that does not have a writing system can be given one, since all spoken languages without exception have rules of pronunciation (of course, these may also be unwritten). A second objection is that it is useless to teach a mother tongue, since a child already knows it. There are two parts to the reply to this objection: first, children know their mother tongue well enough to serve a child's purposes, but their facility in it needs to be increased; and second, the point is not so much that the school would be teaching the mother tongue as teaching other subjects *in* the mother tongue. It is especially important to keep the second point in mind.

The third objection that the Committee deals with is that to teach in the mother tongue will make it more difficult for a youngster to learn a second language later. Those who raise this objection believe that to learn a second language well, it is important that it be used as a medium of instruction right from the start. In fact, some schools use this reasoning to forbid the use of mother tongues on school grounds; this happened at one time to speakers of Gaelic in the Scottish Highlands, to cite one example we have come across. The response to this objection is that 'recent experience in many places' suggests that a better way to introduce a second language may be to teach it first as a subject, using the mother tongue as a medium (Unesco 1968:692). Finally, it seems to some critics that using vernacular languages would impede national unity. Although the Unesco Committee concedes that it is easier to govern a country where everyone speaks the same language, the members doubt that insisting on the national language as a universal educational medium would necessarily produce that result. On the contrary, they suggest, too strong an insistence on the national language might cause some minorities to resent their national government and refuse to accept the national identity. The Committee's responses to the first three objections would, I think, be endorsed by most linguists.[3] The last objection is more sociopolitical than linguistic, but seems to have at least some merit.

In a section called 'Practical limitations in the use of the vernacular in school' (Unesco 1968:693–7), the Report turns to what amounts to another set of objections. These objections are more serious than the first four and the Committee's responses are less successful. Four of these are connected with how ready a language is to be used in education: (1) the lack of textbooks and other educational material; (2) the lack of general reading material; (3) a shortage of trained teachers and; (4) inadequacy of vocabulary. The Report has two basic suggestions to make in response to all four objections: either supply what is lacking, or use the vernacular as far into the educational process as possible and then make a carefully planned transition to a second language. The second recommendation is made with extreme reluctance, since it contradicts the Report's fundamental point. Therefore, the Committee urges governments to remedy shortcomings in readiness by encouraging the printing of books, magazines, newspapers and official notices in bilingual versions, and by training mother-tongue speakers of vernaculars to teach in their native languages, including practice teaching opportunities using the vernacular. The Report seems almost to give up in despair on the problem of vernaculars with almost no school materials (Unesco 1968:694):

> The difficulty is to find or train competent authors or translators; to obtain supplies of materials (such as paper, type and machinery) in days of general shortage; to distribute the finished product under conditions of great distances and poor communications; and above all to find the money. These are practical problems, extremely difficult and of the highest importance. We are not, however, competent to advise on those problems and we strongly urge that Unesco should investigate them. . . .

Somewhat surprisingly, the Report does not recommend vocabulary expansion in cases where a vernacular language does not have a sufficient vocabulary. Instead, it says that a second language will have to be introduced at an early stage. This suggestion is made with the utmost caution. First, the second language should be taught through the first. The transition should be gradual and not necessarily complete. If the language is adequate to support study in some subjects but not others, then the mother tongue should be retained as the instruction medium for those subjects. The same suggestion is offered if a lack of reading material, both educational and general, cannot be remedied.

Another set of pragmatic objections is more sociolinguistic in nature. These are concerned with the multiplicity of languages in: (1) a locality; and (2) a country; (3) the advisability of the use of lingua francas; and (4) popular objection. If a locality within a country is very linguistically diverse, it may be necessary to teach some children in a language that is not their mother tongue. This should be done, however, only after every effort has been made to arrange instruction groups by mother tongue, and then in such a way that it means the least hardship for the bulk of the pupils. Special help should be available for youngsters who do not speak the school language. The same suggestion is made if the country as a whole is linguistically diverse, but here it is seen as a temporary solution. The country should offer education in as many of its languages as will support it and constantly work toward the 'ideal' of mother-tongue education for all.[4]

As far as lingua francas go (the Report explicitly mentions Swahili in East Africa), the Committee seems rather skeptical of their use as media of primary education. The members are prepared to approve such usage, only if 'nearly all the children have some knowledge of the lingua franca as well as of their mother tongue before they come to school.' (Unesco 1968:696). If the children aren't at least familiar with the lingua franca, the Committee would not recommend its use at the early educational stages. Even at later stages, the use of a lingua franca 'would have to be weighed against the claims of a world language' (Unesco 1968: 697).

As surprising as it may seem, speakers of some vernaculars are very much opposed to their own languages being used in their children's education. They may feel that the only path to advancement is via a national or world language, and their own language is nothing but a barrier. If a particular group has this opinion, the Committee recommends that educators try to win the confidence of the people and convince them of the advantages of mother-tongue instruction. If a total program in the vernacular is not acceptable, perhaps some parents can be persuaded to accept an experimental program, which the Committee believes will convince the skeptical that vernacular-language education is sound policy. The Committee accepts the right of the people of a country to choose the language their children will be instructed in, but only 'in the last resort' (Unesco 1968: 696).

The impression the Unesco Report leaves is that it is advising countries to go to great lengths to provide mother-tongue education for all of their children. Although inadequate language development, a lack of teachers and materials, extreme diversity and popular opposition may present serious problems, these problems are to be overcome if at all possible. If they simply cannot be solved, a second language may have to be used as a medium of instruction, but with the minimum number of children, as late as possible in a child's educational career, and only after every effort has been made to minimize the hardship the child will face.

EVALUATION

Since its original publication, the Unesco recommendation has come under considerable critical review (for example, Bull 1955; LePage 1964:19–28; Dakin, Tiffen, and Widdowson 1968:20–40). Bull, in particular, challenges the basic assumption that the major criterion should be benefit for the individual child (Bull 1964:528):[5]

The Committee, rather obviously, strongly believes that what is best for the child psychologically and pedagogically should be the prime point of departure in planning for universal education. This proposition appears, however, to be somewhat unrealistic. What is best for the child psychologically may not be what is best for the adult socially, economically or politically and, what is even more significant, what is best for both the child and the adult may not be best or even possible for the society.

It seems reasonable to ask the following three ordered questions about the Unesco proposal, or, for that matter, about any innovative proposal. First, is it possible? If a plan of action cannot be carried out, there is no point in discussing the benefits and problems there would be if it *could* be carried out. Second, if the proposed action is possible, does it work? In other words, would we actually get the benefits that the proposal is designed to provide? Finally, if it is possible and would work, is it worth it? If the suggestion can be put into effect and would give the promised results, it still would not be a good idea if there were side effects that were worse than not getting the benefits at all, or if the cost and difficulty in carrying out the idea are out of proportion to the results.)

Is it possible?

If the question is 'is it possible to provide every child in the world with initial education in her mother tongue?', the answer is quite clearly 'no'. Some countries are so diverse linguistically that to carry out the Unesco suggestion literally would imply developing materials and training teachers in scores or hundreds of languages. We have seen something of what it would mean in India with its 200 or so languages; it would scarcely be better in Tanzania with its 135 languages. There are numerous other countries that would face similar problems. To make things worse, there is the inescapable fact that the really diverse countries, for whatever reason, are almost always among the poorest ones. To quote Bull (1964:529) once more:[6]

it is apparent that the vast enterprises required to provide a modern education and to sustain a modern state cannot be carried out in excessively polyglot societies. Mexico, for example, which does not have an adequate school system even for its Spanish-speaking inhabitants, can hardly afford to support 49 more projects patterned on the Tarascan experiment.

Quite apart from the staggering effort that it would take to set up even primary education facilities in scores or hundreds of languages, there is the problem of language development itself. Most linguists, as I have said, would agree that there is no reason why the grammar and phonology of any language on earth would not support discussion of any topic from seeds to space exploration. We cannot avoid the fact, however, that the vocabulary for a lot of modern concepts and devices already exists in a handful of 'world' languages, but in a vernacular the vocabulary would have to either be coined or borrowed. Vocabulary development, as language-planning projects go, is not among the most difficult, but it is far from easy. Furthermore, literature and textbooks on many subjects exist in a relatively few languages and would have to be created or translated into all the others before it would be feasible to use them beyond the early months of primary education. Tanzania, by dint of hard work, dedication, and good luck, has made great strides in developing Swahili as a language of education. It is barely conceivable that the nation could repeat that achievement 135 times.

However, to say that it is out of the question to provide vernacular-language education in every single language in the world is not to say that no efforts in that direction are worthwhile. (Of India's approximately 200 languages, the 14 recognized in Schedule VIII of the constitution account for 90 per cent of the population (this becomes 13 languages if we exclude the few native speakers of Sanskrit, and 12, if we consider Hindi and Urdu to be actually one language). This pattern is typical in polyglot countries; although there may be a large number of languages, a small fraction of them are the mother tongues of the vast majority of the population. The use of these vernaculars in education might be within the realm of the possible. It could well turn out to be the case that, if we can't have the whole Unesco Report loaf, half a loaf is better than none.)

Does it work?

The Unesco Committee said it was 'axiomatic' that the best language for a child to be instructed in is his mother tongue.(It seems, on the face of it, hardly to be doubted that a child will find it easier to learn if he fully understands the language the teacher is speaking and the language in the books he has to learn to read.)It is hard to disagree with Spolsky's (1977b:20) statement that:

It must be obvious to all that incomprehensible education is immoral: there can be no justification for assuming that children will pick up the school language on their own, and no justification for not developing some program that will make it possible for children to learn the standard language and for them to continue to be educated all the time that this is going on.

In other words, 'axiomatic' does not appear to be too much of an exaggeration.

Bear in mind that the Unesco Committee met in 1951, some thirty years ago. You might expect that in this amount of time the merits of vernacular-language education might have been tested numerous times and its value for children proven beyond a doubt. In actual fact, the idea has been the subject of quite a number of experiments and research projects. It isn't possible in an introductory text to review all these in detail, but we will examine the conclusions of four researchers, each of whom, in turn, has reviewed several of these experiments. Their conclusions appear below:

However, in view of the lack of satisfactory evidence, perhaps the wisest counsel to follow at the present time is to say that the linguistic effects of teaching in a second language are unknown. (Macnamara 1966:133, after five studies were reviewed, including Macnamara's own)

The evidence about the difficulties of a foreign medium at the school stage thus seems inconclusive. The superiority of the mother tongue has not been everywhere demonstrated . . . (Dakin, Tiffen and, Widdowson 1968:27; four studies reviewed)

The twenty-four studies or reports summarized varied in every conceivable way, and most provided no substantial evidence as to which approach is better. (Engle 1975: 26; 24 studies reviewed)

For a number of years, many educators have accepted as axiomatic the idea that the best medium of instruction for a child is his mother tongue . . . Are there empirical data which unequivocally support this position? The answer would seem to be *no*. Does this mean the position is untenable? Once again, the answer would seem to be *no*. (Tucker 1977:37–8; three studies reviewed)

Thirty years and numerous studies after the publication of the Unesco Report the unanimous opinion seems to be that nobody knows whether using the mother tongue as the medium of instruction is better than using a second language or not. This is an astounding result for an 'axiomatic' idea. To get a feel for the impact of it, imagine a genuine axiom, like Euclid's axiom: 'if equals are added to equals, the sums are equal.' From this axiom, it follows that if A=B, then A+C will be equal to B+C. This law is so obviously true that it would seem superfluous to 'try it out'. Of course, if it were tested, by substituting different numbers for A, B, and C, it would come out true every time, unless there were errors in calculation. Imagine that mathematicians had tried for thirty years to demonstrate that Euclid's axiom is true by testing it on various numbers and had to conclude that they just don't know if it is true or not! This scenario is almost unthinkable. Granted, the Unesco Committee's use of the term 'axiomatic' might have been something of a metaphor, but still, if the metaphor was at all apt, it should have been possible to demonstrate the superiority of mother-tongue education by this time.

Apparently, something has gone wrong. To discover what it might be, it is necessary to know what sort of experiment has been used to test the Unesco recommendation. These experiments are basically of two types. One type tests the use of the mother tongue as the medium of instruction, the approach that Engle (1975) calls the 'Native Language' method. The other kind of experiment tests the use of a language that is not the students' mother tongue, Engle's 'Direct Method'. A well-designed experiment to test the Direct Method would take one or more 'experimental' groups – those who are going to be taught through the medium of a language they do not speak. There would also be 'control' groups; students who are going to be taught in some other way. Ordinarily, one control group consists of students who have the same mother-tongue as the experimental group, but are being taught in that language. Another consists of students who are mother tongue speakers of the language the experimental group is using as a medium, and are using their own language as a medium. After the program has been in effect for a while, the experimental and control groups are tested for educational accomplishments in reading, language skills in both languages, and in general educational achievement. A well-known example of this kind of research design is the St Lambert experiment (cf. Tucker, Hamayan, and Genesee 1976 and the references cited there). In this experiment, native speakers of English were placed in a voluntary program in which they are taught in French from the beginning of their educational experience. Their accomplishments have then been compared with the accomplishments of both French and English native speakers who have been instructed in their own languages.

Numerous tests have been conducted with children in the St Lambert project and similar projects in Canada. The general result is that the experimental groups can function in English, including reading and writing, as well as English Canadian students who have had English-language education. They also do as well as the English-educated students in subject matter and cognitive tests. They are far superior in ability in French than are

English Canadians who have studied French in the usual second-language programs. However, they are not so competent in French as are the French-speaking control groups.

The Native-Language experiments usually have control groups who are being instructed by means of the Direct Method. In other words, most studies of the Native-Language approach compare it to the Direct Method. Typically, comparable groups of students, both having the same mother tongue, are selected. One group is instructed through their mother tongue; the other is instructed through the national language, or whatever language is the usual medium of education in that location. At the end of the experiment, both groups are tested for their ability in both languages, and in other subjects.

An often-cited example of an experiment like this is the Iloilo project in the Philippines (Ramos et al. 1967; Engle 1975). The experimental group was instructed through their native language, Hiligaynon, for the first two grades, and then they switched to English. The control group was taught through English for all six years in the traditional manner. At the end of six years, both groups were given a battery of tests in English. The experimental group scored significantly higher in social studies achievement than the control group. No other achievement test results were significant, although the experimental group was slightly higher in arithmetic and reading and the control group was a little higher in language. The experimental group also reported itself significantly higher on certain parts of a 'Personality Inventory'.

It is clear that in order to conduct research of either type, at least two educational programs have to be in existence – an experimental program and a control program. These programs are not very likely to be set up to comply with the requirements of social science research. As a result, more often than not it is impossible to control for all the variables. Recall that in our discussion of statistics we used an example that was concerned with raising tomatoes with two kinds of fertilizer. The way this hypothetical experiment was set up, we could conclude that one kind of fertilizer was better than the other, if larger tomatoes grew when it was used compared to the other kind. But this conclusion was only valid, *if fertilizer was the only difference between the two gardens*. The example we gave of this condition being violated was if one gardener, in addition to using a different fertilizer, also had planted a different strain of tomatoes. If one of the gardeners grew bigger tomatoes in that case, we wouldn't know if it was because of the variety of the tomato plants, the fertilization practices, or a combination of the two.

In mother-tongue education research, other aspects of the experimental and control-group experience might be different, in addition to the difference in the language of instruction. Some uncontrolled variables that have kept research on this question from being conclusive are the social class of the children, the quality of the teachers, urban versus rural location of the schools, and 'the Hawthorne effect'. The Hawthorne effect is a factor that works in favor of *any* experimental method, whatever its intrinsic merits. For example, if I were able to convince a school system that children would learn to read better if they were put in a green-walled classroom and allowed to take off their shoes, and if the 'green room' teachers really believed in the program and the children came to think of themselves as something special, they would probably learn to read significantly better. Of course, there is no reason to believe that being barefoot and having green walls in a reading room have anything to do with teaching reading, so gains of this sort would come only from the aura of excitement that was associated with the experiment. The best way to overcome the Hawthorne effect is to test the results of the experiment after it has been in operation for several years. By this time, the 'specialness' will have worn off, and any gains the experimental group show are much more likely to be the result of the experimental conditions. Much of the research on the Native-Language, or mother tongue, approach has been tested after only one year. This can cut both ways; the Hawthorne effect can cause inflated benefits for the experimental group, or the length of time might be too short for the benefits to have taken hold.

A very common uncontrolled variable is teacher quality. The quality of instruction that the control group received in a frequently cited test of the Native-Language approach was so bad that Engle's conclusion was that the study 'clearly favored the Native Language Approach over poor instruction (not the Direct Method as described)' (Engle 1975:14). In another study described by Engle (1975:11), no differences could be found in the achievements of Ugandans who had begun their education in their mother tongues compared to those who had begun in English. However, *teacher* variables accounted for 83 per cent of the variance in the subjects' test scores, when subjected to a regression analysis.

The success that seems to be demonstrable for the Direct Method in the Canadian immersion experiments, however, cannot be taken as a clear indication that this method is better.[7] These cases all involve speakers of the nationally dominant language (English) learning through the medium of another national language that is dominant locally (French). In addition, the students who participate in these experiments are most often middle class, they enter the program voluntarily, and their parents work hard to make the program a success. It cannot be assumed that the same thing would work in a country where speakers of a rural small-group vernacular were 'immersed' in a national or world language.

Part of the reason that Unesco's 'axiomatic' proposal has not been consistently and convincingly demonstrated is that it has been so difficult to control other variables and exclude spurious factors such as the Hawthorne effect. Perhaps a series of three or four tightly controlled experiments in different parts of the world would definitively show the superiority of mother-tongue medium instruction. On the other hand, it is hard to avoid the feeling that, after thirty years, a discernible trend in favor of mother-tongue instruction should have emerged, even with less-than-perfect research designs.

That trend is not evident.

Maybe it is necessary to consider the possibility that mother-tongue instruction just isn't as important as 'common sense' would indicate. Bear in mind the fact that most researchers of this issue are North Americans or West Europeans. Many of them have not had first-hand experience with the tremendous linguistic diversity that is a day-to-day fact of life for so much of the world's population. In diverse settings, it is a commonplace for people to become bilingual or multilingual, even without schooling. Even if we grant that the acquisition of a second or third language might not happen when a child is very young, even a small youngster will *expect* to learn a new language as part of growing up. No doubt an American (or German) child would be shocked to find himself under the authority of an adult he can't even understand when he starts school, if practically everyone he has ever met speaks English (or German). But the same is not necessarily true for Indian or Tanzanian children. To them, being in a situation where someone is talking to them in a language they have not learned yet might well be a sign that they are considered grown up. Of course, that doesn't help them understand any better, but it would make a big difference psychologically.

On the other hand, a child might learn a second language very early in life. This seems to be true of the Tiwa Indians who we mentioned in chapter 8. When asked their opinion on the language of instruction, there was considerable support for *bilingual* teachers, but very little for Tiwa-medium instruction, even in elementary school. Of those who responded to the question: 'Would you want to be taught (have your children taught) by teachers speaking only Tiwa, at least in elementary school, or by teachers speaking both Tiwa and English?', 91.7 per cent chose Tiwa and English and only 8.3 per cent answered Tiwa only. The Old Order Amish learn Pennsylvania German at home, but acquire English at an early age. Old Order Amish children attend parochial schools controlled by their own community, but the medium of instruction is invariably English. Furthermore, this fact seems not to have any ill effects on their achievement levels (Huffines 1980). Situations like this exist in many parts of the world. In them, mother-tongue instruction would not be at all advantageous.[8]

Another factor is the matter of language relatedness. In several parts of the world, for example, the Paraguayan Chaco and northern India, language varieties may be partly similar and partly different to such a degree that it becomes really hard to say whether they should be called separate languages, or whether they are better described as dialects of the same language. In East Africa, the Bantu languages, although clearly not co-dialects with Swahili, are similar enough in general structure to soften the transition from native ability in one of them to education through Swahili. In cases where the medium of instruction is an indigenous language, even if it is not the mother tongue, general linguistic similarity might make instruction in a second language less odious than it would otherwise be.

The answer to the question 'Does it work?' is every bit as obscure as the quotations at the beginning of this section make it seem. Although the experimental results are not definitive, the experiments are virtually never adequately controlled. On the other hand, it is possible that mother tongue medium instruction is really *not* a substantial advantage to children. At least, there are many settings in the world where it would not be.

Is it worth it?

As Tucker (1977) says, it's true that we cannot demonstrate unequivocally that mother-tongue education is superior, but we don't know it is *not* either. In other words, it is possible to conclude that it does work. Supposing that some degree of mother-tongue education is possible, even if the mother tongue is a 'vernacular' and that it might be beneficial, we should still ask if it's worth it. As in other language-planning decisions, cost–benefit thinking ought to come into the picture, even if there is no formal cost–benefit analysis.[9] Here, Bull's comment on the good of the society compared with the good of the individual child is worth thinking about. It seems clear enough that the two might be in conflict. Which one gets priority, I would think, depends on the particular nation's value system and resources. It is also clear that setting up a vernacular language to be used as an instructional medium is an expensive business. The benefits would have to be considerable to justify the cost.

World, national and small-group languages. The notion of a tripartite layering of languages is a concept that keeps cropping up in case studies of developing countries. For many countries, India and Tanzania being only two examples, languages seem to be found at three functional levels. At one end of the continuum, there are languages that serve the interactive needs of small groups of native speakers. In India, these are the tribal languages and some of the other languages not mentioned in Schedule VIII of the constitution. In Tanzania, they are the 135 or so languages mentioned in the last chapter.[10] Most of them are only slightly standardized at best, having maybe an alphabet, a short dictionary, and a few primers. Kloss (1968) would call these languages 'preliterate' or 'unstandardized, alphabetized' languages, although some might be in his 'young standard' category. Some countries have a few languages in this group that are fully standardized and may have a substantial literary tradition, but have so few speakers that they have no chance of functioning nationally or world-wide. This last subcategory consists of the languages that Kloss calls 'small-group standard' languages.

At the next level, we find languages that I will call *national* languages, but in a sense somewhat different from the meaning we have given to the term so far. In the present context, a 'national' language serves the nationalist function, not only for *nations*, but for the larger subnational *nationalities*, in Fishman's sense. They may be a functioning national language in some country, like

Swahili or Guaraní. They may be officially declared national languages, like Hindi in India or Pilipino (Tagalog) in the Philippines, that do not really serve the nationalist function for the whole country in the fullest sense. Or they may be one of several indigenous languages that are potential contenders for national language status, like Kikuyu in Kenya or Igbo in Nigeria. Finally, they may be languages that have a substantial number of speakers and considerable development, but no real chance of becoming declared national languages in the countries where they are located. Telegu in India would be an example. Had geopolitical history taken different turns, some of the languages in this last group might have been the national language of some nation that does not exist, but might have. Most of these languages would fit into Kloss's 'young standard' class, although some would fit, somewhat uneasily, into his 'small group standard' category.

The *world* languages, for one reason or another, have over the course of time become the medium for most of the world's technology, commerce, and diplomacy and a large part of its internationally recognized literature. Only a handful of the world's languages qualify; Stern (1963:13) quotes the opinion of the British scholar J. L. Williams that there are only five (which five they are, Stern doesn't say). Although world languages are often colonial languages, the status they have often makes it impossible for newly independent states to remove them from official and educational domains, in spite of their association with the former colonial power. Some nations that have never been colonies still find it to their advantage if at least some of their citizens know a world language. English has this position in Thailand, for example.

In actual fact, the medium of education issue is often presented as a choice between the language that is already in place, usually a world language, and one or more small-group vernaculars. Perhaps a reasonable compromise would be to give special priority to *national* languages over small-group vernaculars, as media of instruction where an alternative to a world language is needed. National languages, in the sense I am using here, have several considerable advantages over small-group vernaculars. First, they are usually spoken as native languages by very much larger populations than are small group vernaculars (Swahili in Tanzania is an exception). Secondly, they are usually not so severely underdeveloped (for purposes of education), as small-group vernaculars so often are. Finally, in many cases, national languages have either already been learned as second languages by school-aged children, or will be learned in the natural course of events, even if the children never go to school.

Many leaders in developing multilingual countries are in favor of this very course of action. The following is an excerpt from a speech by Rajendra Prasad, who was President of India in 1961 (Dakin, Tiffen, and Widdowson 1968:34):

[a mother tongue policy] is feasible only if the linguistic group is of an appreciable size and forms a compact region. It cannot be reasonably demanded by those who are very small in numbers or are scattered in different parts of other linguistic regions . . . The financial and other implications of accepting such a demand can be easily perceived.

Bokamba and Tlou (1977:47) propose the following as a possible language policy for Africa:

Our proposal is that each Sub-Saharan African state select a national language from the pool of its linguae francae on the basis of a statistical and attitudinal language survey, and use this language as the medium of instruction.

It is clear that Bokamba and Tlou are not advocating mother-tongue instruction, but the replacement of the colonial language by a single African language in each country. Although they are probably too optimistic about the possibility of selecting *one* indigenous language to serve as the only medium of instruction, it is important to note that only 'linguae francae', national languages in the broad sense I am employing in this context, are candidates. Ansre (1978) advocates the 'use of indigenous languages' in education in Africa, but apparently this does not necessarily mean mother-tongue education. Ansre (1978:292) cites Tanzania as one of two examples of African nations 'fully committed to UIL' (use of indigenous languages), although we know that Swahili is the mother tongue of a small minority of Tanzanians.

Some suggested criteria. The use of vernacular mother tongues in education in the large majority of the countries of the world is quite simply outside the realm of the possible. Nevertheless, some increased use of indigenous languages instead of world languages is desirable in many settings. This means that decisions have to be made about which indigenous languages will and which will not be used in schools. I suggest the following five criteria for making these decisions.

(1) Use as a medium of wider communication. If a language is already one of those that are used as the medium of communication among subgroups who don't share mother tongues, it should be preferred over languages that are not. One way of determining this is to observe how many people learn the language as a *second* language, relative to its size. Weinreich (1957) has developed a formula, which he calls the measurement of functional importance, that allows a numerical value to be assigned to this factor.

(2) Numbers of speakers. Languages with a large number of native speakers should be preferred over small-group languages. Indisputably, this criterion implies discrimination against children who happen to be born into small ethnolinguistic groups, but it also means that the resources that have to be used to install a language in an educational system will benefit large numbers of people. The meaning of 'large numbers of native speakers' would vary from country to country, but I would think that a language spoken by 10 per cent of

the population or more, or by at least a million speakers would be a reasonable candidate. Languages spoken by fewer than 100,000 speakers should probably not even be considered, except perhaps in wealthier nations.

(3) Language development. A language that is equipped to serve as a school language without extensive language engineering should be preferred over those that need a large development effort. Besides the size and nature of the vocabulary, development means whether or not the language has a writing system, how suitable the writing system is for print technology, the degree of language standardization beyond orthography, whether or not there is a literary tradition in the language, whether or not there are existing pedagogical materials for the language (for example, those that have been prepared by missionaries, or by the community itself), and how easy it will be to recruit and train teachers who can teach through the language.

(4) Group preference. The Unesco Report mentions the possibility that some communities might not even want their language used as the medium of instruction. Sociolinguistic forces of one kind or another may have brought about the attitude that the mother tongue is the best language for home and community, but to use it in school is simply not appropriate. The Unesco Committee suggests that governments ought to try to persuade communities like this of the advantages of mother-tongue education. It seems to me that the persuasion effort, on top of what has to be done to get a language into an educational system, would be so great that a language that is not acceptable to its own speakers should not even be considered as a potential medium of instruction.

(5) The drop-out factor. One important sign that an education system is not working well is a large drop-out rate in the early years of schooling. There is no doubt that the number of drop-outs is a serious problem in many countries. In chapter 1, we saw that Paraguay is one such country, and the use of Spanish as the school language in areas of Guaraní monolingualism seems to be a major cause (Rubin 1968a). Bokamba and Tlou (1977:45) report that in Ghana only 5 per cent of all children who leave elementary-school go on to secondary school. In Zaire, only 30 per cent of the children who enter elementary school complete the first four grades. The authors attribute this to 'inability to master the language of instruction'. Where this situation exists, a change in the medium of instruction might well be indicated: 'There are many situations, however . . . where children for whatever reason do not remain in school beyond grades three or four. In these situations, it would seem perfectly reasonable and well advised to initiate children to formal schooling and to provide initial literacy training in the mother tongue' (Tucker 1977:39). On the other hand, if the educational system is functioning adequately enough so that children remain in school even though they have to learn through a second language, there is probably no educational reason to make the effort to switch to the mother tongue. In this case, Tucker recommends 'a large concentration of instruction in the target language accompanied by support activities in the

mother tongue'. In other words, don't apply an expensive fix where there is no serious problem.

THE CASE OF FRISIAN

So far, we have approached the question of vernacular language education as a conflict between educational benefit and the scarcity of resources. The implication has been that if benefits to the children could be demonstrated and the country could afford it, mother-tongue education is to be recommended. Conversely, if children could be shown *not* to benefit, or if the cost is too great, mother-tongue education would not be advised. However, the pedagogical merits of one or another educational medium are often a minor consideration when decisions are actually made. This point is illustrated very clearly in the case of Frisian, a minority language in the Netherlands.

Background

Frisian is a Germanic language spoken primarily in Friesland, a province in northeastern Holland, although other dialects of Frisian are also spoken in parts of Germany (see map 11.1).[11] Frisian is only distantly related to Dutch and is not mutually intelligible with it. Friesland has a population of 550,000 people, about 4 per cent of the population of the Netherlands (Pietersen 1978:354). Friesland is thoroughly bilingual; virtually the entire population speaks Dutch and most also know Frisian.

Dutch had been the language of the High functions for centuries, but language became an issue in Friesland in the nineteenth century. At that time an active Frisian movement began. Evidence for the persuasiveness and political skill of the movement can be found in the fact that an impressive list of their goals has been achieved in this century. The first church service in Frisian took place in 1915, and a Frisian Bible was published in 1943 (a new ecumenical translation was in preparation during the 1970s). A Frisian Academy was established in 1938 and spoken Frisian (but not its written use) has been permitted in Friesland courts since 1955.

Dutch is the traditional language of education in Friesland, as it is throughout the Netherlands. In 1907, permission was granted to allow the study of Frisian, but it was optional and had to be done outside the normal curriculum. In 1937, a clause was included in the Dutch elementary-school law, that in effect, made it possible to introduce Frisian as a school subject. According to Wijnstra (1978), 100 schools began Frisian studies within a year. An experiment in the use of Frisian as the medium of instruction in the first two grades, involving nine schools, was set up in 1950. The results were apparently satisfactory since a law was passed in 1955 making it legal to use regional languages such as Frisian as the medium of instruction in the first three grades. The number of schools electing to use Frisian as the medium of

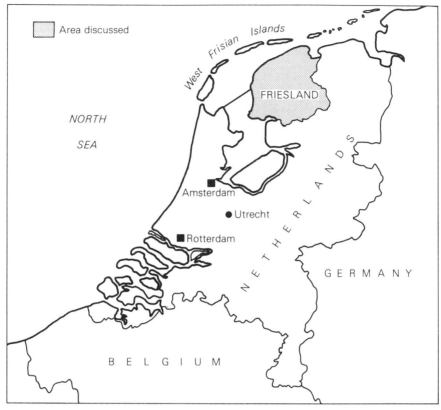

Map 11.1   The Netherlands, showing Friesland

instruction increased to 84 in 1968, although it has since declined somewhat (Wijnstra 1978). In 1972, a law was passed making Frisian an obligatory school subject in Friesland, beginning in 1980.[12]

Data collected by a survey sponsored by the Frisian Academy in 1969 indicate that Frisian is well established in the province. The data indicate that 83 per cent of the population of Friesland speaks Frisian and 97 per cent understand it at least 'fairly well'. Answers to the survey questions indicate a fairly typical pattern of diglossia between Dutch and Frisian. Table 11.1, adapted from Pietersen's (1978:365) table II, shows the distribution by occupational group and also by one High and one Low domain.[13] For all groups, more Frisian is reported in the Low domain and more Dutch in the High domain. In general, it is also true that people with higher-status occupations report more overall use of Dutch than people with lower-status occupations. Frisian seems to be particularly strong in the agricultural occupations, indicating that it is more likely to be spoken in the country. This is an accurate impression. Of respondents who live in the country, 81 per cent report that they use Frisian at home whereas the figure for city-dwellers is 49

*Table 11.1 The percentage use of Dutch and Frisian in Friesland, 1969,
by occupational status and High versus Low domain*

	Language at home		Language with notables*	
Occupational group	Dutch	Frisian	Dutch	Frisian
Leaders/well-to-do	64	28	81	19
Employed middle classes	27	51	74	21
Small shopkeepers	7	68	52	39
Workers	7	77	52	44
Agricultural laborers	0	84	36	56
Farmers	1	96	33	66

*'Notables' are high-status professionals, such as doctors and ministers
Source: data from Pietersen (1978:365)

per cent. Frisian is a written language and there are books published in it, but it is largely used for spoken purposes; 83 per cent of the sample reported that they could speak Frisian, but only 69 per cent could read it at least 'fairly well' and only 11 per cent reported that they could write it more than 'a little' (Pietersen 1978).

It does not seem that the Frisian population is in the process of shifting to Dutch. Although Pietersen (1978:385) reports that 'older people are more involved with the language ideology than younger people', a new survey sponsored by the Frisian Academy and a daily newspaper in 1979 shows the same overall figures as were reported in 1969 (*Frisian News Items* 35:2, 1979).[14] In particular, 96 per cent (compared with 97 per cent in 1969) can understand the language and 77 per cent (compared with 83 per cent) can speak it. As we know, ten years is too short a period of time for an intergenerational shift to start showing up. However, the newer survey shows that there is no difference in knowledge of Frisian between younger and older people. Reported attitudes toward the Frisian language are very positive. Frisian was rated higher than Dutch on a 'niceness' scale. When asked to rate Dutch, Frisian, two Dutch dialects (Limburgs and Gronings), and three world languages (English, German, and French) as languages to be retained, Dutch was rated higher than Frisian, but Frisian outranked the world languages, as well as the Dutch dialects (Pietersen 1978:376).

Effects of Frisian-medium education

In the early 1970s, a research project, reported on by Wijnstra (1978), was initiated to test the educational advantages of bilingual schooling in Frisian and Dutch. The study focused on three groups of Frisian schools and a control group of monolingual Dutch speakers from a rural area near Utrecht. All three groups of Frisian schools were in areas that had high concentrations of Frisian-speaking families (over 90 per cent according to 1956 figures). The three groups differed in the following ways:

Group 1   Kindergarten predominantly Frisian and the first three grades taught in both Frisian and Dutch.

Group 2   Kindergarten predominantly Frisian and the first three grades taught in Dutch.

Group 3   Kindergarten predominantly Dutch and the first three grades taught in Dutch.

Group 1 comes the closest to the Unesco ideal of early instruction in the mother tongue, so the results it achieved will be particularly interesting. The Utrecht group, like group 3, used all Dutch.

The four groups were comparable on measures of intelligence before the study began, and this relationship didn't change. At the end of each year, the subjects were tested on Dutch vocabulary and grammar, oral proficiency in Dutch, Dutch reading speed and comprehension, language usage and composition (also in Dutch) and arithmetic. The scores were statistically analyzed by an analysis of variance, with test scores as the dependent variable and membership in one of the four groups as the independent variable. In the tests of various aspects of Dutch grammar and vocabulary administered at the end of kindergarten and grade 1, the group 1 subjects repeatedly had the lowest scores. On several tests, their scores were significantly lower than the scores of any other group. This is hardly surprising, since their formal exposure to Dutch is the least of any of the groups. By the end of the second grade, the number of tests they scored the lowest on began to decrease and by the end of the third grade, group 1 scores were not significantly lower than the scores of any other group. In two tests for which Wijnstra provides detailed data (one on oral proficiency in Dutch and one on language usage) group 1 third-graders scored higher than any of the other Frisian groups and on the second one, they scored higher than the Utrecht control group as well. These scores were not *significantly* higher, though. In fact, by the end of grade 3, there were hardly any significant differences among the groups at all.[15] There isn't a single significant difference between group 1 and the other two Frisian groups.

In the final analysis, it seems that mother tongue instruction for Frisian children slows down their proficiency in school uses of Dutch for a short period, but that it is neither an advantage nor a disadvantage by the end of the third grade. A large part of the reason for this is that Frisian children are bilingual in Dutch anyway, and there are few cultural differences between them and the rest of the Dutch population. If the educational effect were the only consideration, Frisian-medium instruction would not be worth the trouble. It requires special planning, training, and materials, and seems to produce no measurable pedagogical benefits.

Political benefits

Educational benefits, however, are never the only consideration, and may not even be the most important. Remember that there is an influential movement in Friesland in favor of the preservation of Frisian. Many Frisians see themselves as 'an ancient and freedom-loving people' who are constantly involved in 'wrenching concessions from a highly centralized and essentially foreign government' (*Frisian News Items* 35(1) 1979). Provision for local-option mother-tongue/bilingual education has apparently proved a sufficiently inexpensive political price to pay to prevent the further alienation of the Frisian population. An indication of what the political climate might be was given in a *Frisian News Items* article (35(2) 1979) on a Bill passed by the Dutch parliament in October 1979. The Bill provided for the addition of Frisian to the curriculum of teacher training colleges in Friesland. According to the article, the Bill was passed by a large majority. In addition, a few non-Frisian members of parliament, including the Minister of Education, gave speeches in favor of the Bill in Frisian. It appears that a conciliatory stance toward the advocates of the Frisian language is the best one to take. For social and political reasons, the Frisian mother-tongue policy is fully justified, especially when we realize that: (1) although Frisian-medium instruction doesn't seem to produce direct educational benefits, it doesn't do any harm either; and (2) Frisian is a fairly well-developed 'small-group standard' language.

The Frisian case is not unique in this respect. In the Philippines, both English and Pilipino are still officially languages of instruction, in spite of research that fails to demonstrate educational benefits for Pilipino medium instruction over English (Tucker 1977:34). Tanzania's decision to use Swahili in its educational system was not motivated by the principles that the Unesco Committee advocated. The Irish language educational policy in Ireland has even less to do with the kind of thinking in the Unesco Report.   )

SUMMARY

One of the most critical language planning decisions that can be made is the language to use as a medium of instruction. A Unesco Committee of Experts, meeting in 1951, took the point of view that the well-being of individual children is the most important consideration in making this decision. This led them to recommend that the mother tongues of learners should be used as the language of instruction from the beginning of school and should continue to be used as long as possible. The Committee anticipated four initial objections to their recommendation, and dealt with them in a reasonable manner. Further objections, which the Report calls 'practical limitations', were much more difficult to deal with, although the Report does have something to say about them.

The Unesco recommendation has been a center of controversy ever since. To evaluate its suggestion, it seemed reasonable to ask if it would be possible to follow its implementation, if implementing the recommendation would work, and if the benefits would be worth the effort. To implement the recommendation for every ethnolinguistic group in the world is obviously not possible. At best, the Unesco ideal can only be approximated in most multilingual countries. In spite of the fact that common sense would indicate that children would learn better if they were taught in their native language, the research that has been carried out in the past thirty years is amazingly inconclusive. A large part of the reason is that the difficulties inherent in large-scale social science research make it next to impossible to control all possible confounding variables, and almost all of the research projects leave important variables uncontrolled. Nevertheless, at least a mild trend in favor of mother-tongue education might be expected, even in imperfectly executed research. However, it seems that for every research report that indicates that mother-tongue education is effective, there is another one that indicates that it is not. The consensus on the question of whether or not it works is 'we just don't know'.

If a language-planning agency should conclude that the Unesco recommendation would work in a certain setting, we are still left with the question of whether the benefits would make the effort worth it. A sociolinguistic tripartite classification of the languages of the world gives us a basis for trying to answer this question. The three divisions are: (1) small-group languages; (2) 'national' languages (in a specially defined sense); and (3) world languages. Very often, the decision is presented as a choice between a small-group language and a world language. A reasonable compromise in some settings might be to use a national language in education as a replacement for a world language and as an alternative to trying to use numerous vernaculars. In fact, this sort of solution has been advocated by political leaders and scholars in several multilingual countries. Five criteria that might be used to help to decide on the language or languages to be used in education were concerned with: (1) use as a medium of wider communication; (2) numbers of speakers; (3) language development; (4) group preference; and (5) the drop-out factor. Applying these criteria tends strongly to point to 'national' languages.

In actual practice, the educational benefit for school children is often not the major factor that influences the decision to use one language or another in education. The recent history of the introduction of Frisian, a regional language of the Netherlands, into Friesland provincial schools is an illustration of this fact. The Frisian language has been used as a medium of instruction in a bilingual program in some Friesland schools for the past few decades. Research results indicate that using the Frisian language in initial instruction ultimately neither helps nor hinders students in school achievement. If the results of educational research were the only important consideration, it would seem that Dutch might as well serve as the only instructional language, as it does in the rest of the country. However, the use of Frisian in Friesland schools has continued and was even expanded in 1980. The reasons for this course of action are social and political rather than educational, but the policy seems to be a sound one none the less. In this respect, the Frisian case is typical of educational language planning.

BIBLIOGRAPHICAL NOTES

General discussions of bilingual education, most of which address the question of medium of instruction to some extent, include Fishman (1977), Spolsky (1972), Kloss (1977), and Lewis (1977). In Tosi (1979), there is a review of the literature on mother-tongue education of immigrants and the book has a valuable bibliography. Recent case studies include Spolsky and Cooper (1978) (a collection of articles), Cohen (1975) (Redwood City, California), Mackey and Beebe (1977) (Cuban immigrants in Miami, Florida), Sibayan (1978) (the Philippines), Berry (1976) (cases involving creole languages), Spolsky (1977b), Rosier and Farella (1976) (both on American Indians), and Bamgbose (1976) (West Africa). Included on the long list of studies of French language immersion programs in Canada are: McDougall and Bruck (1978), Stern (1978), Pitts (1978), Swain (1978), Genesee et al. (1978), and Bruck, Lambert, and Tucker (1977) (see also Tucker, Hamayan, and Genesee (1976) and the references cited there).

NOTES

1   Citations from the Unesco Report will, where possible, be made from the more accessible excerpt in Fishman (1968c), rather than from the original publication.
2   Notice that the Unesco definition differs from the one used by Ferguson (1966) in his discussion of profile formulas. Ferguson used standardization as a major criterion; vernacular languages had native speakers, but were not standardized. Unesco replaces standardization with official status in some country of the world. In my opinion, Ferguson's criterion is superior. Take, for example, the languages mentioned in Schedule VIII of the Indian constitution. Most of them are standardized to about the same degree. But whereas Hindi, for example, would not be a vernacular by the Unesco definition because of its status as official in India, nor would Urdu because it is official in Pakistan, Tamil *would* be a vernacular because it is no nation's official language (it does have some *regional* official status in Sri Lanka). Tamil, however, is approximately as well developed as Hindi and Urdu are. The Unesco Report recognizes in a footnote (Unesco 1968:689) that its definition may not be universally applicable. In any case, both definitions will give the same languages in the majority of cases.
3   With respect to the objection about use of the mother tongue preventing the later learning of a second language, not all linguists would agree that teaching a second language through the medium of the first is necessarily the best way. We will see that there is considerable evidence that using a language as a medium of instruction can, in some circumstances, be an effective means of imparting that language. However, I doubt that any linguist would want to say that using the mother tongue as a medium of instruction *prevents* the acquisition of another language.

4   At this point, the Report is a little hard to follow. Local diversity might lead to instruction in a language which is not the mother tongue of some children, and the Committee seems to accept this, however reluctantly, as a permanent solution. The same solution at the national level is presented as a temporary one, falling short of the ideal. Of course countries are made up of localities. Perhaps the implicit idea is that extremely small mother-tongue groups may never get vernacular-language education, but countries ought never to give up the attempt to use all their moderate- to large-group languages in education.

5   Quotations from Bull's article are taken from its reprint in Hymes (1964).

6   The Tarascan experiment that Bull refers to is a vernacular-language education project cited with favor in the Unesco Report.

7   The method used in these experiments is called 'immersion' because students are 'immersed' in French throughout the school day.

8   Le Page (1964:21–8) and Dakin, Tiffen, and Widdowson (1968:33–5) discuss the implications of widespread bilingualism for mother-tongue medium education.

9   Tadadjeu's (1977) cost–benefit analysis leads him to conclude, in essence, that vernacular-language education *is* worth it, in many African countries.

10 Sukuma, the Tanzanian language with the greatest number of native speakers, is marginally a 'national' language under the definition I am about to develop.

11 My description of the Frisian situation is based primarily on Pietersen (1978).

12 The 1980 target was still in effect as late as January 1979 (*Frisian News Items* 35:1, 1979).

13 The percentages do not add up to 100 per cent because, besides Dutch and Frisian, some respondents indicated that they spoke a Frisian 'dialect' or 'Town Frisian', a variety in which a largely Dutch vocabulary is used with Frisian grammar and pronunciation (Pietersen 1978:357).

14 I am indebted to Florence Kuipers for making copies of two issues of *Frisian News Items* available to me, as well as a copy of Wijnstra (1978). *Frisian News Items* is a bulletin published by the Frisian Information Bureau in Grand Rapids, Michigan.

15 One result that Wijnstra finds puzzling is that the Utrecht group scored significantly higher than the three Frisian groups in arithmetic, even though they show no advantages over the Frisian children in reading or listening comprehension in Dutch.

OBJECTIVES

1   Be able to list the three main requirements of a successful medium of education.

2   Be able to state the major suggestion of the Unesco Committee with respect to initial education.

3   Be able to give the Unesco Report's responses to the four objections it anticipated to its suggestion (pp. 293-4).

4   Be able to recognize the UNESCO Committee's suggestion for dealing with the 'practical limitations' concerning inadequate eductional materials in some languages and the lack of teachers available to teach in those languages.

5   Be able to recognize the Unesco suggestion for dealing with situations in which the vocabulary of the vernacular is inadequate for curriculum needs (p. 295).

6   Be able to recognize the Unesco suggestions for dealing with multiplicity of languages in localities and whole countries (be sure you know the subtle difference between the 'locality' and 'whole country' cases).

7   Be able to recognize the Unesco suggestion for dealing with the problem of popular opposition.

8   Be able to recognize the gist of Fasold's answer to the question 'Is it possible?'.
9   Be able to recognize the gist of Fasold's answer to the question 'Does it work?'.
10 Most of the experiments that attempt to answer the question 'Does it work?' fail to control all variables. Be able to recognize a definition of the term 'uncontrolled variables' (pp. 300-1).
11 Be able to identify 'a very common uncontrolled variable' (p.301).
12 Be able to name the situation in which mother tongue education 'would not be at all advantageous' (p. 302).
13 Be able to recognize the gist of Fasold's answer to the question 'Is it worth it?'
14 Be able to recognize definitions of *small-group, national*, and *world* languages.
15 Be able to recognize three reasons why national languages are a reasonable alternative to both small-group and world languages as languages of education in many developing countries.
16 Be able to list the five suggested criteria for deciding which languages will be used in schools.
17 Be able to identify the most valid reason for justifying Frisian-medium education in Friesland.

Bibliography

Abdulaziz Mkilifi, M. H. 1978. Triglossia and Swahili–English bilingualism in Tanzania. In Fishman 1978:129–52.

_____ 1980. The Ecology of Tanzanian national language policy. In Polomé and Hill 1980:139–75.

Adler, Max. 1977. *Welsh and Other Dying Languages in Europe: A Sociolinguistic Study.* Hamburg: Helmut Buske Verlag.

Agheyisi, Rebecca and Fishman, Joshua. 1970. Language attitude studies: a brief survey of methodological approaches. *Anthropological Linguistics*, 12(5):137–57.

Agnew, John. 1981. Language shift and the politics of language: The case of the Celtic languages of the British Isles. *Language Problems and Language Planning*, 5(1):1–10.

Aksornkool, Namtip. 1980. EFL Planning in Thailand: a case study in language planning. Unpublished doctoral dissertation, Georgetown University.

Alatis, James (ed.). 1978. *Georgetown University Round Table on Languages and Linguistics 1978.* Washington, DC: Georgetown University Press.

Alisjahbana, S. Takdir. 1972. Writing a normative grammar for Indonesian. *Language Sciences* (February 1972), 11–14.

_____ 1976. *Language Planning for Modernization: The Case of Indonesian and Malaysian.* The Hague: Mouton.

Anshen, Frank. 1978. *Statistics for Linguists.* Rowley, MA: Newbury House.

Ansre, Gilbert. 1978. The use of indigenous languages in education in sub-Saharan Africa: presuppositions, lessons, and prospects. In Alatis 1978:285–301.

Apte, Mahadev. 1976. Multilingualism in India and its sociopolitical implications. In O'Barr and O'Barr 1976:141–64.

_____ 1979. Review of Sharma, P. Gopal and Kumar, Suresh (eds.). Indian Bilingualism: Proceedings of the Symposium Held under the Joint Auspices of Kendriya Hindi Sansthan and Jawaharlal Nehru University, February 1976. *Language*, 55(4):924–8.

Asuncion-Landé, Nobleza and Emy Pascasio. 1979. Language maintenance and code switching among Filipino bilingual speakers. In Mackey and Ornstein 1979:211–30.

Bailey, Charles-James. 1973. *Variation and Linguistic Theory.* Arlington, VA: Center for Applied Linguistics.

_____ 1975. The new linguistic framework and language planning. *Linguistics*, 158:153–6.

Bamgbose, Ayo (ed.). 1976. *Mother Tongue Education: The West African Experience.* London: Hodder and Stoughton.

Bell, Allan. 1982. This isn't the BBC: colonialism in New Zealand English. *Applied Linguistics* 3.

Bender, M. L., Cooper, R. L., and Ferguson, C. A. 1972. Language in Ethiopia: implications of a survey for sociolinguistic theory and method. *Language in Society*, 1(2):215–33. Also in Ohannessian, Ferguson, and Polomé 1975:191–208.

Berry, Jack. 1968. The making of alphabets. In Fishman 1968c:737–53.

_____ (ed.) 1976. Language and Education in the Third World. *International Journal of the Sociology of Language*, 8.

Blom, Jan-Petter and Gumperz, John. 1972. Social meaning in linguistic structure: code-switching in Norway. In Gumperz and Hymes 1972:407–34.

Bloomfield, Leonard. 1933. *Language*. New York: Holt, Rinehart, and Winston.

Bodine, Ann. 1975. Androcentrism in prescriptive grammar: singular 'they', sex-indefinite 'he', and 'he or she'. *Language in Society*, 4:129–46.

Bokamba, Eyamba and Tlou, Josia. 1977. The consequences of the language policies of African states vis-à-vis education. In Kotey and Der-Houssikian 1977:34–53.

Bourhis, Richard and Giles, Howard. 1976. The language of cooperation in Wales: a field study. *Language Sciences*, 42:13–16.

_____ 1977. Children's voices and ethnic categorization in Britain. *Mondo Lingvo Problemo*, 6(17):85–94.

_____ and Lambert, Wallace. 1975. Social consequences of accommodating one's style of speech: a cross-national investigation. *International Journal of the Sociology of Language*, 6:55–71. (=*Linguistics*, 166)

Branko, Franolic. 1980. Language policy and language planning in Yugoslavia with special reference to Croation and Macedonian. *Lingua*, 51(1):55–72.

Bright, William. 1966. *Sociolinguistics*. The Hague: Mouton.

_____ 1976. *Variation and Change in Language*. Stanford, CA: Stanford University Press.

Browning, Robert. 1982. Greek diglossia yesterday and today. *International Journal of the Sociology of Language*, 35:49–68.

Bruck, Margaret, Lambert, Wallace, and Tucker, G. Richard. 1977. Cognitive consequences of bilingual schooling: the St Lambert project through grade six. *Linguistics*, 187:13–33.

Brudner, Lilyan and White, Douglas. 1979. Language attitudes: behavior and intervening variables. In Mackey and Ornstein 1979:51–98.

Bull, William. 1955. The use of vernacular languages in fundamental education. *International Journal of American Linguistics*, 21:288–94. Also in Hymes 1964:527–33.

Byron, J. L. 1976. *Selection among Alternates in Language Standardization: The Case of Albanian*. The Hague: Mouton.

Carranza, Michael and Ryan, Ellen Bouchard. 1975. Evaluative reactions of bilingual Anglo and Mexican American adolescents towards speakers of English and Spanish. *International Journal of the Sociology of Language*, 6:83–104. (=*Linguistics*, 166).

Chong Hoi Kong. 1977. A study of language maintenance and shift in Singapore as a multilingual society. *RELC Journal*, 8(2):43–62.

Cohen, Andrew. 1974. Mexican-American evaluation judgements about language varieties. *International Journal of the Sociology of Language*, 3:33–52. (=*Linguistics*, 136)

_____ 1975. *A Sociolinguistic Approach to Bilingual Education*. Rowley, MA: Newbury House.

Cooper, Robert. 1974. Language Attitudes, 1. *International Journal of the Sociology of Language*, 3. (=*Linguistics* 136).

_____ 1975. Language Attitudes, 2. *International Journal of the Sociology of Language*, 6. (=*Linguistics* 166).

———— (ed.). 1982. *Language Spread: Studies in Diffusion and Social Change.* Blooming-ton, IN: Indiana University Press.

———— and Danet, Brenda. 1980. Language in the melting pot: the sociolinguistic context for language planning in Israel. *Language Problems and Language Planning,* 4(1):1–28.

———— and Fishman, Joshua. 1974. The study of language attitudes. *International Journal of the Sociology of Language,* 3:5–19. (=*Linguistics* 136).

Coupland, Nikolas. 1980. Style-shifting in a Cardiff work setting. *Language in Society,* 9(1):1–12.

Cronin, Sean. 1978. Nation building and the Irish language revival movement. *Eire-Ireland,* 13:7–14.

Dahlstedt, Karl-Hampus. 1977. Societal ideology and language cultivation: The case of Swedish. *International Journal of the Sociology of Language,* 10:17–50.

Dakin, Julian, Tiffen, Brian, and Widdowson, H. G. 1968. *Language in Education.* London: Oxford University Press.

d'Anglejan, Alison and Tucker, G. Richard. 1973. Sociolinguistic correlates of speech style in Quebec. In Shuy and Fasold 1973:1–27.

Davidson, T. T. L. 1969. Indian bilingualism and the evidence of the census of 1961. *Lingua,* 22:176–96.

DeFrancis, John. 1972. Language and script reform (in China). In Fishman 1972a:476–510.

———— 1977. *Colonialism and Language Policy in Vietnam.* The Hague: Mouton.

Denison, Norman. 1977. Language death or language suicide? *International Journal of the Sociology of Language,* 12:13–22. (=*Linguistics* 191).

Dewees, John. 1977. Orthography and identity: movement toward inertia. In Kotey and Der-Houssikian 1977:120–34.

Dorian, Nancy. 1978. The dying dialect and the role of the schools: East Sutherland Gaelic and Pennsylvania Dutch. In Alatis 1978: 646–56.

———— 1980. Language shift in community and individual: the phenomenon of the laggard semi-speaker. *International Journal of the Sociology of Language,* 25:85–94.

———— 1981. *Language Death: The Life Cycle of a Scottish Gaelic Dialect.* Philadelphia: University of Pennsylvania Press.

Dressler, Wolfgang. 1972. On the phonology of language death. In *Papers from the Eighth Regional Meeting of the Chicago Linguistic Society,* 448–57. Chicago: Chicago Linguistic Society.

———— and Wodak-Leodolter, Ruth. 1977. Language preservation and language death in Brittany. *International Journal of the Sociology of Language,* 12:31–44. (=*Linguistics* 191).

El-Dash, Linda and Tucker, G. Richard. 1975. Subjective reactions to various speech styles in Egypt. *International Journal of the Sociology of Language,* 6:33–54. (=*Linguistics,* 166).

'Element'. *Encyclopedia Americana,* 10:203–9. 1976.

Emmeneau, Murray. 1956. India as a linguistic area. *Language,* 32(1):3–16.

Engle, Patricia. 1975. *The Use of Vernacular Languages in Education: Language Medium in Early School Years for Minority Language Groups.* Arlington, VA: Center for Applied Linguistics.

Fasold, Ralph. 1980. The amazing replicability of a sociolinguistic pattern. *Papers in Linguistics,* 13(2–4):515–28.

Fellman, Jack. 1973. *The Revival of a Classical Tongue: Eliezer Ben Yehuda and the Modern Hebrew Language.* The Hague: Mouton.

———— 1975. On 'diglossia'. *Language Sciences,* 34:38–9.

Ferguson, Charles. 1959a. Diglossia. *Word,* 15:325–40. Also in Giglioli 1972:232–51 and in Hymes 1964:429–39.

———— 1959b. Myths about Arabic. In *Georgetown University Round Table on Languages and Linguistics 1959*, pp. 75–82. Washington, DC: Georgetown University Press. Also in Fishman 1968c:375–81.

———— 1962. The language factor in national development. *Anthropological Linguistics*, 4(1):23–7. Also in Rice 1962:8–14.

———— 1966. National sociolinguistic profile formulas. In Bright 1966:309–24.

———— 1968. Language development. In Fishman, Ferguson, and Das Gupta 1968:27–36.

Fishbein, M. 1965. A consideration of beliefs, attitudes and their relationships. In Steiner and Fishbein (eds.), *Current Studies in Social Psychology*, 107–120. New York: Holt, Rinehart, and Winston.

Fishman, Joshua. 1964. Language maintenance and language shift as fields of inquiry. *Linguistics*, 9:32–70.

———— 1965. Who speaks what language to whom and when? *Linguistics*, 2:67–8.

———— 1966. *Language Loyalty in the United States*. The Hague: Mouton.

———— 1967. Bilingualism with and without diglossia; diglossia with and without bilingualism. *Journal of Social Issues*, 32:29–38.

———— 1968a. Some contrasts between linguistically homogeneous and linguistically heterogeneous polities. In Fishman, Ferguson, and Das Gupta 1968:53–68. Also in *Sociological Inquiry*, 36(2):146–58. (1966).

———— 1968b. Nationality–nationalism and nation–nationism. In Fishman, Ferguson, and Das Gupta 1968:39–52.

———— (ed.). 1968c. *Readings in the Sociology of Language*. The Hague: Mouton.

———— 1968d. Sociolinguistics and the language problems of developing countries. In Fishman, Ferguson, and Das Gupta 1968:3–16.

———— 1968e. Sociolinguistic perspective on the study of bilingualism. *Linguistics*, 39:21–49.

———— (ed.). 1971. *Advances in the Sociology of Language*, Volume 1. The Hague: Mouton.

———— (ed.). 1972a. *Advances in the Sociology of Language*, Volume 2. The Hague: Mouton.

———— 1972b. Domains and the relationship between micro- and macro-sociolinguistics. In Gumperz and Hymes 1972:435–53.

———— 1972c. *Language and Nationalism: Two Integrative Essays*. Rowley,MA: Newbury House.

———— 1972d. Societal bilingualism: stable and transitional. Section VI of *The Sociology of Language*, 91–106. Rowley, MA: Newbury House. Also in Fishman, Joshua. *Sociolinguistics: A Brief Introduction*, 73–90. Rowley, MA: Newbury House.

———— (ed.). 1974. *Advances in Language Planning*. The Hague: Mouton.

———— 1975. The 'official languages' of Israel: their status in law and police attitudes and knowledge concerning them. In Savard, J. and Vigneault, R. (eds.), *Multilingual Political Systems: Problems and Solutions*, 497–535. Quebec: Les preses de l'Université Laval.

———— 1976. The spread of English as a new perspective for the study of 'language maintenance and language shift'. *Studies in Language Learning*, 1(2):59–104.

———— 1977. *Bilingual Education: An International Sociological Perspective*. Rowley, MA: Newbury House.

———— (ed.) 1978. *Advances in the Study of Societal Multilingualism*. The Hague: Mouton.

———— and Cooper, Robert. 1976. The sociology of language in Israel. *Language*

Sciences, 40:28–31.

———— and Fellman, Jack. 1977. Language planning in Israel: solving terminological problems. In Rubin et al. 1977:79–95.

———— and Fishman, David. 1978. Yiddish in Israel: a case study of efforts to revise a monocentric language policy. In Fishman 1978:185–262.

———— Cooper, Robert, and Conrad, Andrew, et al. 1977. *The Spread of English*. Rowley, MA: Newbury House.

———— Ferguson, Charles and Das Gupta, Jyotirindra (eds.). 1968. *Language Problems of Developing Nations*. New York: John Wiley and Sons.

Flint, E. H. 1979. Stable societal diglossia in Norfolk Island. In Mackey and Ornstein 1979:295–334.

Ford, Jerome. 1974. Sociolinguistic-geographic profiles. *Georgetown University Working Papers on Languages and Linguistics*, no. 8, 99–116. Washington, DC: Georgetown University Press.

Frender, Robert and Lambert, Wallace. 1973. Speech style and scholastic success: the tentative relationships and possible implications for lower social class children. In Shuy 1973:237–72.

Frisian News Items, 35(1). (January–February 1979). Grand Rapids, MI: Frisian Information Bureau.

Frisian News Items, 35(2). (March 1979). Grand Rapids, MI: Frisian Information Bureau.

Gal, Susan. 1978a. Peasant men can't get wives: language change and sex roles in a bilingual community. *Language in Society*, 7(1):1–16.

———— 1978b. Variation and change in patterns of speaking: language shift in Austria. In D. Sankoff (ed.), *Linguistic Variation: Models and Methods*, pp. 227–38. New York: Academic Press.

———— 1979. *Language Shift: Social Determinants of Linguistic Change in Bilingual Austria*. New York: Academic Press.

Gardner, Robert. 1979. Social psychological aspects of second language acquisition. In Giles and St Clair 1979:193–220.

Garvin, Paul. 1973. Some comments on language planning. In Rubin and Shuy 1973:24–33.

———— and Mathiot, Madeleine. 1956. The urbanization of the Guaraní language. In Wallace, A. F. C. (ed.), *Men and Cultures: Selected Papers from the Fifth International Congress of Anthropological and Ethnological Sciences*, pp. 365–74. Philadelphia: University of Pennsylvania Press. Also in Fishman 1968c:365–74.

Genesee, Frederick, Lambert, Wallace, and Tucker, G. Richard. 1978. An experiment in trilingual education: Report 4. *Language Learning*, 28(2):343–65.

Giglioli, Pier Paolo. (ed.). 1972. *Language and Social Context*. Harmondsworth, England: Penguin Books.

Giles, Howard. 1973. Accent mobility: a model and some data. *Anthropological Linguistics*, 15:87–105.

———— 1977. *Language, Ethnicity and Intergroup Relations*. London: Academic Press.

———— and Bourhis, Richard. MS Voice and racial categorization in Britain. Mimeographed.

———— and Bourhis, Richard. 1976. Methodological issues in dialect perception: some social psychological perspectives. *Anthropological Linguistics*, 187:294–304.

———— and Powesland, P. 1975. *Speech Style and Social Evaluation*. London: Academic Press.

———— and St Clair, Robert. 1979. *Language and Social Psychology*. Oxford: Basil Blackwell Publisher.

———— Bourhis, Richard, and Taylor, Donald. 1977. Towards a theory of language in ethnic group relations. In Giles 1977:307–49.

Gold, David. 1981. An introduction to English in Israel. *Language Problems and Language Planning*, 5(1):11–56.

Gould, Philip. 1977. Indonesian learners' attitudes towards speakers of English. *RELC Journal*, 8(2):69–84.

Greenberg, Joseph. 1956. The measurement of linguistic diversity. *Language*, 32(2): 109–15.

Greenfield, Lawrence. 1972. Situational measures of normative language views in relation to person, place and topic among Puerto Rican bilinguals. In Fishman 1972a:17–35. Also in *Anthropos*, 65:602–18 (1970).

Griffen, Toby. 1980. Nationalism and the emergence of a new standard Welsh. *Language Problems and Language Planning*, 4(3):187–94.

Grimes, Barbara. (ed.). 1978. *Ethnologue* (9th edn). Huntington Beach, CA: Wycliffe Bible Translators.

Guilford, J. P. 1956. *Fundamental Statistics in Psychology and Education*. New York: McGraw-Hill, Inc.

Gumperz, John. 1962. Types of linguistic communities. *Anthropological Linguistics*, 4(1):28–40. Also in Fishman 1968c:460–72 and in Gumperz 1971:97–13.

_____ 1964. Linguistic and social interaction in two communities. *American Anthropologist*, 66:6 (Part 2) 137–53.

_____ 1971. *Language in Social Groups*. Stanford, CA: Stanford University Press.

_____ 1977. The sociolinguistic significance of conversational code-switching. *RELC Journal*, 8(2):1–34.

_____ and Hymes, Dell (eds.). 1972. *Directions in Sociolinguistics*. New York: Holt, Rinehart, and Winston.

_____ and Naim, C. M. 1960. Formal and informal standards in Hindi regional language area. *International Journal of American Linguistics*, 26(3):92–118 (III). Also in Gumperz 1971:48–76.

Harries, Lyndon. 1968. Swahili in modern East Africa. In Fishman, Ferguson, and Das Gupta 1968:415–31.

_____ 1976. The nationalization of Swahili in Kenya. *Language Sciences*, 5(2):153–64.

Hatch, Evelyn and Farhady, Hossein. 1982. *Research Design and Statistics of Applied Linguistics*. Rowley, MA: Newbury House.

Haugen, Einar. 1959. Planning for a standard language in modern Norway. *Anthropological Linguistics*, 1(3):8–21.

_____ 1966a. *Language Conflict and Language Planning: The Case of Modern Norwegian*. Cambridge, MA: Harvard University Press.

_____ 1966b. Linguistics and language planning. In Bright 1966:50–71.

_____ 1968. Language planning in modern Norway. In Fishman 1968c:673–86.

_____ 1971. Instrumentalism in language planning. In Rubin and Jernudd 1971: 281–92.

Heath, Shirley Brice. 1980. Standard English: biography of a symbol. In Shopen and Williams 1980:3–32.

Heller, Monica. 1978. Bonjour, hello?: Negotiations of language choice in Montreal. *Papers from the Fourth Annual Meeting of the Berkeley Linguistics Society*, pp. 33–51. Berkeley, CA: Berkeley Linguistics Society.

Helwig, Jane. 1978. *SAS Introductory Guide.* Cary, NC: SAS Institute, Inc.

Herman, Simon. 1968. Explorations in the social psychology of language choice. In Fishman 1968c:492–511.

Hill, C. P. 1980. Some developments in language and education in Tanzania since 1969. In Polomé and Hill 1980:362–409.

Hill, Jane and Hill, Kenneth. 1980. Metaphorical switching in Modern Nahuatl:

change and contradiction. *Papers from the Sixteenth Regional Meeting of the Chicago Linguistic Society*, pp. 121–33. Chicago: Chicago Linguistic Society.

Hinnebusch, Thomas. 1979. Swahili. In Shopen 1979:209–94.

Hofman, John E. and Fisherman, Haya. 1972. Language shift and language maintenance in Israel. In Fishman 1972a:342–64. Also in *International Migration Review*, 5:204–26 (1971).

Hoover, Mary Rhodes. 1978. Community attitudes toward Black English. *Language in Society*, 7(1):65–87.

Hopkins, Tometro. 1977. The development and implementation of the national language policy in Kenya. In Kotey and Der-Houssikian 1977:84–96.

Householder, Fred W., Jr. 1963. Greek diglossia. In Woodworth and DiPietro 1963:109–32.

Huffines, M. Lois. 1980. Pennsylvania German: maintenance and shift. *International Journal of the Sociology of Language*, 25:42–58.

Hughes, Everett. 1972. The linguistic division of labor in industrial and urban societies. In Fishman 1972a:296–309.

Hymes, Dell. 1964. *Language in Culture and Society*. New York: Harper and Row.

———— (ed.). 1971. *Pidginization and Creolization of Languages*. Cambridge: Cambridge University Press.

———— 1974. *Foundations in Sociolinguistics: An Ethnographic Approach*. Philadelphia: University of Pennsylvania Press.

Jaakkola, Magdalena. 1976. Diglossia and bilingualism among two minorities in Sweden. *Linguistics*, 183:67–84.

James, Linda. 1976. Black children's perceptions of Black English. *Journal of Psycholinguistic Research*, 5(4):377–87.

Jernudd, Bjorn. 1971. Notes on economic analysis for solving language problems. In Rubin and Jernudd 1971:263–76.

———— 1973. Language planning as a type of language treatment. In Rubin and Shuy 1973:11–23.

———— and Das Gupta, Jyotirindra. 1971. Towards a theory of language planning. In Rubin and Jernudd 1971:195–216.

Johnson, Bruce. 1975. More on diglossia. *Language Sciences*, 37:37–8.

———— 1977. Language functions in Africa: a typological view. In Kotey and Der-Houssikian 1977:54–67.

Jones, R. M. 1979. Welsh bilingualism: four documents. In Mackey and Ornstein 1979:231–46.

Kachru, Braj. 1977. Linguistic schizophrenia and language census: A note on the Indian situation. *Linguistics*, 186:17–33.

Kachru, Yamuna and Bhatia, Tej. 1978. The emerging 'dialect' conflict in Hindi: a case of glottopolitics. *International Journal of the Sociology of Language*, 16:47–58.

Kahane, Henry and Kahane, Renée. 1979. Decline and survival of Western prestige languages. *Language*, 55(1):183–98.

Kavugha, Douglas and Bobb, Donald. 1980. The use of language in the law courts in Tanzania. In Polomé and Hill 1980.

Kaye, Alan. 1970. Modern Standard Arabic and the colloquials. *Lingua*, 24:374–91.

Kazazis, Kostas. 1968. Sunday Greek. In *Papers from the Fourth Regional Meeting of the Chicago Linguistic Society*, pp. 130–40. Chicago: Chicago Linguistic Society

———— 1976. A superficially unusual feature of Greek diglossia. In *Papers from the Twelfth Regional Meeting of the Chicago Linguistic Society*, pp. 369–75. Chicago: Chicago Linguistic Society.

———— MS. Partial linguistic autobiography of a diglossic person. Unpublished.

Keller, Fred S. 1968. Goodbye teacher ... *Journal of Behavior Analysis* 1:79–89.

Kelley, Gerald. 1966. The status of Hindi as a lingua franca. In Bright 1966:299–308.

Kelz, Heinrich. 1981. Sprachplanung auf den Philippinen und die Entwicklung einer philippinischen Nationalsprache. *Language Problems and Language Planning*, 5(2):115–36.

Khubchandani, Lachman. 1977. Language ideology and language development. *Linguistics*, 193:33–52.

———— 1978. Distribution of contact languages in India: a study of the 1961 bilingualism returns. In Fishman 1978:553–86.

Kimple, J., Jr. 1968. Language shift and the interpretation of conversations. In Fishman 1968c:598–610. Also in *Lingua*, 23:127–34.

Kirk, Dudley. 1946. *Europe's Population in the Interwar Years*. Princeton: Princeton University Press.

Klein, Harriet Manelis and Stark, Louisa. 1977. Indian languages of the Paraguayan Chaco. *Anthropological Linguistics*, 19(8):378–98.

Kloss, Heinz. 1966. Types of multilingual communities: A discussion of ten variables. *Sociological Inquiry*, 36:135–45.

———— 1968. Notes concerning a language–nation typology. In Fishman, Ferguson, and Das Gupta 1968:69–86.

———— 1977. *The American Bilingual Tradition*. Rowley, MA: Newbury House.

———— and McConnell, Grant. 1974. *Linguistic Composition of the Nations of the World*, Vol. 1, *Central and Western South Asia*. Quebec: Les Preses de l'Université Laval.

———— 1977. *The Written Languages of the World: A Survey of the Degree and Modes of Use*. Quebec: Les Preses de l'Université Laval.

Knab, Tim and Hasson de Knab, Liliane. 1979. Language death in the valley of the Puebla: a socio-geographic approach. *Papers from the Fifth Annual Meeting of the Berkeley Linguistics Society*, pp. 471–83. Berkeley, CA: Berkeley Linguistics Society.

Kola, C. V. 1977. Hybrid conversational Malayalam. *Anthropological Linguistics*, 19(6):265–73.

Kotey, Paul and Der-Houssikian, Haig. (eds.). 1977. *Language and Linguistic Problems in Africa*. Columbia, SC: Hornbeam Press.

Kroch, Anthony. 1978. Towards a theory of social dialect variation. *Language in Society*, 7(1):17–36.

Krysin, Leonid. 1979. Command of various language subsystems as diglossic phenomenon. *International Journal of the Sociology of Language*, 21:141–52.

Kuo, Eddie C. Y. 1979. Measuring communicativity in multilingual societies: the case of Singapore and West Malaysia. *Anthropological Linguistics*, 21(7):328–40.

Labov, William. 1966. *The Social Stratification of English in New York City*. Washington, DC: Center for Applied Linguistics.

———— 1971. The notion 'system' in creole languages, in Hymes 1971:447–72.

———— 1972a. *Sociolinguistic Patterns*. Philadelphia: University of Pennsylvania Press./ Oxford: Basil Blackwell Publisher.

———— 1972b. *Language in the Inner City*. Philadephia: University of Pennsylvania Press./Oxford: Basil Blackwell Publisher.

Ladefoged, Peter, Glick, R., and Criper, C. 1972. *Language in Uganda*. London: Oxford University Press.

Lambert, Wallace. 1967. A social psychology of bilingualism. *Journal of Social Issues*, 23(2):91–109.

———— 1979. Language as a factor in intergroup relations. In Giles and St Clair 1979:186–92.

———— Gardner, R., Olton, R., and Tunstall, K. 1968. A study of the roles, attitudes and motivation in second-language learning. In Fishman 1968c:473–91.

—— Giles, Howard, and Picard, Omer. 1975. Language attitudes in a French-American community. *International Journal of the Sociology of Language*, 4:127–52. (=*Linguistics* 158)

—— Hodgson, R., Gardner, R., and Fillenbaum, S. 1960. Evaluative reactions to spoken language. *Journal of Abnormal and Social Psychology*, 60:44–51.

Lamy, Paul (ed.). 1979. Language planning and identity planning. *International Journal of the Sociology of Language*, 20.

Laosa, Luis. 1975. Bilingualism in three United States Hispanic groups: contextual use of language by children and adults in their families. *Journal of Educational Psychology*, 67(5):617–27.

Le Page, Robert. 1964. *The National Language Question*. London: Oxford University Press.

—— 1972. Preliminary report on the sociolinguistic survey of the Cayo District, British Honduras. *Language in Society*, 1(1):155–72.

—— Christie, P., Jurdant B., Weekes, A. J., and Tabouret- Keller, Andrée. 1974. Further report on the sociolinguistic survey of multilingual communities: survey of Cayo District, British Honduras. *Language in Society*, 3(1):1–32.

Lewis, E. Glyn. 1972a. Migration and language in the USSR. In Fishman 1972a:310–41.

—— 1972b. *Multilingualism in the Soviet Union: Aspects of Language Policy and Implementation*. The Hague: Mouton.

—— 1975. Attitude to language among bilingual children and adults in Wales. *International Journal of the Sociology of Language*, 4:103–25.

—— 1977. Bilingualism in education-cross-national research. *Linguistics*, 198:5–30.

—— 1978. Migration and the decline of the Welsh language. In Fishman 1972a:263–352.

Li, Charles and Thompson, Sandra A. 1979. Chinese: dialect variations and language reform. In Shopen 1979:295–332.

Lieberson, Stanley. 1964. An extension of Greenberg's linguistic diversity measures. *Language*, 40:526–31. Also in Fishman 1968c:546–53.

—— 1967. Language questions in censuses. In Lieberson, Stanley (ed.), *Explorations in Sociolinguistics*, pp. 134–51. The Hague: Mouton. Also in *Sociological Inquiry*, 36(2):134–51. (1966).

—— 1972. Bilingualism in Montreal: a demographic analysis. In Fishman 1972a:231–54.

—— 1980. Procedures for improving sociolinguistic surveys of language maintenance and language shift. *International Journal of the Sociology of Language*, 25:11–27.

—— and Hansen, Lynn. 1974. National development, mother tongue diversity, and the comparative study of nations. *American Sociological Review*, 39:523–41.

—— and McCabe, Edward. 1978. Domains of language usage and mother tongue shift in Nairobi. *International Journal of the Sociology of Language*, 18:69–82.

—— Dalto, Guy, and Johnston, Mary Ellen. 1975. The course of mother-tongue diversity in nations. *American Journal of Sociology*, 81(1):34–61.

Lind, E. Allan and O'Barr, William. 1979. The social significance of speech in the courtroom. In Giles and St Clair 1979:66–87.

Linn, L. 1965. Verbal attitudes and overt behavior: A study of racial discrimination. *Social Forces* 43:353–64.

Lorwin, Val. 1972. Linguistic pluralism and tension in modern Belgium. In Fishman 1972a:386–412.

Lunt, Horace. 1959. The creation of standard Macedonian: Some facts and attitudes. *Anthropological Linguistics*, 1(5):19–25.

McConnell, Grant. 1979. Constructing language profiles by polity. In Mackey and Ornstein 1979:23–50.

McDougall, A. and Bruck, Margaret. 1978. English reading within the French immersion programme: a comparison of the effects of the introduction of English reading at different grade levels. *Language Learning*, 26(1):37–43.

Mackay, Donald. 1980. On the goals, principles, and procedures for prescriptive grammar: singular they. *Language in Society*, 9(3):349–68.

Mackey, William. 1978. Cost–benefit quantification of language-teaching behavior. *Die Neueren Sprachen*, 1(2):2–32.

_____ and Beebe, Von Nieda. 1977. *Bilingual Schools for a Bicultural Community: Miami's Adaptation to the Cuban Refugees*. Rowley, MA: Newbury House.

_____ and Cartwright, Donald. 1979. Geocoding language loss from census data. In Mackey and Ornstein 1979:69–96.

_____ and Ornstein, Jacob. 1979. *Sociolinguistic Studies in Language Contact: Methods and Cases*. The Hague: Mouton.

Macnamara, John. 1966. The effects of instruction in a weaker language. *Journal of Social Issues*, 23(2):121–35.

_____ 1971. Successes and failures in the movement for the restoration of Irish. In Rubin and Jernudd 1971:65–94.

Magner, Thomas. 1978. Diglossia in Split. *Folia Slavica*, 1(3):400–36.

Meeus, Baudewijn. 1979. A diglossic situation: standard vs. dialect. In Mackey and Ornstein 1979:335–46.

Meisel, John. 1978. Values, language, and politics in Canada. In Fishman 1978: 665–718.

Mills, Harriet. 1956. Language reform in China: Some recent developments. *Far Eastern Quarterly*, 15:517–40.

Milroy, Lesley. 1980. *Language and Social Networks*. Oxford: Basil Blackwell Publisher.

_____ and Margrain, Sue. 1980. Vernacular language loyalty and social network. *Language and Society*, 9(1):43–70.

Morag, Shelomo. 1959. Planned and unplanned development in Modern Israeli Hebrew. *Lingua*, 8:247–63.

Moulton, William. 1963. What standard for diglossia? The case of German Switzerland. In Woodworth and DiPietro 1963:133–48.

Nadel, Elizabeth, Fishman, Joshua, and Cooper, Robert. 1977. English in Israel: A sociolinguistic study. *Anthropological Linguistics*, 19(1):26–53.

Nakir, Moshe. 1978. Normativism and educated speech in Modern Hebrew. *International Journal of the Sociology of Language*, 18:49–68.

Neustupný, Jiri. 1970. Basic types of treatment of language problems. *Linguistic Communications*, 1:77–98.

_____ 1977. Language planning for Australia. *Language Sciences*, 45:28–31.

Nie, N. H., Hull, C. H., Jenkins, J. G., Steinbrenner, K., and Brenk, D.H . 1975. *Statistical Package for the Social Sciences*, 2nd edn. New York: McGraw-Hill, Inc.

Noss, Richard. 1971. Politics and language policy in Southeast Asia. *Language Sciences* (August 1971), 25–32.

Nyerere, Julius. 1968. *Ujamaa* – Essays on Socialism. London: Oxford University Press.

O'Barr, Jean. 1976a. The evolution of Tanzanian political institutions. In O'Barr and O'Barr 1976:49–68.

_____ 1976b. Language and politics in Tanzanian governmental institutions. In O'Barr and O'Barr 1976:69–84.

O'Barr, William. 1976a. Language use and language policy in Tanzania: an overview.

In O'Barr and O'Barr 1976:35–48.

⎯⎯⎯ 1976b. Language and politics in a rural Tanzanian council. In O'Barr and O'Barr 1976:117–36.

⎯⎯⎯ and O'Barr, Jean (eds.). 1976. *Language and Politics*. The Hague: Mouton.

O Cuiv, Brian (ed.). *A View of the Irish Language*. Dublin: Stationery Office.

Ohannessian, Sirarpi, Ferguson, Charles, and Polomé, Edgar (eds.). 1975. *Language Surveys in Developing Nations: Papers and Reports on Sociolinguistic Surveys*. Arlington, VA: Center for Applied Linguistics.

Ó Huallacháin, Colmán. 1962. Bilingualism in education in Ireland. *Georgetown University Round Table on Languages and Linguistics 1962*, pp.75–84. Washington, DC: Georgetown University Press.

⎯⎯⎯ 1970. Bilingual education program in Ireland: recent experiences in home and adult support, teacher training, provision of instructional materials. *Georgetown University Round Table on Languages and Linguistics 1970,* pp. 179–93. Washington, DC: Georgetown University Press.

Omar, Asmah. 1975. Supranational standardization of spelling system: the case of Malaysia and Indonesia. *International Journal of the Sociology of Language*, 5:77–92.

Osgood, Charles, Suci, C., and Tannenbaum, Percy. 1957. *The Measurement of Meaning*. Urbana: University of Illinois Press.

Pandit, Prabodh. 1975. The linguistic survey of India – perspectives on language use. In Ohannessian, Ferguson, and Polomé 1975:71–86.

Parasher, S. N. 1980. Mother-tongue-English diglossia: a case study of educated Indian bilinguals' language use. *Anthropological Linguistics*, 22(4):151–68.

Perez-Alonso, Jesus. 1979. Catalan – an example of the current language struggle in Spain: sociopolitical and pedagogical implications. *International Journal of the Sociology of Language*, 21:109–25.

'Periodic Law'. *Encyclopedia Americana*, 21:587–91. 1976.

Pietersen, Liewe. 1978. Issues and trends in Frisian bilingualism. In Fishman 1978:353–400.

Pitts, Ruth Ann. 1978. The effects of exclusively French-language schooling on self-esteem in Quebec. *Canadian Modern Language Review*, 34(3):372–80.

Platt, John. 1977. A model for polyglossia and multilingualism (with special reference to Singapore and Malaysia). *Language in Society*, 6(3):361–78.

Poll, Solomon. 1980. The sacred–secular conflict in the use of Hebrew and Yiddish among ultra-orthodox Jews of Jerusalem. *International Journal of the Sociology of Language*, 24:109–26.

Polomé, Edgar. 1975. Problems and techniques of a sociolinguistically oriented language survey: the case of the Tanzania survey. In Ohannessian, Ferguson, and Polomé 1975:31–50.

⎯⎯⎯ 1980a. The languages of Tanzania. In Polomé and Hill 1980:1–25.

⎯⎯⎯ 1980b. Tanzania: a socio-linguistic perspective. In Polomé and Hill 1980:103–38.

⎯⎯⎯ 1982. Rural versus urban multilingualism in Tanzania: an outline. *International Journal of the Sociology of Language*, 34:167–81.

⎯⎯⎯ and Hill, C. P. 1980. *Language in Tanzania*. Oxford: Oxford University Press for the International African Institute.

Pool, Jonathan. 1972. National development and language diversity. In Fishman 1972a:213–30.

⎯⎯⎯ 1979. Language planning and identity planning. *International Journal of the Sociology of Language*, 20:5–21.

Poplack, Shana. 1978. On dialect acquisition and communicative competence: the case of Puerto Rican bilinguals. *Language in Society*, 7(1):89–104.

Rabin, Chaim. 1974. *A Short History of the Hebrew Language*. Jerusalem.

Ramos, M., Aguilar, J. V., and Sibayan, Bonifacio. 1967. *The Determination and Implementation of Language Policy*. Dobbs Ferry, NY: Oceana Publications.

Ray, Punya Sloka. 1963. *Language Standardization*. The Hague: Mouton.

―――― 1968. Language standardization. In Fishman 1968c:754–65.

Rey, Alberto. 1977. Accent and employability. *Language Sciences*, 47:7–12.

Rice, Frank. 1962. *Study of the Role of Second Languages in Asia, Africa and Latin America*. Washington, DC: Center for Applied Linguistics.

Rona, José Pedro. 1966. The social and cultural status of Guaraní in Paraguay. In Bright 1966:277–98.

Ros, Maria and Giles, Howard. 1979. The Valencian language situation: an accommodation perspective. *ITL*, 44:3–24.

Rosier, Paul and Farella, Merilyn. 1976. Bilingual education at Rock Point - some early results. *TESOL Quarterly*, 10(4):379–88.

Rubin, Joan. 1968a. Language education in Paraguay. In Fishman, Ferguson, and Das Gupta 1968:477–88.

―――― 1968b. Bilingual usage in Paraguay. In Fishman 1968c:512–30.

―――― 1968c. *National Bilingualism in Paraguay*. The Hague: Mouton.

―――― 1971. Evaluation and language planning. In Rubin and Jernudd 1971:217–52. Also in Fishman 1972a:476–510.

―――― 1973. Language planning: discussion of some current issues. In Rubin and Shuy 1973:1–10.

―――― (ed.). 1977. Language Planning in the United States. *International Journal of the Sociology of Language*, 11.

―――― 1978. Toward bilingual education for Paraguay. In Alatis 1978:189–201.

―――― and Jernudd, Björn (eds.). 1971. *Can Languages be Planned?* Honolulu: University Press of Hawaii.

―――― and Shuy, Roger (eds.). 1973. *Language Planning: Current Issues and Research*. Washington, DC: Georgetown University Press.

―――― Jernudd, Björn, Das Gupta, Jyotirindra, Fishman, Joshua, and Ferguson, Charles. 1977. *Language Planning Processes*. The Hague: Mouton.

Rustow, Dankwart. 1968. Language, modernization and nationhood – an attempt at typology. In Fishman, Ferguson, and Das Gupta 1968:87–106.

Ryan, Ellen Bouchard and Carranza, Michael. 1977. Ingroup and outgroup reactions to Mexican American language varieties. In Giles 1977:59–82.

―――― and Giles, Howard (eds.). 1982. *Attitudes Towards Language Variation: Social and Applied Contexts*. London: Edward Arnold.

Ryan, Thomas A., Jr., Joiner, Brian, and Joiner, Barbara. 1976. *Minitab Student Handbook*. North Scituate, MA: Duxbury Press.

Sage, J. C. (ed.). 1980. Standardization of Nomenclature. *International Journal of the Sociology of Language*, 23.

Sankoff, Gillian. 1980. Language use in multilingual societies: some alternate approaches. In G. Sankoff, *The Social Life of Language*, pp. 29–46. Philadelphia: University of Pennsylvania Press. Also in Pride and Holmes (eds.), *Sociolinguistics*, pp. 33–51. Harmondsworth, England: Penguin Books, 1972.

SAS User's Guide, 1979 edn. 1979. Raleigh, NC: SAS Institute, Inc.

Saville-Troike, Muriel. 1982. *The Ethnography of Communication*. Oxford: Basil Blackwell Publisher.

Scherer, Klaus. 1979. Voice and speech correlates of perceived social influence in simulated juries. In Giles and St Clair 1979:88–120.

Schmidt, Richard and McCreary, Carol. 1977. Standard and super-standard English:

recognition and use of prescriptive rules by native and non-native speakers. *TESOL Quarterly*, 11(4):415–29.

Scotton, Carol Myers. 1978. Language in East Africa: linguistic patterns and political ideologies. In Fishman 1978:719–60.

―――― and Ury, William. 1977. Bilingual strategies: the social functions of code-switching. *International Journal of the Sociology of Language*, 13:5–20.

Seligman, C., Tucker, G. Richard, and Lambert, Wallace. 1972. The effects of speech style and other attributes on teachers' attitudes towards pupils. *Language in Society*, 1:131–42.

Shaffer, Douglas. 1978. Afrikaans as a case study in vernacular elevation and standardization. *Linguistics*, 213:51–64.

Shaklee, Margaret. 1980. The rise of standard English. In Shopen and Williams 1980:33–62.

Shavelson, Richard. 1981. *Statistical Reasoning for the Behavioral Sciences*. Boston: Allyn and Bacon.

Shopen, Timothy (ed.). 1979. *Languages and their Status*. Cambridge, MA: Winthrop Publishers.

―――― and Williams, Joseph (eds.). 1980. *Standards and Dialects in English*. Cambridge, MA: Winthrop Publishers.

Shukla, Shaligram. 1974. *Phonological change and dialect variation in Middle Indo-Aryan*. In Anderson, J. and Jones, C. (eds.), *Historical Linguistics* II, pp. 391-401. Amsterdam: North-Holland Publishing Co.

Shuy, Roger (ed.). 1973. *Georgetown University Round Table on Languages and Linguistics 1972*. Washington, DC: Georgetown University Press.

―――― 1977. Problems of communication in the cross-cultural medical interview. *ITL: A Review of Applied Linguistics*, 35.

―――― and Fasold, Ralph (eds.). 1973. *Language Attitudes: Current Trends and Prospects*. Washington, DC: Georgetown University Press.

―――― and Williams, Frederick. 1973. Stereotyped attitudes of selected English dialect communities. In Shuy and Fasold 1973:85–96.

―――― Baratz, Joan, and Wolfram, Walter. 1969. *Sociolinguistic factors in speech identification*. Project Report No. MH 1504801, National Institute of Mental Health. Washington, DC: NIMH.

Sibayan, Bonifacio. 1978. Bilingual education in the Philippines: strategy and structure. In Alatis 1978:302–29.

Sjoberg, Andree. 1966. Socio-cultural and linguistic factors in the development of writing systems for preliterate peoples. In Bright 1966:260–76.

Sotiropoulos, Dimitri. 1977. Diglossia and the national language question in modern Greece. *Linguistics*, 197:5–31.

Southworth, Franklin. 1977. Functional aspects of linguistic heterogeneity. In Sharma, P. Gopal and Kumar, Suresh (eds.). *Indian Bilingualism: Proceedings of the Symposium Held under the Joint Auspices of Kendriya Hindi Sansthan and Jawaharlal Nehru University*, February 1976, pp. 210–31. Agra: Kendriya Hindi Sansthan.

Spolsky, Bernard. 1972. *The Language Education of Minority Children: Selected Readings*. Rowley, MA: Newbury House.

―――― 1977a. American Indian bilingual education. *Linguistics*, 198:57-72.

―――― 1977b. The establishment of language education policy in multilingual societies. In Spolsky and Cooper 1977:1–21.

―――― and Cooper, Robert. (eds.). 1977. *Frontiers of Bilingual Education*. Rowley, MA: Newbury House.

―――― (eds.). 1978. *Case Studies in Bilingual Education*. Rowley, MA: Newbury House.

Sreedhar, M. V. 1979. The functions of bilingualism in Nagaland. *International Journal of the Sociology of Language*, 22:103–14.

Sridhar, S. N. 1978. On the functions of code-mixing in Kannada. *International Journal of the Sociology of Language*, 16:109–18.

Stern, H. H. 1963. *Foreign Languages in Primary Education*. Hamburg: Unesco Institute for Education.

———— 1978. French immersion in Canada: achievements and directions. *Canadian Modern Language Review*, 34(5):836–54.

Stewart, William. 1962. An outline of linguistic typology for describing multi-lingualism. In Rice 1962:15–25.

———— 1963. Functional distribution of Creole and French in Haiti. In Woodworth and DiPietro 1963:149–62.

———— 1968. A sociolinguistic typology for describing national multilingualism. In Fishman 1968c:531–45.

Swain, Merrill. 1978. French immersion: Early, late or partial? *Canadian Modern Language Review*, 34(3):577–85.

Tabouret-Keller, Andre. 1968. Sociological factors of language maintenance and language shift: a methodological approach based on European and African examples In Fishman, Ferguson, and Das Gupta 1968:107–18.

———— 1972. A contribution to the sociological study of language maintenance and language shift. In Fishman 1972a:365–76.

Tadadjeu, Maurice. 1977. Cost-benefit analysis and language education planning in sub-Saharan Africa. In Kotey and Der-Houssikian 1977:3–34.

Tauli, Valter. 1968. Introduction to a theory of language planning. In *Acta Universitatis Upsaliensis, Studia Philologiae Scandinavicae Upsaliensia*, 6. Uppsala: University of Uppsala.

Taylor, Donald, Meynard, Roch, and Rheault, Elizabeth. 1977. Threat to ethnic identity and second-language learning. In Giles 1977:99–118.

Taylor, Orlando. 1973. Teachers' attitudes toward Black and nonstandard English as measured by the Language Attitude Scale. In Shuy and Fasold 1973:174–201.

Thelander, Mats. 1976. Code-switching or code-mixing? *Linguistics*, 183:103–24.

Thompson, Roger. 1974. Mexican American language loyalty and the validity of the 1970 census. In Fishman 1972a:213–30.

Thorburn, Thomas. 1971. Cost-benefit analysis in language planning. In Rubin and Jernudd 1971:253–62. Also in Fishman 1972a:511–19.

Timm, Lenora. 1980. Bilingualism, diglossia and language shift in Brittany. *International Journal of the Sociology of Language*, 25:29–42.

Tosi, Arturo. 1979. Mother-tongue teaching for the children of migrants. *Language Teaching and Linguistics: Abstracts*, 12(4): 213–31.

Trudgill, Peter. 1974. *Sociolinguistics: An Introduction*. Harmondsworth, England: Penguin Books.

———— and Tzavaras, George. 1977. Why Albanian-Greeks are not Albanians: language shift in Attica and Biotia. In Giles 1977:171–84.

Tucker, G. Richard. 1977. Bilingual Education: Current Perspectives, Vol. 2, *Linguistics*. Arlington, VA: Center for Applied Linguistics.

———— Hamayan, Else, and Genesee, Fred. 1976. Affective, cognitive and social factors in second-language acquisition. *Canadian Modern Language Review*, 32(3):214–26.

Unesco. 1953. *The Use of Vernacular Languages in Education*. Paris: Unesco. Excerpt in Fishman 1968c:688–716.

Valdman, Albert. 1968. Language standardization in a diglossia situation: Haiti. In Fishman, Ferguson, and Das Gupta 1968:313–26.

———— 1971. The language situation in Haiti. In Hymes 1971:61–4.

Vallee, Frank and de Vries, John. 1978. Trends in bilingualism in Canada. In Fishman 1978:761–95.

Verdoodt, Albert. 1972. The differential impact of immigrant French speakers on indigenous German speakers: a case study in the light of two theories. In Fishman 1972a:377–85.

Verma, S. K. 1976. Code-switching: Hindi–English. *Lingua*, 38(2):153–65.

Weinreich, Uriel. 1957. Functional aspects of Indian bilingualism. *Word*, 13(2):203–33.

———— 1968. *Languages in Contact: Findings and Problems*. The Hague: Mouton. Originally published as *Publications of the Linguistic Circle of New York*, no.1, 1953.

Wexler, Paul. 1981. Jewish interlinguistics. *Language*, 57(1):99–149.

White Paper on the Restoration of the Irish Language. 1965. Dublin: Stationery Office.

Whiteley, Wilfred. 1968. Ideal and reality in national language policy: a case study from Tanzania. In Fishman, Ferguson, and Das Gupta 1968:327–44.

———— 1969. *Swahili: The Rise of a National Language*. London: Methuen.

———— 1971a. Some factors influencing language policies in Eastern Africa. In Rubin and Jernudd 1971:141–58.

———— (ed.). 1971b. *Language and Social Change: Problems of Multilingualism with Special Reference to Eastern Africa*. London: Oxford University Press.

———— 1973. Sociolinguistic surveys at the national level. In Shuy 1973:167–80.

———— (ed.). 1974. *Language in Kenya, Ethiopia, Tanzania, Uganda, Zambia*. Nairobi: Oxford University Press.

Wijnstra, Johan. 1978. Education of children with Frisian home language. Paper presented at the 19th International Congress of Applied Psychology, Munich, 1978.

Williams, Frederick. 1968. *Reasoning with Statistics: Simplified Examples in Communications Research*. New York: Holt, Rinehart, and Winston.

———— 1973. Some research notes on dialect attitudes and stereotypes. In Shuy and Fasold 1973:113–28.

———— 1974. The identification of linguistic attitudes. *International Journal of the Sociology of Language*, 3:21–32. (=*Linguistics* 136)

———— and associates. 1976. *Explorations of the Linguistic Attitudes of Teachers*. Rowley, MA:Newbury House.

———— Whitehead, J., and Miller, L. 1971. *Attitudinal Correlates of Children's Speech Characteristics*. OSOE Research Report Project No. 0–0336. Washington, DC: United States Office of Education.

———— 1972. Relations between language attitudes and teacher expectancy. *American Educational Research Journal*, 9:263–77.

Wölck, Wolfgang. 1973. Attitudes toward Spanish and Quechua in bilingual Peru. In Shuy and Fasold 1973:129–47.

———— 1976. Community profiles: an alternative approach to linguistic informant selection. *International Journal of the Sociology of Language*, 9:43–7. (=*Linguistics* 177).

Wolff, Hans. 1959. Intelligibility and inter-ethnic attitudes. *Anthropological Linguistics*, 1(3):34–41. Also in Hymes 1964: 440–45.

Wolfram, Walt. 1973. Objective and subjective parameters of language assimilation among second-generation Puerto Ricans in East Harlem. In Shuy and Fasold 1973:148–73.

———— 1974. *Sociolinguistic Aspects of Assimilation: Puerto Rican English in New York City*. Arlington, VA: Center for Applied Linguistics.

———— and Fasold, Ralph. 1974. *The Study of Social Dialects in American English*. Englewood Cliffs, NJ: Prentice-Hall.

Wood, Richard. 1980. Language maintenance and external support, the case of the French Flemings. *International Journal of the Sociology of Language*, 25:107–20.

Woodworth, Elisabeth and DiPietro, Robert (eds.). 1963. *Georgetown University Round Table on Languages and Linguistics 1962*. Washington, DC: Georgetown University Press.

Yuker, Harold. 1958. *A Guide to Statistical Calculations*. New York: G. P. Putnam.

Zughoul, Muhammed. 1980. Diglossia in Arabic: investigating solutions. *Anthropological Linguistics*, 22(5):201–17.

Index

Abdulaziz Mkilifi, Mohammed 8, 42,
44-6, 52, 56-7, 218, 268, 275
Albanian 159
Amharic 124
Angaité 18-19
Arabic 35, 39, 61, 63, 75, 78, 130-1, 149,
165-8, 189, 199, 249, 267, 270
Assamese 20, 28

Bahasa Indonesia 287
Bahasa Malaysia 48-9, 137, 287
Basque 214
Bengali 20, 22, 24, 43
Berber 130-1
Bhojpuri 27
Bihari 116

Cantonese 136
Chinese 48, 136
    Mandarin 48-50, 76, 136
Chulupi 18-19, 81-2
continuum 71-3, 82, 181, 183, 224

diglossia 34, 36-46, 47, 49, 51-8, 63-4,
66, 71-5, 164-5, 166, 170, 176, 180,
186-8, 190, 193, 207, 231, 308
    broad 53, 71, 165, 194;
        definition of 53
    classic 54, 57
    classical 54-5
    definition of 38-9
diglossic community 44, 47, 51, 52,
153, 158, 169, 170, 183-4, 213

diversity, linguistic 6, 85, 87, 95, 113,
118-19, 125, 127-8, 130, 132-6, 140,
142-3
domain 49, 55, 183-8, 201, 202, 207,
213, 224-5, 227, 231, 233, 241-2,
246, 257, 304
Dorian, Nancy 192-4, 202, 214, 216-18,
222-7, 231
Dutch 307-11

education 3, 5, 17, 27, 41, 42, 46, 52-3,
63, 69, 70, 75-6, 79-80, 170, 183,
184-5, 225, 271, 273, 279-82, 283-6,
292-3, 295-6, 299-300, 305
    language of 16, 19, 35, 52, 62, 69, 76,
79, 196, 221, 225-6, 247, 269, 292,
297, 307
Estonian 249
ethnic group 2-3, 8-9, 17, 19-20, 23,
29-30, 56, 69, 123, 136

Ferguson, Charles 25, 34, 36-7, 38-43,
46, 49, 52-3, 54-6, 62-7, 72, 75, 77,
80, 124, 164, 248-50, 258, 261
Fishman, Joshua 2, 3, 16, 18-19, 29-30,
40-3, 49, 52, 74, 95, 148-9, 152-4,
183, 193, 218, 247, 272, 303
Flemish 11
fluidity 23, 28, 45-6, 116
French 11, 12, 35, 39, 41-2, 43, 50-1, 73,
75-6, 117, 120-2, 130-1, 150, 158,
162-4, 181, 189, 215-18, 227-31,
233, 241, 253, 259, 299-301, 309

Frisian 307-13
functions, unifying and separatist 3, 19, 73-4, 158, 161, 248

Gaelic 214, 222, 224-7, 247, 253, 259, 266, 275, 278, 294
Gal, Susan 192-3, 196-8, 200, 203-5, 207-8, 216-18, 220-2, 233-4, 240
Galla 124
Garvin and Mathiot 3, 15, 161, 248
German 11, 12, 14, 35, 38, 40-4, 75-6, 82, 115, 181, 195-200, 203-6, 208, 214, 216, 218-22, 226, 231, 240, 251, 253, 259, 267-8, 274, 276, 302, 309
Greek 35, 38-9, 51, 54-6, 160-1, 279
Guaraní 14-19, 24, 40, 57, 61, 73, 75, 78-9, 81-2, 115, 117-18, 138-9, 161, 201-2, 217, 253, 304, 306
   tribal 19, 213
Gujerati 20
Gumperz, John 40, 44, 46, 47, 52, 180, 192-5, 202-6, 258

Haitian Creole 35, 37
Hebrew 78, 149, 188, 250, 287
Hiligaynon 300
Hindi 5, 20, 22, 23-7, 29, 46-8, 51, 61, 66, 74, 79-80, 116-17, 137-8, 141, 181-3, 185-6, 205-6, 256, 277, 287, 297, 304
Hindi-Urdu, *see* Hindi
Hokkien 136
Hungarian 195-200, 204-5, 208, 213-14, 218-22, 226, 231, 240, 274

Icelandic 73
Igbo 304
Irish 49, 69, 278-87, 292, 311
Italian 11

Japanese 73, 286

Kannada 20
Kashmiri 20, 25, 26
Khubchandani, Lachman 20-5, 27-8, 116, 119, 138, 141
Kichagga 274
Kikuyu 304
Kurdish 123

language maintenance 133, 143, 148, 213-14, 218, 227, 233, 239-42, 258, 260

language shift 133, 137, 143, 213-19, 220, 227, 239-42, 259-60
Lappish 69
Latin 77-8, 251, 279
Lieberson, Stanley 114-16, 118, 120-2, 124, 130-2, 134-5, 137, 141, 143, 215-19, 221, 227-32, 241
Lithuanian 249

Magahi 27
Maithili 22, 26
Malay 48, 136-7, 252
Malayalam 20, 25, 119
Manx 73
Marathi 20, 141
Mascoi 17-18
Mataguayo 18

Nagassamese 28
Nahuatl 181, 204
nation 2, 3, 30, 68-9, 72-3, 75, 95, 116, 120, 130, 135-6, 247-8, 287, 297, 303-4
national language 4, 5, 15, 19, 24-5, 29, 39, 45, 57, 61, 73-5, 78-9, 114-15, 124, 133, 136-7, 142-3, 247-8, 252-7, 266, 268-9, 271-4, 276-8, 282-8, 292, 294, 300-1, 303-5, 312
nationalism 3, 5, 16, 19, 24, 26, 29-31, 39, 57, 142, 247, 274, 287
nationalist 9, 57, 72-5, 139, 272, 278, 282, 292, 304
nationalist language 138, *see also* national language
nationality 2, 3-5, 9-11, 19-20, 29-30, 62-74, 247, 285, 303
nationism 3-5, 16, 30, 247
nationist 4-5, 8-9, 15-19, 24, 27, 29-30, 73, 255, 272, 282
naturalism 68, 72, 82
naturalist 71, 76, 257
Norwegian 132, 194-5, 247

official language 5, 8, 11, 15-16, 25-6, 27, 40, 61-3, 69-70, 72-3, 80, 87, 136-7, 142, 247, 256, 271, 278, 282, 287
Oriya 20

Panjabi 20, 22, 26, 117
Persian 43, 249
Pilipino 287, 304, 311, *see also* Tagalog
Portuguese 286

Quechua 74

Rajasthani 23. 116
Romansch 11
Rona, Jose Pedro 14-16, 42, 79, 115-16, 118, 139
Rubin, Joan 15-17, 115, 118, 180, 192, 201-2, 250-2, 262, 306
Russian 41, 51, 76, 255

Sanskrit 1, 20, 22, 27, 47, 49, 78, 297
Sindhi 117
Spanish 14-19, 27, 40, 46, 57, 61, 73-7, 79, 81-2, 114, 116-17, 138-9, 158, 161, 165, 168-70, 181-4, 186, 190, 201-6, 217, 231-4, 239, 242, 297, 306
speech community 36, 41-4, 53, 63, 70, 148, 190, 213, 214
standard language 34, 42-4, 63-4, 66, 70, 76, 279
Stewart, William 42, 50-1, 62-5, 66, 68-70, 71-3, 77, 80, 258

Swahili 8, 42, 45-6, 56-7, 61, 75, 80, 124, 248, 266-77, 284-7, 292, 295, 297, 302, 304-5, 311
Swedish 132

Tagalog 287, *see also* Pilipino
Tamil 20, 24, 119, 136
Telegu 20, 141, 304
Thai 73
Tiwa 231-9, 241-2, 260, 302
Tok Pisin 206
Turkish 123, 249

Urdu 20, 22, 24, 26, 66, 297

vernacular 45-6, 56-7, 61-3, 65, 70, 114-15, 124, 272-6, 292-5, 296-7, 298, 304-5

Welsh 155-7, 164, 181, 248, 253-4, 259

Yiddish 115